COMPARATIVE LITERATURE IN BRITAIN
NATIONAL IDENTITIES, TRANSNATIONAL DYNAMICS
1800-2000

LEGENDA

LEGENDA is the Modern Humanities Research Association's book imprint for new research in the Humanities. Founded in 1995 by Malcolm Bowie and others within the University of Oxford, Legenda has always been a collaborative publishing enterprise, directly governed by scholars. The Modern Humanities Research Association (MHRA) joined this collaboration in 1998, became half-owner in 2004, in partnership with Maney Publishing and then Routledge, and has since 2016 been sole owner. Titles range from medieval texts to contemporary cinema and form a widely comparative view of the modern humanities, including works on Arabic, Catalan, English, French, German, Greek, Italian, Portuguese, Russian, Spanish, and Yiddish literature. Editorial boards and committees of more than 60 leading academic specialists work in collaboration with bodies such as the Society for French Studies, the British Comparative Literature Association and the Association of Hispanists of Great Britain & Ireland.

The MHRA encourages and promotes advanced study and research in the field of the modern humanities, especially modern European languages and literature, including English, and also cinema. It aims to break down the barriers between scholars working in different disciplines and to maintain the unity of humanistic scholarship. The Association fulfils this purpose through the publication of journals, bibliographies, monographs, critical editions, and the MHRA Style Guide, and by making grants in support of research. Membership is open to all who work in the Humanities, whether independent or in a University post, and the participation of younger colleagues entering the field is especially welcomed.

ALSO PUBLISHED BY THE ASSOCIATION

Critical Texts
Tudor and Stuart Translations • New Translations • European Translations
MHRA Library of Medieval Welsh Literature

MHRA Bibliographies
Publications of the Modern Humanities Research Association

The Annual Bibliography of English Language & Literature
Austrian Studies
Modern Language Review
Portuguese Studies
The Slavonic and East European Review
Working Papers in the Humanities
The Yearbook of English Studies

www.mhra.org.uk
www.legendabooks.com

STUDIES IN COMPARATIVE LITERATURE

Editorial Committee
Chairs: Dr Emily Finer (University of St Andrews)
and Professor Wen-chin Ouyang (SOAS, London)

Dr Ross Forman (University of Warwick)
Professor Angus Nicholls (Queen Mary, University of London)
Dr Henriette Partzsch (University of Glasgow)
Dr Ranka Primorac (University of Southampton)

Studies in Comparative Literature are produced in close collaboration with the British Comparative Literature Association, and range widely across comparative and theoretical topics in literary and translation studies, accommodating research at the interface between different artistic media and between the humanities and the sciences.

ALSO PUBLISHED IN THIS SERIES

20. *Aestheticism and the Philosophy of Death: Walter Pater and Post-Hegelianism*, by Giles Whiteley
21. *Blake, Lavater and Physiognomy*, by Sibylle Erle
22. *Rethinking the Concept of the Grotesque: Crashaw, Baudelaire, Magritte*, by Shun-Liang Chao
23. *The Art of Comparison: How Novels and Critics Compare*, by Catherine Brown
24. *Borges and Joyce: An Infinite Conversation*, by Patricia Novillo-Corvalán
25. *Prometheus in the Nineteenth Century: From Myth to Symbol*, by Caroline Corbeau-Parsons
26. *Architecture, Travellers and Writers: Constructing Histories of Perception*, by Anne Hultzsch
27. *Comparative Literature in Britain: National Identities, Transnational Dynamics 1800-2000*, by Joep Leerssen
28. *The Realist Author and Sympathetic Imagination*, by Sotirios Paraschas
29. *Iris Murdoch and Elias Canetti: Intellectual Allies*, by Elaine Morley
30. *Likenesses: Translation, Illustration, Interpretation*, by Matthew Reynolds
31. *Exile and Nomadism in French and Hispanic Women's Writing*, by Kate Averis
32. *Samuel Butler against the Professionals: Rethinking Lamarckism 1860–1900*, by David Gillott
33. *Byron, Shelley, and Goethe's Faust: An Epic Connection*, by Ben Hewitt
34. *Leopardi and Shelley: Discovery, Translation and Reception*, by Daniela Cerimonia
35. *Oscar Wilde and the Simulacrum: The Truth of Masks*, by Giles Whiteley
36. *The Modern Culture of Reginald Farrer: Landscape, Literature and Buddhism*, by Michael Charlesworth
37. *Translating Myth*, edited by Ben Pestell, Pietra Palazzolo and Leon Burnett
38. *Encounters with Albion: Britain and the British in Texts by Jewish Refugees from Nazism*, by Anthony Grenville
39. *The Rhetoric of Exile: Duress and the Imagining of Force*, by Vladimir Zorić
40. *From Puppet to Cyborg: Pinocchio's Posthuman Journey*, by Georgia Panteli
41. *Utopian Identities: A Cognitive Approach to Literary Competitions*, by Clementina Osti
43. *Sublime Conclusions: Last Man Narratives from Apocalypse to Death of God*, by Robert K. Weninger
44. *Arthur Symons: Poet, Critic, Vagabond*, edited by Elisa Bizzotto and Stefano Evangelista
45. *Scenographies of Perception: Sensuousness in Hegel, Novalis, Rilke, and Proust*, by Christian Jany
46. *Reflections in the Library: Selected Literary Essays 1926–1944*, by Antal Szerb
47. *Depicting the Divine: Mikhail Bulgakov and Thomas Mann*, by Olga G. Voronina
48. *Samuel Butler and the Evolutionary Debate: Science, Literature and Unconscious Memory*, by Cristiano Turbil
49. *Death Sentences: Literature and State Killing*, edited by Birte Christ and Ève Morisi
50. *Words Like Fire: Prophecy and Apocalypse in Apollinaire, Marinetti and Pound*, by James P. Leveque

Comparative Literature in Britain

National Identities, Transnational Dynamics
1800-2000

Joep Leerssen

LEGENDA
Studies in Comparative Literature 27
Modern Humanities Research Association
2019

Published by Legenda
an imprint of the Modern Humanities Research Association
Salisbury House, Station Road, Cambridge CB1 2LA

ISBN 978-1-78188-713-4 (HB)
ISBN 978-1-78188-576-5 (PB)

First published 2019
Paperback edition 2021

All rights reserved. No part of this publication may be reproduced or disseminated or transmitted in any form or by any means, electronic, mechanical, photocopying, recording or otherwise, or stored in any retrieval system, or otherwise used in any manner whatsoever without written permission of the copyright owner, except in accordance with the provisions of the Copyright, Designs and Patents Act 1988, or under the terms of a licence permitting restricted copying issued in the UK by the Copyright Licensing Agency Ltd, Saffron House, 6–10 Kirby Street, London EC1N 8TS, England, or in the USA by the Copyright Clearance Center, 222 Rosewood Drive, Danvers MA 01923. Application for the written permission of the copyright owner to reproduce any part of this publication must be made by email to legenda@mhra.org.uk.

Disclaimer: Statements of fact and opinion contained in this book are those of the author and not of the editors or the Modern Humanities Research Association. The publisher makes no representation, express or implied, in respect of the accuracy of the material in this book and cannot accept any legal responsibility or liability for any errors or omissions that may be made.

Trademark notice: Product or corporate names may be trademarks or registered trademarks, and are used only for identification and explanation without intent to infringe.

© Modern Humanities Research Association 2019

Copy-Editor: Dr Susan Tilby

CONTENTS

	List of Illustrations	ix
	Acknowledgements	xi
	Introduction	1
1	Patterns (1800–1848)	7
	The comparative method: Nationality and language, empire and race	
	Nationality politics and cultural faultlines	
	Universities in England and Scotland	
	Cultural transfer: A German-type university in London	
	Literature: Criticism, history, philology	
	Historicism, Anglo-Saxonism and the turn towards German-style philology	
	Comparative philology, anthropology, and ethnicity: J. C. Prichard and the Celts	
	Literary internationalism and John Bowring	
	The new history-writing and Henry Hallam	
	Wales, the 'matière de Bretagne' and Thomas Price	
	Summary, outlook	
2	Matthew Arnold (1848–1869)	55
	Arnold, education and ethnicity in the mid-century	
	Critical judgements: Hellenism, Hebraism and the Philistines	
	Coining 'Comparative Literature'	
	Literary ethnicities: Celticism, Saxonism, and English	
	Summary, outlook	
3	Henry Buckle and H. M. Posnett (1857–1886)	70
	The impact of positivism: Henry Thomas Buckle	
	Comparative history, anthropological stadialism, and the Empire	
	Posnett's 'Comparative Literature' (1886)	
4	Reviewers, Critics, Academics (1860–1914)	84
	Journals and critics	
	Literary intellectuals and the universities: Sidney Lee and Edward Dowden	
	Asymmetrical developments: Criticism, intellectual history, ethnology	
	Biographical positivism and history of ideas	
	Saintsbury and his associates: European periods and the encyclopaedic approach	
	Methodological crossroads: Positivism and criticism	
	Summary, outlook	
5	Comparatist Trends within Literary Studies (1914–1950)	109
	German Studies and John George Robertson	
	Gender and foreign languages	
	English and the resilience of criticism	
	Literary anthropology at Cambridge	

Modern languages, joint honours and 'littérature comparée'
Bridging the Second World War: *Comparative Literature Studies*

6   Consolidation and Crises (1950–2000) 134
National continuities and mid-century internationalism
The ICLA, the challenge of Wellek, and the New Criticism
Postwar criticism and Eng.Lit.
The postwar generation and the new universities
Challenges post-1968
International crosswinds: The new approaches
Postcolonialism and the new interest in World Literature
Literary history, literary reception and the transnational perspective
Modes of transfer: Remediation and translation
By way of conclusion; outlook

Source References 169
1. Obituaries and articles from the 'Oxford Dictionary of National Biography'
2. Works cited in the text

Appendix: A Chronological List of British Publications of Comparatist Interest, 1800–1975 181

Index 252

LIST OF ILLUSTRATIONS

In my search for portrait illustrations I was kindly aided by various colleagues and librarians. Warm thanks go to Rebecca Beasley, Steffan Davies, Máire Ní Mhaonaigh, Martine Prange, Fiona Stafford, Roger Stephenson and Daniel Wilson; and in particular to Helen Conger at Case Western Reserve University, Andrea Meyer Ludowisy at the University of London, Kate O'Donnell at Somerville College Oxford, Judy Quinn at Newnham College Cambridge, Michael Riordan and Dr Graeme Salmon at The Queen's College Oxford, and Karen Syrett at the British Academy.

FIG. 1.1. Henry Crabb Robinson, engraving by by William Holl Jr, after Maull & Co, 1869. (© National Portrait Gallery, London)

FIG. 1.2. Thomas Campbell, drawing by Daniel Maclise originally published in *Fraser's Magazine*, reprinted in *The Maclise Portrait Gallery* (1883). (Archive.org)

FIG. 1.3. Joseph Ritson ('Impiger iracundus inexorabilis acer'), aquatint caricature by James Sayers, 1803 (© National Portrait Gallery, London)

FIG. 1.4. Sharon Turner, painting by Sir Martin Archer Shee, c. 1817 (© National Portrait Gallery, London)

FIG. 1.5. Christian Karl Josias von Bunsen, from *Die Gartenlaube*, 1858 (Wikimedia Commons)

FIG. 1.6. Friedrich Max Müller, from *Cassell's Universal Portrait Gallery* (London: Cassell 1895)

FIG. 1.7. James Cowles Prichard, from the *Journal of the Royal Anthropological Institute of Great Britain and Ireland*, 38 (1908)

FIG. 1.8. Sir John Bowring, painting by John King, 1826 (© National Portrait Gallery, London)

FIG. 1.9. Henry Hallam, stipple engraving by William Holl jr and George Richmond (© National Portrait Gallery, London)

FIG. 1.10. Title page of Hallam's *Introduction to the Literature of Europe*, vol. 1, Paris, 1839 (University Library Amsterdam)

FIG. 1.11. Rev. Thomas Price, Carnhuanawc, lithograph by Lowes Dickinson after drawing by Charles Lucy (National Library of Wales; reproduced under Creative Commons license)

FIG. 1.12. Lady Llanover, painting, 1862 (Amgueddfa Cymru and peoplescollection.wales, reproduced under Creative archive license).

FIG. 1.13. Lady Charlotte Schreiber (née Bertie, then Guest), photograph (albumen print) by Camille Silvy, 1861 (© National Portrait Gallery, London)

FIG. 1.14. Visualization of the personal connections in the Llanover circle, generated by the *Encyclopedia of Romantic Nationalism in Europe*, http://ernie.uva.nl

FIG. 2.1. Matthew Arnold, caricature by James Jacques Tissot, *Vanity Fair*, 11 November 1871 (© National Portrait Gallery, London)

FIG. 3.1. Henry Thomas Buckle, frontispiece to vol. 1 of A. H. Hutt, *The Life and Writings of Henry Thomas Buckle* (3rd. ed.; 2 vols; London: Sampson Low, Marston, Searle & Rivington, 1880)

FIG. 3.2. Edward Augustus Freeman, photograph by Elliott & Fry, 1886 (© National Portrait Gallery, London)

FIG. 3.3. Sir Henry Sumner Maine, photograph by Herbert Rose Barraud (albumen carte de visite), 1882-88 (© National Portrait Gallery, London)

FIG. 3.4. Cover of H.M. Posnett's *Comparative Literature*, London: Routledge Kegan Paul, 1886 (photograph © Joep Leerssen)

FIG. 4.1. John Mackinnon Robertson, photograph by Bassano, 1920 (© National Portrait Gallery, London)

FIG. 4.2. Sir Sidney Lee, chalk drawing by Francis Dodd, 1920s (© National Portrait Gallery, London)

FIG. 4.3. Edward Dowden, from *Cassell's Universal Portrait Gallery* (London: Cassell 1895).

FIG. 4.4. George Saintsbury, photograph by Elliott & Fry, 1900s (© National Portrait Gallery, London)

FIG. 4.5. Sir Edmund Gosse, drawing by Frank Dicksee, 1912 (© National Portrait Gallery, London)

FIG. 4.6. John Churton Collins (Library of Congress, George Grantham Bain collection)

FIG. 5.1. John George Robertson (courtesy of the Institute for Modern Language Research, Senate House Library, University of London)

FIG. 5.2. Edna Purdie, photograph by Bassano Ltd., 1963 (© National Portrait Gallery, London)

FIG. 5.3. Eliza Marian Butler, photograph by Elliott & Fry, c. 1958 (© National Portrait Gallery, London)

FIG. 5.4. Nora Kershaw Chadwick (courtesy of the British Academy)

FIG. 5.5. Wiliam James Entwistle, photograph by Walter Stoneman, 1950 (© National Portrait Gallery, London)

FIG. 5.6. Enid Starkie, photograph by Henry Parker (courtesy Principal and Fellows, Somerville College, Oxford)

FIG. 5.7. Leonard Ashley Willoughby, photograph by Lotte Meitner-Graf, 1965 (© The Lotte Meitner-Graf Archive, Ltd.)

FIG. 6.1. Elizabeth Mary Wilkinson (courtesy of the British Academy)

FIG. 6.2. Donald Davie (courtesy of the British Academy)

FIG. 6.3. Siegbert Salomon Prawer in 1981 (courtesy of the British Academy)

FIG. 6.4. Lilian R. Furst as Flora Stone Mather Visiting Professor at Case Western Reserve University, 1978. Image 02294, CWRU Archives (courtesy Case Western Reserve University)

ACKNOWLEDGEMENTS

A book whose origins go back to my graduate student days contains, visibly or invisibly, all the moral, emotional and intellectual debts that I have incurred over almost half a century: inspiring encounters and supportive companions for the best part of a lifetime. To do justice to them all would require nothing less than an autobiography. Here I can only single out a few, and I mention only in passing the most important of all these: my parents and my wife, to whom I am indebted for so much more than just this book.

My career as a comparatist was shaped and fostered by Hugo Dyserinck, my professor in Aachen and supervisor of the MA thesis from which this book grew; and by Elinor Shaffer, who generously provided information while I was conducting my initial research in the 1970s, and who, as editor of the BCLA's house journal *Comparative Criticism*, invited me to become its Bibliography Editor in the 1980s. Dyserinck initially helped the MA thesis into print as a book in his house series *Aachener Beiträge zur Komparatistik*; Shaffer stimulated and facilitated its reworking for a 21st-century English-language public.

Substantial parts of the historical bibliography appended to this book draw gratefully on the work of the late Glyn Tegai Hughes, first British lecturer in Comparative Literature (at Manchester 1953), as Bibliography Editor for *Comparative Criticism*.

In addition, Graham Nelson of Legenda Publishers has been a firm support, as were many generous colleagues in the BCLA. I am most grateful to Susan Bassnett for engaging with the text; her feedback greatly enriched my understanding of academic developments in the UK over the recent decades. In helping me she reprised, unwittingly perhaps, her kindness of 1978, when she kindly shared information from Warwick when I began research on the original MA thesis.

At the core of this reworked book lies, still, the original archival research done in Aachen. During the translation and revisions I was constantly reminded of the friendship, guidance and support (not least in matters of German idiom) of my fellow students at Aachen's Comparative Literature department. It is to them, *quondam commilitonibus*, that this book is dedicated.

J. L., Amsterdam, May 2019

Every *True Critick* is a Hero born, descending in a direct Line from a Celestial Stem, by *Momus* and *Hybris*, who begat *Zoilus*, who begat *Tigellius*, who begat *Etcaetera the Elder*, who begat *B-tley*, and *Rym-r*, and *W-tton*, and *Perrault*, and *Dennis*, who begat *Etcaetera the Younger*.

And these are the Criticks from whom the Commonwealth of Learning has in all Ages received such immense benefits, that the Gratitude of their Admirers placed their Origine in Heaven, among those of *Hercules, Theseus, Perseus*, and the other great Deservers of Mankind.

— JONATHAN SWIFT, *A Tale of a Tub*

Nay, is not the diseased self-conscious state of Literature disclosed in this one fact, which lies so near us here, the prevalence of Reviewing! [...] now your Reviewer is a mere taster; who tastes, and says, by the evidence of such palate, such tongue, as he has got, It is good, It is bad. Was it thus that the French carried out certain inferior creatures on their Algerine Expedition, to taste the wells for them, and try whether they were poisoned? Far be it from us to disparage our own craft, whereby we have our living! Only we must note these things: that Reviewing spreads with strange vigour; that such a man as Byron reckons the Reviewer and the Poet equal; that at the last Leipzig Fair, there was advertised a Review of Reviews. By and by it will be found that all Literature has become one boundless self-devouring Review; and, as in London routs, we have to do nothing, but only to see others do nothing. — Thus does Literature also, like a sick thing, superabundantly 'listen to itself'.

— THOMAS CARLYLE, 'Characteristics' (*Edinburgh Review*, 1831)

INTRODUCTION

This book is based on the MA thesis which I completed in 1979 for the Department of Comparative Literature at Aachen University under Hugo Dyserinck, and which in 1984 was published in reworked form under the title *Komparatistik in Grossbritannien:1800–1950*. These German forerunners could draw on existing outlines of the history of comparatism which had appeared since the 1950s in articles and handbooks; but the principal basis was — and still remains for this English version — the admirable archive of the disciplinary history of Comparative Literature, which Dyserinck had built up at his Aachen department in the 1970s.[1] That, forty years later, an English version should appear is due to the encouragement and enthusiasm of Elinor Shaffer, who generously urged the present book into being.

In the interval, some developments have contributed to a more congenial scholarly climate for a book like this. The massive benchmark of the *Cambridge History of Literary Criticism* has appeared,[2] to complement, expand and deepen René Wellek's heroic earlier work. Archival material is in the process of being repertoried and is increasingly becoming available online.[3] The history of knowledge production has moved far beyond the *Fachgeschichte* of 1970s Germany. Following the work of Michel Foucault, Peter Burke and others, knowledge production is now seen as a vital part of the dynamics of cultural production in the larger sense, and an exciting point of overlap between intellectual history and the social history of institutions. The new interest in World Literature (signalled in particular by American scholars like Emily Apter, David Damrosch and Haun Saussy) was made possible by the postcolonial turn that set in just as I was submitting my MA thesis. It has involved reflections on the history of scholarly eurocentrism and on the history of theorizing about global and transnational literature; in the process it has shed fresh light and provided a new interpretive frame for the history of Comparative Literature. Finally, the period since 1975 has seen a robust consolidation of the discipline in Britain which is all the more remarkable since it occurred in an increasingly parlous situation for the Humanities in general — or even academic scholarship and the universities as a whole. Ironically, in this generalized sense of crisis, the ingrained habit to proclaim specific existential emergencies for Comparative Literature has ceased to make much sense, and the situation of the discipline at this time (surveyed also by Hambrook 2014) is a good one for reassessing the past two centuries.

However, while I could continue to rely on the unrivalled archival resources built up by Hugo Dyserinck's Aachen Programme, turning a 1979 German thesis into a 2019 English book required much more than a straightforward literal translation from the original — or rather forerunner. Not only have new historical connections, new relevant studies and theoretical perspectives emerged in the intervening four decades, with Comparatism going through important theoretical, methodological, and institutional changes since the original 1950 cut-off point, my own way of viewing the discipline and its core business has gone through changes as well. *Non sum qualis eram bonae sub regno Cynarae.*

Most fundamentally, a conceptual re-think was necessary when moving from one language to another. The German survey had been written from the view of *Vergleichende Literaturwissenschaft*, and had tried to make sense of British developments in a *literaturwissenschaftlich* frame of reference. The German notion of *Wissenschaftlichkeit* distinguishes academic scholarship from knowledge-at-large, or from cultural commentary or cultural analysis, by a specific set of methods and procedural rules. *Wissenschaft* was memorably discussed by Max Weber as a *Beruf*: something between a vocation and a profession. It is given a specific professional status in a social and education-institutional framework on that basis; and it was within that semantic, methodological and institutional framework that the original book attempted to render account of the emergence of Comparatism from a British tradition of *literary criticism* during a tardy and haphazard process of academic institutionalization in the decades between 1880 and 1950.

As a German book about a British subject, *Komparatistik in Grossbritannien* was constantly negotiating the semantic and methodological differences between *Wissenschaft* and criticism, between the social and institutional positions of literary scholarship in the two countries. To maintain, even in an English-language version, that analytic frame might place British developments in a grotesquely uncongenial light. What is more, such an approach might become normative and programmatically prescriptive — distinguishing between 'right' and 'wrong' ways of doing Comparatism, and filtering the discipline's history through a Sellars and Yeatman filter of 'Good Things' vs. 'Bad Things'. Yet, on the other hand, to fully abandon an underlying analytical focus would yield, not a history, but a disparate mass of dates, facts and anecdotes. Moreover, to think that British developments can only be understood properly in a British frame of reference would be a form of methodological nationalism ill-suited to this, of all topics. And in any case, we need to know what this book is about, and what we mean, if anything, by Comparative Literature.

It is necessary to define our subject in order to give focus to this book, and in doing so I maintain an emphasis on the fact [a] that Comparative Literature is the study of literature as a multinational topic from a supranational standpoint (this being Hugo Dyserinck's pithy definition), and [b] that as an academic discipline, it is taught and conducted according to the formal and informal rules that set academic scholarship apart from cultural reflection at large.

To maintain this emphasis means, from the outset, to thematize the way in which the early development of Comparatism in Britain differed from that in other countries — how, though often in intense dialogue with developments in other European countries, it followed different lines from different source-traditions in different institutional settings.

Most general surveys of comparatist history (e.g. Weisstein 1977: 22–87, Dyserinck 1991: 17–85), after having traced the discipline's intellectual roots and interests among intellectuals like Herder and Madame de Staël, are firmly anchored in academic institutional history. French origins are located in the new philological chairs established in the late 1820s and early 1830s at the Sorbonne, with incumbents like Jean-Jacques Ampère, Abel-François Villemain, or Claude Fauriel, and indeed the coinage of the phrase *littérature comparée* took place during a lecture at the Sorbonne in 1816. German developments are traced as fanning out from the University of Göttingen in the opening decades of the nineteenth century (Bouterwek, Eichhorn) and then move firmly within the general history of the philological sciences and their academic departments. And although the budding discipline got the wind in its sails from more general literary debates about notions like Goethe's *Weltliteratur*, names (later in the century) of early representatives like De Sanctis, Graf and Farinelli in Italy, Monnier or Betz in Switzerland, or Brandes in Denmark are all firmly linked to the institutional pursuit of literary history in a university setting.

Such an approach would be fruitless in a British context. There were no Modern Languages departments at the British universities which could offer a similar academic framework (although the existence and importance of isolated professorial chairs in Poetry, Rhetoric and Belles Lettres, or Anglo-Saxon will be encountered). What makes Comparatism in Britain different from its sister disciplines in many Continental countries is that it did *not* emerge from the academic institutionalization of the modern philologies, as a counterbalance to the fact that these were all compartmentalized on a national-linguistic basis. Indeed, Comparatism emerged on the Continent as an academic form of literary cosmopolitanism, counterbalancing the rise of the national-linguistic paradigm in the nineteenth century. To trace the intellectual roots of British Comparatism, we must, by contrast, survey a preoccupation with literature whose transnationalism was imperial rather than cosmopolitan, in which language and nationality were coincidental rather than fundamental qualities of the text; where the study of literary texts was conducted as a mode of cultural criticism and intellectual connoisseurship rather than as a philological specialism; where the academic institutionalization of the Modern Languages, and the professionalization of the philologist, occurred much later and much more hesitantly.

* * * * *

It was not until 1953 that Comparative Literature in Britain was institutionally established, in the form of a lectureship at the university of Manchester; nonetheless the pursuit itself had been around for decades, and had received its baptism as early as 1886 with Hutcheson Macaulay Posnett's book *Comparative Literature* — one of the first of its kind world-wide. The present book will be centrally concerned with investigating the curious time-lag between Posnett's early presentation, and academia's tardy adoption, of Comparative Literature.

Disciplines (and here I follow Posner 1988) evolve by way of crystallization, from the fluid sphere of intellectual interest into the institutional fixity of university departments. They usually emerge out of a successful combination of a corpus, an argued-out set of research questions (theory), and a defined set of analytical procedures (method). The stages of development and consolidation lead from ad-hoc encounters of like-minded scholars to self-identifying publications, conferences, ongoing collaborative research projects, dedicated periodicals, and university courses (first optional, then curricular). Crucially, at some point a transgenerational continuity and generational awareness sets in, where practitioners reflect on, and position themselves vis-à-vis, their scholarly antecedents.

Such a process takes time, as the emergence of other new disciplines such as Women's Studies or European Studies has shown, and is never smoothly linear. But the time-lag between 1886 and 1953 is remarkable by any standard. To understand it, the powerful presence of the cultural institution of the *critic* must be taken into account. Literary criticism, an intellectually refined reflection on moral and literary matters, stands in the tradition of the essay and is more closely linked to the praxis of 'belles lettres' and 'literature' proper (as a verbally expressed art form) than to the world of scientific discovery. The critic counts among his direct ancestors men like Dryden, Johnson, Coleridge, and (most importantly for this book) Matthew Arnold. Twentieth-century critics like T. S. Eliot, or for that matter many eminent literati who were appointed to the Professorship of Poetry at Oxford (as successors to Matthew Arnold), are part of a literary rather than an academic system. The pre-eminent institution in the British literary system is not the university, but rather the review: that important type of periodical which from the days of the *Edinburgh Review* to the *London Review of Books*, from the *Criterion* to *Times Literary Supplement*, has attracted the contributions of Britain's finest prose writers, most insightful readers, and cleverest minds. Under that richly thriving panoply, the academic departments of literary studies could not but be etiolated, starved of sunlight. The most inspiring role models, the most enticing career prospects for young intellectuals with literary interests, lay in the field of criticism rather than academic scholarship. As H. V. Routh put it in 1913:

> [...] the critic is really an artist, not necessarily of words but of facts. Whether he is studying an author, an age or the history of a type of literature, he has to gather together a mass of sometimes apparently incongruous knowledge, often penetrating far into other ages and languages or digressing into history, economics, sociology and arts, and he weaves all this learning around his theme, till it stands out in a new garb.

And Routh concludes, bluntly:

> It is obvious that in such a scheme of study there can be no place for comparative literature. (Routh 1913, 10)

This, then, is the general outline of what will be charted in the following pages: the idea and development, between the uncongenial source traditions of academic learning and literary criticism, of Comparative Literature (and, more generally, of the idea of a transnationally comparative method). That process formed part of developments in the humanities and in intellectual history generally, in the university system, and even in the constitutional system of the United Kingdom itself, which, as a realm comprising four nations with different languages and cultures, and ruling a globally extended colonial empire, had resisted the modernizations of the French Revolution and of Napoleonic vintage, but which came to experience the rise of national thought both in the wider European context and within its own populations.

The book is divided into six chapters which, despite the dates in the title, are largely thematic, and have a good deal of chronological overlap through tracing different run-ups, aftereffects, antecedents and repercussions. A first chapter will set the scene by outlining the state of literary criticism and scholarship prior to the foundation of the University of London in 1828. Chapter Two deals with the period 1828–1848 (in which year Matthew Arnold is on record as having used the phrase 'comparative literature'), while Arnold himself, and the period until his death in 1888, is the subject of Chapter Three. Chapter Four discusses post-Arnold critics in the period until 1914; Chapter Five deals with the period between 1918 and 1953 (when Glyn Tegai Hughes as appointed to the comparatist lectureship at Manchester); Chapter Six with the discipline in the decades of its academic establishment.

The bibliography contains, not only the references to works used and cited,[4] but also a chronological list of materials documenting the development of Comparative Literary Studies in Britain in the period 1800–1975. The list is based on the similar list of 'Zeugnisse englischer Komparatistik 1800–1950' in *Komparatistik in Grossbritannien* (and hence on the Aachen archive mentioned at the beginning of this introduction), as completed for publication in the BCLA's yearbook *Comparative Criticism: An Annual Journal*. In the completion, I was kindly aided by my predecessor as *Comparative Criticism*'s Bibliography Editor, Glyn Tegai Hughes.[5] A certain amount of overlap between the 'works cited' and the 'chronological list' was unavoidable.

Notes to the Introduction

1. On the historical importance of Dyserinck's Aachen Programme, see Schmidt 2017. Various monograph studies based on the Aachen archive appeared, like *Komparatistik in Grossbritannien*, in the book series 'Aachener Beiträge zur Komparatistik' (ed. H. Dyserinck; Bonn: Bouvier); mention should also be made of the *Internationale Bibliographie zu Geschichte und Theorie der Komparatistik*, ed. H. Dyserinck with M. S. Fischer (Stuttgart: Hiersemann, 1985). Among previous work on the history of comparatism in general, and of British comparatism in particular, I mention Dyserinck 1991 (17–85); Leithmann 1977; Prawer 1973; Roe 1954; Shaffer 1979; Thorlby 1969; Watson 1964; Weisstein 1968 (22–87); Wellek 1941 and 1961–92. More recently, an excellent intellectual history of comparatism has been provided by Antoni Martí Monterde (2011, in Catalan). There is also the very valuable methodological survey by Domínguez, Saussy and Villanueva (2015).
2. The volumes dealing with the period under review here are nos 4–8: Nisbet & Rawson 2008, Brown 2008, Habib 2013, Litz Menand & Rainey 2000, and Selden 1995. The volumes as a whole have informed and enriched my understanding generally; the bibliography cites only those articles specifically engaged with or relied upon.
3. The Germanic Papers at the School of Advanced Studies, for example, include the E. M.

Butler papers, the Leonard W. Forster papers, the Waterhouse Papers, and the Archive of the English Goethe Society (<https://modernlanguages.sas.ac.uk/library/germanic-archives>). Biographical data have become more easily accessible since the necrologies of British Academy Fellows and *Times* obituaries have been placed online, and as a result of the completion and online availability of the new edition of the *Oxford Dictionary of National Biography* (cf. p. 169 below).

4. Use has been made throughout of the British Academy's obituaries of its Fellows, and of the *Oxford Dictionary of National Biography*, for information concerning the scholars presented here. That use has not in each separate instance been separately referenced; a list of entries and their authors is given as a separate section in the Bibliography.

5. The bibliography as given here has been compounded from the ones in *Comparative Criticism* 7 (1985): 303–16 (covering 1800–1950); 8 (1986): 341–59 (covering 1951–1960); 9 (1987): 339–64 (covering 1961–1965); 11 (1989): 277–98 (covering 1966–70) and 15 (1993): 293–313 (covering 1971–1974). *Comparative Criticism* from its incipience in 1975 began to carry annual bibliographies of Comparative Literature, to which the reader is referred for post-1975 developments.

CHAPTER 1

Patterns (1800–1848)

The comparative method: Nationality and language, empire and race

The decades around 1800 saw the break-up of Enlightenment universalism and a spreading belief that vernacular language communities are the natural categories for human culture. The classical concept of literature had tended to use that word in the singular, with the plurality of men and periods as a mere accidental.[1] After Herder, that plurality becomes the very core of what makes human culture different from animal instincts: humankind's capacity to proliferate into different language communities, different traditions of poetic expression, different literatures, different cultures. All those words (languages, literatures, cultures) become countable, plural. Following Macpherson's Ossian and the modern editions of the Eddas, a growing interest focused on the vernacular ('modern') languages and literatures and on Celtic, Germanic, and Slavic myths, sagas and epics, until they ranked equal with the classical, Graeco-Roman tradition. In Germany, the philologist Karl Lachmann can with equal gravitas edit the *Nibelungenlied,* Catullus or the New Testament. In linguistics, Hebrew is ousted from its central position as the primordial language of reference, and Sanskrit takes its place (generally Leerssen 2012).

This amounts to a scientific revolution in the root meaning of the term; philologists came to see Europe as a mosaic of vernacular languages, in a redefined (Indo-European) family-tree system of relationships, each with its own literature, and each literature with its own epic-heroic point of origin. Greek and Latin, the Iliad and the Aeneid, the 'Classics' of Classicism, were reduced to the status of mere branches on the Indo-European tree. The *Nibelungenlied*, Beowulf, the *Chanson de Roland* and many others were retrieved by philologists from dusty, hitherto undisturbed libraries, and presented in printed editions to an eager European readership (the *Nibelungen* by Von der Hagen in 1807, *Beowulf* by Thorkelin in 1814, the *Chanson de Roland* by Francisque Michel in 1836). Goethe, who saw the lower slopes of his Parnassus being settled by Teutons and Goths, remarked how 'each nation that wants to stand tall now seems to require its own epic'; but by the 1820s he was fighting a rearguard action against the rising tide of national literatures by urging the need for something loftier: World Literature.

> I see increasingly that poetry is a common possession of humankind, and that it appears everywhere and in all periods in hundreds upon hundreds of people [...] if we Germans do not turn our gaze beyond the narrow circle of

our own environment, we will all too easily end up in pedantic obscurity [...] National literature does not mean much these days, the time has come for world literature. (*Maximen und Reflexionen*, 1829: Goethe 1985–1999, II: 12, 224–25; trl. JL)

But Goethe was, as Nietzsche would call it, *unzeitgemäss*, out of his time. His 'world literature' concept, though it would continue to reverberate and provoke reflection in literary circles across succeeding generations until the very present, went against the rising tide of a national paradigm which had also found academic institutionalization in the notion of the 'modern' philologies. Indeed the concept of 'philology' (more on which on p. 21 below), the institutional backbone of the new Humboldt-style university, came to weave strands of inquiry together which until then had been in widely separate scholarly departments: textual scholarship, palaeography and etymology on the one hand, and the criticism of poetics, rhetoric and 'belles lettres' on the other.

'Literatures' (countably, in the plural) were defined first and foremost by their language of expression, indeed by their demotic rootedness. Unlike the free-floating, universal hypercanon of the older 'Classics', such literatures carried a specific name: *national*. That word described two things at once: a social constituency and a cultural tradition. Socially, the nation referred to the 'people at large' (as empowered in that new French institution which baptised itself the *Assemblée Nationale* in 1789); culturally, it signified the transgenerational cultural continuity that bonds ancestors and offspring, forefathers and contemporaries, in a diachronic continuity (as in Fichte's *Reden an die deutsche Nation*). The nation was both a social and a historical contract. What held it together was its language; and what made that language more than the barking of dogs or the occasional grunts of inarticulate savages was its capacity to become the vehicle of memory, of commemoration, of reflection — indeed, of literature. That is how Friedrich Schlegel put it in his 1812 lectures on the *Geschichte der alten und neuen Literatur*.

The notion of literary nationality arises, then, in the decades of emerging democracy (the idea of popular sovereignty) and emerging historicism, between the storming of the Bastille and the publication of *Waverley*. It arises conjointly with the rise of the nation-state: both involve a recognition of the national collective as a mandate-giving power in human affairs. This view was resisted, precisely, by the *ancien régime* empires, for whom nationality was a minor shoulder-shrugging irritation in their multi-ethnic, dynastic inertia. The multi-ethnic imperial capitals of Europe, from Istanbul and St Petersburg to London by way of Vienna, would have understood Goethe better than did the fervent intellectuals and literati of Germany, France, and Scandinavia. The British Empire, with its Burkean rejection of the new ideology, was as little preoccupied with the question of nationality as it was with a written constitution, or a decimal system of weights and measures. It managed the deep-rooted divisions between its different cultural traditions (both in the colonies and within the United Kingdom) by benign neglect. What identity politics there were, were largely of a religious nature: the most salient differences around 1800 between Ireland, England, Wales and Scotland were labelled Catholicism, Anglicanism, Methodism and Presbyterianism — *pace* Macpherson, Walter Scott and the receding memory of Jacobitism.

Thus, while intellectuals in France and Germany around 1810–1820 were fixated on what made nations and their literatures separate and special (and needing, for that very reason, a method to place these nations in a comparative juxtaposition), the issue was as yet far less urgent in the British intellectual context. That is ironic, because Britain itself consisted of very different national traditions. It had reconstituted itself into a four-nation United Kingdom, comprising England, Wales, Scotland and (as of 1801) Ireland. The long wars with France superimposed a shared British solidarity on these nations (prefigured by the way Shakespeare had brought his captains Pistol, Fluellen, Jamie and Macmorris together in the intensely patriotic *Henry V*). Britishness depended, not on shared language or a social or transgenerational 'contract', but on the religious or quasi-religious factors of Protestantism and venerability: the almost liturgical organicism, patina and prestige of its ancient and enduring state traditions and institutions.

The point needs stressing because literary critics from this British tradition for a long while remained wholly unconcerned with questions of literary nationality — in stark contrast with Continental literary scholars like Georg Gottfried Gervinus in Germany or Hippolyte Taine in France. While literary studies on the Continent worked firmly within a national paradigm, classifying and ordering literary corpuses primarily by language and 'nationality', there is a strong tradition in British criticism that remains blithely heedless of nationality. When Matthew Arnold defines criticism as 'the best that is known and thought in the world', he is almost Goethean in his holistic vision of an undifferentiated, whole-world literature. It is not even 'literary cosmopolitanism' — if we understand by that term the attempt to transcend the national; because the national category is hardly noticed, and ignored rather than transcended. This nationless view is pre-national, imperial, rather than post-national. It is unreflected, and, of course, naively ethnocentric and Eurocentric: 'the world' for Arnoldian critics is mainly English, with the underlying inheritance of the Greek and Roman classics, the addition of a bit of 'Europe', and quite possibly a nod towards the 'ancient epics' East of the Bosphorus, or Suez.

In such a scheme of things, it is hard to put the 'Comparative' into Comparative Literature. Why should comparison between Chaucer and Boccaccio be of a different status from that between Chaucer and Malory? Why should a critic take a deeper breath before referring to Dante or Calderón than to Shakespeare or Donne? On the Continent, and particularly in Germany, a supranational perspective on literature as a multinational praxis was necessary, since the default type of study took place within explicitly national, language-bounded traditions, and might therefore fall victim to national tunnel vision. The tunnel vision among British critics was of a different nature; and the notion of transnational comparison was not an obviously-felt desideratum.

What did develop in Britain, as in other empires, was an increasing sense of ethnicity. When Welsh and Irish literary history were discovered and placed on the British cultural and literary-historical map, this happened under the marker 'Celtic', a notion which was then also extended to the Highland culture celebrated since the days of Ossian and Scott; conversely, English literature itself began to identify its roots increasingly in 'Anglo-Saxon' terms. Cultural diversity in Britain, from the mid-nineteenth century onwards, was seen in the racial terms of the traditions of Celt, Anglo-Saxon and Norman-French. Words like 'Welsh' and 'Irish' continued to refer primarily to races and territory, rather than to language, and uneasy coinages like 'Erse' or 'Kymric' failed to clarify the terminology. It was in this racial/ethnic, rather than linguistic/cultural taxonomy, that the first initiatives towards a philological and possibly comparative study of literary traditions emerged. From the days of Max Müller to those of Jessie Weston and Hector and Nora Chadwick, an anthropologizing tradition has remained pronounced in British literary studies.

Nationality politics and cultural faultlines

Even so, nationality politics would develop within the United Kingdom. The notions of Britishness and Englishness were never quite clearly distinguished, but the non-English portions of the British Isles would each come to develop their national particularisms, in varying gradations of regionalist or nationalist intensity.

Ireland, which had merged into the United Kingdom in 1801, was burdened by the legacy of that country's early-modern subordination to the English Crown — the expropriation of its lands from their native owners, the settlement of English (and, in Ulster, Scottish) colonists and land-owning gentry, and the reduction of the native population to disenfranchised cheap labour. This colonial-style system (known as 'landlordism') was kept in place by laws that denied non-Protestants legal standing and which in the eighteenth century in effect established a type of religious apartheid regime. Similar restrictions affected non-Protestants (and nonconformist Protestants) in England as well, but the demographics were different: the Irish population was overwhelmingly Catholic, and thus in Ireland (unlike in England) it was the overwhelming majority of the population that was reduced to a subaltern and disenfranchised status, and excluded from public institutions and offices, in their own country. Confessional politics accordingly dominated Irish affairs until the granting of Catholic Emancipation in 1828, and even afterwards. However, after 1828, a new type of nationalism emerged in Ireland; one which invoked a non-religious argument in its demands for independence: culture. Ireland could never be an integrated whole of the United Kingdom, it was argued, because its culture, its linguistic roots, literary traditions and historical memories, were Gaelic, and utterly dissimilar from the cultural root-system and historical experience and recollections of England. Thus, cultural differences, and the possible need for transcultural comparison, within the British Isles leapt to the eye as soon as the presence of Ireland was taken into account.

Something similar can be said concerning Wales. Here, too, a combination of linguistic/cultural and religious differences from England was at work, though with far less virulence. Wales had been incorporated into the English state (including its legal and episcopal structure) from an early date onwards, had participated in the Protestant Reformation, and was therefore to a large extent a reconciled part of Britain despite its different language. However, here, too, a sense of national-cultural separateness arose, which first gained a public foothold because it overlapped with the salient Welsh turn (stronger than anything in other parts of the United Kingdom) towards Methodism, and, what is more, towards a particular type of Methodism, more Calvinist than Arminian in its flavour. Methodist chapels were established in all villages of the principality; Methodist services were by and large conducted in Welsh wherever that was the language of the locality. Hymns, tracts and religious services, as well as the educational activities developed by Methodist clergy, thus gave a Welsh cultural colouring to what was in effect becoming a Welsh church, and gave to Wales, which in any case had a robust tradition of widely-disseminated print culture, a sense of a separate public sphere.

Scotland had maintained a high degree of institutional autonomy even after the Union of the Crowns (1603) and the Parliamentary Union of 1707. On the surface there was the eye-catching local colour of Highland culture, tartan and bagpipe. By 1820 this was being redeemed from its Jacobite, anti-Hanoverian and seditious connotations, and domesticated and commodified into a romantic component of the greater British whole, under the influence of Sir Walter Scott. More fundamentally, under this tartan surface, Scotland had preserved its legal system and many public institutions intact, both secular and religious (Presbyterian rather than Episcopalian/Anglican), in a separate system from that of England/Wales. Among the secular institutions, importantly, there were Scotland's universities — a topic warranting closer scrutiny.

Universities in England and Scotland

In the first quarter of the nineteenth century, the United Kingdom had seven universities. One of these was in Ireland (the University of Dublin, consisting of a single college, Trinity College), two in England (Oxford and Cambridge), and four in Scotland (Edinburgh, Glasgow, Aberdeen, St Andrews). Oxford and Cambridge were at this time in a state of elegant, tradition-wreathed decrepitude. Despite occasional endowments of colleges and professorships and the prestige that could attract fine minds to their cloisters, they had failed to catch the tide of the new scientific age. The BA course of studies in Oxford, even in the mid-nineteenth century, followed a statute from 1636 to the effect that

> The Student in the first year was to attend lectures on Grammar [...] The Student was also to attend Lectures of Rhetoric, founded on the works of Aristotle, Cicero, Hermogenes, or Quintilian. The Ethics, Politics, and Economics of Aristotle, and Logic, were to be the subjects of the second year. Logic, Moral Philosophy, Geometry, and the Greek Language under the Professor of Greek, of the third and fourth.

The MA, in addition, required three years 'devoted to the study of Geometry, Astronomy, Metaphysics, Natural Philosophy, Ancient History, Greek, and Hebrew' (Royal Commission 1852, 56). This was a course of study almost exclusively suitable for theologians or aspiring clergymen. Those training for professions such as medicine or the law followed an institutional route bypassing Oxford or Cambridge altogether. There were 23 professors in Oxford, but professorial appointments were often granted as a pension or sinecure. According to William Wordsworth, two thirds of the professors never fulfilled the duties of their office. Cambridge degrees (both BA and MA) were often granted without examination, while examinations in Oxford were often entrusted to ignorant examiners, both parties relying on set lists of ritual questions and answers (Godley 1908, 43 and 174). And the new, empirical sciences were conducted in academies such as the Royal Institution, while Oxbridge colleges increasingly gained a reputation of preparing young gentlemen of leisure for positions in an Anglican church largely run by patronage. As one observer summarized the situation for the early decades of the century:

> To social exclusiveness must be added the still more serious bar of religious tests. At Oxford members were on admission to subscribe to the Thirty-nine Articles and to take the Oath of Supremacy. On taking a degree this had to be repeated [...] At Cambridge admission was free, but in order to proceed to the degree of BA, BCL, BM, a declaration was required [...] In addition, by the Act of Uniformity it was required no form of prayer, or administration of sacraments or ceremonies, should be used in either of the two universities unless in accord with the Book of Common Prayer of the Church of England; and by the statutes of the University of Oxford, members of the university were forbidden to have any communication with any society of dissidents from the doctrine or discipline of the Church of England, or to be present at any sermon or religious service except in places consecrated or licensed by the bishops. Jews, catholics, and protestant dissenters were thus effectively excluded. (Bellot 1929, 5)

Things were far different north of the Tweed. Neither the Anglican Church with its Thirty-nine Articles and its Book of Common Prayer, nor the Act of Uniformity and other English laws, had the legal status in Scotland that they had in England. To be sure, St Andrews, Glasgow and Aberdeen were, like Oxford and Cambridge, rooted in late-medieval curricular practice (and St Andrews in addition was organized, like Oxford, Cambridge and Trinity College Dublin, as a 'residential college'); but it was generally agreed (at least among Scots) that the Scottish universities never fell 'into such troughs of intellectual sloth as did the older universities of England in the seventeenth and eighteenth centuries'. One reason for this was that Scottish students were on the whole poorer than those at Oxford and Cambridge, drawn from a wider social spectrum, relied on a proper university training for professional and career purposes and

> [...] were spurred on by the opportunities for advancement which their university training ensured for them [...] This tradition of grim dedication to the acquisition of knowledge implanted itself also in the younger university of Edinburgh. Until quite recently, seven subjects had to be passed for the ordinary degree in Scotland, and the breadth of this curriculum, in which philosophy was rigorously embedded, gave a special quality to the Scottish graduate. (Mountford 1966, 12)

Other advantages lay in

> the lecture-system, the non-residence of the students, their admission to single courses, the absence of religious tests, the dependence of professors upon fees, and the democratic character of the institution. (Bellot 1929, 8)

Finally, there was the legacy of the Scottish Enlightenment, and the fact that there were intensive contacts between the Scottish universities and the Calvinist universities of the Continent, such as Leiden. This international orientation stood in contrast to the academic isolation of England, where

> the older traditions which clung to the two great universities, and the higher practical interests of a select class which upheld those traditions, prevented any of the Continental ideals, be it the philological of F. A. Wolf, or the philosophical of Fichte, or the scientific of Laplace and Cuvier, from establishing themselves in the older seats of learning. And they were, after all, the only organisations for higher culture which possessed a historical character and continuity. (Merz 1903–14, 1: 263–64)

Merz's reference to Oxbridge's heedlessness of F. A. Wolf (he who had launched the 'Homeric Question' in the 1790s and contributed so importantly to the rise of the comparative paradigm in the philologies; cf. Maufroy 2011) is a telling one. It is borne out by Hans Aarsleff's point that, although the importance of Sanskrit as a comparative touchstone for European languages was originally a British insight (gained in Calcutta by Sir William Jones in his capacity as a judge for the East India Company), this insight was, ironically, eagerly adopted in Paris and Berlin but remained tenuous for a while within Britain, where, ironically, it tended to be seen as a German-philological discovery (Aarsleff 1967).

At any rate, innovations in British learning and in British literary scholarship could not be expected from the heartland of the Home Counties or from the 'established seats of learning'; we must search for their early traces elsewhere. The literary journalism of Edinburgh's 'Scotch Reviewers' (especially Francis Jeffrey's and Sydney Smith's *Edinburgh Review*, established in 1802), the amateur historians working in their quiet studies in London, and even the cultural eisteddfod festivals of Wales are the hatching ground for a new type of learning and for a new, historical-comparative approach to literature. And academically, a new-fangled institution was trying its wings in the capital itself.

Cultural transfer: A German-type university in London

Many factors contributed to the remarkable interest in German life and culture in the late-eighteenth and early-nineteenth century. To begin with, there was the ingrained dislike for anything that was French. Around the middle of the eighteenth century, a pose and *habitus* had taken shape in patriotic celebrations of homegrown, anti-aristocratic values (such as honesty, stalwartness and unaffected dignity) as being 'nationally English' and as such opposed to the refinement of France, with which Britain was almost uninterruptedly at war. As Germany itself underwent its remarkable cultural upsurge of the Kant-Goethe decades, it attracted to itself that interest which was now turning away from France. Authors like

Wieland, Bürger and the young Schiller were to exercise a powerful influence over English Romanticism, either directly (in poets like Scott or Coleridge), through mediators (Scott's amanuensis Henry William Weber, or the Norwich-born men of letters William Taylor and Henry Crabb Robinson) or in a more generalized taste for the 'gothic'. What is more, Britain between 1715 and 1837, under monarchs from George I until Victoria, was in personal union with an important German state: the electorate (and, as of 1814, kingdom) of Hanover. There, in Göttingen, George II had founded a university which by 1800 had gained great European renown.

Around 1800, the German university system was in flux, with medieval foundations falling into desuetude and new (re)foundations being necessitated by the dynastic pride of princes or the changing borders of their principalities. Bavaria had Munich, Bohemia had Prague, Württemberg had Tübingen, and Hesse had Marburg; so too, Saxe-Weimar had Jena — the academic counterpart to its literary Parnassus at Weimar. However, after the battle of Jena in 1806, many of its students (as well as professors like Hegel) trailed away, to the benefit of the university of Heidelberg (acquired by the newly-created kingdom of Baden in 1803). Following the Jena defeat, Prussia lost the city of Halle a/d Saale with its university, and in its stead founded a new university in its capital, Berlin, in 1809. And Berlin (followed by other Prussian foundations in Breslau, 1811, and Bonn, 1818) became a model university for all of Europe in the nineteenth century.

The design for that new university was entrusted to one of the great intellectuals of German Romanticism, Wilhelm von Humboldt, who used the occasion to consolidate the many new ideas that were in the air concerning the holistic intellectual formation and cultivation (*Bildung*) of young men's minds, and the constellation of faculties around the common central core of Philosophy. What is more, the new Humboldt-style university firmly took on board the modern languages as *philologies* — twinning linguistic and textual-literary studies, aiming to elucidate a nation's cultural anthropology by studying its language and its imagination as expressed in literary texts. Humboldt himself, a prominent linguist of the Romantic generation, was firmly convinced that a language was its nation's mental 'operating system' (Sweet 1978–80).

The 'Humboldt model' came to embody the academic achievements of Germany in the early decades of the nineteenth century. For much of the nineteenth century, German academic learning was to carry the prestige of being high-quality, theoretically rigorous (even philosophically abstruse, but never complacent or facile), and based on massive amounts of erudite source-study. The environment of the *seminar*, while close to that of the Oxbridge tutorial, involved students into research from undergraduate days onwards and was a prominent feature of the German historical sciences following its systematic application by Leopold von Ranke. And the notion of *Bildung* (the fostering and stimulating of the maturing mind) was to influence educational reformers from Thomas Arnold, headmaster of Rugby School from 1828 onwards, to John Henry Newman's *The Idea of a University* (1852).

Through various conduits, the German university ideal began to penetrate into English educational circles. Coleridge's experiences on his German trip of 1798 may

Fig. 1.1. Henry Crabb Robinson, engraving by by William Holl Jr, after Maull & Co, 1869. (© National Portrait Gallery, London)

Fig. 1.2. Thomas Campbell, drawing by Daniel Maclise originally published in Fraser's Magazine, reprinted in *The Maclise Portrait Gallery* (1883). (Archive.org)

have played a role in establishing the high reputation of the German universities, as well as Madame de Staël's *De l'Allemagne* (which after all was published in London, 1813, following the seizure of the original Paris 1810 edition by Napoleon's police). A more concrete influence, which was ultimately to lead to the foundation of a new university in London, is connected with the names of Henry Crabb Robinson and of Thomas Campbell.

Crabb Robinson (1775–1867) is remembered nowadays as the English Goncourt, a meticulous diarist and chronicler of his age; his extensive literary and cultural network, his bachelor lifestyle and his abilities as a conversationalist meant that in the course of his long life he spent many evenings privately socializing with the leading public figures of his time, leaving valuable records of these encounters in his diaries and correspondence. What is more, he was a cardinally important mediator between England and Germany (generally Crabb Robinson 1869, 2010; Norman 1930; Stelzig 2009). Born in Bury St Edmunds, his interest in German literature was awakened by an early encounter with the Norwich translator and man of letters William Taylor — who, like Crabb Robinson, was a staunch Nonconformist. Between 1800 and 1805 Crabb Robinson toured Germany. He stayed with the Brentano family in Frankfurt for a while, studied law and philosophy in Jena (he followed Schelling's lectures on aesthetics, and his letters to his brother evince a thorough grasp of Kant's thought) and in Weimar he became friendly with Madame de Staël, with Goethe and with Goethe's daughter-in-law Ottilie. After his return to England, he kept up these German contacts. A barrister himself, he corresponded with the great legal scholar and statesman Savigny, and early on translated Savigny's essay on educational politics which would later (in 1832) appear in Ranke's *Historisch-politische Zeitschrift*. That translation was submitted to the *Monthly Register* as early as 1802. These interests culminated, in 1828, in his attempts to establish a Humboldt-style university in London. In these attempts, he joined forces with the Scottish poet Thomas Campbell, a fellow-traveller to Germany in the brief lull between 1800 and 1806.

Like Robert Southey and Thomas Moore, Thomas Campbell (born in 1777 in Glasgow; he died in 1844 in Boulogne; generally Beattie 1850) was one of those 'minor Romantics' whose works are nowadays read by few, but whose stature in the Regency period was very high indeed. In his early life he moved in the Edinburgh literary circles around Francis Jeffrey, Henry Brougham and Walter Scott, and undertook his first trip to Germany as correspondent of the *Morning Post* in 1800–01, visiting Klopstock in Hamburg and Heyne in Göttingen (as did Coleridge) and getting caught up, as a British subject, in wartime difficulties. This and subsequent journeys also led to a friendship with August Wilhelm Schlegel and a keen interest in the Humboldt-style university.

Significantly, this dovetailed with Campbell's literary-historical interests: he meant to give an ambitious series of lectures on 'the subject of Modern Literature', comprising 'an entire view of Greek, Roman, French, Spanish, Italian, and German literature'. The project was probably inspired by the famous lecture series by the Schlegel brothers, with which Campbell was familiar. August Wilhelm's public

Vorlesungen on belles lettres and art (*Schöne Literatur und Kunst*) had been held in Berlin in 1804; although very influential among the literati and budding philologists in attendance, they remained unpublished until 1884. Much wider and immediate fame was enjoyed by his lectures on *Dramatische Kunst und Literatur* held in Vienna in 1808 (published 1809–10 and later translated by Carlyle). As for his brother Friedrich, his Vienna lectures on the *Geschichte der alten und neuen Literatur* of 1812 (published 1815), were scarcely less celebrated. They count as the beginning of modern literary history, tracing formal and thematic developments as part of the culture-historical development of societies rather than discussing the merits of successive authors, and applying to literature that linguistic-comparative view which Schlegel had already promulgated in his *Über die Sprache und Weisheit der Indier* of 1808.

Campbell's lecture series started off at the Royal Institution in 1811–12 but got bogged down in the Biblical and Classical period. Aborted after its first season, it failed to cover the 250 volumes of Italian classics which Campbell claims to have read in preparation. By this time he was contemplating the possibility of applying, at Walter Scott's behest, for the Professorship of Literature at Glasgow University — one of those free-floating professorial chairs (like the Professorship of Poetry at Oxford or the Chair of Rhetoric and Belles-Lettres at Edinburgh) which provided regular lecture series and an academic platform for meritorious literati, without necessarily corresponding to a regular course of studies or academic discipline. Much later, when Campbell had been given the prestigious post of Lord Rector of Glasgow University, he returned to his Schlegelian ambitions and began a series of *Letters on the History of Literature: Addressed to the Students at the University of Glasgow*; owing to ill health that, too, was aborted after an initial volume (1829) dealing with Greek and Latin antiquity. Campbell's enduring literary-historical work is a historical anthology, *Specimens of the English Poets* from Chaucer onwards, and preceded by an 'Essay on English poetry' (1819).[2]

Both Campbell and Crabb Robinson were Whigs of the Holland House circle, with a romantic interest in the self-determination of peoples; both sympathized with the Liberal side in the Spanish civil wars, Campbell also writing verse in solidarity with the national causes of the Greeks and Poles. Both men had visited Germany; both also felt the need for a new university that was less tightly controlled by the Church and the Tory establishment, and less onerous financially for enrolled students. Berlin seemed to furnish a template, as did Berlin's offshoot Bonn, the university founded in 1818 after the Rhineland had come under Prussian rule. Campbell visited Bonn (where A. W. Schlegel was then a professor) in 1820, and in the course of discussions there developed the idea that founding a new university might be an easier course of action than reforming the existing ones.

In the early 1820s Campbell began to canvass this idea, initially privately, and later in public. Around 1825 a series of publicly printed letters exchanged between him and his erstwhile old friend from Edinburgh days, Henry Brougham, massaged public opinion on the topic. Brougham had since 1810 (the year of his election to the House of Commons as a Whig) been on various educational reform committees (where he had been influenced by the 'Rockfish Gap report' drawn up by Jefferson for a new university in Virginia[3]), and had since his defence of Princess Caroline in her divorce trial from the Prince Regent pursued an increasingly high-profile public career. That career would culminate in his support for the 1832 Reform Bill, the 1833 Abolition of Slavery Act, and the peerage that went with the office of Lord Chancellor.

By the time the plans for a new university matured, in 1828, Campbell had been called away from London to take up the office of Lord Rector of Glasgow University; Crabb Robinson took his place. Initial problems concerning the teaching and examination powers of the new establishment were resolved when 'London University' was reorganized as 'University College, London'.[4] University College, together with a Tory counter-foundation (King's College) became the nucleus of the University of London, which obtained its charter in 1836, one year before the break-up of the personal union between the United Kingdom and Hanover.

Deeply influenced by its Scottish, Nonconformist and German source traditions (some of the initial appointments, especially in philology, were from Hanover), the University of London was an important breakthrough on the English academic scene, doing for scholarship what the great Reform Bill did for politics. It was here that modern languages (English, French, German and Italian) were first taught academically, and its mere presence opened up English scholarship towards a continental style of studying literature philologically. What that means will be more closely discussed in the next section.

Literature: Criticism, history, philology

What were the ways and modes in which 'literature' could be studied in early nineteenth-century Britain? To begin with, it would be anachronistic to understand the word 'literature' itself in our present-day usage (in its narrowest meaning: a verbal art-form; in its widest meaning: the textual form of culture) when discussing developments two centuries ago. Literature had in Godwin's *Inquiry concerning Political Justice* been defined as 'the diffusion of knowledge through the medium of discussion, whether written or oral' and could refer in the broadest sense to the condition of 'being literate'. To study literature could take the form, then, of something we might class, as the case might be, as cultural sociology, moral reflection, or textual commentary. It may not lead to general, abstract truths or insights. The person studying literature might not, therefore, make so bold as to call himself a philosopher and would prefer the appellation of *critic* — someone of discernment, taste, erudition and judgement. Accordingly, the pursuit was called *criticism* and embraced literary reflection from Aristotle's *Poetics* to the book reviews in monthly or quarterly periodicals, including even controversialism on matters of literary taste or on the function and proper pursuit of literature. The practice of literary criticism straddled the Aristotelian fields of poetics and aesthetics, might attract both poets and philosophers, was, indeed, a meeting ground between the two. Before 1800, it had come to include, not only Dryden's 'Essay of Dramatick Poesie', Pope's 'Essay on Criticism', Dr Johnson's vindication of Shakespeare as a 'classic genius', and Wordsworth's Preface to the *Lyrical Ballads*, but also David Hume's 'On the Standard of Taste' and Edmund Burke's essay on the Sublime and the Beautiful.

Such criticism could include cross-national comparisons. When Francis Meres in his commonplace-book *Palladis Tamia* (1588) collected witticisms and apophthegms on literary topics, some of these revolved around 'A comparative discourse of our English poets with the Greeke, Latine and Italian poets'. The notion of 'discourse' should not, however, mislead the reader: Meres merely lists quips and one-liners juxtaposing a foreign classic and an Elizabethan ('As Anacreon died by the pot, so George Peele by the pox'). Almost a century later, and with an established tradition of neo-Aristotelianism to fall back on, Dryden's 'Of Dramatick Poesie' involved a more sustained use of ancient and modern criticism, the latter culled from French and Italian sources as well as English. Dryden's essay was, explicitly, 'to vindicate the honour of *English* Writers, from the censure of those who unjustly prefer the *French* before them' (Dryden 1971, 7). Around this time, the juxtaposition of 'ancients' and 'moderns' became, first a famous literary offshoot of the French *querelle des anciens et des modernes*, and then a habitual heuristic contrast (Mme de Staël still uses it in her *De la littérature* of 1800).

Throughout the eighteenth century, asserting the nation's stature in the world of letters at large was the chief reason for critics to embark upon comparative forms of criticism. As Peter Leithmann puts it, 'eighteenth-century poets and critics such as Pope and Dr Johnson utilized foreign literature in vindicating the superiority of English literature as well as showing how the native literature could be enriched by judicious imitation of foreign literatures' (1977, 110).

Criticism could attract (and continues to attract) the finest minds and pens. But at the same time it is intensely personal, essayistic, indeed itself almost 'literary': a genre of literary disquisition on literary topics, as in Coleridge's metaliterary essays and table talk, or the essays of Hazlitt, or Thomas De Quincey's famous distinction between the literature of power and the literature of knowledge. As metaliterature, 'literature about literature', criticism was also the very opposite of a 'discipline': its lacked an institutional framework, a collectively accepted set of procedures of methodology, or a meta-theory on the basis of which the merits or defaults of divergent opinions can be compared and assayed. Literary criticism is, in short, a cultural field rather than a scholarly discipline, and there should be no more need to pursue this in a university setting than to teach courses in wine-tasting or after-dinner-speeches (except possibly as an ancillary specialism: textual exegesis and the use of 'rhetoric and belles lettres', e.g. in theology).

To be sure, this situation was not unique to the British Isles or the English language. However, those academic and intellectual changes which we might call the 'philological turn' (and which were briefly referred to in the Introduction) affected the Continent (France and Germany) earlier and more intensely than they affected British intellectual life. New types of source criticism, historicism, reflections on the taxonomy and the historical development of language, created a generation of historians, linguists and textual scholars on the Continent that was as yet without counterpart in the United Kingdom. What was crucial in this philological turn was the insight that literature was part of a historical dynamics and of an anthropological process of providing societies with an ambience of cultural reflection. The early parts of Friedrich Schlegel's Vienna lectures of 1812 are concerned precisely with this 'humanizing' function of literature: societies that reflect on their past and present, on their position in the world, by that very gesture evolve from brute savagery to humane civility, and it is literature (the power of poetic reflection on experiences) that, quite literally, makes the difference between the two, almost as language makes the difference between humans and animals (Schlegel 1988 [1815], 7–9). Following as it did Herder's principle that the essence of human culture was its diversity, its capacity to be different from place to place and from society to society, Schlegel's anthropology of literature was centrally concerned with following its different courses, different modalities and different phases in different languages.

The 'differentness' of those languages had been realigned in a true scientific revolution, in the root sense, which took place around 1800 when the study of linguistic relations was placed on a new footing (Aarsleff 1967, Davies 1998). Since the emergence of 'Comparative Literature' is inconceivable without the conjoint rise of its scientific twin, 'Comparative Linguistics', this deserves closer attention.

Sir William Jones's description of Sanskrit[5] led to a tendency to compare European languages, not with the religious *Ursprache* Hebrew (as had been the tendency before) but with Sanskrit, and paved the way for a phylogenetic-comparative method full of new insights. It made possible, indirectly, the reclassification of linguistic variations as resulting from historically specific vowel or consonant shifts, and a systematic description of such shifts. Grimm's famous 'laws' of *Lautverschiebung*[6] modelled the regularities in historical sound-shifts; they were the first example of a nomothetic description of law-like regular patterns in the field of human communication rather than for inanimate nature.

This paradigm shift implied a sudden and complete change in the scholarly status of philology and etymology. *Philology* had been, until the eighteenth century, an obsolete byword for well-read but useless erudition (cf. Hummel 2003), while *etymology* was notorious for giving free reign to speculative analogy-hunting between unrelated but superficially similar words from different languages. The paradigm shift is illustrated tellingly by the vehemence with which Friedrich Schlegel, in his *Über die Sprache und Weisheit der Indier* (1808), in order to vindicate the new Sanskrit-informed and systematic comparatism, denounces happy-go-lucky old-school etymologists. Schlegel sets out, as he states at the conclusion of Book I, to show

> on which principles a comparative grammar and a properly historical family-tree, a true history of linguistic development, could be designed to replace the old-fashioned speculative theories on linguistic origins. (Schlegel 1995 [1808], 189)

The same Schlegel, in his diaries and around the same time, begins to describe his own work as 'philology', the first sign that that term was being retrieved from near-oblivion. Giambattista Vico had, in his *Scienza Nuova* of 1823, opposed philosophy (the study of the externally created world, or facts) to philology (the study of human meaning-making). After an obscure and latent afterlife in the following century, that distinction was resurfacing in the years 1800–1810 to describe the new turn towards the study of languages and literary traditions. By 1820, the notion of philology was being institutionally enshrined as the very core of what the humanities were all about in Humboldt's new university model. The study of language (until then a mere adjunct for classicists and biblical scholars) was yoked to the study of literature (until then an adjunct for rhetorical studies), and the new twin science of 'Lang. & Lit.', under the new label of 'Philology' became the very backbone of the new humanities faculties.

Both in its linguistic and in its literary orientation, philology worked, centrally, with a phylogenetic-comparative method. Variants of language or of texts were compared and ordered into a 'family tree'. In language and largely through the work of Franz Bopp, the 'trees' of the Germanic, Romance and Slavic languages were collated with Sanskrit into the master 'tree' of the Indo-European languages, as were, in the course of these decades, languages like Armenian, Albanian, Lithuanian and the Celtic complex. In literary studies, the editorial method pioneered by the towering figure of Karl Lachmann (1793–1851) proceeded in a similar fashion: textual variants in various manuscripts were compared and grouped until a 'tree' or *stemma* of codical relationships could be established springing from a common root or '*Urtext*' (Timpanaro 1963). Just as linguists could extrapolate vanished words from dead languages by comparing their various descendants, so too editors could extrapolate what must have been in the 'Urtext' by systematizing the various derivative manuscripts. (The method was so all-pervasive that it would also be applied to the realm of living organisms (by Friedrich Haeckel), influenced by the thought of Darwin later that century; cf. Dayrat 2003.)

Between 1810 and 1840, men like Jacob Grimm applied their new philological method to a variety of fields which are now considered to be widely separate: not only linguistics, textual scholarship and literary history, but also legal studies (especially jurisprudential history) and history-writing, as well as the investigation of folktales and folk beliefs, often with a view towards establishing their roots in ancient mythological belief-systems. In short, philology in these decades had the ambition to be an all-embracing cultural anthropology of the various nations of Europe in their primordial origins, establishing a nation's cultural profile and outlook by the investigation of its language, poetry, myths and sagas, historiography and legal system.

In developing this programme, the scholars concerned worked very closely along the lines that had been suggested by Giambattista Vico for such a *scienza nuova* in 1725; not only did they use the name of *philology*, which Vico had employed as an unfamiliar quasi-neologism to refer to such a *scienza nuova*; they also began to see each historical civilization in world history as the separate development of an autonomous epic origin, a cultural 'big bang' of primal self-articulation marking the start of a society's civility and historical presence in the world. All that was following Vico's model; yet most of them did so in almost total ignorance of Vico's work, life or even name. Exactly how Vico's agenda and nomenclature managed to survive their author's obscurity, and came to influence the philological renewal of the humanities three generations after the appearance of the *Scienza nuova*, is a complex challenge in intellectual history (Leerssen 2012a, b). Suffice it here to point out, firstly, that the new learning combined a keen sense of historical development (as opposed to static typology) and was closely linked to the rise of historicism — the tendency to see things as the outcome of growth-processes, and the recognition that these processes must be studied in their own, preterite frame of reference; secondly, that the comparative-historical method emerging from that insight was applied with equal cogency in the study of language and in the study of literature; and thirdly, that this developed in Italy, Germany and France well before it took hold in Britain.

Ulrich Weisstein (1968, 32) points out (and the reader will at this point recognize the truth of that observation) that in France and Germany, literary studies developed as literary *history* rather than literary *criticism*. So as not to draw up an overly lopsided comparison, we should realize that Britain, too, had its literary history; indeed, that literary history does constitute the breeding ground in which later developments towards Comparative Literature were to originate. René Wellek has traced this development, and has usefully distinguished between literary history in a more narrow sense (which was slow to get off the ground), and a broader form of literary antiquarianism which flourished vigorously in the decades around 1800:

> Literary history in the more narrow sense developed, by an obvious process of specialization, from established forms like biography — which was not, of course, confined to literature — and from the criticism of individual works or the poetics of specific genres, which were slowly expanded to include a historical survey of the past. Literary history as a distinct discipline arose only when biography and criticism coalesced and when, under the influence of political historiography, the narrative form began to be used. (Wellek 1941, 1)

Old-style criticism had evinced little sense of literature as a diachronic, developing process and pronounced its judgements on literature by surveying a static corpus of canonical texts. Meres and Dryden refer to 'ancients' (authors from classical antiquity) as canonical contemporaries of modern authors. The famous 'Battle of ancients and moderns', which spilled over from France to England around 1700, rattled this static sense of literary timelessness, and allowed for something like progress in the world of learning and literature. Critics embarked on theories concerning the 'original genius' (i.e. a poet standing at the very mainspring of a literary tradition, like Homer or Dante), and formulated stadial notions on literary development that came to a head around the Ossianic controversies of the 1760s and 1770s; Robert Wood's *Essay on the Original Genius of Homer* (1769) is a case in point. Irish antiquaries were provoked to claim Oisín as a legendary hero from Irish Gaelic literature, as against the figure's transmogrification into 'Ossian', a putative Caledonian bard in the Homeric vein. In the process of these antiquarian rivalries, important Gaelic textual traditions were retrieved from semi-oblivion, and literary-antiquarian investigations were published such as Joseph Cooper Walker's *Historical*

Memoirs of the Irish Bards (1788) An antiquarian interest in English balladry was flourishing at the same time. After Young's *Conjectures on Original Composition* (1759) and Hurd's *Letters on Chivalry and Romance* (1762), Bishop Percy brought out the hugely important collection of *Reliques of Ancient English Poetry* (1765), with an introduction ('An Essay in the Ancient Minstrels in England') which attempted to sketch a diffusionist model for courtly minstrelsy, claiming Northern Europe as its region of origin. The combination of criticism and antiquarianism yielded inspiring results, and triggered attempts at literary history-writing that looked to the vernacular Middle Ages rather than to Classical antiquity as the nation's literary mainspring. Thomas Warton's *History of English Poetry* (1774–1781), Charles Dibdin's *Complete History of the English Stage* (1800), and J. P. Collier's *History of English Dramatic Poetry up to the Time of Shakespeare* (1831) can be mentioned; bibliophile societies like the Roxburghe Club and the Percy Society were dedicated to the reprinting of rare ancient texts; anthologies and editions were published by Romantics like Scott (*Minstrelsy of the Scottish Border*), Southey (*The Book of Kynge Arthur*), Hazlitt and Coleridge.

Such antiquarian criticism presents a fascinating run-up to the development of literary history proper; but a run-up, no more. Antiquarianism is not history. If in some cases we even see a scope that ranges comparatively across the European landscape, this should not lure us into hailing these works as early forms of comparatism. Dibdin, for instance, may present his *Complete History of the English Stage* as an 'Introduction by a comparative and comprehensive review of the Asiatic, the Grecian, the Roman, the Spanish, the Italian, the Portuguese, the German, the French and other theatres'; but that 'comparative and comprehensive review' is still in the mode of national self-vindication such as we have encountered it with Dryden and Francis Meres. Tellingly, when some decades later Thomas Campbell was preparing his lectures on 'Modern Literature' with their comprehensive view 'of Greek, Roman, French, Spanish, Italian, and German literature', it was to August Wilhelm Schlegel that he turned for a model, and not to his countryman Dibdin: the new approach that inspired him was philological and romantic historicism rather than antiquarian criticism.

Yet, on the other hand, the inspiration and influence of the antiquarian critics does carry over into the 1830s. If René Wellek is to be followed in hailing Thomas Warton as the first proper literary historian of England, we should realize that Warton's work is still concerned deeply with the eighteenth-century post-Ossianic debates on 'original genius'. But the 1824 edition carries a foreword by Richard Price, which, according to Wellek, updates and re-contextualizes it into the new paradigm, introducing the notion

> [...] of general literature as a huge treasure house of themes, which spread, multiply, and migrate according to laws similar to those established for language by the new Germanic philology of the Grimms. (Wellek 1961–92, 3: 88–89)

Still, England in the 1820s, amidst all the intellectual richness of antiquarians and critics, had no Grimm, no Villemain, no Bouterwek.

Historicism, Anglo-Saxonism and the turn towards German-style philology

The late 1820s and 1830s are usually seen as an 'in-between' period: between the Regency and Victorianism, between the death of Byron and the debut of Dickens. Intellectually, it is dominated by the figure of Thomas Carlyle, who combined the influences of Scottish Presbyterianism and of German idealism to forge a type of high-minded, hard-bitten moralism. Expressed in a prose style that ranged from the craggy to the cranky, Carlyle's anti-frivolous outlook (artists and intellectuals have the duty of guiding society through the metaphysical and ethical uncertainties of modern life) put a heavy stamp on the 'Victorian' attitudes of the next generation. Poets like Tennyson and Browning, historians like Froude, were all formatively influenced by the 'sage of Cheyne Walk'.

In literary scholarship, historicism began to take hold — less noticeably than on the Continent, and obscured from the general public's view, perhaps, by the limelight-stealing genre of the historical novel as developed by Walter Scott — but steadily increasing nonetheless.

Various trends coincided and overlapped in this development: the taste among Romantic poets for the exotic setting of long-ago periods; a penchant for 'national-patriotic' verse thematizing different nations (Thomas Campbell, to recall him, had penned poems like 'Men of England', the philhellenic 'Song of the Greeks', and 'Stanzas in support of the Spanish Patriots'); the ongoing antiquarian tradition of editing ancient ballads (by Joseph Ritson, George Ellis, Robert Southey, and others); and a slowly growing awareness of the place of England's Anglo-Saxon roots in a comparative-philological family tree of languages.

The evocation of old 'national' poetic settings (as opposed to ancient settings in Biblical or Classical antiquity) had been on the increase since the early-eighteenth-century rediscovery of Alfred the Great and King Arthur as appealing protagonists. Tellingly, the treatments of these historical monarchs avoid the Romantic or quasi-medieval genre of the 'romance' and opt instead for the classical genre of the 'epic poem', invoking the grandeur and prestige of the national-historical topic rather than the beguiling exoticism of the distant past with its colourful lifestyle.[7]

Together with these instances of poetic recycling, there were also the re-editions of the old texts themselves, in the continuing tradition of Bishop Percy. Arthurian interest, for instance, was boosted by the bibliophile reprint or re-edition of three medieval texts: Walter Scott's *Sir Tristrem: A Metrical Romance of the Thirteenth Century by Thomas of Ercildoune, Called the Rhymer* (1804); the anonymous *The History of the Valiant Knight Arthur of Little Britain. A Romance of Chivalry* (1814), and Robert Southey's *The Byrth, Lyf, and Actes of Kyng Arthur* (1817). Southey published a good deal of historical anthologies and historicist epics, and his role as a man of letters in the rising tide of 'literary historicism' (Leerssen 2004a, b) has recently been gaining recognition, thanks in no small part to Lynda Pratt's editions of his works and correspondence. The rediscovery and refreshed production of texts styling themselves either Epics, or Romances, or (in the case of Scott's prose fictions) Novels, sparked critical reflections on the meaning of such genre labels in historical and contemporary usage. Scott himself (who from *Waverley* to *Guy Mannering* to

FIG. 1.3. Joseph Ritson ('Impiger iracundus inexorabilis acer'), aquatint caricature by James Sayers, 1803 (© National Portrait Gallery, London)

Ivanhoe called his prose fictions, variously, Novels or Romances) contributed a penetrating and influential article to the 1820 Encyclopaedia Britannica on the varying degrees of realist verisimilitude in the Romance and the Novel.

Antiquarian editions of, and disquisitions on, older English literature had become a thriving business since Bishop Percy. Percy's adversary Joseph Ritson (*Pieces of Ancient Popular Poetry*, 1791; *Ancient Songs*, 1792; *Robin Hood, A Collection of all the Ancient Poems, Songs, and Ballads now Extant Relating to that Celebrated English Outlaw*, 1795) had established an interest which carried over into the Regency and beyond, and with a shift from 'popular balladry' to medieval romance.[8] Meanwhile, a new term emerged to denote the oldest linguistic and textual relics of the English past: *Anglo-Saxon.*

The notion that England had 'Saxon' roots was nothing new, and a Professorship in Anglo-Saxon (named after Richard Rawlinson, who had endowed it) was established in Oxford in 1799. Sharon Turner's epoch-making *History of the Anglo-Saxons* (4 vols, 1799–1805) was a veritable eye-opener. As Southey put it, 'so much information was probably never laid before the public in one historical publication'. What is more, Turner's history played into long-standing ideas that England before 1066 had been a tribal democracy with quasi-parliamentary institutions, only later to be burdened by the 'Norman yoke' of feudal aristocracy and an autocratic monarchy (Walter Scott's novel *Ivanhoe* testifies to Turner's influence on the Romantic revival of this historical myth).[9] How important this historicist Anglo-Saxonism was, becomes obvious from the 1803 inaugural lecture (on the 'Utility of Anglo-Saxon Literature') given by James Ingram as Rawlinson Professor of Anglo-Saxon. In the year of the great Napoleonic invasion scare, Ingram advocated the continuing importance of the Anglo-Saxons' legacy:

> what are our present Parliaments, but the revival of the free and simple *witena-gemotes* of our Saxon ancestors? [...] for, however historians may differ with respect to the precise æra of the first assembling of a Parliament, we may well rest assured, that there is nothing French or Norman in it but the name. (quoted Aarsleff 1967, 170–71)

That type of democratic primitivism was, of course, in the air. Opponents of Napoleon throughout Europe resented the technocratic modernization of state constitutions imposed by a 'Corsican usurper', and instead highlighted native traditions of liberty and resistance against foreign tyranny.[10] Homegrown liberties and institutions were celebrated as icons of identity against hegemonic encroachment, and could involve scholars defending native customs and laws, native traditions and native culture generally. Savigny and Grimm are obvious examples in Germany (Rothacker 1913). What is more, the native-philological turn was made from nationalist motives, but with a comparative vision: the nation's vernacular was being placed in the phylogenetic, philological, Indo-European root system of the European nations. It is highly significant, therefore, that Ingram in the same lecture advocates a comparative linguistics, with Cuvier's Comparative Anatomy as a methodological template: he pleads for studying, 'if I may use the expression, the *comparative anatomy of human language*' (quoted Aarsleff 1967, 170–71; my emphasis).

Fig. 1.4. Sharon Turner, painting by Sir Martin Archer Shee, c. 1817
(© National Portrait Gallery, London)

To sum up: the discovery of Anglo-Saxon literature involved English literary historians in debates that were methodologically informed by the new comparative paradigm, that saw the philological study of literature as a textual form of historical scholarship, and that involved questions of national appurtenance requiring a comparative scrutiny.

The growth of Anglo-Saxon studies, is, then, the most significant development in literary studies in the early decades of the nineteenth century. It was impelled and provoked by the publication of *Beowulf*, in 1815, by the Danish philologist Grímur Thorkelin. Thorkelin had discovered and copied the sole surviving manuscript while on a research mission in Britain, and published it as a 'Danish poem in the Anglo-Saxon dialect'. His edition was faulty and raised the question of which contemporary literature could claim *Beowulf* as its own — the language being obviously Old English, the tribal and geographical setting obviously not. German philologists, in their increasingly chauvinistic national enthusiasm, went as far as claiming this to be a German (Saxon!) poem, taken across the North Sea by the Saxons who conquered Britain...[11] English philological appropriations appeared from the mid-1820s onwards, invariably placing Beowulf in the 'Anglo-Saxon' nomenclature which had been nationalized by Sharon Turner: thus as part of John Josias Conybeare's *Illustrations of Anglo-Saxon poetry* (1826), in J. M. Kemble's edition of 1835 and his translation of 1837, and Benjamin Thorpe's edition/translation of 1855. In the process, *Beowulf* was canonized as England's primeval 'national epic', and Anglo-Saxon as the oldest stratum, indeed the bedrock, of the nation's language.

By the 1830s, English Anglo-Saxon scholars (J. M. Kemble foremost among them) had caught up with the new philological expertise of Grimm-style *Germanistik*, and took the new modern philology into the English universities. As with most scholarly paradigm changes, this involved considerable controversy. As Kemble introduced the 'new' Grimm-style philology in Britain (he had studied under the Grimms in Göttingen in the mid-1830s, and kept up a correspondence with them), he did so by acerbically criticising an older generation of incumbents of the Rawlinson Professorship at Oxford. This sparked off the so-called 'Saxonist Controversy', fought mainly in the pages of the *Gentleman's Magazine* in the mid-1830s, and ostensibly revolving around the most suitable typography for text editions of Old English. (Traditionally, a 'Saxon' type had been used to approximate the MS handwriting; this was denounced as bibliophile foppery, and an austerely scientific use of modern type was promoted instead.) Underneath this surface, the real debate was, of course, about the adoption of Continental-style comparative philology in English academia. For German-style philology was making its presence felt in various places. The chair of Sanskrit in the newly established University of London had in 1828 been given to Friedrich August Rosen (1805–1837); his lectures influenced the classicists trained there. When the Taylorian Institution opened in Oxford in the late 1840s, it initially entailed a Professorship in Modern Languages. Its first incumbent was the Swiss-born Heinrich Trithen, who had gained his PhD in Berlin; he was in due course succeeded by the famous Friedrich Max Müller, after whose re-appointment to the Chair of Comparative Philology the Professorship in Modern Languages lapsed. (A Taylorian Professorship in German

Fig. 1.5. Christian Karl Josias von Bunsen, from *Die Gartenlaube*, 1858 (Wikimedia Commons)

was established in 1907, followed by professorships in French and other modern languages from 1909 on.) The duties of the Taylorian Professor included regular lectures on 'the philology and literature of the principal languages of Europe'; it meant that modern European languages (and, in its wake, modern literatures) were gaining an institutional foothold in Oxford itself (Firth 1929).

By 1840, the constitutional union between Britain and Hanover was broken (Victoria, who was crowned in 1837, could not inherit the Hanoverian kingship under Salic law), but another, stronger Anglo-German link was forged instead through her marriage with Albert of Saxe-Coburg-Gotha. On the basis of a now-common 'Saxon' ancestry and a present-day dynastic intertwinement, England developed close ties of self-identification with the 'German Cousin', indeed came to see its own ethnic roots increasingly in 'Saxonist' terms — a self-image approved of, and indirectly fostered, by Carlyle[12]). The presence of German intellectuals on the English philological scene played its role in this process. The Prussian amateur scholar and Niebuhr-adept Christian Karl Josias von Bunsen (1791–1860), who had an English, Welsh-educated wife (Frances Waddington), was appointed Prussian ambassador in 1842; he took an active role in the religious, cultural and scholarly life of the 1840s (we shall note his presence at a Welsh eisteddfod) and functioned as Max Müller's patron, aiding his philological career at Oxford.

Müller (1823–1900) was, like Rosen, a Sanskritist with a deep interest in the Rig-Veda (he was to make use of the East India Company's resources for his enormous project of an annotated edition/translation in six volumes, 1849–74). In the course of his long English career he came to incorporate German-style comparative philology both in academic circles and for the public at large. Although, to his resentment, he was passed over for the regular professorship of Sanskrit, and had to remain Taylorian Professor, his public lectures and popularizing books on Indo-European languages and comparative mythology (e.g. Müller 1994 [1861–64]) made his name a household word and contributed hugely to the general acceptance of the comparative-historical method (Nicholls 2015).[13]

Comparative philology, anthropology, and ethnicity: J. C. Prichard and the Celts

Much later in the century (1888), Müller would in a famous, often-quoted disclaimer bitterly denounce the confusion between linguistic and ethnological nomenclature. It was an annoying error, he felt, to equate languages with the peoples who spoke them.

> To me an ethnologist who speaks of an Aryan race, Aryan blood, Aryan eyes and hair, is as great a sinner as a linguist who speaks of a dolichocephalic dictionary or a brachycephalic grammar. It is worse than a Babylonian confusion of tongues — it is downright theft. We have made our own terminology for the classification of languages; let ethnologists make their own for the classification of skulls, and hair, and blood.[14]

Really, Professor Müller? A bit rich, coming from someone who himself had written that 'the blood which circulates in their grammar [*i.e.* that of the languages

Fig. 1.6. Friedrich Max Müller, from *Cassell's Universal Portrait Gallery* (London: Cassell 1895)

of Northern India, JL], is Arian blood' (Müller 1854, 8). Müller's wrath is selective and disingenuous, for he himself, and indeed the entire linguistic school that he spoke for, had actively connived in the confusion that by 1888 he presumed to denounce. He had also forgotten, perhaps, his own comments in his popular *Lectures on the Science of Language* (1861–64), which constantly slipped from the linguistic to the anthropological and the ethnographical by way of the mythological. Müller had then propounded a cultural/mythological familiarity between the 'Aryan races' as much as a linguistic one: 'a family likeness between the sacred names worshipped by the Aryans of India and the Aryans of Greece' (Müller 1994, 2: 408). 'In the hymns of the Rig-Veda we still have the last chapter of the real Theogony of the Aryan races' (2: 410).

Despite Müller's belated and disingenuous bluster, the confusion between language and race is not an anomaly, but a systemic feature of the comparative-historical paradigm of those early decades. While the nomenclature of modern languages (Spanish, Danish, Bulgarian, Finnish) is usually geographical, overlapping with names of countries and regions where those languages are spoken, the nomenclature of older languages and of the larger language families has traditionally been ethnic, referring to the tribes or 'races' by whom these languages were spoken: Semitic, Celtic, Slavic, Germanic, and, indeed, Aryan and Anglo-Saxon. The comparative method in philology was paradigmatically and in its historical emergence linked to the comparative method in anthropology (Wilhelm von Humboldt) and anatomy (Georges Cuvier) — the reader will recall Ingram's programme, as early as 1803, for what he calls, by analogy, 'the comparative anatomy of human language'. A similar link was made between comparative ethnology and comparative philology by Nicholas Wiseman in 1835; in a lecture 'On the comparative study of languages', Wiseman advocated the new, Continental, comparative methodology, and spoke of 'the sister sciences' of 'philological and physiognomical ethnography'.[15]

In the emerging philological paradigm, the tendency to equate language and ethnicity was structural rather than incidental. Linguistic and cultural diversity in the British Isles was, as a result, from the beginning placed under the heading of 'race' (Augstein 1996; it should be understood that the notion of 'race' was as yet a fairly fluid one and not as biologically rigid as it would become later on.) In its ethnological and anthropological overtones, the comparative method was a challenge to the Biblical account of the descent of man (as descended from a single pair of ancestors, Adam and Eve, and sprung from a single nuclear family, that of Noah and his fellow-survivors of the Deluge). Regardless whether the Biblical account was interpreted literally or metaphorically, it imposed a view of humankind as in its entirety belonging to a single 'family tree' — the so-called 'monogenist' view. That view came under pressure from the comparatists, whose taxonomy of closer and more distant relations (the twigs, boughs and branches of the family tree) could accommodate no familiarity beyond the 'Indo-European' or 'Aryan' category. Accordingly, the comparatist view played into the hands of Anglo-Saxonist, imperialist triumphalism, as well as Eurocentric or 'white' exclusivism and ethnocentrism: it excluded Semitic and non-European languages and 'races'

Fig. 1.7. James Cowles Prichard, from the Journal of the Royal Anthropological Institute of Great Britain and Ireland, 38 (1908)

from the central, Indo-European category, which was habitually considered superior in its cultural achievements and civilization to the rest of humanity. Anthropological 'polygenism' (the counterpart to the monogenism of the Biblical model) would later in the century harden into outright racism and give to racism a quasi-scientific lustre (Gould 1981, Stocking 1987). While the polygenists had the scientific wind in their sails, owing to the great advances and discoveries made in comparative linguistics, there were rearguard actions by monogenist-minded scholars, who, significantly, tended to have a theological background or links to the church: Nicholas Wiseman, Thomas Arnold, and, importantly, James Cowles Prichard (cf. generally Augstein 1997).

Prichard had received his medical doctorate at the University of Edinburgh for a thesis addressing the 'varieties of mankind' (*De generis humani varietate*), a topic which was to engross him for the rest of his life, and in which he would combine evidence from physical anthropology (skull-shapes and cranial measurements) with data from comparative linguistics. As such, he was an important voice in that conceptual confusion between 'race' and 'language' which was later exacerbated and subsequently denounced by Max Müller.

Prichard's specific importance for our topic of interest lies in the fact that he took the question of ethnicity into the bosom of the British Isles. He had, through his mother, a Welsh background, and wrote his thesis (and its monograph spin-off, *Researches Into the Physical History of Mankind*, 1813) when the place of the Celtic languages in the Indo-European family was as yet undecided (like Albanian or Armenian). Friedrich Schlegel himself had voiced doubts on that score, and it was only in the late 1830s that Continental scholars would demonstrate the relationship.[16] In that uncertainty, and in the growing tension between polygenist and monogenist views, Prichard was much concerned with the place of the Celtic races/languages in that 'physical history of mankind'. That doubt led to the publication of his *Eastern Origin of the Celtic Nations* (1837), which drew on many Welsh sources and literary data.

Prichard was, to some extent, an eccentric stray in the history of science; but the influence of his work permeates the discussions surrounding the birth of Comparative Literature in Britain, as we shall see further on, in the cases of Thomas Price and Matthew Arnold. The place of the Celtic languages and literatures was a contentious point, given the Victorians' dominant Anglo-Saxonism and their unease and scorn when confronted with Irish nationalism; and the dispute over the relative weight of Anglo-Saxon and Celtic literary influences in British literary life was to be one of the formative experiences for emerging British comparatism.

FIG. 1.8. Sir John Bowring, painting by John King, 1826
(© National Portrait Gallery, London)

Literary internationalism and John Bowring

In the study of *ancient* languages, myths and epics, then, the comparative method was in the air, imported from German academia by a number of remarkable mediators. It did not yet, however, make itself felt in the study of *modern* (i.e. non-ancient, non-Classical) literatures. The notion that Europe consisted of different nations, each with its own literature, enjoyed some popularity among the Whigs of the Holland House circle, who resented the Metternich-style restoration of a Europe divided into divinely ordained monarchical realms, and supported the calls of subject peoples for a measure of self-determination. Spearheading that anti-Metternich patriotism was, of course, philhellenism, which in Byron had its most famous champion and martyr (Spencer 1954; St Clair 1972). To support the Greek insurrection against Ottoman rule was (like abolitionism) a coded liberal-democratic stance: against the divine right of princes and for democratic self-determination. The Holland House circle (which included Campbell and Crabb Robinson) generated literary support for national movements in many European countries; literary figures under its penumbra like Mrs Hemans, Lady Morgan and Thomas Moore wrote liberal- and patriotically-minded tales and verse on Ireland, Belgium, Greece, Spain and Italy; young John Kemble even travelled to Malaga by way of Gibraltar in 1831 to support General Torrijo's ill-fated Constitutionalist revolt against the autocratic-restorative Ferdinand VII.

Such a romantic enthusiasm for the cause of national patriotism and the Mazzini-style solidarity of oppressed nations in Europe was to find a continuation when the refugees of failed national-democratic movements arrived in London in the 1840s: people like Alexander Herzen, Kyrstyn Lach-Szyrma (father of the Cornish revivalist) and Gabriele Rossetti (father of Dante Gabriel and Christina). This stance often went together with an interest in the folk songs of the nations in question: philhellenes had taken an interest in Greek klephtic songs, while the Serbian oral epic collected by Vuk Karadžić was attracting attention all over Europe (Leerssen 2012a).

How these various interests could coalesce into a general, comparative interest in popular literature is shown in the case of John Bowring. Bowring (1792–1872), now known mainly as a Benthamite, radical MP and ultimately Governor of Hong Kong, on his many travels across Europe familiarized himself with many languages, cultures and patriotisms, all of which he presented to the liberal English readership in (largely plagiarized) anthologies: *Specimens of the Russian Poets* (1820), *Batavian Anthology*, *Ancient Poetry and Romances of Spain* (both 1827), *Specimens of the Polish Poets* and *Servian Popular Poetry* (both 1830), *Poetry of the Magyars* and *Cheskian Anthology* [sic] (1832). He saw all of these as building blocks in what should become an anthology of the 'national literatures' of Europe. (In this phraseology, 'national' obviously meant 'popular, demotic, folk'.)

On his travels, he 'networked' to ensure the collaboration of leading scholars and literati in all the countries he visited: Rasmus Rask and Finnur Mágnusson for Icelandic, Adam Oehlenschläger for Danish, Ferenc Toldy for Hungarian, Nikolai Karamzin for Russian, Julian Ursyn Niemcewicz and Adam Mickiewicz for Polish,

Vuk Karadžić for Serbian, Václav Hanka and František Čelakovský for Czech (all of them famous names in the literary revivals of their respective countries, cf. ERNiE 2018); also among his contacts were important comparative philologists and translators such as Talvj (Therese von Jakob) and Claude Fauriel.[17]

The Max Müller-style comparative method of the antiquarian philologists dealt with ancient languages and texts, without interest in modern literary multinationality; conversely, the Bowring-style modern interest in literary multinationality had no comparative method or sense of historical growth and exchange processes. Neither of these, then, could develop into something we would recognize as 'comparatist'. A comparative literary history that focused on post-Classical Europe did, however, begin to arise in other fields. We can trace its incipience in two remarkable individuals: Henry Hallam and Thomas Price.

The new history-writing and Henry Hallam

History-writing had in its traditional form chronicled affairs of state: space was divided by realm, time by great turning points (military battles, dynastic successions and political crises). In the eighteenth century history had in addition come to be seen as a vast storehouse of data on human choices and experiences, and as such as 'philosophy teaching by example'. Following the French Revolution and the break-up of the Enlightenment, various alternative historiographical trends competed. The new emphasis on source criticism meant that many historians (the Ranke school) turned to archives, which focused their attention on 'social changes directed from above' (as Peter Burke has felicitously phrased it, 2012); at the same time, an Idealist view took hold (e.g. with Michelet) which attempted to see, beyond the man-made and government-driven incidents of each period, the manifestation of more deep-rooted and transcendent forces, and which saw as the protagonists of a nation's history not the monarch or his ministers and generals, but the nation itself. And finally there was a trend, rooted in antiquarianism, which took an interest in the details of everyday life and in the experiences, manners and customs of the common people. That trend was most successfully applied in the narratives of Walter Scott, whose powers of evoking, and bringing to life in the reader's mind, the experience of living in the past, were the envy of professional historians (Rigney 2001). This trend, which is very close to what nowadays we would call cultural history, used a great variety of sources, many of them of a 'literary' nature (in a broad definition of that term, including reminiscences, ballads and so on). Indeed, the possibility may be fruitfully entertained that many of the early 'literary histories' originated, not so much as 'histories of literature', but as 'cultural histories based on literary sources' (cf. some of the cases covered in Spiering 1999). These new 'cultural histories based on literary sources' supplanted older forms of literary chronicling, which were mainly concerned with inventorying works and authors, and writing 'Lives of the Poets'.

Someone who came very close to this type of historiography in the English context, and one of the most direct precursors of comparatism in Britain, was

Fig. 1.9. Henry Hallam, stipple engraving by William Holl Jr and George Richmond (© National Portrait Gallery, London)

Henry Hallam (1777–1859). The only son of a high-ranking churchman (erstwhile Canon of Windsor and Dean of Bristol), Hallam was educated at Eton and Christ Church, Oxford. He was a barrister and MP (on the conservative wing of the Whigs), but devoted most of his energies to history-writing. His *View of the State of Europe During the Middle Ages* (1818) had sprung from a constitutional comparison between Anglo-Saxon and Norman England, which he further pursued in his *Constitutional History of England from the Accession of Henry VII to the Death of George II* (1827). Most important for the present context is, however, his *Introduction to the Literature of Europe in the Fifteenth, Sixteenth, and Seventeenth Centuries*, which appeared in four volumes between 1837 and 1839. The title promises, and the book delivers, a broad sweep encompassing various languages and literary traditions; but it should not be confused with the great synoptic works of later comparatists like Georg Brandes or Paul Van Tieghem, in that the humanist and neoclassical canon that Hallam surveys did not see itself as nationally compartmentalized; not does Hallam himself reflect on the necessity for a comparative procedure that his synoptic view entails. That the work was a synoptic one, Hallam acknowledges: he defines it as 'a synoptical view of literature [displaying] its various departments in their simultaneous conditions through an extensive period, and in their mutual dependency'.

More importantly, Hallam defines 'literature' in a very broad sense, as the textual form of culture. This is how he defines his corpus:

> Some departments of literature are passed over, or partially touched. Among the former are books relating to particular arts, as agriculture or painting, or to subjects of merely local interest, as those of English law. Among the latter is the great and extensive portion of every library, the historical. Unless where history has been written with particular beauty of language, or philosophical spirit, I have generally omitted all mention of it [...] I have not given its numerical share to theology. (Hallam 1837–39, 1: xiv ff.)

What we see here is a definition of literature in transition. Traditionally, a wide, inclusive definition of literature had encompassed historiography, philosophy, criticism, theology and other forms of learned discourse as well as fictional narrative and the poetic genres: epic, dramatic and lyrical. It had, of course, been prevalent until Romanticism (and is still used when we deal with ancient and classical literature). By 1837 this wide definition was becoming old-fashioned in its application to modern letters: Romantics themselves had begun to distinguish between (as Thomas De Quincey phrased it) the 'literature of knowledge and the literature of power', the former of which was beginning to disappear from the purview of literary critics and, after Hallam, literary historians. Hallam still adheres to the wide definition (and as such is firmly a 'cultural historian working on a literary corpus'), but is already beginning to apply restrictions based on aesthetic merit: 'beauty of language', 'philosophical spirit'.

Yet, on the other hand, Hallam is far removed from literary criticism, which places the text's 'merit' at the very centre of its concerns; such merit, for Hallam, is incidental at best, a secondary consideration besides the overriding aspect of historical importance and influence in intellectual and cultural life.

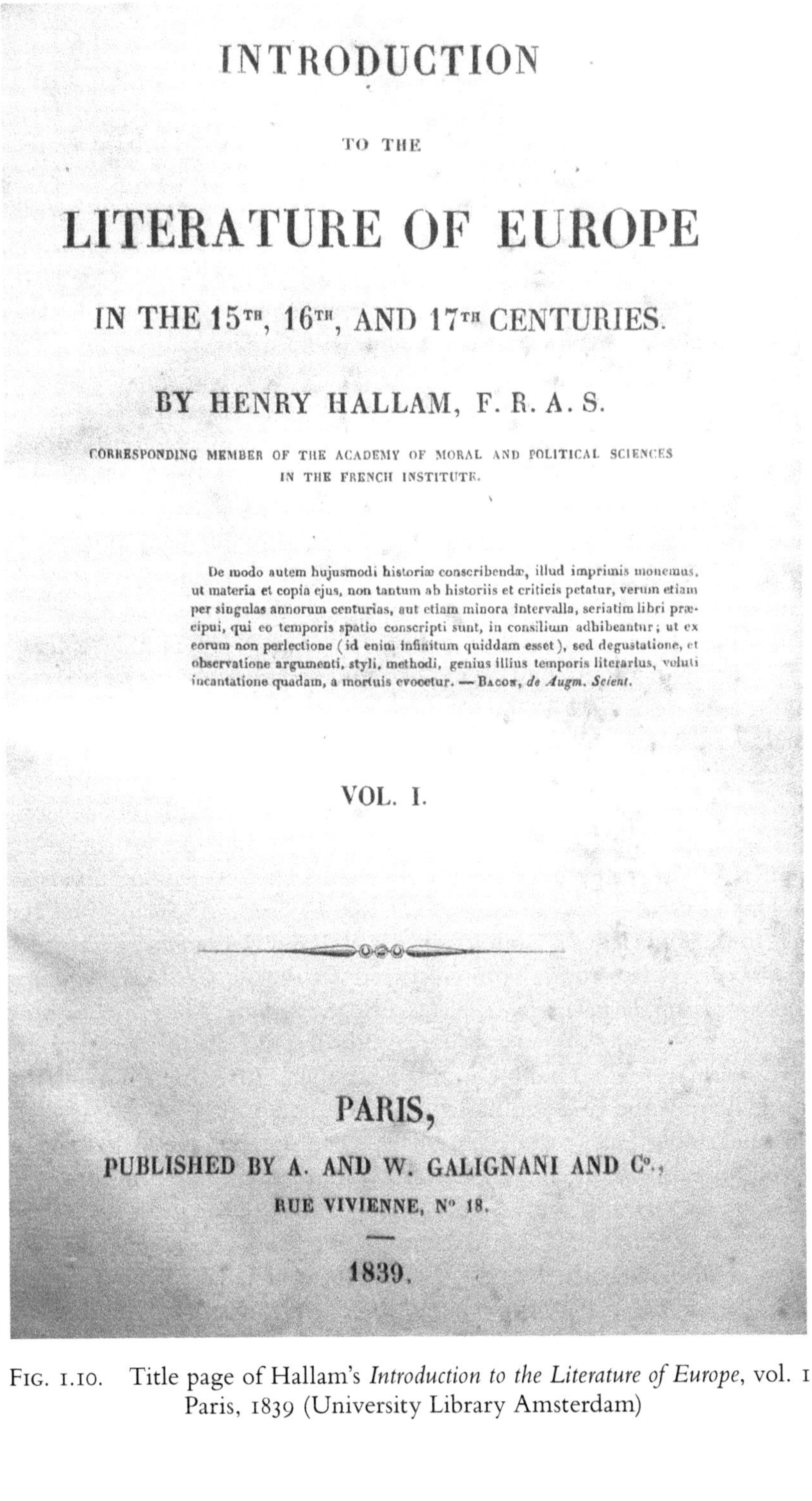

INTRODUCTION

TO THE

LITERATURE OF EUROPE

IN THE 15TH, 16TH, AND 17TH CENTURIES.

BY HENRY HALLAM, F. R. A. S.

CORRESPONDING MEMBER OF THE ACADEMY OF MORAL AND POLITICAL SCIENCES
IN THE FRENCH INSTITUTE.

> De modo autem hujusmodi historiæ conscribendæ, illud imprimis monemus, ut materia et copia ejus, non tantum ab historiis et criticis petatur, verum etiam per singulas annorum centurias, aut etiam minora intervalla, seriatim libri præcipui, qui eo temporis spatio conscripti sunt, in consilium adhibeantur; ut ex eorum non perlectione (id enim infinitum quiddam esset), sed degustatione, et observatione argumenti, styli, methodi, genius illius temporis literarius, voluti incantatione quadam, a mortuis evocetur. — BACON, *de Augm. Scient.*

VOL. I.

PARIS,

PUBLISHED BY A. AND W. GALIGNANI AND C°.,
RUE VIVIENNE, N° 18.

1839.

FIG. 1.10. Title page of Hallam's *Introduction to the Literature of Europe*, vol. 1, Paris, 1839 (University Library Amsterdam)

In one crucial respect Hallam's historiographical procedure distinguishes his book, as an academic-scholarly study, from mere criticism or chronologically-ordered literary commentary: he anchors his own work in his primary and secondary sources. Hallam's preface aims to 'state [his] general secondary sources of information, exclusive of acquaintances I possess with original writers' (1: xiv). This, of course, is the very essence of academic scholarship (as opposed to cultural commentary): the idea that one contributes to an ongoing, accumulative tradition of knowledge, and that one's comments on the primary corpus (with which one is directly 'acquainted', as Hallam phrases it) proceeds on the basis of an awareness of the *status quaestionis*, and an ongoing acknowledgement of the accumulated body of previous, secondary studies on the topic. To highlight that ingrained *habitus* is not quite to belabour the obvious. For one thing, its 'obviousness' has lost ground in recent decades. Historicist source-anchoring has in literary studies been largely replaced by the edgier, more iconoclastic merits of subversive originality and theoretically-informed acumen. More importantly, it is in this habitus that Hallam departs also from the practices of criticism, literary commentary of an interpretative or evaluative nature, and places the study of literature in the methodological context of the historical and philological sciences.

Hallam's survey of his secondary sources groups them into various categories.

The first of these comprises 'General histories of literature, embracing all subjects, all ages, and all nations'. As Hallam wrily puts it, 'We possess little of that kind in our language'. Among the examples which Hallam invokes is Juan Andrés's remarkable *Dell' origine, progresso e stato attuale d'ogni letteratura* (1782–99, now gaining fresh recognition as one of the first works emphasizing the deep impact of Arabic literature on Europe, by way of Moorish Spain; Andreu 2016). Hallam calls it 'an extraordinary performance, embracing both ancient and modern literature in its full extent'. Hallam's other examples are the well-known German universal-history surveys: Daniel Georg Morhof's *Unterricht von der deutschen Sprache und Poesie* and *Polyhistor* (1682/88); Friedrich Bouterwek's 12-volume *Geschichte der neuern Poesie und Beredsamkeit* (1801–1819) and Johann Gottfried Eichhorn's *Geschichte der Literatur von ihrem Anfänge bis auf die neuesten Zeiten* (5 vols, 1805–1812). These are acknowledged classics in the prehistory of general literary history, at least in their impact within their own country (e.g., Tiraboschi and De Sanctis in Italy); for their impact in England, Hallam is the first and most important conduit.

Hallam next mentions 'national histories so comprehensive as to leave uncommemorated no part of [a country's] literary labour', again noticing that Britons are in no position to 'claim for ourselves a single attempt of the most superficial kind'.

The 'history of particular departments of literature' acknowledges Sismondi's classic *De la littérature du Midi de l'Europe* (1813). Hallam would have known Sismondi's famous treatise on the republican constitutions of the Italian city-states, *Histoire des républiques italiennes du Moyen Âge* (1809–1818); the Geneva-born author, one of Mme de Stael's intimates, was, like Hallam, one of the new generation of liberal historians of national culture and political thought.

Finally, there are the biographical compendia. Here, Britain has various examples to show, which Hallam makes use of, but which he clearly sees as the mere raw materials to process, synthesize and transcend.

From the array of authorities that Hallam engages with, and the spread of their provenance, the reader may judge how intense his engagement with the European world of learning was; not only his topic, but also his own command of the relevant sources, is Europe-wide in scope. Hallam is aware of his pioneer position, his attempt to break new ground. He sees no precursors within Britain, but introduces from European forerunners something that has advantages 'too manifest to be disputed': the 'synoptical view' of a multinational literary system defined in its 'various departments', 'simultaneous conditions through an extensive period', and 'mutual dependency'. What better definition of Comparative Literature? But how could that method take root if it was the leisure-time pursuit of professional gentlemen?

Wales, the matière de Bretagne *and Thomas Price*

The Romantic interest in vernacular cultures also affected Britain's 'Celtic Fringe'. In Wales, the colourful figure of Iolo Morganwg (1747–1826), with his enticing, often fanciful evocations of bardic/druidic traditions, exerted a powerful influence, and literary gatherings called *eisteddfodau*, which since the Middle Ages had dwindled into insignificance, were revived in a climate of modern sociability, often under genteel or aristocratic patronage.

A crucially important figure in this nascent Welsh revival was Thomas Price (1787–1848), an Anglican clergyman who admired Prichard's monogenist work on Celtic origins (he published an essay 'On the physiognomy of the inhabitants of the British Isles'), and who shared the ideas and enjoyed the support of the powerful cultural patron Lady Llanover (1802–1896).[18]

Two aspects here are worth probing. One is the social setting: the network in which Price and Lady Llanover managed to lift the eisteddfod from a local, popular-cultural event into a prestigious philological and national-cultural one. The other is Price's comparative and pan-Celtic interest, which allowed the local Abergavenny network to reach across Brittany into France and into philological circles which were at the time going through a process of academic professionalization.

Augusta Hall, wife of the Welsh industrialist Sir Benjamin Hall (after whom the 'Big Ben' clock tower in Westminster is named), became, upon her husband's ennoblement in 1859, known as Lady Llanover. Under that name she gained fame as a colourful figure in the romantic revival of Welsh culture, designing, for example, what she considered a Welsh national costume and requiring her tenants and employees on her estate near Abergavenny to wear it. What is more, she maintained a convivial network at her estate which attracted relatives by marriage, friends, and acquaintances, and which reached from the local and intimate to the far-flung and global.[19] Wales at that time and place did not have the institutional infrastructure of London that could carry new cultural and intellectual developments, but Lady Llanover's circle provided, in that absence, an alternative platform.

Fig. 1.11. Rev. Thomas Price, Carnhuanawc, lithograph by Lowes Dickinson after drawing by Charles Lucy (National Library of Wales; reproduced under Creative Commons licence)

Lady Llanover, née Augusta Waddington, was the sister of that Frances Waddington who, while on the Grand Tour in Rome, married a young Prussian diplomat posted there: none other than the Baron Bunsen (cf. above, 31) who later became Prussian Ambassador to the Court of St James, and (with Max Müller) the very embodiment of the closeness of German-British relations in the mid-nineteenth century. Bunsen had philological interests and, as with many of his generation, this revolved around the 'Aryan' relations between Northern Europe and British India. He was particularly intrigued to see his in-laws' Welsh background as the Celtic, Westernmost outrider of the Indo-European linguistic family, counterpart to India, the two united under the imperial aegis of Anglo-Saxon England (cf. Young 2008). We shall encounter other instances of this imperial-Aryan globalism further on. It was Bunsen who would encourage his German philological contacts to participate in the revived eisteddfods that were organized in Abergavenny in the 1830s (Gruber 2014).

But the network ramified further. It involved a noblewoman from the Dowlais estate at nearby Merthyr Tydfil, Lady Charlotte Guest (1812–1895), who has won lasting fame as translator of the Welsh cycle of medieval romances, the Mabinogion. She resided near the mining works of her husband, Sir John Josiah Guest (another wealthy industrialist, like the Hall and Waddington families). Apt at languages, Guest had learned Welsh after her marriage; her translation of the Mabinogi tales, taken from the Red Book of Hergest, were made under Price's inspiration from 1838 on and appeared in three volumes as *The Mabinogion* in 1849.[20] Part of the Mabinogion's appeal lay in the fact that some of its tales featured King Arthur, drawing attention to the Welsh background of that English literary icon. It was a symbolical trump card for Welsh culture that would be relied upon heavily by the cultural actors in this circle. And these involved, not only the German-philological contacts of Bunsen, but also Breton and Welsh men of letters. Price himself had commissioned the Breton lexicographer Le Gonidec to translate the Bible for the British and Foreign Bible Society; that contact led to a Breton-French cultural axis which in turn proved the germ of later pan-Celtic alliances. The Breton network thickened after Frances Waddington Bunsen, while in Rome (where her husband had a diplomatic posting at the time) furnished a Breton art historian, Alexis-François Rio, with an introduction to Lady Charlotte Guest. While there, Rio met and married a Catholic Welshwoman, Apollonia Jones, took up residence in Wales, became a member of the Llanover Circle, and it was due to him that for subsequent eisteddfods prominent Bretons were invited, among them the philologist and ballad collector Théodore de La Villemarqué (1815–1895). He caught the Arthurian-bardic bug from Guest and Price, and paid Lady Charlotte the compliment of plagiarizing her work for his *Les Bardes bretons du VIe siècle* (1850).

By this time, the informal friends-and-relatives coterie around Lady Llanover had found a wider social outlet in a club, the *Cymmreigiddion y Fenni* or Abergavenny Welsh Society, established in 1833, which became the organizer of cultural and scholarly festivals called by the time-hallowed name of *eisteddfod*. The intellectual mover of these initiatives was the historian/clergyman Thomas Price.

What made Price stand out among other Welsh cultural enthusiasts was precisely

Fig. 1.12. Lady Llanover, painting, 1862 (Amgueddfa Cymru and peoplescollection.wales, reproduced under Creative archive licence).

Fig. 1.13. Lady Charlotte Schreiber (née Bertie, then Guest), photograph (albumen print) by Camille Silvy, 1861
(© National Portrait Gallery, London)

his wider comparatist interest. He visited and corresponded with Irish cultural historians and antiquaries and, more importantly, visited Brittany, where he was deeply struck by that region's obvious linguistic and cultural kinship. These comparative pan-Celtic interests Price instilled into his revivals of the eisteddfod-gatherings.

With the support of Lady Llanover's prestige, money, and network, the eisteddfods in which Price played an ever more influential role (starting with Carmarthen, 1823; Welshpool, 1824; Brecon 1826 and 1828; culminating in those he organized in Abergavenny as of 1833) grew in literary, cultural and scholarly status. Addresses were read out from Sir Walter Scott, Thomas Moore, Robert Southey and Lamartine; Breton delegates like La Villemarqué attended, eager to bolster the Celtic connection; and when Bunsen's diplomatic posting in Rome came to an end in 1838, he too became a regular guest. It was he who recommended the eisteddfod, on the basis of common Aryan roots, to the Calcutta tycoon Dwarkanath Tagore, then visiting Britain (grandfather of the poet Rabindranath, and instigator of the 'Bengal Renaissance'[21]). And ultimately, it was an eisteddfod experience that inspired Matthew Arnold for his lecture series 'On the Study of Celtic Literature' (below, pp. 61 ff.).

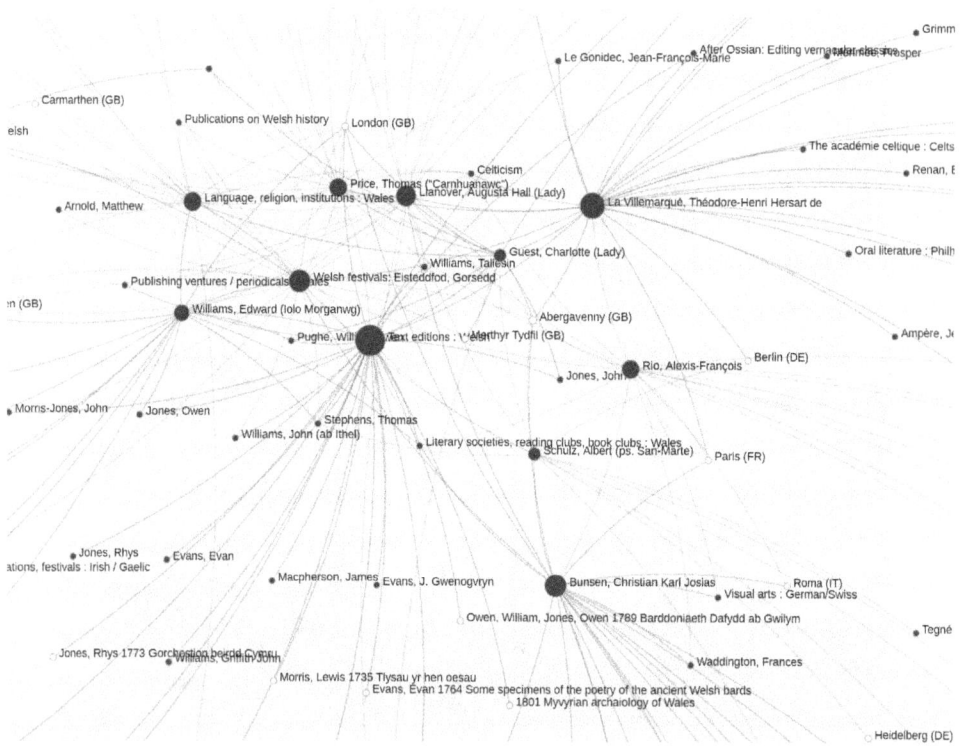

FIG 1.14. Network visualization of the Llanover Circle

The eisteddfod meetings, like other associations and gatherings at the time, habitually tried to improve public knowledge and learning by means of prize essays on set topics. The themes suggested by Price (who was by now known largely under his bardic name 'Carnhuanawc') were frequently of a comparative-philological nature, involving the Prichard-derived topic of the place of the Celtic traditions in human civilization. What specifically interested Price was the role of Wales in the European spread of Arthurian romance.

In this interest, Price also had the example of George Ellis to go by. Ellis (1753–1815), a celebrated literary antiquary with Welsh interests, had in 1805 published his three-volume *Specimens of Early English Metrical Romances, to which is Prefixed an Historical Introduction on the Rise and Progress of Romantic Composition in France and England*. In the introduction he had ventured the suggestion, then a fairly novel one, that there was a genetic line that led from the semi-legendary Welsh king Arthur, mentioned by the medieval chronicler Geoffrey of Monmouth, to the various romances involving King Arthur and his Knights of the Round Table, culminating in the work of Chrétien de Troyes, which was re-introduced into England by way of an Anglo-Norman conduit. Ellis's friend Walter Scott had given this book a very extensive and positive review in the *Edinburgh Review* in 1806, and the theory had also elicited keen interested on the Continent: Grimm referred to Ellis in his correspondence from 1810 onwards, and French scholars from the 1830s onwards classified Arthurian chivalric romance as the 'Matter of Britain', *matière de Bretagne*.[22] That the appellation *Bretagne* could refer to Great Britain and Little Britain (Brittany) was grist to the mill of pan-Celtic Bretons — and also Price.

It was against this background that Price set, as the prize essay for the 1838 Abergavenny eisteddfod, the theme of 'the influence which the Welsh traditions have had on the literature of Europe'. The title is pregnant with comparatist interest. The budding study of Arthurian romance obviously saw its theme as a transnationally ramifying literary phenomenon and as a matter of what nowadays would be called 'cultural transfers'; that is noteworthy, as is the phraseology of a 'Literature of Europe' in which various national traditions such as the Welsh can mesh and participate. But what lifted the prize essay out of its amateur-regionalist and parochially Welsh setting was the effect it had on scholars wider afield. Bunsen and Tagore were in attendance, and the jury was chaired by none other than Henry Hallam. Among the competitors were, not only Price himself (his lengthy essay is in his *Literary Remains*, 1859 1: 235–303), but also the German philologist Albert Schulz (1802–1893), friend of Bunsen and better known under his pseudonym 'San-Marte' (Gruber 2014), and the aforementioned La Villemarqué, who was then on a government-sponsored philological mission to the British Isles.

These factors turn the 1838 Abergavenny eisteddfod into a nodal point for comparatist cross-currents across Europe. Its outreach spanned local, regional and global levels: the private conviviality of the Llanover Circle, the local cultural patriotism of the Welsh revivalists, the Aryan-imperial connections of the Bunsen-Tagore axis as well as contacts with the emerging medievalist and philological traditions of Germany and France. True, its influence for Celtic Studies in the German direction proved abortive; Schulz/San Marte published on Arthurian and chivalric romance, but remained marginal to the academic mainstream. (After the publication of Zeuss's *Grammatica Celtica* of 1854, the development of Continental Celtology was to follow a more hard-edged philological course, with names like Zimmer and Thurneysen, and with a greater interest in the more primitive-archaic, rather than medieval-romantic themes.) But the Welsh-Arthurian entanglements with French medieval and comparative studies were more momentous.

French medievalists were at this moment scrutinizing cross-channel exchanges between Norman-dominated England and France. The *Chanson de Roland* was in these years rediscovered in the Bodleian Library, and it was in hope of similar discoveries, of a more Arthurian nature, that La Villemarqué had undertaken a semi-official mission to Wales and, indeed, the Bodleian.[23] Its philological impact was hampered by La Villemarqué's slapdash and speculative approach — *Les bardes bretons du VIe siècle* is not only a derivation of Guest's work, but also off-beam in its periodization and historical theories. Worse, La Villemarqué's Breton ballad collection *Barzaz breiz* would soon after come under suspicion as to its authenticity; nonetheless, he was at the time a fairly highly-regarded philologist, correspondent of Jacob Grimm, and linked to the circles around Claude Fauriel, first professor of *littératures étrangères* at the Sorbonne (Guiomar 1997; Constantine 2007). Fauriel and other harbingers of French comparatism such as Abel Villemain, Jean-Jacques Ampère and Philarète Chasles picked up the interest, and in 1842, the Académie française,

> with Villemain as its representative, proposed, as the subject of the 'Concours extraordinaire', the *Histoire Comparée des Littératures espagnole et française*. The prize fell to Adolphe de Puibusque, who in the following year published his thesis in two volumes; this work, of which the subject had perhaps been suggested by that of the Abergavenny Eisteddfod of 1838 [...] constitutes the earliest really long attempt at comparative criticism as we understand it nowadays. (Partridge 1926, 170–71)

And the intra-British impact? Price's own eisteddfod essay (which, in the event, failed to obtain the first prize) vindicates the importance of Wales in European literary history. In Price's view, Wales was spared the post-Roman upheavals of the early Middle Ages, repelled the encroaching Saxon conquest and entered with its ancient culture almost intact into the Norman feudal period. Hence, Price concludes,

> as far as regards modern Europe, with the exception of the Principality of Wales, prior to the twelfth century, either no national literature existed at all, or else, where it did exist, as among the Saxons of England, or the aborigines of Ireland, it became entirely extinguished in the general commotion — the erection of new states, and the formation of new languages, which took place at that extraordinary epoch. It is therefore to this period that we are to look for the first dawn of modern literature [...]

It was from this nationally undisturbed sanctuary that, as Price saw it, Arthurian impulses (mediated by Bretons) could reach continental poets like Chrétien de

Troyes and exercise their rejuvenating inspiration on the chivalric literature of medieval Europe.

Price's model has obvious flaws, shortcomings and a localist *parti pris*, but it remains remarkable in its vision of literary developments as a transnational European dynamic. The literary-historical map of Europe that Price studies undoubtedly lists erroneous or incomplete data read in a slanted manner, but the map as he unrolls it is in itself a perfectly comparatist one, and employs parameters still used in present-day Arthurian and medieval studies.

Price's attempts to vindicate his native literature involve, deliberately, a comparative treatment: he places that literature in a wider European context and studies the relative importance by weighing each against other counterparts. That was also the procedure he followed in a later, similar but more ambitious 100-page essay, which was awarded a prize at the 1845 Abergavenny eisteddfod: 'On the Comparative Merits of the Remains of Ancient Literature in the Welsh, Irish, and Gaelic Languages, and their Value in Elucidating the Ancient History and the Mental Cultivation of the Inhabitants of Britain, Ireland, and Gaul' (Price 1859 1: 113–232). The use of the comparative principle is here signalled explicitly by the use of that word in the title. Although 'comparative' refers to literary 'merits' rather than to investigative procedure, that procedure is systematically contrastive and synoptic. The application of that procedure, and of the judgement as to 'merits', is, however, in the direction of a comparative anthropology of Celtic-speaking cultures, Prichard-style, rather than towards an understanding of the dynamics of literature. But the idea of a Celtic cultural undercurrent, itself transnationally enmeshed in wider European patterns, enriching the repertoire of English literary history, and to be identified and assessed philologically, was to be taken up by Matthew Arnold ten years later.

Summary, outlook

By the mid-century, comparatist perspectives and tendencies could be noticed in a wide array of settings and locations, from the Llanover estate in Wales to the reviews and reviewers in and around literary life, and around the new University of London. They drew on a wide tributary system of source traditions, from antiquarianism to Anglo-Saxon studies, and from literary criticism to the more recently emerging ethnological and philological interest; and they were involved in different transfers from and to other parts of the world, mainly Germany and France. Vernacular literatures, often with ancient roots (such as Anglo-Saxon or Welsh) were now documented and studied with all the expertise that had previously been the monopoly of the Classics; their linguistic complexities and interrelatedness were being arranged into a taxonomy derived from the new science of comparative linguistics; and a historicist mode of studying literary remains resulted from the application of new comparative-philological methods to the older tradition of antiquarianism.

However, none of these trends was dominant; they were almost invariably subsidiary flavourings of pursuits defining themselves in wholly different terms.

In most of these cases, the interest was not in itself a literary one. Literature was studied for historical purposes, as illustrative of the manners and customs of remote ancestors and cultures. The study of literature as a verbal art-form, characterized by its poetics and by its aesthetic function, was left to the literary critics, connoisseurs who were more interested in artistic judgement than in historical context or importance. Literary criticism was fiercely judgemental, often controversialist and deeply influenced by the political parti-pris of the writer; it was, as we shall see in the following chapters, pursued in contentions, journals and periodicals rather than in academic settings. These academic settings were only slowly beginning to accommodate the study of the vernacular ('modern') languages.

It was against this background that Matthew Arnold was to offer his seminal ideas on 'the function of criticism at the present time', and to reserve a space for a specifically pedagogic, transnational and comparative element in such criticism.

Notes to Chapter 1

1. 'Para el concepto clásico, la pluralidad de los hombres y de los tiempos es accesoria, la literatura es siempre una sola'; Jorge Luis Borges, 'La postulación de la realidad' (1930), in Borges 1985, 1:155–60.
2. Beattie 1850, 2: 315, 348 ff., 356. On Campbell's personal contacts with the Schlegels and his proposal for a German-style university in London: Redding 1860, esp. 1: 54–55 and 2: 1–28. On the lecture series: Redding 1860, 2: 98–130.
3. When Thomas Jefferson conceived of a new university for the state of Virginia, his preparatory report (the 'Rockfish Gap' report of 1818) envisaged a university offering subjects such as Astronomy, Architecture and Philosophy, to be based on 'the illimitable freedom of the human mind', and dedicated to a critical quest 'to follow truth wherever it may lead, nor to tolerate any error so long as reason is left free to combat it.' Cf. Bellot 1929, 9–11.
4. Some flanking developments in academic institutions can be mentioned: the foundation of the University of Durham, in 1832, and the consolidation of St Patrick's College in Maynooth (Ireland, founded in 1795), and of St David's College near Lampeter (Wales, founded 1822). These were all conceived as ecclesiastical foundations (Maynooth as a Catholic seminary) but would in due course come to function as part of the wider, secular university system.
5. On Jones: Cannon 1990 and Franklin 2011; specifically on the colonial context of his work: Mukherjee 1968 (a book which antedates Edward Said's critique of Jones in his *Orientalism*).
6. Examples of the Germanic consonantal shift include p>f, k>h, t>th (Latin *pes, pullex, plenus* vs. foot/*Fuß*, flea/*Floh*, full/*voll*; *canis, centum, cor* vs. hound/*Hund*, hundred/*hundert*, heart/*Herz*; *tres, tu, tenuus* vs. three/*drei*, thou/*du*, thin/*dünn*). A second-stage consonantal shift similarly modeled the p>pf, k>kh and t>ts differences setting High German off against the other Germanic languages (pipe/*Pfeife*, book/*Buch*, tongue/*Zunge*).
7. Alfred treatments (cf. generally Parker 2007): Richard Blackmore, *Alfred: An Epic Poem*, 1723; James Thompson and David Mallet, *Alfred*, 1740; John Home, *Alfred*, 1778; Ebenezer Rhodes, *Alfred: An Historical Tragedy*, 1789; Joseph Cottle, *Alfred: An Epic Poem in 24 Books*, 1800; Henry James Pye (the poet laureate), *Alfred: An Epic Poem in 6 Books*, 1801; John Fitchett, *Alfred: an Epic Poem*, 1808, 1834, 1841–42; Thomas Dibdin: *Alfred the Great*, 1813; James Sheridan Knowles, *Alfred the Great: or, The Patriot King*, 1830. Arthur treatments are less frequent in the period 1800–1830 (Thomas Warton, *The Grave of King Arthur*, 1777; Walter Scott's anonymously published *The Bridal of Triermain*, 1813) but burgeon with Tennyson: *The Lady of Shalott*, 1833; *Morte d'Arthur*, 1842; *Idylls of the King*, 1859 ff.). Bulwer-Lytton chipped in with *Arthur: An epic poem* (1848).
8. e.g., Henry Weber, *Metrical Romances of the Thirteenth, Fourteenth, and Sixteenth Centuries*, 1810; John Merridew, *The Noble and Renowned History of Guy Earl of Warwick*; William J. Thoms, *A Collection of Early Prose Romances*, 1823.

9. There is a sizeable body of literature on Saxonism and the myth of the 'Norman Yoke', going back to Kliger 1952 and including, more recently, Frantzen & Niles 1997, Oergel 1998 and Parker 2015.
10. The classic study tracing the growth of British nationalism in these decades is Linda Colley's *Britons* (1992). More generally for the European context, my own *National Thought in Europe* (Leerssen 2018) and the *Encyclopedia of Romantic Nationalism in Europe* (ERNiE 2018).
11. Thus the remarkable title of Heinrich Leo's *Beowulf, das älteste deutsche, in angelsächsischer Mundart erhaltene Heldengedicht [...] Ein Beitrag zur Geschichte alter deutsche Geisteszustände* (1839); there are similar sentiments in the introductions to Ludwig Ettmüller's translation *Beowulf. Heldengedicht des achten Jahrhunderts*, 1840, and Karl Simrock's translation *Beowulf. Das älteste deutsche Epos*, 1859. The various claims and controversies surrounding Beowulf have been admirably collected by Haarder & Shippey 1998; cf. also Shippey 2008.
12. For Carlyle's Saxonism, see Horsman 1981 and Chandler 1998.
13. His distinguished career would see him naturalized a British subject in 1855, and a member of the Privy Council in 1869. On him, see Chaudhuri 1974; Davis & Nicholls 2016 and 2017.
14. Quoted MacDougall 1982, 121. Generally, on Aryan racial terminology in the context of Britain's Imperial link with India, Trautmann 1997; also Arvidsson 2006.
15. Wiseman 1866; the author (1802–1865) was appointed Roman Catholic Cardinal-Archbishop of Westminster in 1850.
16. This uncertainty was in fact unnecessary: the relationship between Welsh/Irish and German had already been demonstrated by seventeenth- and eighteenth-century scholars like Marcus Boxhorn, Edward Lhuyd and Leibniz; in fact, the very category 'Celtic' to comprise the Welsh/Breton and Irish/Scottish Gaelic languages, alongside Gaulish, had emerged in the wake of Lhuyd's work, in the decades after 1710. But in the subsequent paradigm shift towards the historical-comparative method, these older insights had been lost from view. The matter was settled by the Geneva scholar Adolphe Pictet (later teacher of Saussure) and by Franz Bopp in 1837–38, and by the great *Grammatica Celtica* (1854) of Johann Caspar Zeuss.
17. Bowring's contacts are mentioned in George Barnett Smith's article in the 'old' Dictionary of National Biography, which is more informative on this aspect than Gerald Stone's in the 'new' Oxford Dictionary of National Biography. Although Bowring's British career as a radical politician has been well studied, a full survey of his European literary contacts and activities is as yet outstanding. Cf. generally Leerssen 2011.
18. Generally, on Price and what follows: Price 1859; some comments in Young 2008, and above all the relevant chapter in Constantine 2007. On Lady Llanover and her network: Fraser 1962, 1966, 1968.
19. Elsewhere in Europe, a similar role for salons and convivial semi-domestic networks, with a concomitantly important role for women as 'hubs', cultural producers and linking agents, can be observed. Known examples seem to come from a sociohistorical setting with a literate elite culture but little academic professionalization or metropolitan centralization: thus the Bökendorf circle in Germany c. 1805, and the role of the Tengström women in Finland (cf. Van der Linden 2016 and Eiranen 2014, respectively), or the role of Rosalía de Castro and Emilia Pardo Bazán in Spanish Galicia.
20. Some aspects of her intriguing personal life, reminiscent of *Downton Abbey* plotlines, are worth mentioning in passing (generally Revel & John, 1989). Née Lady Charlotte Bertie, daughter of the Earl of Lindsey, she became mother of ten children following her marriage to Guest in 1833. Her family successfully negotiated the class difference between nobility and trade: her children were all ennobled and/or married into the aristocracy. After Sir John Guest's death in 1852, her re-marriage in 1855 caused scandal: her second husband, Charles Schreiber (1826–1884) was the Oxford tutor of one of her sons, and fourteen years her junior (her first husband had been 27 years older than she). Although the scandal led to a rupture with Lady Llanover, her considerable wealth and influence got her second husband elected as an MP, and allowed her to spend much of the rest of her life travelling and putting together a fine porcelain collection, which she bequeathed to the Victoria and Albert Museum along with her collection of fans. She supported philanthropic causes and kept an extensive diary throughout her life.

21. This Imperial dimension to British nineteenth-century cultural studies is further indicated by the fact that Price published, in 1847 an essay on *The Geographical Progress of Empire and Civilization*, subscribing to the world-historical theory of a 'westward course' from pre-Antiquity to Britain and America. On Tagore and on the Bengal Renaissance: Kling 1977, Kopf 1969, Chatterjee 2010, Dasgupta 2011.
22. The labeling was coined in the 1830s by the medievalist Paulin Paris, in contradistinction to the *Chansons de geste* (cf. Ridoux 2001).
23. We may surmise that La Villemarqué's entry for the prize essay incorporated parts of the report he was then submitting to the French minister Salvandy on his MSS-consultation mission at Oxford, 1837.

CHAPTER 2

Matthew Arnold (1848–1869)

Arnold, education and ethnicity in the mid-century

Matthew Arnold (1822–1888) is the foremost representative, along with Thomas Carlyle, of those Victorians who grappled with the moral 'condition of England' and with English culture. Author of *Culture and Anarchy* (1870) and 'The Function of Criticism at the Present Time' (1865), Professor of Poetry at Oxford, inspector of education, adept of French positivism, anguished agnostic and great crusader against what he termed *philistinism* (the stolidity and narrow-mindedness of the Victorian moral outlook), Arnold during his lifetime was already a *maître à penser*. His poetry voiced the existential anxieties of his time, torn between science and religion and sensing that high moralism only deepened personal unhappiness; his critical writings evinced a firm belief in society's capacity for moral and intellectual progress. Most important of all, perhaps, was his educational stance. It was Arnold, more than anyone else, who in the British context formulated and successfully propagated the idea (derived from the Romantic German notion of *Bildung*) that cultural literacy is a valuable and indispensable part of the education of young people, despite its lack of pragmatic applicability. Anyone who tries to improve young minds by sending schoolchildren to an art gallery or a Beethoven concert is indebted to Matthew Arnold.

In his educationalism, Arnold followed in the footsteps of his father, the reforming headmaster of Rugby School, Dr Thomas Arnold (famously celebrated in the pages of Thomas Hughes's juvenile classic *Tom Brown's School Days*, 1857). The idea of the 'Christian gentleman' — that middle-class Victorian revival of chivalric notions of self-control and high moral virtue linked to physical courage — is due in no small part to Arnold *père*, as is the idea that the formation of the English boy's character takes place on the sports field as much as in the classroom. The moral preoccupation with values and mores in society became (as Hughes's *Tom Brown* books show) a national/imperial cultivation of Englishness: Victorian values as a matter of national character.

Arnold junior adopted his father's *Bildung* notion of education as being not only instruction but also character building, but added to this his specific belief in the morally uplifting power of culture and taste. After his studies at Balliol College he became private secretary to the Whig statesman Lord Lansdowne, and was in 1851 appointed Inspector of Schools; by this time he had also begun to publish poetry.

Fig. 2.1. Matthew Arnold, caricature by James Jacques Tissot, Vanity Fair, 11 November 1871 (© National Portrait Gallery, London)

Fact-finding trips to the Continent acquainted him with the German and French educational systems and led to his *Schools and Universities on the Continent* (1868, prefaced by a motto taken from Wilhelm von Humboldt), an endorsement and amplification of the liberal educational ideas of John Henry Newman's *Idea of a University* (1852, revised 1873).

The institutional history of the British university in these decades was marked by the 1852 report of the *Oxford University Commission*, which gave fresh impulses to university reform and prepared the way for the wave of new establishments towards the end of the century (the 'redbrick universities', see below 87). Already in 1850, new universities were founded in Ireland: the federated 'Queen's Colleges' of Belfast, Cork and Galway. The first of these persists (as 'Queen's University Belfast') as a direct continuation of its original foundation; together with a Catholic counter-foundation in Dublin (1854, with John Henry Newman as its first Rector and Gerard Manley Hopkins, briefly, as a lecturer) these colleges merged into a federal 'Royal University of Ireland' in 1880. There was little or no scope for anything like Comparative Literature in these Irish colleges, but indirectly, the Continental mode of philological studies found an institutional footing there through the professorial appointment of leading Celtic scholars in Belfast and Dublin. The Dublin lectures of Eugene O'Curry, especially, became an important Gaelic counterpart to the Anglo-Saxon work of Kemble at Cambridge; we shall see their influence in Matthew Arnold's lectures as Oxford Professor of Poetry in 1867.[1] Within Oxford, the Taylor Institute, founded shortly after 1845, was to become a landmark for modern language studies, and invited literary scholars from the Continent to give guest lectures. The first of these was, in 1871, the renowned Hippolyte Taine, whose seminal *Histoire de la littérature anglaise* of 1864 was then famous (and is now notorious) for its positivistic belief that all literature could be explained in the determining parameters of 'race, milieu and moment'.

Critical judgements: Hellenism, Hebraism and the Philistines

Arnold was a poet before he became a critic. It was probably to his poems that he owed his appointment to the Oxford Professorship of Poetry in 1857.[2] In the course of this Professorship (held until 1867, and declined when offered again in 1877), Arnold developed the lines of critical thought that were published as *On Translating Homer* (1858) and *On the Study of Celtic Literature* (1867); during this tenure he also published his *Essays in Criticism* (1865), of which the opening essay seminally addressed 'The function of criticism at the present time'. Much of this essay was still to echo in Arnold's most sustained reflections of culture, the 1870 volume *Culture and Anarchy*, on which his reputation as the main cultural critic of High Victorianism rests.

Arnold's criticism remains inspiring, even for present-day readers, mainly because of its fundamental insistence on the variety of culture and on the interconnectedness of culture's variations. A text or thought is never studied atomistically, but always as part of a web of allusions and contextual or situational implications. As he himself phrased it in his opening lecture as Professor of Poetry, 'On the Modern Element in Literature':

> The spectacle, the facts, presented for the comprehension of the present age, are indeed immense. The facts consist of the events, the institutions, the sciences, the arts, the literatures, in which human life has manifested itself up to the present time: the spectacle is the collective life of humanity. And everywhere there is connexion, everywhere there is illustration: no single event, no single literature is adequately comprehended except in its relation to other events, to other literatures. (Arnold 1960 [1857], 20)

This arresting thought crops up in passing as an *obiter dictum*, an incidental general reflection in the margins of a different line of reasoning. It has not been widely influential or often quoted, and therefore its historical importance should not be over-emphasized. But it does throw light on Arnold's way of looking at things, and also on his way of looking at literature: no text, no literary tradition is an island, and the connections between literatures are what give them their position and meaning. No comparatist programme could wish for a better intellectual starting point.

By the same token, Arnold the critic was no island; nor was he narrowly English in his cultural views. He was deeply influenced by Sainte-Beuve, whom he met on his continental travels, and by French positivists like Edmond Schérer and (as we shall see) Ernest Renan. And, last but not least, he was a committed Goethean (cf. Schirmer 1947, 113–22), and like Goethe believed that culture could only flourish by means of literary cosmopolitanism rather than on the basis of national introspectiveness. That sounds like a truism nowadays, but at the time, when national chauvinism was rampant, Goethean literary cosmopolitanism was out of step with the times, a case that needed to be made. Arnold thus belongs to the generation of early comparatists of the period who took Goethe's *Weltliteratur* and the idea of literary cosmopolitanism as the starting point of their reflections. (Cf. also Anderson 1971).

Arnold's literary cosmopolitanism also shines through in his memorable and often-quoted definition of criticism. It was the cornerstone of his argument in the essay 'On the function of criticism at the present time' (1865) and was echoed in *Culture and Anarchy* (1870). The definition is a double, recursive one, defining criticism in terms of the culture which is criticism's object. Culture being 'the best that is known and thought in the world', criticism accordingly is defined as the 'disinterested endeavour to learn and propagate the best that is known and thought in the world.' Both elements are heavy with implications.

Arnold's views on culture, which he developed in many directions and contexts, have been the subject of much debate and study. In *Culture and Anarchy* the idea of 'the best' is taken both in an ethical and aesthetic sense. Culture is both intellect and art, admirable achievement and enriching joy, uniting the qualities of goodness and beauty, or, as Arnold famously phrased it, 'sweetness and light'.[3] This almost Platonic combination of 'kalos kai agathos' Arnold sees as being supremely embodied in Classical Greece. Accordingly, his cultural mission is to propagate this Greek ideal in contemporary society: to 'Hellenize' Victorian England. This mission is necessary, Arnold argues, because of the overwhelming moralism and pragmatism of his time — the sort of attitude Dickens was already satirizing in the figure of Mr Gradgrind (*Hard Times* had appeared in 1854). The England of platitudinous utilitarianism and stifling moralism he denounced as 'philistine', a term now generally current but introduced by Arnold.[4] To add to the complexity, the actual counterpart to 'Hellenism' in *Culture and Anarchy* is 'Hebraism'. This denotes a tendency, linked by Arnold to Jewish-Biblical morality, to improve the world, not by seeking the pleasures of sweetness and light, but by avoiding sin and its contamination. (DeLaura 1969; as the reader will have noticed by now, Arnold has a strong tendency to describe moral positions by way of ethnic metaphors.)

Arnold's definition of culture is, then, transnational, or at least a-national ('the world'); axiological, i.e. predicated on ethical and aesthetic value judgements; and pedagogical, in that culture connotes an upward counterforce in a world dominated by a gravitational downward pull, a 'hellenistic' ideal of sweetness and light in a society of philistines. The critic is accordingly both a connoisseur and a missionary: it is the critic's task to 'learn and propagate'.[5] Finally, that mission requires high moral standing, in that the critic's endeavour should be 'disinterested' — i.e. without parti pris, ulterior motives, prejudice or controversialist bias.

For contemporary readers, Arnold's definition seems almost embarrassingly high-minded. After Terry Eagleton's timely and insightful *Criticism and Ideology* (1976, new edn 2009), literary scholars have become highly sensitive to the complacent, status-quo-affirming and liberal-elitist tradition in English literary criticism; over the last decades, they have developed a special aptitude for detecting the ideological blind spots in the idealistic universals of Arnoldian vintage. Arnold's use of 'the world' is obviously imbued with Eurocentric triumphalism, all the more objectionable for not being explicitly reflected. His invocation of implicit, unargued value judgements as cognitive fundamentals is question-begging and, what is worse, elitist: complacent, and designed to shore up the prestige and cultural capital of educated upper-middle-class males. Modern-day readers can still derive a pleasurable sense of self-righteousness from blaming Arnold for being a Victorian — as if he had much choice in the matter.

A fairer estimate would judge Arnold by the standards of his time, rather than ours. Intervening as he did in a critical praxis dominated by the fierce party politics of the periodical reviews, and the stifling cultural tyranny of a moral conformism that makes 'political correctness' appear frivolous in comparison, Arnold was less arguing *for* a critical programme than *against* the hidebound pieties of his times. That the critic should be disinterested, and his working field 'the world', was not a complacent thing to say in 1865, and deserves better than pedantic second-guessing from hindsight. All the more when we read a conclusion that, allowances made for historical distance, should give contemporary readers food for thought:

> But, after all, the criticism that I am really concerned with — the criticism which alone can help us for the future, the criticism which, throughout Europe, is at the present day meant, when so much stress is laid on the importance of criticism and the critical spirit, — is a criticism which regards Europe as being, for intellectual and spiritual purposes, one great confederation, bound to a joint action and working to a common result; and whose members have for

their outfit, a knowledge of Greek, Roman, and Eastern antiquity, and of one another. (Arnold 1962 [1865] 283)

The statement was not an incidental flourish, but reiterated in 1879, in Arnold's preface to a Wordsworth edition:

> Let us conceive of the whole group of civilised nations as being, for intellectual and spiritual purposes, one great confederation, bound to a joint action and working towards a common result; a confederation whose members have a due knowledge both of the past, out of which they all proceed, and of one another. This was the ideal of Goethe [...] (cf. Shaffer 1979, x)

Arnold did not develop an academic programme, and for that reason alone it would be problematic to consider him an early comparatist. But his supranational vision and his awareness of the transnational connectedness of literary traditions placed him in the best company of the intellectual precursors of comparatism. What is more, his prestige (as the most respected critic between Coleridge and T. S. Eliot) was such that his example gave at least moral support and standing to all endeavours to study literature transnationally. How important this was to the early generation of academic comparatists can be gauged from the fact that he has been credited even with coining the name 'Comparative Literature' — a complex matter which deserves a brief digression.

Coining 'Comparative Literature'

There are various assertions in circulation that it was Arnold who coined the phrase 'Comparative Literature' for the transnational study of literature; and they have found their way into the discipline's various handbooks. In fact there are two scenarios to choose from: the first (mentioned by Wellek 1970) derives ultimately from a 1950 lecture by Leonard Willoughby, who claimed that Arnold used the phrase when translating sections of an *Histoire comparative* by J.-J. Ampère (Willoughby 1950, 21). The reference to Villemain is unclear,[6] and Weisstein (1968, 63) casts doubt upon it. Instead, Weisstein identifies another passage in Arnold's writings where the fateful phrase is used: a letter written to his sister in 1848. The passage runs as follows:

> How plain is it now, though an attention to the comparative literatures for the last fifty years might have instructed any one of it, that England is in a certain sense far behind the continent. (quoted Weisstein 1968, 63)

Is this, then, the place where we see a French influence, possibly the influence from Ampère put forward by Willoughby (cf. Shaffer 1979, ix; Anderson 288)? Does this throwaway phrase amount to a newly-minted term denoting 'the comparative study of literature', as Leithman (1977, 113) puts it? There are good reasons to doubt this, summarized as follows by Anderson (1971).

> Arnold speaks not of a discipline but of a plurality of 'comparative literatures', specified as being those of England and the Continent. Moreover, he places them together not for comparison but for contrast. Finally, the epithet

> 'comparative' as he uses it bears no strong technical sense. It is hardly stronger, in its context, than 'several' or 'respective' would have been. (288)

Decades, later, H. M. Posnett (1901, 856) felt it necessary to defend his usage 'Comparative Literature' as a deliberate, albeit problematic neologism: to call a scholarly discipline by the name of its object (see below, 80). That possible confusion between discipline and object is what we see at work in these various phraseological confusions around Arnold's throwaway remark. Arnold was referring offhand to an aggregate of literary traditions, not to a method of studying them.

What this does show, however, is that by the mid-century, the topic was in the air, and the phrase was waiting to be coined, as it were, discernible in pre-echoes, phraseological straws in the wind. We have by now registered various close encounters between the words or notions of literature and comparison. More momentous in that crystallization process was Arnold's final lecture series as Professor of Poetry, *On the Study of Celtic Literature* (1867).

Literary ethnicities: Celticism, Saxonism, and English

On the Study of Celtic Literature enjoys a good deal of fame in the field of Irish Studies, influential as it was in the development of the literatures of Britain's Celtic Fringe. It signals the early stirring of a Celtic interest or 'Celticism' among mainstream English intellectuals in the mid-nineteenth century; it directly triggered the establishment of a Chair of Celtic at Oxford University (whose first incumbent was Sir John Rhys, as of 1877). Arnold's lectures also had a formative effect on the development of a Celtic stereotype, and on the literary revival of Ireland and Britain's 'Celtic Fringe'. It gave prestigious endorsement to Celtic revivalism in Wales, centred around the eisteddfod festivals; it anticipated the Irish Literary Revival of the 1890s which we link with the name of W. B. Yeats; and it fixed a number of characterological traits and stereotypes which have since then been habitually attributed to a 'Celtic' mentality: a propensity for dreamy fantasy and otherworldliness, and a 'stubborn rebellion against the despotism of fact' (cf. Leerssen 1996, 2008).

More importantly for our purposes, it marks the point of intersection, in British literary studies, between the philological Saxonism of Turner and Kemble, and the cultural Celticism of Thomas Price.

The beginning of *On the Study of Celtic Literature* lies in a series of lectures which Arnold held in 1867, his last year as Professor of Poetry at Oxford.[7] The lectures were published in *Cornhill Magazine* and afterwards in book form. Their publication intervened at a crucial moment in the still-dominant but slightly *passé* discourse of Victorian Anglo-Saxonism, which has been signalled above (28–31; and cf. Frantzen & Niles 1997). By the 1860s, following various political periods of unrest in Ireland, Saxonism found itself in a complex three-cornered standoff. 'Anglo-Saxon' Englishness could be contrasted wither with a Romance (Norman-French) or with a Celtic (Irish/Welsh/Highland) counterpart. In one opposition, it was defensive (Anglo-Saxon England had been overthrown by the Normans in 1066), in the other, it was triumphalist (the Saxons had pushed back Britain's Celts to the Atlantic fringes). When contrasted with the Normans (as per *Ivanhoe* and J. M. Kemble), the Anglo-Saxons were seen as demotic, tribal-democratic natives; when contrasted with Britain's indigenous Celts, they were seen as stalwart invaders ousting a primitive race of underdeveloped aboriginals. The result of these compounded binary oppositions was a great semantic ambivalence. The Saxon-Norman contrast was mainly invoked in European affairs (especially the long-standing rivalry with France). The Saxon-Celtic opposition was mainly for domestic and colonial use (in vindicating the hegemony of England in the British Isles, or England's destiny to rule its colonial empire).[8]

Arnold himself partook, as we have seen, of the racial discourse and the ethnic essentialism that characterized his day and age. Much as his culture-critical essays are replete with Hellenes, Philistines and Hebraism, this lecture series is predicated on the polarity between 'Saxon' and 'Celt', presented here as the opposing-but-complementary halves of English culture.

Arnold opens with an evocation of how he witnessed an eisteddfod at Llandudno, then just entering its heyday as a Victorian tourist resort on Wales's north coast. The promontory at Llandudno offers vistas eastward, towards Liverpool, and westward, towards Anglesey, and Arnold's contrastive description of these Eastern and Western vistas, with which the essay opens, is one of the classic formulations of what is now called Celticism (Celtic exoticism). Eastward lies Liverpool, modern, commercial and industrial, dynamic, full of business sense and material progress; westward lies Wales, dreamy and quiet, timeless, otherworldly, given to ethereal meditation.

Thus, Arnold's encounter with Welsh culture invokes an underlying opposition between metropolis and countryside, dynamism and quietude, materially-minded pragmatism and otherworldly dreaminess. The former (Liverpudlian, English) is called 'Saxon', the latter Celtic. Arnold positions himself clearly as a mediator between the two. He addresses an audience of 'My brother Saxons' and attempts to instil in them a certain interest in 'the Celtic genius'. In establishing a common base with his English ('Saxon') audience, he admits that this 'Celtic genius' is a thing of the past. Modernity and national unity will absorb and obliterate it:

> I must say I quite share the opinion of my brother Saxons as to the practical inconvenience of perpetuating the speaking of Welsh. It may cause a moment's distress to one's imagination when one hears that the last Cornish peasant who spoke the old tongue of Cornwall is dead; but, no doubt, Cornwall is the better for adopting English, for becoming more thoroughly one with the rest of the country. The fusion of all the inhabitants of these islands into one homogeneous, English-speaking whole, the breaking down of barriers between us, the swallowing up of separate provincial nationalities, is a consummation to which the natural course of things irresistibly tends; it is a necessity of what is called modern civilisation, and modern civilisation is a real, legitimate force; the change must come, and its accomplishment is a mere affair of time. The sooner the Welsh language disappears as an instrument of the practical, political, social life of Wales, the better; the better for England, the better for Wales itself. (296–97)

These sentiments are proffered by Arnold as an echo of the commonsensical public opinion of the time. More Carlyle than Herder, this: we recognize an ethnocentrism that imposes absorption, assimilation and loss of identity on other cultures in the name of a 'historical progress' or 'march of history' which is vested in the English nation.

It is important to realize, however, that Arnold invokes this style of ethnocentrism in order to qualify and query it ('a terrible way [...] of wanting to improve everything but themselves off the face of the earth', 297). His paraphrase of Anglocentric triumphalism serves, rather, to establish a kicking-off point, his goal is to mitigate and change this attitude. Unlike his 'brother Saxons' who, Arnold surmises, 'will have nothing to do with the Welsh language and literature on any terms [and] would gladly make a clean sweep of it from the face of the earth', Arnold himself claims a positive cultural interest for the non-English languages of Britain:

> I, on certain terms, wish to make a great deal more of it than is made now; and I regard the Welsh literature, — or rather, dropping the distinction between Welsh and Irish, Gaels and Cymris, let me say Celtic literature, — as an object of very great interest. My brother Saxons have, as is well known, a terrible way with them of wanting to improve everything but themselves off the face of the earth; I have no such passion for finding nothing but myself everywhere; I like variety to exist and to show itself to me, and I would not for the world have the lineaments of the Celtic genius lost. (297–98)

The rest of his essay is dedicated to showing that there is a cultural, historical and anthropological interest (if not a practical one) in the presence of Celtic traditions in the British Isles, and that the greatest achievements of English literature allowed a 'Celtic' sense of fancy and fantasy to leaven a 'Saxon' sense of pragmatic realism.

In attempting to mediate between partialities of 'Celt-haters' and 'Celt-lovers', Arnold clearly wants to establish a neutral middle ground. His defence of Britain's Celtic literary heritage is studiously 'disinterested' (to use his own key qualification for the critic's ideal stance) and invokes, wherever possible, academic works of scholarship. Celtic culture for him is not interesting as a living tradition: predicated as Celticism is on its pastness, Arnold dismisses any claims to survival or revival for Celtic culture in the modern age. Indeed, the more strident manifestations of Celtic intransigence (in contemporary Irish politics, e.g. separatist Fenianism) are cited by Arnold mainly as an example of what can go wrong, and what needs to be remedied (the 'Anarchy' that results from a lack of Culture). Far more sympathetic to him is the mild regionalism of Wales, better integrated in the British political scheme, less virulent in its vindications. Even here, he dismisses the revivalist implications of eisteddfod festivals as quixotic. Celtic interest is *antiquarian*. Hence his use of specifically philological sources on Celtic antiquity: translations of the Welsh Mabinogion, the text editions of Eugene O'Curry, John O'Donovan and other Irish scholars. These are respectable, sober, learned, and removed from the sordid strife of political activism. Similarly, also, he sees the sphere of high scholarship as the starting position for a reconciliation move between Celt and Saxon. The concluding call of the essay is typically top-down in its Victorian cultural elitism and idealism:

> Let us reunite ourselves with our better mind and with the world through science; and let it be one of our angelic revenges on the Philistines, who among their other sins are the guilty authors of Fenianism, to found at Oxford a chair of Celtic, and to send, through the gentle ministration of science, a message of peace to Ireland. (386)

The gentle ministration of science... Arnold's belief that scientific progress will dispel the darkness of misunderstanding and ignorance invokes in particular the recent achievements of Comparative Linguistics. It was, after all, only recently that the Celtic position in the Indo-European family tree had been definitively established by the German grammarian Johann Caspar Zeuss, in his *Grammatica Celtica* (1854). For Arnold, Zeuss represents a perfect instance of the power of scientific analysis with its 'gentle ministration' to demonstrate a familial relationship between Celts and other (Indo-)Europeans. He approvingly endorses a 'German' sense of methodical procedure:

> One thing, and one thing alone, led to the truth: the sheer drudgery of thirteen long years spent by Zeuss in the patient investigation of the most ancient Celtic records in their actual condition, line by line and letter by letter. (299n.)

And again:

> Philology, however, that science which in our time has had so many successes [...] has brought, almost for the first time in their lives, the Celt and sound criticism together. The Celtic grammar of Zeuss, whose death is so grievous a loss to science, offers a splendid specimen of that patient, disinterested way of treating objects of knowledge, which is the best and most attractive characteristic of Germany. (328)

Arnold goes on to celebrate at length the achievement and beneficial influence of comparative linguistics, German-style; indeed this reflects to some extent his reliance, for some of the more technical passages, on the expert advice of Max Müller, whom we have encountered as leading philologist at Oxford and every Victorian's favourite German scholar. Such a careful, comparative analysis was also needed, Arnold feels, for the ethnological study of culture and literature: 'The literature of the Celtic peoples has not yet had its Zeuss, and greatly it wants him.' (70).

Of course, this comparatism is not as 'disinterested' as Arnold would have it: the unity it establishes between Saxons and Celts is, after all, an Aryan, Indo-European one, and invokes an undercurrent of Aryanism which, combined with certain reservations vis-à-vis 'Hebraic' moralism, make for uncomfortable reading nowadays.[9] The nomenclature of language families, is, after all, a racial one; as Arnold blithely asserts, 'philology carries us towards ideas of affinity of race which are new to us' (71), his essay goes a good deal towards that physical ethnography which, after the earlier work by Prichard, was taken to new heights by John Beddoe (*The Races of Britain*, 1885), and which forms part of the development of pseudo-scientific racism in Europe (Fischer-Tiné 2011, Leerssen 2008).

Against all this is must be observed that in each and every instance, Arnold aims to reconcile rather than to denigrate; and that his use of racial categories appears *metonymical* rather than literal — a bit like those contemporary nostrums about 'men being from Mars and women from Venus'. Arnold is, after all, a critic, not an ethnologist. A given cultural profile or stance may be labelled 'Saxon', 'Celtic', 'Latin, 'Hellenic' or 'Philistine', not because Arnold seriously wants to argue that racial descent determines cultural proclivities, but because these ethnic terms function as handy ad-hoc labels, in a shorthand characterization. It is for this reason that the ethnic nomenclature proliferates so freely in his discourse: it is a stenography of predicative metaphors, not a taxonomy. Ethnic nomenclature merely *describes*, even *invokes* culture, it does not classify it. For Arnold to call an author 'Teutonic' or 'Celtic' says less about that author's DNA, descent or innate/inherited genotype and ethnocultural phenotype, than about an ingrained, recognizable and even stereotyped national characterology which supplies handy predicates.

Arnold accordingly holds up the chief poets of the English literary tradition as a felicitous merger between 'Saxon' and 'Celtic' sensibilities, between realism on the one hand and 'rebellion against the despotism of fact', a sense of natural magic, on the other: Byron and Shakespeare are cited in evidence. The ethnic appellations become blurred to such an extent that the opposition Hebraic-Hellenic is aligned with Saxon-Celtic: In some Shakespearean lines, Arnold identifies 'the very point of transition from the Greek note to the Celtic'; and elsewhere he invokes the need for an acknowledged Celtic personality-strain 'to give us delicacy, and to free us from hardness and Philistinism'.

Arnold wants to subvert the type of pig-headed chauvinism which he links with a Saxonist attitude. Saxonism was still a very strong force in the 1860s, but it was declining even as Arnold lectured. The year immediately preceding Arnold's lectures, 1866, was the eighth centenary of the Battle of Hastings, and such commemorations as this elicited (which were comparatively few and muted) had, it is true, a Saxonist, anti-Roman undertone.[10] Charles Kingsley's novel *Hereward the Wake*, about the last Saxon warrior resisting Norman dominance, appeared in 1866. (Hereward had made his debut in nineteenth-century historical fiction as a character in Walter Scott's *Count Robert of Paris* of 1832; as for Kingsley, he had given a sample of his Saxonist attachment in the earlier lecture series 'The Teuton and the Roman', delivered in Cambridge in 1860).

However, 1866 had been preceded two years earlier by the devastating defeat of Denmark at the hand of Prussia; and 1866 itself was marked by the war Prussia waged against Austria, and the annexation, by Prussia, of the Kingdom of Hanover, until recently in personal union with the British Crown. In 1863, Princess Alexandra of Denmark had become the consort of the Prince of Wales; she brought with her an inveterate dislike of Prussia and Germany, marking a sharp change in court circles from the Germanophilia of Prince Albert, who had died in 1861. The real rise of anti-Germanism would only emerge after the reconstitution of the German Empire in 1871 and its development of colonial ambitions; but by the late 1860s, a Bismarckian chill was already in the air, and many Victorians were beginning to turn from a German interest towards a Nordic (Scandinavian, Viking) one (cf. Wawn 2000).

The Saxonist with whose shade Arnold takes issue most directly in *On the Study of Celtic Literature* is likewise the representative of a previous, mid-Victorian generation: it is his own father, Dr Thomas Arnold. Thomas Arnold was known, and is remembered, as one of the leading Saxonists of his generation, someone with a great affection for the Teutonic roots of the English 'race' and a corresponding disdain for Britain's Celtic traditions.[11] We know that there was some friction between father and son, and against that background it becomes significant that Thomas Arnold's wife, Matthew's mother, was of Cornish extraction, with the very Cornish maiden name of Penrose; Matthew himself was, in other (Victorian) words, a Saxon-Celtic 'half-breed'.

Arnold's discovery of England's disregarded Celtic roots is, then, an extension of his private, familial sense of identity: he himself, like his country, descends from a mixed Saxon-Celtic ancestry. The analogy is reinforced by Arnold's insistence to genderize the Saxon-Celtic binary by classifying the Celts (his mother's side) as 'an essentially feminine race'. Indeed, Arnold's discovery of Celtic culture does have some interesting biographical concomitants. It began, not in Llandudno (where *On the Study of Celtic Literature* opens), but in Brittany.

During the 1840s, Arnold had encountered in the *Revue de Paris* some of La Villemarqué's materials based on Breton and Arthurian themes; his own 1852 poem 'Tristram and Iseult' reflects this. In subsequent years, Arnold read an essay by his admired Ernest Renan whose title and theme closely foreshadow *On the Study of Celtic Literature*: 'La poésie des races celtiques' (1854).[12] Arnold had encountered Renan on his missions to the Continent, undertaken to report on educational systems.

Arnold started to develop *On the Study of Celtic Literature* during a visit that he made to Renan's homeland, Brittany, in 1859. On that occasion (emotionally fraught because his wife and children, who had originally accompanied him, had returned to England for health reasons, and Arnold here heard of his brother's death) Renan's essay reverberated with a meditation on his own family roots. Towards the end of that year, Arnold wrote to his sister Lucy as follows:

> I have long felt that we owed far more, spiritually and artistically, to the Celtic races than the somewhat coarse Germanic intelligence readily perceived, and been increasingly satisfied at our own semi-Celtic origin, which, as I fancy, gives us the power, if we will use it, of comprehending the nature of both races.
> (quoted Machann, 1998, 65–66)

The unspecificity of the first-person plural is telling: it could refer to as narrow a circle as the Arnold siblings, Matthew and Lucy, with their mixed Cornish-English ancestry, or to as wide a circle as the English nation at large. It makes no difference: Arnold extrapolates from his private family meditations towards a reflection on national culture.

Arnold's Celts have, then, a partially Breton-French background. And another French aspect of *On the Study of Celtic Literature* is the way this Celticity is activated in order to combat Saxonism. In France, a Celtic/Gaulish self-image was increasingly feeding into the rising tensions with Germany, soon to culminate in the 1870/71 war (Beller & Leerssen 2018), with Renan playing a leading part among the *intellectuels*. From this, Arnold's *On the Study of Celtic Literature* imbued, not only a nostalgic Celticism, but also emerging reservations vis-à-vis things Germanic. 'Englishness' was beginning to be weaned from its partnership with the German Cousins.

Summary, outlook

Matthew Arnold occupies a truly cardinal position in the development of literary studies in Britain: the entire process hinges around him. His definition of the critic's role in the relationship between literature and society, as the arbitrator of cultural values and of their social importance, gave decisive public standing to what had until then been a form of meta-literary dilettantism and connoisseurship. Before Arnold, the educational and academic institutionalization of literary criticism (apart from free-floating Professorships in 'Poetry' or 'Rhetoric and Belles-Lettres') would have raised puzzled eyebrows; after Arnold, it became an obvious necessity. What is more, Arnold linked criticism (a 'disinterested' endeavour in *Lehre und Forschung*, research and teaching, 'learning and propagating') to the cool and meticulous working methods of philology, yoking the two together into what might become a scholarly-academic literary discipline rather than just an exercise in formulating evaluative commentary. The philological role model at least implicitly also hinted at a historicist working method, or a study of literature in its historical context.

At the same time, Arnold's criticism intervened at a juncture when the study of cultural diversity and the very craft of philology were in large measure ethnologically oriented; the demarcations between cultural or physical anthropology, ethnology, and philology were still fluctuating, still coming to terms with the shock of Darwinism. Accordingly, we can see that Arnold habitually couches cultural or ethical patterns (or the social-epistemic phenomena nowadays called 'mentalities') in ethnic terms, from 'Celts' to 'Philistines', and that for him the idea of cultural diversity, and the connections between cultural variants, is more an ethnic than a linguistic-national one. While on the continent, early comparatists were comparing national-literary categories, primarily linked to languages and states, and only in the second place to ethnic ones, that relationship is different for Arnold. The cultural landscape he surveys and within whose context he tries to situate his ideal of 'Englishness' is primarily mapped out with ethnic labels.

And finally, Arnold, for all his importance in proclaiming scholarly-philological 'disinterestedness' and erudition, still sees criticism as an exercise of sound judgement, involving, centrally, ethical and aesthetic value judgements, and giving to the critic the public status of a moral and artistic arbitrator. These elements were to continue as formative influences in his legacy.

Notes to Chapter 2

1. The appointment of John O'Donovan in Belfast was an empty gesture since there were no students with Celtological interest in that city. Newman's Catholic University, however, gave an important platform to the erudition of Eugene O'Curry (*Lecturers on the Manuscript Materials of Ancient Irish History*, 1861, and the posthumously published lectures *On the Manners and Customs of the Ancient Irish*, 1873).

2. The Professorship is largely an honorific appointment given for a limited time (5–10 years) to prestigious literati, who are expected to give three public lectures per year.
3. The reference is to Jonathan Swift's parable of the spider and the bee, where the bee is praised for using its powers of flight and collaborative work in order to provide humankind with honey (sweetness) and candlewax (light).
4. He borrowed it, through Carlyle, from German student slang, where it was used in town-and-gown conflicts to deride the uneducated townspeople. In Arnold's usage: 'The people who believe most that our greatness and welfare are proved by our being very rich, and who most give their lives and thoughts to becoming rich, are just the very people whom we call the Philistines' (*Culture and Anarchy*, chapter 1).
5. Here Arnold shows the influence of Carlyle, who in his essay 'Characteristics' (1831) had thematized the uncertainties of the age ('man begins in darkness, ends in darkness: mystery is everywhere around us and in us, under our feet, among our hands. Nevertheless so much has become evident to every one, that this wondrous Mankind is advancing some-whither'), to conclude: 'Man's task here below, the destiny of every individual man, is to be [...] Scholar, Teacher, Discoverer.'
6. Jean-Jacques Ampère is generally acknowledged as an early French comparatist. He published *De la littérature française dans ses rapports avec les littératures étrangères au moyen âge* in 1833, and already in his *Discours sur l'histoire de la poésie* (1830) speaks of 'l'histoire comparative des arts et de la littérature'; but what precise paper-trail Willoughby had in mind he does not specify, either as regards the Ampère provenance or as regards the usage in Arnold's own writings.
7. Page references are to Arnold 1962[b]. For the biographical and historical context: Super's editorial 'Critical and explanatory notes' in Arnold 1962[b], 491–98; Coulling 1974, esp. 134; Honan 1981, esp. 297–99; Machann 1998, 8–9 and 65–66. Generally also Leerssen 2006.
8. This gives anglocentric thought the character of 'internal colonialism'; a phrase coined by Hechter 1975. For an analysis of the racialist denigration of the Irish, see Curtis 1968 and 1997. Also, Young 2008.
9. Indeed, the Indo-Europeanism of Wilhelm von Humboldt and Jacob Grimm does coincide with a degree of anti-Semitism; there was a sense of relief to have the Semitic, Biblical languages *excluded* from the linguistic taxonomy of Europe. Arnold himself comments: '[...] the tendency is in Humboldt's direction; the modern spirit tends more and more to establish a sense of native diversity between our European bent and the Semitic bent, and to eliminate, even in our religion, certain elements as purely and excessively Semitic, and therefore, in right, not combinable with our European nature, not assimilable by it.' (26) This is even juxtaposed with a growing sense of kinship with the Irish, now recognized as fellow-Indo-Europeans. For suggestive comments on this topic, see Faverty 1968, chapter 6 ('The Semitic vs. the Indo-European Genius'), esp. 163–64. Faverty also (227–28) gives an interesting sourcing for Arnold's reference to Humboldt, which indicates that, while Arnold misremembered the precise nature of Humboldt's preference for Greek and Indian over Judaic thought, this certainly informed his usage of terms like *hellenism* and *hebraism*.
10. Other echoes of mid-century Saxonism: Bulwer-Lytton had written a novel on Harold, the last Saxon king vanquished by William the Conqueror in 1066 (1844); the theme was to be picked up by Tennyson in his 1876 poem on Harold. Tennyson himself was to publish a version of the Battle of Brunanburh in 1880. Cf. Scragg & Weinberg 2000; on the nineteenth-century cult of the centenary: Leerssen & Rigney 2014. On the relative lack of interest for 1066 in 1866: Briggs 1985.
11. Even so, there is room for nuance. As a clergyman and a monogenist, Thomas Arnold believed in the ultimate unity of all humanity under God; accordingly, he evinced a much more liberal attitude on the Irish question than did Carlyle (cf. Leerssen 1996, 99–100).
12. In *La poésie des races celtiques*, Renan (who had trained for the priesthood for a while before losing his religious faith) had sentimentally celebrated Brittany as the land of his childhood and as the homeland of his childhood's simple, devout piety. The influence of *La poésie des races celtiques* falls heavily on even the very rhetoric of *On the Study of Celtic Literature*: both essays construct, in their evocative opening pages, the Celtic West (Brittany or Wales) as a place of nostalgia,

non-progress, spirituality and otherworldliness (cf. McCormack 1985); both aim to revalorize, in the name of scientific philology, a region which in terms of cultural politics was denigrated and marginalized.

CHAPTER 3

Henry Buckle and H. M. Posnett (1857–1886)

The impact of positivism: Henry Thomas Buckle

Cultural movements cut both ways. The onset of Romanticism and the spread of transcendent *Naturphilosophie* triggered, on the rebound, a scientistic tendency that came to valorize physical, measurable facts as the only sure foundation of certainty and reliable knowledge. Not only did Hegel's idealistic dialectics pave the way for Marx's dialectical materialism, the positivist school of Auguste Comte came to see all of human history as a long struggle of intellectual, fact-based understanding against superstitious speculation, science against myth, 'positive' knowledge against vague conjecture.

Comte's lectures on 'positive philosophy', developed in the 1820s and 1830s, mark the incipience of this school of thought, which was spread in Britain by those 'progressive Victorians' who also espoused Darwinism (George Eliot, George Henry Lewes, Harriet Martineau, John Stuart Mill, Herbert Spencer). Comte's positivism was also a formative first step in the development of sociology: the idea that the totality of human relations, which bind individuals together into something called a 'society', are systemic, and can be therefore described and analysed systematically and scientifically. Such a scientific understanding of society can in turn furnish an explanatory framework and make objective analyses possible for specific historical and cultural phenomena — such as literature.

The attempt to explain literature in terms of the social structures out of which it emanates is, of course, older than the sociological discipline: we see its early stirrings in the writings of Herder and in Madame de Staël's tellingly-titled *De la littérature considérée dans ses rapports avec les institutions sociales* of 1800. But unlike the ad hoc connections made by Herder and de Staël, the literary sociology that developed after Comte (say, in Hippolyte Taine's *History of English Literature* of 1864) was much more scientific. It was 'nomothetic' (to use Windelband's still-useful distinction[1]): directed towards the identification of general patterns and laws, rather than accounting for the specificity and root causes of individual phenomena. The new, positivist-inspired school of literary analysis was looking for society-based laws and patterns determining the historical development of culture and literature. The idea of 'literary autonomy' — a phrase never used except to decry or denounce it — so prominent in the thought of Matthew Arnold, was here replaced by its very opposite: the idea of literature as 'societal epiphenomenon' or, to phrase it more politely, literature as a 'mirror of society'.

Fig. 3.1. Henry Thomas Buckle, frontispiece to vol. 1 of A. H. Hutt, *The Life and Writings of Henry Thomas Buckle* (3rd. ed.; 2 vols; London: Sampson Low, Marston, Searle & Rivington, 1880)

One prominent, but somewhat eccentric, adept of Comtean positivism was Henry Thomas Buckle (1821–1862), a self-taught polymath based in London who by 1850 could read eighteen foreign languages. Supported by private wealth, unmarried and slightly hypochondriac, Buckle lived a retired life, dictated by a rigid daily routine involving much reading and writing and punctuated by numerous travels (he died on one of his journeys, in Damascus). This life-style made for a formidable erudition, but also for a certain rigidity of thought untempered by academic collegiality with its daily exposure to dissenting opinions. Buckle's master theory, that human behaviour and the development of culture can be accounted for by 'fundamental laws of human progress', was the basis of his main work, a *History of Civilization*. It occupied fourteen years of his life. Although unfinished in its planned entirety, the two volumes that did appear (in 1857 and 1861) gained considerable renown. They were republished in 1866; many reprints followed under various titles (*An Introduction to the History of Civilization in England* or *A History of Civilization in England, France, Spain, and Scotland*) and translations appeared in Russian, German and French. The book's programme is clear from the very outset; even in the first chapter's title, it is stipulated that human actions 'are governed by mental and physical laws: therefore both sets of laws must be studied, and there can be no history without the natural sciences.' The book's main argument was aptly summarized by its later editor, John Mackinnon Robertson:

> climate and soil in early civilizations determined [a] the food supply, and so [b] the degree of population, and [c] their economic condition; besides further affecting them as regards the regularity or intermittence of their industry.

This in accordance with the notion that 'accumulation of wealth [is] antecedent to that of knowledge'. (Buckle 1904, xvii, vii, x)

Besides the sociological dimension, Buckle's work is relevant in the present context for two reasons. To begin with, Buckle continues Henry Hallam's work in what might broadly be called cultural or intellectual history, which, no matter how socially-deterministic the view, provides a congenial historical basis for the study of literary developments. Indeed, Buckle might be considered a stepping-stone in the tradition which led from Henry Hallam to later works like W. E. H. Lecky's *History of European Morals from Augustus to Charlemagne* (1869) and Leslie Stephens's *History of English Thought in the Eighteenth Century* (1876). We should recall, once more, that at the time the demarcation between what we would now distinguish as 'literary history', 'cultural history' and 'intellectual history' was fluid, porous and indistinct, literature still being seen, to a large extent, as culture or civilization in its textual manifestation.

Secondly, there is the book's comparative slant. Buckle's nomothetic ambition can only work on the basis of data and case studies adduced from different contexts, and that alone means that England cannot be studied in isolation, even though it stands at the centre of attention. It was in this respect that his book was an acknowledged inspiration for early Continental comparatists such as Louis-Paul Betz, who praised Buckle's capacity to 'survey his own national literature by adducing foreign connections or parallels'.[2]

Comparative history, anthropological stadialism, and the Empire

As mentioned before, the imperial nature of the British state and its overseas colonies tended to favour an ethnological rather than a 'national' view on questions of culture, literature and society. The positivistic impulse of sociology was almost automatically applied, not only to the analysis of British social and constitutional affairs (as, for instance, in the critical writings of Walter Bagehot and the historical work of E. A. Freeman), but also in more far-flung comparison with non-European, especially South-Asian, societies and culture. William Jones's 1780s 'discovery' of Sanskrit for comparative purposes while posted in Calcutta as a judge for the East India Company, was replicated in the mid-19th-century comparative constitutional studies of Henry Sumner Maine and Whitley Stokes. If the ultimate focus of this present chapter is Hutcheson Macaulay Posnett's classic 1886 book *Comparative Literature*, it is against this background that we must approach it.

Edward Augustus Freeman, one of the most reputable historians of the mid-century, is nowadays remembered chiefly for his insistence on rigorous source fidelity and for his *History of the Norman Conquest* (1867–76). As the topic of that work might already hint (in the light of what was outlined in the previous chapters), Freeman was a product of Saxonism, indeed one of its last great representatives. He deliberately avoided words of Latin/Romance derivation and attempted to use a purified Germanic English (a widespread trend at the time, which led to coinages such as 'folklore' and 'foreword' in order to avoid 'popular culture' and 'preface'), and is notorious for his statement that the USA would be much improved 'if only every Irishman would kill a negro, and be hanged for it'. His appointment as Regius Professor of History in Oxford (in which capacity he was undistinguished) came late in his life, 1884, and at a time when his type was already out of fashion (cf. generally Bremner & Conlin 2015, Hesketh 2012). But Freeman's importance for our purpose lies elsewhere: in his now-neglected *Comparative Politics* of 1873. It stands at the very beginning of what is now a thriving specialism in political science, and is duly acknowledged as such in the classic 1971 article by Arend Lijphart, 'Comparative politics and the comparative method'. Freeman, too, had become enthusiastic for a nomothetic, Comte-style type of research, and saw a viable programme for longitudinal historical research in the convergence of four types of inquiry: a constitution-historical one in the tradition of Henry Hallam; an ethnological one as in the work of Prichard; a positivist-sociological one (Buckle); and a systematically applied comparative method, which he hailed (obviously with linguistics and Darwin in mind, like Matthew Arnold) as the 'greatest intellectual achievement of his time'. What *Comparative Politics* aimed to achieve, both as a book and as an agenda for a scholarly discipline, was a worldwide comparative history of state systems: their varieties in space (across the globe) and varying evolutions in time (over the course of history). Freeman proposed nothing less than a world-encompassing (though Europe-based) view.

Thus Freeman's scope tends to study analogies 'between the political institutions of times and countries most remote from one another' (Lijphart 1971, 687), that is to say: much more widely than the state systems of Europe which evolved on the

FIG. 3.2. Edward Augustus Freeman, photograph by Elliott & Fry, 1886 (© National Portrait Gallery, London)

ruins of the Roman Empire (as studied by Hallam, for instance). This ethnological, trans-European view, closer to Prichard's, was boosted by the fact that the scholarly frame of reference by the mid-nineteenth century quite naturally included Britain's overseas colonies. The natural political taxonomy for scholars of Freeman's generation was not a national one (such as might be foregrounded in Germany or France) but an imperial one.³

The Indian Mutiny of 1857 made it clear that the colonial exploitation of the subcontinent through the instrumentality of the East India Company was due for an overhaul. The East India Company was abolished, a new imperial governance model was imposed, and Victoria was crowned Empress of India in 1876. The 'British Raj' had begun, object of Orientalist triumphalism in the later Victorian period and romantically imagined in a Kiplingesque mode; and the cultural imagination of its 'ancient civilization' was part of it. From Sir William Jones to Max Müller and Freeman, India had proved to be a treasure-trove also for comparative-minded British scholars. In the Arnold decades, we see the scholarly importance of the Indian connection also in the career of Whitley Stokes (1830–1909), eminent Celtologist and prominent civil servant in the Indian service from 1862 until 1881, and above all in the work of someone who, with Stokes, prepared the imperial codification of Indian law, Sir Henry Sumner Maine (1822–1888). This eminent scholar, who over the course of his career held professorships in both Oxford and Cambridge, combined anthropology and legal scholarship in a manner reminiscent of Freeman's *Comparative Politics*. His main works, *Ancient Law* (1861) and *Lectures on the Early History of Institutions* (1875) relied, not only on the well documented sources of Graeco-Roman and Germanic history, but also on ethnological comparisons between Gaelic clan societies and traditional village administration in the Indian subcontinent, where he served on the Viceroy's council from 1862 until 1869. Meanwhile, the ancient Gaelic ('Brehon') laws of Ireland were being edited by a scholarly committee equally keen to discern parallels with Brahminic India (Hancock et al, *Ancient Laws of Ireland*, 1865 ff.)

Celtic-Indian comparisons provided antiquarians, ethnographers, philologists, and sociologists with a heuristic counterpart, a profiling tool, to contrast with their own sense of modernity. Maine's *Village Communities in East and West* (1871) inspired Frederic Seebohm's *The English Village Community* (1883) and influenced Ferdinand Tönnies's cardinally important typological distinction between the traditional small-scale 'community' and modern large-scale 'society' (*Gemeinschaft* and *Gesellschaft*, as in the classic treatise thus titled of 1881). Maine's own theory saw a universal stadial growth-process of legal systems from 'primitive' status-based and kinship-bound societies to contractually-governed civil societies. And it was this socio-anthropological stadialism which most profoundly affected the first handbook of what was now naming itself as a separate academic specialism: *Comparative Literature*, by Hutcheson Macaulay Posnett (1886).

FIG 3.3. Sir Henry Sumner Maine, photograph by Herbert Rose Barraud (albumen carte de visite), 1882-88 (© National Portrait Gallery, London)

Posnett's 'Comparative Literature' (1886)

The book's fame, which was among the first worldwide to coin the name of the new discipline and to provide it with a methodological agenda, for a long time overshadowed our scant knowledge of its somewhat obscure author. Historical surveys of Comparative Literature habitually cited Posnett as one of the great early harbingers of the discipline — alongside other late-nineteenth-century figures such as the Frenchman Joseph Texte, the Swiss Louis-Paul Betz, the Dane Georg Brandes, the Italians Arturo Graf and Arturo Farinelli, and the German-Transylvanian Hugo Meltzl von Lomnitz. Traditionally, *Comparative Literature* was mentioned in comparatist *Fachgeschichte* as an isolated early harbinger, without much specific context (beyond its publication in a positivistic book series). The author himself was usually seen as what the title page called him: Professor of Classics at the University of Auckland, New Zealand.[4]

However, it was subsequently established that *Comparative Literature* was written in Ireland, and finished in the month before its Irish author obtained his New Zealand professorship.[5] Posnett, born in Co. Antrim in 1855 as the son of an Anglican clergyman, had been educated at Rathmines School in Dublin and had taken both his MA and his doctorate at Trinity College Dublin in 1882.[6] Following publications on *The Historical Method in Ethics, Jurisprudence, and Political Economy* (1882) and *The Ricardian Theory of Rent* (1884), Posnett obtained a professorship in Classics at the recently established University College of Auckland. He relinquished his chair (possibly because his tasks were too numerous and onerous) in 1890. In 1892 he unsuccessfully applied for the professorships of Greek and of Latin at University College London (eventually given to A. E. Housman; cf. Naiditch 1988, 9 and 164), and settled as a barrister in the Dublin suburb then known as Kingstown and now as Dun Laoghaire, from where he wrote an occasional article or letter to the editor of *The Times*.[7] In these letters he positions himself as a 'moderate Liberal', a supporter of Home Rule for Ireland with the exception of Ulster (which should be allowed to remain within the Union). He also shows himself to be still, in 1913, an adept of Sir Henry Maine, in particular in denouncing hunger strikes (at that time a hotly-debated instrument of activism for jailed suffragettes). Writing during the scandals around force-feeding and the 'Cat and Mouse Act', Posnett reminds his readers that hunger strikes were justly suppressed as a form of barbarism in the Indian Penal Code drawn up by Maine. Channelling Maine, Posnett suggests that hunger strikers should be allowed to die of starvation, followed punitively by a posthumous persecution for suicide rendering the hunger striker's property liable to confiscation. Posnett was of course well placed to apply the Empire's Indian law code to contemporary feminist hunger strikes: Maine's (and his own) high Victorian ethnography, comparing ancient Brahminic and Gaelic self-starvation rituals, had facilitated the cultural cross-currents which the hunger strike culturally available as a gesture for modern British activists (cf. Lennon 2009).

The Posnetts, many of them with Hutcheson or Hutchinson as a given name, were a well-established Co. Antrim family with ties to the established church and the Belfast magistrature. Posnett's father Robert (1821–1885) had graduated BA

Fig 3.4. Cover of H.M. Posnett's *Comparative Literature*, London: Routledge Kegan Paul, 1886 (photograph © Joep Leerssen)

from Trinity College Dublin in 1844, and entered the service of the East India Company in 1847, serving as a chaplain in a variety of postings until he resigned due to ill health in 1854. Upon his return to Ireland, he took his MA at Trinity College Dublin in 1859 and became Rector of Laracor, Co. Meath — a parish famous in literary history for having once been in the charge of Jonathan Swift. He died in 1865. The Indian postings of Posnett *père* are of some interest, certainly the one at Bangalore, where he made his mark in 1853–54. Here he established a new church, St John's, in the Bangalore cantonment at Mootoocherry (present-day Cleveland Town / Pulekeshinagar), which is still a landmark of High-Church neo-Gothic architecture in India. The venture was remarkable because it was expressly intended to provide religious service and educational facilities (boys' and girls' parish schools and a library) to 'Eurasian' children, i.e. the offspring of interracial relationships between locals and colonials, who were barred from attending services and following education in existing churches or institutions (McNally 1976; Penny 1922, 3: 206–08).

This background not only explains how effortlessly Posnett junior could feel qualified to offer comparative observations on Celtic Ireland and colonial India, but also places him in his social and ideological context. The author of *Comparative Literature* hailed from the Irish 'Protestant Ascendancy' imbued with paternalistic imperialism, situated between idealistic Anglicanism and secular positivism, in the spirit of Thomas Arnold, Herbert Spencer and Charles Kingsley. Posnett's positivistic belief in progress and scientific improvement may have been less religiously oriented than that of his father, but both seem to have seen the Empire as a great testing ground for the educational power and duties of their class and nation (of whose superiority in morality and development they had no doubt).

For that is what his book propounded as a scholarly agenda. *Comparative Literature* outlined a system of global literature determined by a universally stadial model of societal progression, reflecting at each stage the social relations from which it sprang and of which it forms part. Like Kelso-born Sir Henry Maine, Posnett makes grateful use of the Celto-Sanskrit frame of reference, juxtaposing Gaelic antiquity alongside classical antiquity and assorted other civilizations and cultural traditions.

Thus, although the book's title may phraseologically echo some passages in Matthew Arnold, Posnett is definitely not an Arnoldian. He is not even a 'critic' to begin with. Rather than adjudicating 'the best that is known and thought in the world', Posnett follows Freeman and Maine, and, beyond them, Henry Thomas Buckle in the tradition of a type of 'scientific', positivistic criticism that was concerned with sociological, even anthropological context. The very coinage of the term 'Comparative Literature' situated the endeavour in the nomothetic ambience of Comparative Linguistics and Comparative Politics.

Posnett had in fact positioned himself in those terms in 1884, while still a graduate student. A letter to *The Academy*, dated from Trinity College, shows that he was already contemplating the basic ground-work of his book at that time and in that place. The text is worth reproducing here in full, because it makes use of the phrase 'comparative literature' as an established though underdeveloped pursuit in literary studies, and because it demonstrates how Posnett, in proposing to take that pursuit further, takes his cue from eighteenth-century ethnographic stadialism and from the French positivist Hippolyte Taine.

Clan Poetry

24 Trinity College Dublin: Feb 18, 1884

The effect of primitive communal life on the beginnings of literature is a subject worth the careful attention of any student of comparative literature. Dr Brown, in an attempt to sketch the origin of poetry — an attempt which attracted the attention of Bishop Percy in his remarks introductory to the Reliques — proposed more than one hundred years ago to discover the source of the combined dance, song, melody, and mimetic action of primitive compositions in the common festivals of clan life. The student of comparative literature will probably regard Dr Brown's theory as a curious anticipation of the historical method in a study which, in spite of Mr Taine's efforts, has made so little progress as yet. The clan ethic of inherited guilt and vicarious punishment has attracted considerable attention. But the clan poetry of the ancient Arabs and of the bard-clans surviving in the Hebrew sons of Asaph or the Greek Homeridae has not received that light from comparative enquiry which the closely connected problems of primitive music and metre would alone amply deserve. I should feel deeply obliged to any student of Oriental or Occidental literatures for such evidences of clan poetry as he may have happened to observe.

H. Macaulay Posnett[8]

That, then, is what Posnett, a member of the Linnaean Society, and during his time at Auckland also examiner in Political Economy, stood for: the 'International Scientific Series' in which his book appeared included works by Bagehot and Herbert Spencer, he himself called Comparative Literature a 'Science' which he confessed he would like to 'less exclusively in the hands of literary men'. He also stressed in so many words, in a 1901 article written in self-vindication, that his usage of the term 'Comparative Literature' was in analogy to 'Professor Freeman [...] in his "Comparative Politics", viz., to make the name of the subject-matter do duty for the uncoined name of the study of the subject-matter' (Posnett 1901, 856 and 866).

It is perhaps for this heavily ethnographical and sociological investment that a literary critic and historian like George Saintsbury (1900–1904, 3: 143) would quibble with the term; but it has remained the appellation of what would become a new discipline. There are two ironies at work here. To begin with, Posnett, for all his ethnologically-derived scientism, is in fact much more a *literary* scholar than his predecessors: the corpus he works on is far more specific than that of, for instance, Henry Hallam or Buckle, concentrating as it does on imaginative and poetic texts, 'literary' in the present-day sense, with less attention for history-writing or other forms of prose disquisition. It is perhaps because Posnett was much more literary in his definition of which texts constituted his corpus, that he bent over the opposite way in stressing the non-literary nature of his method.

The other irony lies in the fact that Posnett's book, so utterly isolated in terms of the discipline's institutional development, should have been so formative in coining its name. The explanation of this paradox must be sought across the Atlantic. When comparatist departments were established in the United States, this occurred a mere few years after the appearance of Posnett's book (Harvard 1890, Columbia 1899). The positive notice given to *Comparative Literature* by William Dean Howells (*Harper's New Monthly Magazine* 73.434, July 1886, 318) may have channelled Posnett's nomenclature for these freshly-established and newly-named departments in the US, and the evolutionary approach popular in early American comparatism (Alastair Mackenzie, *The Evolution of Literature*, 1911) took its cue from Taine, Brunetière — and Posnett (Moore 2013, 575). In Japan, too, Posnett's book turned out to have repercussions: it was translated in 1899 by the authoritative playwright, author and critic Tsubouchi Shōyō (1859–1935), Professor of Literature at the modernizing institution that would later become Waseda University. It is tempting to think that Posnett's book may have been brought to Tsubouchi's notice by Lafcadio Hearn (who, incidentally, had spent some of his boyhood years in Dublin). Hearn knew Howells and had also written for the *Atlantic Monthly* shortly before returning to Japan in 1890; from 1894 onwards he taught English literature at Tokyo's other main university, the Imperial University; in 1904, Tsubouchi would headhunt him for Waseda and become a friend.[9]

Within Europe, Posnett's book was noticed by the early generation of comparatists such as Joseph Texte, Edouard Rod, Fernand Brunetière and Louis-Paul Betz; for his part, Posnett in his later 1901 article shows himself aware of these men. A common frame of reference was establishing itself, but there was disagreement as to the direction in which Comparative Literature should develop, and Posnett's scientist, global-imperial stadialism stood alone. Joseph Texte (1893, 253), surely caught the general mood when he saw Posnett as an inspiring, yet isolated and premature case.

On the Continent, comparatists were turning to the notion of 'world literature' in a different sense. Like Matthew Arnold, many early comparatists saw a major justification of their discipline in the Goethe-derived (if not always properly understood) concept of *Weltliteratur* (generally Martí 2011). The tone was set memorably by Joseph Texte's own book *Jean-Jacques Rousseau et les origines du cosmopolitisme littéraire* (1895). Texte's book appeared (and provoked some nationalist irritation) in the intense Franco-German antagonism of the post-1871 years. Indeed, the notion of 'world literature', or else of a trans-national ensemble of mutually entangled literatures, was itself subject to that antagonism, French critics vindicating French cosmopolitanism against the Germans... Such mixed feelings dominated Vogüé's review of Texte, and Ferdinand Brunetière's essay on 'Le cosmopolitisme et la littérature nationale', in the *Revue des Deux Mondes* (1895). It was in that same year, 1895, that Alfred Nobel established the prizes named after him, one of which was dedicated to literature (with the first adjudication going to Sully Prudhomme in 1901). From that moment to the establishment of P. E. N. International in 1921, the Goethean concept functioned as something both enveloping and transcending national literatures, with Comparative Literature claiming a more direct connection to this lofty sphere than the merely nationally oriented writers and critics.

Thus, the early-twentieth-century resurgence of 'world literature' was in the mode of Arnoldian criticism rather than of Posnett-style stadialist positivism. Instead of stadialist, the underlying world-view was, if anything, Darwinian-evolutionist

(Moore 2013, 575–78). The evolution of literature was seen to take place in the tension field between national rootedness and cosmopolitan flourishing, seeing 'world literature' as a wider horizon in which to situate the best that was known, thought and written in the national literatures. Of course, despite the presence of writers like Rabindranath Tagore (Nobel Prize 1913 — six years after Kipling), the hypercanon of this *Weltliteratur* sitting atop the subsidiary national canons was almost wholly European in scope; the occasional nod to (ancient) Persian or Indian epic or Chinese poetry being a mere gesture and in any case situating the literature of the non-European world in a static, ahistorical space of ancient heritage without contemporary vitality or presence.

While most European intellectuals and critics concurred by 1900 in an Arnoldian, elite-idealistic vision of an evolving 'literature beyond frontiers', there was, within that shared vision, a divide between British and Continental attitudes.

Weltliteratur in the 1890s on the Continent meant, in fact, the literary transcendence of chauvinistic French-German enmity. Within Britain the post-Arnold generation moved away from the global-imperial ethnological positivism of Posnett, Freeman and Maine, and continued the connoisseurship and erudition of literary criticism. But the Arnoldian notion of 'learning and propagating the best' was almost wholly absent from continental comparatism. The working method in continental university departments was fundamentally historical: fact- and archive-based, positivistic, detailing the events and connections of *la vie et l'œuvre / Leben und Werk* in their historical context. In Britain, the working method (derived from Arnold) was fundamentally axiological: concerned with forming critical judgements on the artistic and moral merits and shortcomings of literary works. In this respect, it had less of a connection with continental academia than with the great tradition of essayistic criticism and reviewing as pursued in the literary reviews.

Notes to Chapter 3

1. The neo-Kantian philosopher Wilhelm Windelband coined the antonyms 'nomothetic' and 'idiographic' in 1894 in order to define an ideal-typical distinction between the natural and the historical sciences (prefigured also in Vico's distinction between 'philosophy' and 'philology' (above, p. 22): the former accounting for specifics, the latter attempting to extrapolate general laws. Despite our present-day mistrust of facile binary oppositions, the distinction has considerable heuristic value and is instinctively used in our everyday attitudes to the various faculties of academic life (also when it comes to funding).
2. Betz 1901, 660. In the original: 'Wie kein anderer verstand es Henry Thomas Buckle [...] die eigene Literatur durch Herbeiziehung ausländischer Beziehungen und Parallelen zu schildern'. Betz (New York 1861–Zurich 1904) was Professor of Comparative Literature at Zurich.
3. This only applies to the agenda of *Comparative Politics*. As a historian, Freeman's scope was as European as Hallam's, and among his *Essays* (3rd series, 1879) there is a disquisition on 'Race and Language' (1879) which bravely disentangles the various semantic overlaps and ambiguities between the national, ethnic and linguistic categories. In that essay, Freeman shows himself closer to Ernest Renan (whose *Qu'est-ce qu'une nation* was to appear a few years afterwards) than to the Victorian racialists of Max Müller vintage.
4. Dyserinck 1992; Shaffer 1979; Weisstein 1968, chapter 2; Wellek 1961–92 4: 143.
5. A reference to the German original of the present book (Leerssen 1984, 60–61, from which much of the information in these pages is reprised) would be incomplete without reiterating

my gratitude to my Aachen fellow-student Helen O'Connell (herself from New Zealand), who generously put at my disposal information based on Richardson 1968 and on her own archival research. This, with the addition of Sinclair 1983, 34–35, was the *status quaestionis* that has since found its way into further reflections on Posnett, e.g. Damrosch 2006, which also picks up on my idea that a situational parallel links Posnett to Hugo Meltzl von Lomnitz, an early comparatist from the German-speaking communities of Transylvania. (On Meltzl's importance for early comparatism, see also Dyserinck 1991 and Fassel 2005; for a recent juxtaposition between Meltzl and Posnett under the rubric of Goethean *Weltliteratur*: Nicholls 2018). Fresh information on Posnett's colonial family background (also digested in the following pages) was presented in Leerssen 2010. There are now fresh reappraisals of Posnett's work, cross-calibrating his imperial background and outlook with his global scope, in the contemporary context of postcolonialism and globalization interests; these were heralded when Emily Apter in 1995 emphasized *Comparative Literature* as an 'ironic point of interface between world literature as instrument of colonial ideology and world literature as postcolonial answer to the Eurocentric parochialism of comparative literature.' Apter concludes: 'It is as if we have now come full circle to Posnett's originary design though with entirely refashioned political principles and interpretive stakes' (1995: 94). Cf. also During 2004.

6. Rathmines School was a boarding school for boys from a prosperous Church of Ireland background. The TCD graduate records show that Posnett entered the College as a sizar in 1872, being elected scholar in 1877; he took his BA in 1877, winning a moderatorship and working as a tutor during the later years of his study there.

7. Posnett died in Dun Laoghaire in 1927; I gave the date erroneously as 1928 in Leerssen 1984, 61. The letters to *The Times* are: 'What Are We Voting For' (6 Jan. 1910, 5); 'Sitting "Dharna"' (11 Mar. 1913, 14); 'Action of Moderate Liberals' (14 Oct. 1913, 5); 'The Irish Crisis' (29 July 1914, 10); 'Racing and War' (16 Mar. 1915, 11).

8. *The Academy*, 616 (23 February 1884), 184. The 'Dr Brown' mentioned here is John Brown, author of *The History of the Rise and Progress of Poetry* (1764). The letter (previously noted in Leerssen 2015, 206) came to my attention because it was referred to (cheek by jowl with Max Müller and Celtic folklore studies) in Laurence Gomme's *Folklore as an Historical Science* (1908, 96).

9. The department of literature was established in 1890; the university was then still called Tokyo Senmon Gakko. It would be reconstituted as Waseda University in 1902. For Hearn and Howells: Goodman & Dawson 2005, 320.

CHAPTER 4

Reviewers, Critics, Academics (1860–1914)

Journals and critics

The generation of critics that emerged after the death of Matthew Arnold was rooted in the tradition of book reviewing that had flourished in periodicals since the 1820s (generally, Demata & Wu 2002, Parker 2000, Shattock 1989 and 2013). This publishing format in turn reaches back to the great spectatorial tradition of the eighteenth century (*The Spectator, Idler, Tatler,* and so on) and drew on the best writing talents in the country. The reviews increased their importance as a running commentary on public affairs, of a political, literary and social nature, as a result of the great printing technology revolutions of the first half of the nineteenth century. While newsprint was made much cheaper and large-circulation figures became much more easily attainable, the 'reviews' also reached into the very heart of literature itself: alongside discursive prose, they contained poems and original writing, and, as the century moved on, became an important medium for the genre of fictional sketches, stories and the Victorian novel. The 'great tradition' of Victorian novels relied fundamentally on the initial publishing format of periodical instalments: Charles Dickens's periodicals *Household Words* and *All the Year Round* formed the launching pad for novelists like Wilkie Collins, George Eliot, W. M. Thackeray and Thomas Hardy.

But the core of the Review was, somewhat tautologically, the review: extensive accounts of new publications which often ran to considerable length and included substantial passages cited from the works under discussion. The review ultimately turned on an evaluation, either commending or castigating the work, and often the judgements were exceedingly harsh, with displays of merciless mockery or ferocious denunciation. Notorious examples are the diatribes of the staunch Tory John Wilson Croker against the Whiggish novelist Lady Morgan (in the 1820s), and Robert Buchanan's 1871 crusade against the pornographic 'fleshly school of poetry' (for that is how this upright Victorian qualified the Pre-Raphaelites).

The leading reviews of the mid-century can be loosely quartered into four groups using the dual demarcation criteria 'Tory vs. Whig/Liberal' and 'elite vs. middle-class' readership. The *Edinburgh Review* (est. 1802) characterizes the 'up-market Whig' quadrant, the *Quarterly Review* (est. 1809) the 'up-market Tory' quadrant,

Fraser's Magazine (1830) the 'broad-appeal Tory' quadrant and the *Athenaeum* (1829) the 'broad-appeal Liberal' quadrant. However, despite their political and commercial differences these reviews drew on an often-overlapping reservoir of writers and critics.

It was in the pages of these periodicals that the art of literary criticism (i.e. to pronounce judgement on a text in a well-thought-out and well-expressed manner, reflecting erudition, wide reading, sound judgement and intellectual originality) was honed to a fine edge. This tradition of criticism involved some of the century's leading prose writers and cleverest minds: the lineage reaches from Coleridge to Carlyle and included great Victorian *maîtres à penser* such as G. H. Lewes and John Morley, with for a central nodal point Matthew Arnold. From Arnold it continues on, as has been pointed out, to twentieth-century critics like T. S. Eliot, Anthony Powell, V. S. Pritchett and J. B. Priestley, and into magazines like *The Criterion*, *Times Literary Supplement* and the *London Review of Books*. Yet, although this tradition often crossed paths with the development of Comparative Literature, it is not the purpose of this book to trace a history of literary criticism, Wellek-style. More to our point is to trace the interaction between criticism and academic scholarship.

As we have seen, Matthew Arnold, in his inaugural lecture as Oxford Professor of Poetry ('The Function of Criticism at the Present Time'), had called for a more 'disinterested' type of criticism: less judgemental, less doctrinaire than that of the polemicists in the magazines, more studiously sober in the application of erudition and of knowledge concerning literary and historical interconnections — in short: concerned with knowledge production as much as with cultural reflection. How this call was picked up can be exemplified by various late Victorian intellectuals. John Mackinnon Robertson (1856–1933; on him: Dekkers 1998 and Moore 2013, 585–86), Shakespearean scholar, occasional critic, freethinker, and political radical MP, authored a remarkable early work of imagology, *The Saxon and the Celt* (1897). His aim was to deconstruct quasi-anthropological nostrums as to the opposing ethnotypes supposedly running through the British cultural character — a favourite stereotype, as we have seen, since before the days of Matthew Arnold. Indeed, as T. G. Tucker's *The Foreign Debt of English Literature* (1907) shows, such stereotypes at the time had become ingrained even in literary scholarship: Tucker is apt to explain cross-national literary dynamics by means of an English national character whose basis 'is chiefly Teutonic, in some measure Celtic' (Tucker 1907, 1). Robertson's study collects and deconstructs a great number of such characterological tropes and is a forgotten classic of great value for modern postcolonial scholars and imagologists. Along similar lines, but part of a wartime climate, is his denunciation of German racism (*The Teutonic Gospel of Race*, 1916). Other works are *Buckle and his Critics: A Study in Sociology* (1895) and *Montaigne and Shakspere* (1897).

Other great representatives of the period were Sidney Lee and Leslie Stephen, the two initiators of that great Victorian enterprise, the *Dictionary of National Biography*. The DNB (1885–1900) stands alongside the *Oxford English Dictionary* (1884–1933) and the *Encyclopaedia Britannica* in its 9th and 11th editions (1875–1889; 1910–1911) as one of the great monuments of the Victorian dedication to the large-scale collecting

Fig 4.1. John Mackinnon Robertson, photograph by Bassano, 1920
(© National Portrait Gallery, London)

and dissemination of knowledge, also mobilizing and collectivizing the efforts of a great many philologists and historians. Leslie Stephen (1832–1904, immortalized by his daughter Virginia Woolf as 'Mr Ramsay' in *To the Lighthouse*) was an earnest, high-minded Victorian intellectual in the Matthew Arnold mould. As editor of the *Cornhill Magazine* (as successor to Thackeray, from 1871 until 1882), he wrote criticism, which, like that of the generation between Carlyle and the *fin de siècle*, was predicated on ethics rather than aesthetics; his main historical work, a *History of English Thought in the Eighteenth Century* (1876) belongs to the post-Hallam tradition of intellectual history which also includes Lecky and Freeman.

Literary intellectuals and the universities: Sidney Lee and Edward Dowden

Unlike Stephen himself, Stephen's fellow-editor at the DNB, Sidney Lee (born Solomon Lazarus Levy in 1859; educated at Oxford; knighted in 1911; died in 1926), was appointed to a chair at East London College, now Queen Mary University of London. This happened rather late in his life (in 1913): in contrast, Edward Dowden, born in 1843, gained his professorial appointment at the age of 24, in 1867. Between them, and between their appointment dates of 1867 and 1913, Dowden and Lee represent the move of an entire generation from private, popularly-oriented scholarship and criticism towards academic careers.

The move was driven from both ends: there was a great supply of prolific critics in post-Arnold Britain, and a demand for lecturers and professors in newly established universities and university departments. The need for literary intellectuals made itself felt at the universities; after all, the teaching of modern languages at new university departments was philological rather than purely linguistic. It involved the study of the most important works written in the subject-language, which implied a good grasp of the historical relationship in which these works stood to each other and to their time. What is more, new universities, known from the Victorian architecture of their main buildings as 'redbrick' universities, were being established where such philological programmes in modern languages gained a foothold. Manchester in 1880 became a university city with 'branch' colleges in Liverpool and Leeds (which became independent universities in 1903 and 1904). A federal university of Wales, along the lines of the Irish one (cf. above, 57) was set up in 1893, with colleges in Aberystwyth, Bangor and Cardiff (Swansea becoming a fourth college in 1920). Universities were also established in Birmingham (1900), Sheffield (1905) and Bristol (1909). In addition, new colleges were established in Oxford and Cambridge, where modern languages were taught, respectively, at the Taylor Institution and for the Tripos in Medieval and Modern Languages (1886).

The teaching of foreign languages was advocated at grass-roots levels by a 'Modern Language Association of Great Britain', founded in 1890, which published its own quarterly journal from 1897 onwards and urged the introduction of modern-language curricula at university level in places like TCD, Durham and Oxford. One Oxford don (Thomas Case, President of Corpus Christi College and Waynflete Professor of Moral Philosophy) denounced this as a turn away from the

Fig 4.2. Sir Sidney Lee, chalk drawing by Francis Dodd, 1920s
(© National Portrait Gallery, London)

Classics (possibly with men like Kemble and Max Müller in mind) and a triumph of Anglo-Saxon barbarism:

> An English School will grow up, nourishing our language not from the humanity of the Greeks and Romans, but from the savagery of the Goths and the Anglo-Saxons. We are about to reverse the renaissance.[1]

That was a rearguard sentiment. Modern languages and literatures had gained a firm foothold in the universities by the end of the century. The talents that were drawn to this new academic workplace were largely men schooled in the craft of criticism, and accordingly modern languages, and especially the schools of English, became an academic extension of the tradition of literary criticism, prestigious public platforms of good taste and literary erudition.

Sidney Lee and Edward Dowden were both known in their day as Shakespeare experts. Dowden's *Shakespeare, his Mind and Art* (1875) and *Shakespeare Primer* (1877) were translated into various languages and earned him the Royal Irish Academy's Cunningham Medal in 1878; Dowden is also behind many of the Shakespearean debates and allusions in the 'Scylla and Charybdis' episode in James Joyce's *Ulysses*. Lee's work revolved around the role of Italy in Shakespeare's work, and culminated in *The French Renaissance in England* (1910). By that time, there was an established notion of 'Comparative Literature', which could serve as a frame for Lee to present his work in:

> It is as a tentative contribution to a comparative study of literature that I wish the work mainly to be judged. That study has been pursued in this country on a smaller scale and less systematically than abroad. Yet the comparative study of literature is to my thinking a needful complement to those philological and aesthetic studies which chiefly occupy the attention of English scholars. (Lee 1910, v)

Lee places a British type of Comparative Literature explicitly under the auspices of Matthew Arnold. Arnold's call for a disinterested criticism dedicated to the knowledge and propagation of the best that is known and thought in the world leads Lee to observe that

> every great national literature is a fruit of much foreign sustenance and refreshment; however capable the national spirit may prove of mastering the foreign element. The comparative study should therefore form an integral part of any sound analysis of literary achievement. Students of literature who keep their sight fixed exclusively on a single nation's literary work run the risk of narrowing and distorting their critical judgement. No literature can be viewed in a just perspective until the comparative study has brought foreign literary effort within the range of vision. (Lee 1910, vi)

This is a mature, fully established comparatist position, which was reached by Lee and others between 1900 and 1914. None of this was in place when Dowden had begun his professorial career, in the very year of Arnold's *On the Study of Celtic Literature*, 1867.

Dowden, born in Cork in 1843, alumnus of the Queen's College in that city and of Trinity College Dublin, was appointed in 1867, a mere 4 days after his doctoral promotion, to the newly established chair of English Literature in Trinity College Dublin — an indication, not only of his good standing in his college (he had published an essay 'On the Criticism of Literature' while still an undergraduate, in 1864), but also of the career openings provided by this new type of university institution. His main interests were Shakespeare and Shelley (whose biography he published in 1886); he was also an early admirer of Walt Whitman. As a literary authority, he was viewed with a combination of respect and irritation by the young Dublin literati (like W. B. Yeats) who disliked his Victorian literary taste and his preference for English over Irish-born authors. As a literary connoisseur in academic garb, Dowden was the prototype of the professorial critic; his two volumes of *Studies in Literature* (1878 and 1895) represent the type of criticism that was moving from the ephemeral context of the periodicals into the gravitas of book form. That trend had been heralded by John Morley, the statesman-journalist (de Waard 2007), who became editor of the *Fortnightly Review* in, once again, that hinge-year 1867 — the year that Arnold read his *On the Study of Celtic Literature* and Dowden became Professor of English in Dublin. Under Morley, the *Fortnightly* abolished what until then had been standard practice: the anonymity of contributors and critics.[2] Opinions and contributions were no longer given as part of an anonymous round-robin collectivity, but as part of what the personally identified critic felt called upon to communicate to the public. The critic, too, was becoming an author as he gained authority.

Morley's own *Critical Miscellanies* of 1871 and 1877, like Dowden's *Studies in Literature*, also move from journalism to authorship. Observations on literary works are no longer a matter of taste, but of authoritative judgement, and in Dowden's case part of that authority derives from the critic's academic status.

Asymmetrical developments: Criticism, intellectual history, ethnology

Many critics on the crossover to academic status were, then, appointed to the new chairs created in the period. In each case the question needs to be asked, to which extent these critics were aware of the need to incorporate into their criticism [a] a sense of the historicity of literature (as opposed to the immediacy of the work's aesthetic function and its appreciation), and [b] linked to this, some form of cross-national or transnational, comparative awareness, based on the realization that the historical development of literature does not run a uniform course in different language areas.

These questions are weighty in view of two facts. Firstly, criticism before Arnold owed its supranational point of view and comparative method often to the influence of adjoining specialisms like intellectual history and ethnology (or ethnologically inflected philology). Secondly, these adjoining specialisms were not affected in the same way by the institutional opportunities offered by the university renewals of the period. Intellectual history, for instance, which with representatives like Hallam, Buckle, and Leslie Stephen had often been the pursuit of private scholars, felt the academic 'pull' much less strongly than what we shall notice with regard to the literary/journalistic tradition of 'criticism'. As history-writing professionalized into an academic discipline, it gravitated towards 'the archive-based study of changes imposed from above', with a tendency towards methodological nationalism: a thematic focus on the historian's and readers' own country, a tendency to rely largely on sources institutionally available within that country, and hence a proclivity to seek the root causes for historical events and developments within one's own borders. Accordingly, the core business of historians became national rather than transnational history, social or political history rather than cultural or intellectual history.[3] Although some university-based historians, like W. E. H. Lecky, ventured into the *History of European Morals*, the most important late-Victorian / Edwardian representative of this tradition, John Theodore Merz (1840–1922) remained outside the new academic humanities altogether. Born in 1840 in Manchester, he pursued studies in philosophy and the natural sciences at various universities in Germany (where his parents had come from) and became an official in the electricity supply company of Newcastle. His publications (which eventually earned him an honorary doctorate from the University of Durham) usually addressed the interface between philosophy and science; the most outstanding of these, a four-volume *History of European Thought in the Nineteenth Century*, appeared between 1903 and 1914. It emphatically includes science as one of the intellectual fields covered, and in its positivistic belief in science-driven progress as well as in its method and scope, continues the tradition of Hallam and Buckle. It is also significant that this interest in intellectual history remained largely outside the academic disciplines that were consolidating around 1900.[4] What was being institutionally consolidated were the mononational rather than the transnational humanities.

In the social sciences, the comparative-ethnological tradition which, as we noted in the case of Henry Maine and Max Müller, often interacted with interests such as comparative sociology and comparative religion, found a working field between archaeology and folklore studies, between the study of artefacts, practices and belief systems, and between museological display and academic research and analysis, with Augustus Pitt-Rivers (1827–1900) and the historian/folklorist Laurence Gomme (1853–1916), and thus moved away from its earlier philological connections. However, at the very moment where philology parted ways with antiquarianism/ archaeology and with anthropology, a massively influential crossover between them was produced in the venerable Max Müller mode, which would exercise a lasting influence across the twentieth century: James Frazer's *The Golden Bough*. The author, born in Glasgow in 1854, published this ambitious study of the archaic ritual negotiations of power, religion and magic in an initial two-volume version in 1871. The work ultimately grew into twelve volumes appearing between 1907 and 1915, and became a landmark in the anthropology of symbol, magic and myth. Among Frazer's influential successors are comparative mythologists like Mircea Eliade, Georges Dumézil, and Joseph Campbell. *The Golden Bough* also affected the wider literary and cultural imagination, and more immediately within Britain, thanks in no small part through the 'school' that Frazer established in Cambridge (his place of work, where he died in 1941). The impact in literary studies would be most strongly felt in the fields of Celtic Philology, and in the thematization of myth and magic in the study of ancient and early-medieval literatures (see below, 120).

These lines of development diverge widely and the tentative crossovers between them — between literary criticism, intellectual history and comparative ethnology, such as we noticed around the time of Matthew Arnold — were hindered rather than helped by the asymmetrical paths towards academic institutional consolidation. Comparatism, which in the decades after 1880 was beginning to be an established discipline on the European Continent and in the United States, would in Britain become a niche interest for professorially appointed critics. Within their university appointment, their critics' expertise in pronouncing expert judgement on literary texts was to be framed didactically as contributing to the formation of students' minds — training them in the ability to discern literary merit and to formulate this incisively.

That programme was to prove lastingly influential, and was still propounded by C. L. Wrenn in 1968. In his Presidential Address to the Modern Humanities Research Association, in the year before his death at the age of 74, Wrenn (J. R. R. Tolkien's successor as professor of Anglo-Saxon at Oxford) stated his belief 'that the study of comparative literature should sharpen, enlarge, and deepen the student's aesthetic awareness, his sensitiveness and imaginative capacity'. In addition, he denounced 'the dangers and disadvantages of the current emphasis on contemporary literature as an academic discipline' and advocated 'that the main emphasis should be placed rather in medieval and Renaissance literature' (Wrenn 1968, 4 and 16).

That was how an Elder Statesman felt in 1968, at the very eve of a general rebellion when old-school literary criticism came to be perceived as an exclusivist initiation into the prestigious conventions of elite culture. But it shows how long the Arnoldian, *Bildung*-derived style of propagating 'the best that is known and thought in the world' held sway.

Biographical positivism and history of ideas

In the case of Dowden, we note an intensive preoccupation with the historical and social anchoring of literary texts. Already in his published presidential address to the Dublin Undergraduate Philosophical Society, he sees the study of literature as a two-pronged undertaking, involving on the one hand a 'philosophical' analysis, 'leading to the discovery of principles in the philosophy of literature', and on the other a 'biographical analysis' leading to 'the discovery of principles in the history of literature'. The distinction is commonsensical and has (in roughly analogous form, albeit in different terms) often been made in the methodology of literary studies: it prefigures Wellek/Warren famous dichotomy between 'intrinsic study' and 'extrinsic approach' and, *mutatis mutandis*, the later split between literary theory and poetics on the one hand, and literary history on the other. That Dowden should reduce the historical, contextualizing approach to a 'biographical' one is uncongenial to our modern terms of literary engagement, but understandable in a period from well before the 'death of the author', when the duonyms 'life and work', 'l'homme (or 'la vie') et l'œuvre' were universally current. In an article on 'Goethe and the French Revolution', which appeared in 1889 in Morley's *Fortnightly*, and which offers a good example of Dowden tackling a cross-national topic in literary history, the term

Fig. 4.3. Edward Dowden, from *Cassell's Universal Portrait Gallery* (London: Cassell 1895)

'Goethe' unproblematically serves to signify the historical individual experiencing events in his time, and the author-figure whose name underwrites a specific corpus of literature: the biographical is a shortcut to, or even a substitute for, the historical. On the other hand, what Dowden calls the 'philosophy of literature' is not merely a question of poetics or the rhetoric of literary texts, as much as ethics. Dowden was a morally high-minded Victorian and tended to concentrate on those authors who, like him, wrote from an ethical engagement with the world (Shelley, George Eliot, Browning, Walt Whitman).

Goethe, in fact, was one of Dowden's great literary interests; at one point he served as chairman of the English Goethe Society, one of those commemorative literary associations across Europe which helped to spread a notion of literary historicism. It should be recalled that by now, such associations were often of a transnational as much as a national nature: Goethe was, after all, the man behind the concept of 'world literature', and in an established hypercanon of the literary giants of Europe the commemoration of Goethe by an English Society is no more surprising than the commemoration of Shakespeare by a German Society, the *Shakespeare-Gesellschaft,* founded in 1864 in Weimar. A third pan-European classic in this literary commemorative culture was Dante. If, then, Dowden deals as intensively with an author like Goethe as with Shakespeare, this is not necessarily in the awareness that he is thereby crossing a national frontier: Goethe and Shakespeare co-inhabit a transnational Parnassus. Accordingly, it is quite natural for Dowden to extend his interest in the literary impact of the French Revolution from the figure of Goethe to English authors; witness his book *The French Revolution and English Literature,* based on lectures held in Cambridge and Princeton, and published in book form in 1897. That book is in itself a further example of the crossover between literary connoisseurship, a newly emerging academic framework, and the ambition to publish literary criticism in monograph form rather than as journalism. In it, Dowden still pursues his earlier two-pronged approach between evaluative commentary and historical situatedness, which brings him to a remarkable early coinage of the notion of a 'history of ideas': he states as his purpose

> to enter in a disinterested way into the spirit of each writer who comes within the scope of my subject, and to let the meanings of the French Revolution, as they entered into English literature, expound themselves. To present some important figures on a background of history — history of ideas rather than of events — has been my aim. (Dowden 1899: vi)

Dowden's importance for something that might develop into comparatism rests mainly in the essays gathered in his *New Studies in Literature* of 1895. In it, he shows himself aware of contemporary literary studies on the continent: it contains an obituary appreciation of Edmond Schérer (a liberal-protestant literary historian) and an endorsement of Taine-style positivism in the essay 'Literary Criticism in France'. That he applied this European frame of reference to the domestic situation is further exemplified by the essay 'The Teaching of English Literature' and by the introduction to the volume. The fact that literature now becomes a matter of teaching and research means for Dowden (much in the style of Arnold's educational ideas) that English scholarship needs a broader, European horizon in what is becoming a more generally European world of learning:

> amid all their diversities a certain community has been established between the several literatures of Europe. As in the mediaeval period a dominant theology bound together the intellects of the various countries of the West, so now the dominant conceptions of science inhabit English, Italian, French and German brains, and a real society of thinkers, extending beyond the limits of any one nation, has come into existence. (Dowden 1895, 14)

What is more, he sees this type of intellectual cosmopolitanism as an antidote against the growing national chauvinism in Germany and Italy, and the language enthusiasm 'with which Welsh bards are listened to at the national Eisteddfods' (15). Within his own country, Dowden was less than enthusiastic about the Irish literary nationalism of W. B. Yeats and his school in the 1890s, which, a Dublin man of letters himself, he witnessed at close quarters. Against such tendencies towards national particularism Dowden vindicates a more cosmopolitan function of literature itself and of its study.

Remarkably, the comparative historian E. A. Freeman once again emerges as a template, as he had earlier with Dowden's erstwhile student Posnett:

> Had I my way in the teaching of English literature I would have the student start with a 'General Sketch of European Literature' somewhat resembling Mr Freeman's 'General Sketch of European History' in its aim and scope and manner of treatment. Unfortunately, no such book (as far as I am aware) exists, nor does one know where to turn in search of a writer competent to trace such an outline. (421)

That last sentence may or may not be read as a disavowal of Posnett's *Comparative Literature*; but Dowden does mention Hallam as a possible example for such a survey. On the basis of such a general historical-European frame of reference, the trainee critic

> should know where were the headquarters of literature in each successive period — now in Florence or in Rome, now in Paris, now in London, now at Weimar. When Boccaccio is spoken of in connection with Chaucer, when Tasso or Ariosto is spoken of in connection with Spenser or Boileau in connection with Dryden or Pope, or Goethe in connection with Carlyle he ought at least to be able to place Boccaccio and Tasso and Ariosto and Boileau and Goethe aright in the general movement of European literature, and in some measure to conceive aright the relation of each to the literary movement in our own country. (421–22)

Thus we see how the new, academic approach to the 'Teaching of English Literature' triggered the need for at least a Europe-wide peripheral vision in that anglocentric programme. Comparatism may be put forward here as an ancillary discipline, a *Hilfswissenschaft*, but the presentation of a 'general movement of European literature' does call into play a type of scholarship that was to actuate Continental comparatists from Georg Brandes to Paul Van Tieghem. As Dowden put these thoughts forward in his *New Studies in Literature*, Brandes's Shakespearean criticism was just being translated into English by William Archer (it would appear as *William Shakespeare: A Critical Study*, 1898). Brandes's epoch-making *Main Currents in Nineteenth-Century Literature* (*Hovedstrømninger i det 19de Aarhundredes Litteratur*) had already made their mark in Danish (1872–1875) and was in the process of being translated into the major European languages (an English edition appeared in 1906).

Within England, this synoptic period-survey approach was represented most prominently by George Saintsbury.

Saintsbury and his associates: European periods and the encyclopaedic approach

George Edward Bateman Saintsbury was two years younger than Dowden (born in 1845 in Southampton), but his career had a slower start. An undistinguished student at Oxford, he became teacher of Classics on Guernsey; his stint there (1868–1874) overlapped with the final two years of Victor Hugo's Jersey exile (1851–1870). It was in the Channel Island atmosphere that Saintsbury developed an interest in French literature. His initial fame was as a journalist-critic and rested on his contributions on English and French literature to Morley's *Fortnightly*. This journalism saw him develop ties with other critics such as Arthur Symons and Edmund Gosse (with whom he wrote for the *Academy*), and an article on Baudelaire in the *Fortnightly* established his prominence. We should note, incidentally, that he contributed various French-related articles to the ninth edition of the *Encyclopaedia Britannica* — as has been noted, the Encyclopaedia in these decades emerged for many critics as an important platform for the dissemination of literary knowledge — and collected his occasional pieces into books form: *Essays in English Literature, 1780–1860* (2 vols, 1890–1895), *Essays on French Novelists* (1891), *Miscellaneous Essays* (1892), and *Corrected Impressions* (1895). All this eventually paid off: in 1895 he was appointed to the chair of Rhetoric at the University of Edinburgh, which had recently been restructured so as to include the field of English Literature.

To be sure, Saintsbury had combined his journalistic criticism with more historically and pedagogically oriented studies: a *History of Elizabethan Literature* (1887), a *History of Nineteenth Century Literature* (1896), and *A Short History of English Literature* (1898, repeatedly re-issued). All this activity in itself documents the way in which English literature, and English literary history, was becoming something once might call a 'subject' or even a 'discipline', requiring dedicated scholars to conduct research and offer guidance, and in turn offering those scholars academic career prospects. Saintsbury's professorship came later to him than Dowden's, but he immediately followed his appointment through with ambitious, large-scale projects: a *History of Criticism* (1900–1904) and the hugely important, twelve-volume *Periods of European Literature* (1897–1907).

With the *Periods*, Saintsbury gave the type of large-scale conspectus that, obviously inspired by Brandes's great *Hovedstrømninger*, has remained a core business of a certain type of Comparative Literature: the cumulative, macroregional, 'transnational' superhistory often also covering lengthy historical periods and attempting to map

FIG. 4.4. George Saintsbury, photograph by Elliott & Fry, 1900s
(© National Portrait Gallery, London)

the tectonic plate shifts rather than the minutiae of literary developments. Although its roots lie in the encyclopaedic polymath authors of the eighteenth and nineteenth century (e.g. Benito Feijóo's *Teatro crítico universal*, 1729–1736), this synoptic approach by the late nineteenth century began to shade into cultural history in general — a type of endeavour which had been pioneered by Jakob Burkhardt's *Kultur der Renaissance in Italien* (1860; an English translation had appeared in 1878). It is in this tradition we can place later single-author works like Paul Hazard's *La Crise de la conscience européenne* (1935), Erich Auerbach's *Mimesis* (1946) and Ernst Robert Curtius's *Europäische Literatur und lateinisches Mittelalter* (1948). Most often, however, such works are collaborative efforts (e.g. Franco Moretti's *Il Romanzo*, 2004) and many of them have been initiated by the International Comparative Literature Association since that body was established in the 1950s.

The cumulative-synoptic, long-duration, large-scale literary history is, then, a type of flagship of what Comparative Literature would come to mean in the twentieth century, and Saintsbury's enterprise is a remarkable, early example of the genre. Saintsbury saw the project as 'an attempt, original and meritorious if not wholly successful, to exhibit European literature from the comparative point of view' (Saintsbury 1907, vii) — a striking combination of a multinational subject-matter and a transnational approach. Saintsbury also explicitly wanted to re-inscribe literary criticism into the framework of the historical and comparative sciences, and in this saw in Henry Hallam an intellectual ancestor. Although he did not want to go so far as to claim the title of a 'new Hallam', he nevertheless acknowledged the example explicitly:

> To the English student of literary history and of literary criticism, Henry Hallam must always by a name *clarum et venerabile* [...] For Hallam was our first master in English of the true comparative-historical study of literature — the study without which, as one main result of this volume should be to show, all criticism is now unsatisfactory, and the special variety of criticism which has been cultivated for the last century most dangerously delusive. His *Introduction to the Literature of Europe* [...] is the earliest book of the kind in our language: it is not far from being, to this day, the best book of the kind in any. (Saintsbury 1900–04, 3: 462)

Saintsbury's venture into what he himself considered the indispensable 'comparative-historical study of literature' also served to bring the best part of a generation together into collaboration. The first volume, *The Dark Ages*, was by William Paton Ker (1855–1923), who, after appointments in Edinburgh and Wales (as the first Professor of English in Cardiff), had since 1889 held the Chair of English at London, where he also founded Scandinavian studies (in 1917). Ker was a notable expert on the Middle Ages: his *Epic and Romance* (1897) opposed those two literary types in a periodization and characterization which is still current nowadays. Other collaborating professors from 'new' chairs of English were Charles Edwyn Vaughan (1854–1922, Leeds), Oliver Elton (1861–1945, Liverpool), and Gregory Smith (1865–1923, Belfast).

Saintsbury himself contributed three volumes to the *Periods*: the second (*The Flourishing of Romance and the Rise of Allegory*, 1907), the fifth (*The Earlier Renaissance*,

1901) and the concluding twelfth (*The Later Nineteenth Century*, 1907). For the remaining eight volumes, he enlisted the help of Frederick Snell (3: *The Fourteenth Century*, 1899), Gregory Smith (4: *The Transition Period*, 1900), David Hannay (6: *The Later Renaissance*, 1898), Herbert Grierson (7: *The First Half of the Seventeenth Century*, 1906), Oliver Elton (8: *The Augustan Ages*, 1899), J. H. Millar (9: *The Mid-Eighteenth Century*, 1902), C. E. Vaughan (10: *The Romantic Revolt*, 1907), and T. S. Omond (11: *The Romantic Triumph*, 1900).

Of these, the name of Herbert J. C. Grierson (1866–1960) is still best known nowadays for his work on the Metaphysical Poets. Shetland-born and educated at the universities of Aberdeen and Oxford, he became Professor of English at Aberdeen and, as Saintsbury's successor, at Edinburgh. He did little comparatist work besides his participation in the *Periods*.

Gregory Smith, likewise a Scot, worked under Saintsbury as a lecturer at Edinburgh,[5] where he was also editor for the Scottish Texts Society; in 1909 he obtained a professorial appointment as librarian at Queen's University Belfast. Author of a collection of *Elizabethan Critical Essays* as well as articles for the *Dictionary of National Biography* and the *Encyclopaedia Britannica*, his importance for the development of comparatism in Britain would be limited if it were not for his authorship (anonymous at the time[6]) of a trenchant critique regarding the new discipline, and its position vis-à-vis French *littérature comparée*. That intervention warrants slightly closer scrutiny.

Methodological crossroads: Positivism and criticism

Smith's critical article appeared in *Blackwood's Edinburgh Magazine* (1901) under the title 'The Foible of Comparative Literature'. It was occasioned by the *Congrès Internationale d'Histoire Comparée* held in Paris in 1900, within which a workshop was held in the *Section d'histoire de littérature comparée*, with French practitioners like Ferdinand Brunetière and the medievalist Gaston Paris. Such critics dovetailed comparative philology with intellectual history — something that had been noted previously by Leslie Stephen in his 1899 review of Joseph Texte's *Jean-Jacques Rousseau et les origines du cosmopolitisme littéraire* (1895). Texte, usually considered one of the founding fathers of comparatism, was a pupil of Brunetière and obtained an appointment in 1896 to the first chair dedicated to *littérature comparée* (at Lyons); illness and an early death prevented his intended appointment to the Sorbonne (Thieme 1901). What Stephen reviewed in 1899 was an English translation of Texte's book: an essay 'The Cosmopolitan Spirit in Literature', which summarized Texte's argument and discussed its possible application to the English context. Stephen considered the English type of literary intellectual, the *critic*, as an ideal carrier for this new type of cosmopolitan learning:

> Critics, like other people nowadays, are anxious to be scientific. They wish to improve upon the old simpleminded criticism which expressed a mere individual liking or disliking. The personal element, indeed, is essential to all good criticism; to the only criticism which can really open our eyes to unrecognised genius; to such criticism, for instance, as that by which Coleridge

or Lamb revived an interest in our older authors. But the individual taste now requires to be guided by a wide knowledge of the taste of other ages and countries. (Stephen 1899, 379)

This is an Arnoldian attempt to reconcile axiology with historical knowledge and scientific method, in the process adjusting the idea of the critic to a new scholarly and indeed academic climate. But while Stephen attempted to harmonize these contradictory elements, science and taste, Smith's 1901 'Foible' article dismissed the factualist historicism of the French *Congrès Internationale* as unworkable. He sarcastically denounced the programme propounded there as evolutionary-genetic rather than truly comparative. A true comparison should not be the bibliographical record of moments in a historical track record, but should involve the finesse and judgement of the *critic* and embrace artistic realms beyond the purely textual stemmatology of philological *Stoffgeschichte*:

> May there not be a comparative interest in things whose only connection is from analogy, or even in forms and motives, between which there may be not only no admitted or known connection, but not even an obvious hint or likeness? There is, for example, surely something in the examination of parallel forms of folk-tale (if only to disprove some of the extravagant generalisations of the folklorists); yet in nearly all the cases there is not, and there cannot be, a scrap of evidence of derivation or interaction. Whether the different arts have, or do not have, a common aesthetic basis, is a question which need not prevent certain analogies or using one art as a touchstone for the other; and we may do so without being convicted of the quackery of the symphony-in-blue-journalism. And may we not compare such excentric things as a Hindu epic and a French epic? (Smith 1901, 64)

Smith reiterated these strictures in his 1905 essay 'Some Notes on the Comparative Study of Literature', published in the first volume of the newly-founded *Modern Language Review*. But by then, his earlier article had drawn a response from none other than H. M. Posnett, now back from New Zealand. Posnett's 'The Science of Comparative Literature' appeared in the *Contemporary Review* in 1901 as a feisty reply to Smith. It was, in other words, the first methodological altercation of the fledgling discipline. Posnett, even more trans-European in his orientation than Smith, was of course a dyed-in-the-wool positivist, for whom factualism and comparison were part of a method far beyond mere formal appearances or critical appeal; and evolutionary stadialism had always been part of his outlook (Moore 2013, 567–77). Indeed, Posnett, for his part, felt that the Saintsbury school was, if anything, moving the 'science' of comparatism into the ambit of mere literary reviewers and taste-pundits: 'literary specialists, champions of the old and unhistorical criticism, and many amateur critics who are content to echo the sentiments of the old school without enquiry' (Posnett 1901, 866). He had a point. While some of Saintsbury's collaborators were 'redbrick' professors of English, others were private scholars and journalists: Vaughan, Omond, Hannay.

And so Saintsbury's *Periods*, reflect, in British terms, a European debate between factualism (from positivistic and philological antecedents) and a more interpretative approach (involving aesthetics, philosophy and cultural history or *Geistesgeschichte*).

The tension may be generic for Comparative Literature as such, or even literary history in general, and has replicated itself in the 1960s debates between René Wellek and the 'New Critics' on the one hand and the 'French School' on the other, and in the various debates (anti-historicism, poststructuralism, cultural materialism, New Historicism) since then.

In late-nineteenth-century Britain, the tradition of literary criticism tended to favour the evaluative, text-critical type of literary scholarship, important representatives being critics like John Churton Collins (1848–1908) and Edmund Gosse (1849–1928). Gosse is now mainly known as the author of the autobiographical novel *Father and Son* (1907). In *fin de siècle* London, he was loosely connected with that generation of literati who combined a certain aestheticism with a progressive literary taste (be it Arts-and-Crafts-utopianist, or naturalist, or symbolist; often France-oriented). Gosse, essentially a private connoisseur and 'man of letters', eventually became librarian to the House of Lords — a sinecure, rather than a task requiring philological professionalism. The widening gulf between his type of criticism and the new demands of academic scholarship was made obvious by the savage attacks that were levelled at Gosse's collection *From Shakespeare to Pope* (1885) by one John Churton Collins. The incident has become notorious (cf. Cunningham 1991) for precisely that reason: it exemplified the growing divergence between journalistic and academic criticism. With his book, Gosse (a lecturer at Cambridge at the time) had proffered his credentials for one of the new professorial career opportunities (on which cf. Sutherland 1991). Collins's savage review put an end to Gosse's academic prospects. Gosse's literary cosmopolitanism would henceforth be lost to the developing discipline; it found expression in publications like the *Studies in the Literature of Northern Europe*, 1879 and in Gosse's *French Profiles*, containing an essay on 'The Influence of France upon English Poetry'. The project which Gosse had mentioned in a letter to Edward Dowden in 1877 was to remain unfulfilled:

> what I wish to be a distinctive feature [...] constant references to technical influences on our poetry from abroad (from France, Italy, Spain, and Holland), and *vice versa* (on Germany, Sweden, Italy etc.), which to my knowledge has never been attempted. (Dowden & Dowden 1914, 108)

As for John Churton Collins (1848–1908), his critical vehemence became notorious (he also waxed irate over George Saintsbury) and ultimately made him an academic loner. Denounced as a 'louse in the locks of literature' by Tennyson, he is now known in popular culture for having indulged a morbid interest in the Whitechapel Murders, and for having committed suicide. Although his journalistic statements in support of English as a university subject helped bolster the English Honours School at Oxford in 1893, he himself was long unsuccessful in his many applications for the chairs that were being established. When he finally did obtain a chair (Birmingham, in 1904), his final years saw a flourish of literary scholarship. His book on *Voltaire, Rousseau, and Montesquieu in England* was obviously meant as a form of cultural diplomacy in order to bolster the newly-established French-British *entente cordiale* of 1904. His article on 'The literary indebtedness of England to France', in the *Fortnightly Review* of 1908, is almost embarrassingly fulsome

Fig. 4.5. Sir Edmund Gosse, drawing by Frank Dicksee, 1912
(© National Portrait Gallery, London)

FIG. 4.6. John Churton Collins
(Library of Congress, George Grantham Bain collection)

in its francophile rhetoric. The 1904 book is more restrained. Beyond the sober description of the book's three main figures on their English sojourns, a certain methodological vista is opened up:

> I am well aware what a trifling contribution this little volume is to the promotion of a branch of study the significance and interest of which we are only now beginning to understand, I mean the solidarity of the humanities, and the mutual influences which the chief literatures of Europe have exercised on each other both in relation to evolution and in relation to idiosyncrasies. It is only by minute investigation, and by investigation in detail, that real progress can be made in such study. At present it seems to be represented rather by abstract generalisations than by generalisations based on facts; but unless in such enquiries the second precede the first there can be small security for soundness and truth. (Collins 1908, viii)

This sentiment went unheard, alas, and the 'Comparative' in Comparative Literature has all too often been taken as an entitlement to neglect, rather than to accumulate, concrete literary-historical data.

Both Gosse and Collins are part of the literary rediscovery of France that took place at the time. After the Franco-Prussian War of 1870–71, imperial Germany grew into Britain's most powerful Continental rival; the old Saxonist sympathies for the 'German Cousin' evaporated (Firchow 1986) while artistically, an anti-Victorian aestheticism emerged which frequently looked to *fin de siècle* France for inspiration. To some extent, the old interest in 'Northern Europe' persisted (we have seen it exemplified in the person of W. P. Ker[7]), but it now was complemented by a school of literary studies which also looked to the Romance neighbours to the South: Cervantes, Dante[8] and the French. Both Germanic and Romance Philology were henceforth to inform the peripheral vision of comparatist-minded critics. Celtic Philology would, as has been pointed out and as we shall see, maintain itself most strongly as a comparatist inspiration in the more anthropologically-oriented tradition drawing inspiration from Frazer's *The Golden Bough*. Slavic Studies was as yet largely non-existent, despite the critical appreciation of Tolstoy and Turgenev.

Summary, outlook

In 1913, an article appeared in the *Modern Language Review* entitled 'The Future of Comparative Literature' — a poignant title, given what we now know the immediate future held in store. The author, Harold Victor Routh, a Cambridge-educated classicist (1874–1951) felt in a position to look back on the great achievements of the past generations, most notably Saintsbury's *Periods* project, and to outline perspectives for what was now beginning to appear like an emerging discipline. His outline makes eminently sensible reading, even a century later, and steers a middle course between the airy judgementalism of aesthetic criticism, the arid factualism of positivistic historicism, or the collector's instinct of the encyclopaedic compilers. Instead, Routh privileges the notion of literature as a dynamic skein of developments and processes, and as something characterized by its powers of variation. Thus the comparatist's task begins when literary processes become more intriguing than the literary products, and when differences, transitions and changes become more arresting than the fixed patterns. Routh's programme is worth quoting at some length:

> The real value of comparative literature can be appreciated only in the hands of some scholar who has no special author or period in mind, nor any desire to 'give a bird's eye view of the whole field', but whose curiosity is excited by the strange contrasts and deviations of literary development. Such an enquirer will not dream of covering Europe's output in prose and poetry, but will concentrate his attention, almost instinctively, on those authors and schools of expression, that at any time or in any place have unexpectedly differed. Not being distracted by any of the specialist's interests, though availing himself largely of his labours, he will pass from one author to another, wherever contrasts suggest an opening, first of all estimating the art and ideas of the works momentarily in question, then examining the *milieu* which shaped each literary life, then enquiring into causes, whether social, domestic, racial, climatic or political, which turned them severally from one trend of thought and from one form of expression and drew them to another. By and by, as he gradually learns what influences count in the formation of thought and what other influences, though considerable in history or sociology, are powerless, and again what qualities are essential to a particular type of literature, while certain other qualities are accidents of time and place, his apparently erratic footsteps begin to progress along definite lines. He finds that while avoiding the bibliographical and textual minuteness of the specialists, he has himself become a specialist of another sort, who supplements their discoveries by researches just as recondite. His chosen province is neither aesthetics not biography, but the study of literary essence and evolution. Books for him are so much data for investigating the conditions which inspire and the conditions which diversify the written word. (Routh 1913, 5)

Routh later gave an example of this approach with his *God, Man and Epic Poetry* of 1927, which he subtitled *A Study in Comparative Literature* — the first time that phrase was used on the title page of a British monograph since Posnett. Ultimately the work of Donald Davie at Essex in the 1960s (below, 148) can be seen as a continuation of what for Routh was still 'The future of Comparative Literature'. But many things that seemed set fair to prosper in undisturbed development from their Victorian beginnings took a knock after August 1914, and the lack of institutional fixity for the fledgling discipline meant that its continuance was left to a handful of individually dedicated scholars.

The 'post-Arnold' decades, from 1870 until 1914, show a number of trends highly propitious to the development of comparative scholarship. A cosmopolitan outlook took hold after, and because of, Matthew Arnold; critics developed from journalists into literary intellectuals and in many cases secured university appointments, acquiring academic status and an academic outlook; there was growing awareness of a fledgling discipline on the Continent and in the US called Comparative Literature, and even a handbook proclaiming that new discipline under that very name; and a number of important studies were published (by Edward Dowden, Sidney Lee, Saintsbury, Churton Collins) which deliberately ventured into the comparative, trans-national study of literature. There was only one thing missing:

a sense of institutional organization and consolidation — something perpetuating itself through planned projects like recurring conferences, dedicated journals, courses in university curricula, structural faculty appointments, and developing a master-pupil continuity (cf. Posner 1988). Comparatism was a scholarly fashion, not yet a discipline.

The troubled transgenerational and institutional carry-over across the Great War is illustrated by the figures of Arthur Quiller-Couch and Charles Harold Herford. Both were bereaved fathers who lost their sons to the War. For Quiller-Couch (known as 'Q'; Cornish regionalist, one of the great anthologists and 'men of letters' of his time and, from 1912 onwards, Professor of English at Cambridge), this confirmed his francophile-Edwardian preference for what he considered the 'Romance' tradition in English culture (rather than 'Germanic'), and also inspired an enduring Cornish regionalism suffused with fin-de-siècle Celticism. After the war, he was to be the presiding genius for English literature and Modern Languages in Cambridge, until his generational clash with F. R. Leavis (below, p. 116).

As for Herford, his committed Germanophilia (his wife was from Bremen) had led him to give his doomed son the name 'Siegfried' (like the War Poet Sassoon). Born in Manchester in 1853 and educated at Cambridge, Herford was one of the Redbrick appointees of these decades (Aberystwyth 1887–1901), and his 1902 appointment to his native city's university, as the first incumbent of a dedicated chair for English Literature, would see him established and active there until 1921. He died in Oxford in 1931. Herford was known for many text editions in English literature, and was a collaborator of Dowden's in the English Goethe Society; among his scholarly inspirations were the great men of old-school *Germanistik*, Ludwig Geiger and Wilhelm Scherer, whose lectures he had attended in Vienna in 1881–82.

Herford's personal experiences abroad, and the fact that he married outside his native country, bespeaks a new type of academic mobility which helped foster an interest in cross-national themes. We shall see in this and the following generation that an international orientation or experience in one's private life meshes with a choice for transnational topics. Most of Herford's work moved in the Anglo-German realm, such as the *Studies in the Literary Relations of England and Germany in the Sixteenth Century* (1886). That book, like Sidney Lee's *The French Renaissance in England* of 1910, is a good example of what in German became known as *Einfluss- und Beziehungsforschung* and which more recently has attracted fresh attention as *Cultural Transfer*; and it has been praised by later comparatists for defining a new field of study called 'international literature' — which seems, however, to be an exaggerated claim.[9] To be sure, Herford defined his topic as consisting of a literature that was more than mono-national, but he did not draw specific methodological conclusions from that insight except an ambition to thematize these cross-currents in 'a connected and intelligible account' (Herford 1886, xix).

Almost forty years later, in 1925, when Herford reviewed Fernand Baldensperger's comparatist classic *Le mouvement des idées dans l'émigration française* in the *Modern Language Review*, he still showed no awareness that influences, relations and transfers were now the specific object of a dedicated comparatist discipline. Yet, the fact that he was one of the driving forces behind the *Modern Language Review* (established in 1905) constitutes one of his most important contributions to the post-war fresh start of literary studies in Britain. In an obituary by John George Robertson, his fellow-editor of the *Modern Language Review*, Herford's *Studies in the Literary Relations of England and Germany in the Sixteenth Century* were retrospectively praised as an eminent example 'among our none too numerous English works in the field which the French call *la littérature comparée*' (Robertson 1933).

There are a number of important scholars in the interwar years who had started their academic careers pre-1914. Alongside Routh and Robertson, who will be noted in greater detail in the next chapter, we shall also encounter representatives like Leonard Wilson Forster, Gilbert Waterhouse, Leonard Willoughby, and Edna Purdie. All of them worked in a context where 'English' together with 'Modern Languages' (usually French or German) triggered an interest in the literary processes that occurred across and between language areas; and they worked in a context when, at Continental universities, but not in Britain, there were comparatist university departments dedicated to this topic.

That resulted in both a strength and a weakness: a tenuous self-definition within the British institutions and a thriving exchange with foreign universities. While the immediate post-Arnoldians (Dowden and Herford excepted) had attended university in the old style of 'finishing one's education', and had then usually been drafted into academic careers from other, more literary fields, their successor generation, the post-Saintsburyans, had been students at a new type of university, part of a Europe-wide system of professionally-trained scholarship, and had received at least part of their academic training or early career openings at Continental universities: F. E. Sandbach (see note 7) in Strasbourg and Paris, H. V. Routh in Paris, Marburg and Munich, Robertson in Leipzig and Strasbourg, L. W. Forster in Königsberg and Basel. A type of comparatist scholar emerged who not only studied 'literary cosmopolitanism' and international exchanges, but also lived the experience.

Notes to Chapter 4

1. In his 1887 pamphlet 'An Appeal to the University of Oxford against the Proposed Final School of Modern Languages', quoted Firth 1929: 70–71.
2. For most of the nineteenth century, contributions to periodicals went unsigned, and attributing to a specific author was often painstaking or difficult — a task famously undertaken in the *Wellesley Index to Victorian Periodicals*, now best used in combination with the *Curran Index* at <http://victorianresearch.org/curranindex.html>.
3. For the development of academic/national history-writing in the nineteenth and early twentieth centuries, see the historiographical entries in ERNiE 2018 and the various publications in the Palgrave Macmillan series *Writing the Nation* edited by Stefan Berger; for the narrowing-down tendency in this process, Rigney 2007. The qualification of the Rankean moment in history-writing as a turn towards 'the archive-based study of changes imposed from above' I heard from Peter Burke in Göttingen in 2012 during his presentation of Burke 2012.
4. Some studies in intellectual history were produced by chaired philosophers: The *History of the Philosophy of History* published in 1893 by the St Andrews professor Robert Flint (1838–1910), and *The Development of Modern Philosophy* by the Glasgow professor Robert Adamson (1852–1902).
5. John Hepburn Millar (1864–1929), author of the volume *The Mid-Eighteenth Century*, was another Edinburgh connection: he was lecturer, then professor of law at the university there, and known mainly for his *Literary History of Scotland* (1903).

6. Smith's authorship was made known by Eric Partridge in 1926.
7. Generally Leerssen 2019. Ker's London colleague Charles Harold Herford published *Norse Myth in English Poetry* in 1919. Previously, in 1903, the Birmingham lecturer (later professor) Francis Edward Sandbach (1874–1939, born in London, educated at Aberystwyth, Strasbourg, the Sorbonne and Cambridge) published his *The Nibelungenlied and Gudrun in England and America* as 'a modest contribution of material to the future historian of the literary relations between the English and German speaking peoples' (Sandbach 1903, v)
8. F. J. Snell (one of Saintsbury's collaborators in the *Periods* project) had published *Dante in America* in 1896. Interest in Dante crystallized around the work of J. Paget Toynbee, who had published an article on 'English Translations from Dante (Fourteenth to Seventeenth Century)' in the American *Journal of Comparative Literature* in 1903; Toynbee's *Dante in English Literature from Chaucer to Cary* appeared in 1909.
9. Cf. Roe 1954, 5–6. Roe states that Herford 'had every claim to be a comparatist', echoing the 1931 *Times* obituary which had stated that 'A research Chair of Comparative Literature would perhaps have been the ideal appointment for him' (*The Times*, Monday 27 April 1931, 17). Roe cited Herford's Taylorian Lecture of 1879 (*The Influence of Goethe's Italian Journey on his Style*), and some articles in *Ryland's Library Bulletin*, the Manchester University house journal in these years, on 'Dante and Milton' and on Pushkin as 'A Russian Shakespeare' (1924 and 1925).

CHAPTER 5

Comparatist Trends within Literary Studies (1914–1950)

The Great War did not quite bring literary scholarship and criticism to a complete halt, but it did form a caesura of sorts. Also, in the minds of contemporaries, the post-1918 years marked a fresh start and a break with the Victorian and Edwardian past. One voice strenuously holding on to pre-war patterns was that of Arthur Quiller-Couch, who celebrated the aesthetic, gentlemanly, Romance orientation in English literature, and who was later to enter into a generational conflict with the new spirit as represented by F. R. Leavis. Another figure of continuity was the arresting, if somewhat isolated, figure of Laurie Magnus (1872–1933), who directed the Routledge publishing company from 1902 onwards. Magnus was among the few to continue the synoptic tradition of George Saintsbury after the Great War. In 1918 he published *A General Sketch of European Literature in the Centuries of Romance*, followed in 1926 by a *Dictionary of European Literature* and in 1927 by *English Literature in its Foreign Relations, 1300–1800*. *A History of European Literature* appeared posthumously in 1934. Magnus saw Edward Dowden as his great forerunner; Dowden's appeal to serve the study of English literature with a '*General Sketch* [...] somewhat resembling Mr Freeman's *General Sketch of European History* in its aim and scope' (above, p. 95) is used as a motto to Magnus's 1918 book, lending intertextual significance to its title. Magnus also invokes other academic critics of the Dowden generation: Saintsbury, Sidney Lee, W. P. Ker, C. H. Herford and T. G. Tucker (on whom see p. 85 above). However, although Magnus's books were doubtless useful as handbooks and surveys, and deserve to be remembered as interesting phenomena in the early history of British comparatism, they did not establish or consolidate an academic trend, school or method. In its isolation, Magnus's work signifies not only a continuity with such pre-war practice, but also its decline. Greater comparatist continuity within university life was ensured mainly by scholars in German Studies.

German Studies and John George Robertson

In Cambridge, where we have noted the presence of Charles Harold Herford, the aegis for German Studies was the Schröder Professorship, instituted in 1909. Its first incumbent was Karl Breul, born in Hanover in 1860 and tenured at Cambridge since 1884; he died in 1932. Breul's interest in German-English relations during the Romantic period influenced Gilbert Waterhouse's 1914 *The Literary Relations of England and Germany in the Seventeenth Century*,[1] F. W. Stokoe's *German Influence in the English Romantic Period (1788–1818)* (1926), and Violet Stockley's *German Literature as Known in England* (1929).

At Oxford, Hermann Georg Fiedler developed German Literature at the Taylor Institution. Born in 1862 in Saxony, after a career as lecturer in Glasgow, Professor in Birmingham and private tutor at the royal court, Fiedler became Professor at Oxford in 1907. His long tenure formed future Germanists such as Leonard Willoughby, who became professor, first in Manchester, then at University College London in 1931 and who would dominate, with his younger collaborator and eventual successor Mary Wilkinson, Goethe/Schiller studies for most of the century. In Fiedler's monograph series 'Oxford Studies in Modern Languages and Literatures', many young scholars found a publication forum, among them James Boyd with his *Goethe's Knowledge of English Literature* (1932). Boyd was later to become editor of the *Modern Language Review*. In that capacity, he was the successor of the MLR's influential founding editor, John George Robertson.

John George Robertson (1867–1933, noted already in the foregoing pages in a pre-1914 context) stands somewhat apart from his contemporaries. Born in Glasgow in 1867, educated in Glasgow and Leipzig (where he met his future wife,[2] whom he married in Munich in 1894), and briefly tenured at the university of German-occupied Strasbourg, Robertson was in 1903 appointed to the chair of German in London (University and Bedford Colleges), where he inspired a tradition in German Studies that gained prominence from the 1940s on (Flood & Simon 2017). After 1918 he developed into a truly cardinal figure in the history of British comparatism, embodying in his career a continuity of sorts across the 1914–1918 gap. Educated outside Britain, specialist in a subject that was much less fashionable in the early twentieth century than it had been in the mid-nineteenth, Robertson is also the literary academic in Britain who was most vividly aware of critical and comparatist trends on the Continent. Even before 1914 he had published on reception history: an article on 'The Knowledge of Shakespeare on the Continent at the Beginning of the 18th Century' (in an early 1906 volume of the *Modern Language Review*, whose founding editor he was) and a similar topic concerning Milton read before the British Academy in 1907. A chapter on 'Shakespeare on the Continent' was contributed to the 1910 *Cambridge History of English Literature*. It was after the War that Robertson came into his own. His *Studies in the Genesis of Romantic Theory in the Eighteenth Century* of 1923 is no doubt one of the outstanding comparatist publications of the inter-war period. As to its self-awareness as a comparatist study, the opening paragraph speaks for itself:

> It is one of the most tangible achievements of the vaguely defined science of Comparative Literature that it has lifted the veil from the phenomena of analogous development in literary history. We are no longer content to register the fact that, at certain periods of their history, the literature of Italy, France, England and Germany passed through identical metamorphoses and reacted similarly to the same spiritual forces; that great movements like the Renaissance, or Romanticism, moving over the face of Europe, left behind them similar

Fig. 5.1. John George Robertson (courtesy of the Institute for Modern Language Research, Senate House Library, University of London)

effects on every land; we are beginning now to understand the processes and developments involved in such phenomena; to grasp and formulate, in other words, natural laws of literary evolution. Literature is regarded as a living organism, subject to the laws of growth and decay which all living things obey. (Robertson 1923, 1)

We hear echoes of the older, positivistic historicism of the Hallam/Arnold generation, but less deterministically so, and apparently informed by the work of Van Tieghem on Romanticism and Pre-Romanticism. Once again, a sense of literature as a dynamic multinational system goes together with a keen sense of the historicity of the literary text. In the absence of dedicated comparatist chairs or lectureships, Robertson is probably the single-language specialist who went furthest towards a supranational treatment of literature as a multinational topic — becoming not so much a scholar in English, French or German studies who broadens his horizon by factoring foreign influences into his analysis or capitalizing on his knowledge of other languages, but making a deliberate leap towards a transnational analysis of literary dynamics spanning different language areas. What is merely 'peripheral vision' for scholars like Saintsbury, Gosse or the many literary critics of the earlier generation, becomes Robertson's specific focus. His purview encompasses much more than the Germany to which his specialism and chair was dedicated; he aims to locate the roots of what would come to be called 'pre-romanticism' in the interplay between Italy, France and Spain,

> to show that the Italy which led the critical theory of Europe in the sixteenth century, played again a pioneer rôle at the beginning of the eighteenth; that the conception of the 'creative imagination', with the help of which Europe emancipated herself from the pincers of pseudo-classicism, was virtually born in Italy to grow to full maturity in England and Germany. (Robertson 1923, vi)

It was around this time, too, that Robertson took steps to found a department of Comparative Literature, as he later reminisced in a letter to Baldensperger:

> Years ago, I made a determined effort to get a department of Comparative Literature established here [in London]. My plan had the blessing of the Board of Education and went a certain distance towards fulfillment.[3]

Throughout the 1920s Robertson was active in the *Modern Language Review* (which became a forum for many transnationally-oriented articles). In addition, his work with the English Goethe Society and his many occasional lectures and articles (e.g., a contribution to the 1930 *Festschrift* for Baldensperger) regularly reflect his interest in Continental developments. An essay on *Goethe and Byron* (1925, for the English Goethe Society) presents the mutual indebtedness of both poets to each other as marking a new stage in cross-national literary dynamics:

> In most problems of international literary relationships, the investigation is limited to the comparatively simple issue of the influence exerted by one literature or author upon another; the question of a mutual exchange of ideas and mutual indebtedness rarely, for obvious reasons, arises before the nineteenth century. The relationship of Goethe and Byron is of the mutual type. (Robertson 1925: 1)

This observation becomes more suggestive in the light of a Liverpool lecture, likewise from 1925, on 'Literary Cosmopolitanism'. Taking his cue from *Jean-Jacques Rousseau et les origines du cosmopolitisme littéraire* (by Joseph Texte, the first comparatist professor in France), Robertson defines as cosmopolitanism any complex of factors which facilitate the Europe-wide spread of literary works or trends; ironically, the advent of Romanticism, in his view, cut across such cosmopolitan patterns as had been at work in the Middle Ages, the Renaissance and the Enlightenment: 'Romanticism meant individualism, and individualism meant the break-up of the literary cosmopolitanism of the eighteenth century' (in Robertson 1935, 282).

In his late lecture on 'Literature in the Universities' (1932) Robertson tries to mediate between what he sees as a 'British' notion of literary scholarship, 'largely concerned with the appreciation and criticism of poetic qualities — qualities dependent on the exercise, not of the reason, but of the imagination' and (on the other hand) a more historicist tradition coming out of France. Remarkably, Robertson shows himself reluctant to embrace German examples which (according to him) vacillate between dry factualism ('sesquepedalian treatises, mechanical compilations of data, often a futilely misdirected hunting for sources') and speculative quasi-profundity ('an orgy of metaphysics') (in Robertson 1935, 299–314). The language is acerbic, the positioning of a comparatist programme still insightful, even today, setting a historically informed analysis against moral-aesthetic pronouncements of taste and appreciation, dry fact-obsessed antiquarianism, and freewheeling indulgence in abstract reflection.

Gender and foreign languages

In London, in the English Goethe Society and in the *Modern Language Review* (both of which published a good deal of comparatist material[4]), Robertson's work was continued by Edna Purdie (1894–1968), alumna of Somerville College Oxford, who had gained her Master's and doctoral degrees under Robertson's supervision at London. Between 1917 and 1921 she was lecturer at Liverpool and, from 1921 until 1933, at Bangor (where her predecessor had been Thomas Rea). During that period she published a study of direct comparatist importance: *German Influence on the Literary Ballad in England during the Romantic Revival*, in the *Publications of the English Goethe Society* (vol. 3, 1924; the series was at that time under the editorship of Robertson). Purdie was to succeed her erstwhile teacher Robertson (whose posthumous *Essays and Addresses* she edited in 1935) as Professor of German Literature at London (Bedford and Royal Holloway), where she remained one of Britain's most outstanding German scholars well into the 1960s; she retired in 1962 and died in 1968.

The figure of Purdie, who also was among the British contributors to the Parisian *Bibliothèque de la Revue de Littérature Comparée*, exemplifies the advent of women graduates on the scene of British literary studies. Most women academics of the inter-war years had studied at the women's colleges founded in the previous decades; these included Bedford College (1849; a constituent college of the

Fig. 5.2. Edna Purdie, photograph by Bassano Ltd., 1963
(© National Portrait Gallery, London)

University of London as of 1900); Somerville College (1879) and St Hilda's (1893) in Oxford; Girton (1869) and in particular Newnham College (1871) in Cambridge. They produced a cohort of literary scholars who commenced their academic career in this period and who found, in their colleges and departments, a congenial working environment during their early careers. As we shall see (below, 127), there were a number of British women contributors to the Parisian *Bibliothèque de la Revue de Littérature Comparée* during the inter-war years who had read French Literature at their home universities.

While most of these subsequently ran into the glass ceiling of gender, some — like Purdie, and in her wake E. M. (Elsie) Butler, Nora Chadwick and E. M. (Mary) Wilkinson, on whom more below — eventually rose to professorial chairs. (To his credit, George Robertson had encouraged the academic vocation, not only of Purdie, but also of Butler and Wilkinson.)

This advent of women scholars affected, of course, other academic fields besides Comparative Literature, and a fuller treatment would necessitate a look also at those female literary academics whose working field was English — personalities like the formidable Edith Morley (to whom comparatists are indebted for her early benchmark editions of Henry Crabb Robinson's writings): suffragette and eventually Professor of English at Reading (cf. Morley 2016). On the whole, however, the incipient rise of women academics seems to be more pronounced outside the narrow ambit of English Studies — in Classics or Modern Languages (mainly German and French), and despite the presence of critics like Morley and Q. D. Leavis. On the whole, there seems also to be a certain divergence of approaches between literary studies as they developed in these respective fields. I do not want to heighten these nuances into overriding schematizations, since my own concern is merely to tease out the run-up to comparative literary studies, and the impressions gleaned here would need to be put to the test of more sustained historical investigation. But it appears to me that comparatist interest is most firmly situated in the field of the modern foreign languages, accompanied by a growing anthropological interest mainly among Classical scholars and specialists in ancient vernaculars (Germanic, Celtic; cf. below, 120; also Chance 2005). Both fields had a noticeable involvement of a pioneer cohort of women academics. Conversely, female involvement and a transnational interest both appear to play a less conspicuous role in the emerging academic discipline of English Literature.

English and the resilience of criticism

That discipline, 'Eng.Lit.' as it came to be known, had had its own development and antecedents (Palmer 1965). It had first taken root in the newly established University of London and in the developing chairs for Rhetoric and Belles Lettres (Sutherland 1998, McMurtry 1985) and had fought to establish its own position between literary criticism and university professionalization, obtaining an institutional footing in Oxford and Cambridge from the 1880s on and spawning dedicated textbooks in the process (Goldie 2013, esp. 46–49). As Small notes in his insightful study

(Small 1991; also Guy & Small 2000) it struggled to establish its academic authority between the moral pundits of cultural life and the factual experts of the philologies. How precarious this was, we can see from the position of John Churton Collins, who found it necessary to anathematize the aesthetic appraisal-criticism of Gosse (above, 101; Cunningham 1998) but had himself to fend off the dismissive scorn of historians like E. A. Freeman (Goldie 2013, 65–66).

As Eng.Lit. moved from textual review to textual survey and textual criticism, the assumption of authority was always asserted in the axiological habit: the notion, ultimately Arnoldian, that the critic sat in judgement over the text. Whether that axiology should be merely aesthetic or also pedagogical became the battleground in the new century of the generational clash between Quiller-Couch (representative of the old gentlemanly school of fine criticism) and F. R. Leavis; it was also marked by the spreading influence of I. A. Richards. 'Eng.Lit.' would calibrate literary achievement in a combination of close-reading analysis and social contextualization. It remained hybrid, continuing the Arnoldian tradition of combining fine judgement with an equally Arnoldian pedagogical high-mindedness, believing firmly in the need for English Literature scholars to dispense sweetness and light across society (cf. Baldick 1987); this played into the older proclivity to disseminate expertise in review journalism (cf. Gross, 1969).

A departure from the Arnoldian legacy, however, lay in the tendency to abandon Arnoldian cosmopolitanism in favour of a certain methodological nationalism. Quiller-Couch himself (on him, Brittain 1947) had authored, largely in the fervent climate of the Great War, his essays on 'Patriotism in English Literature' (published in *Studies in Literature*, 1918), and carried that commitment with him for the rest of his life. More generally, for him and other anglicists, the English-language corpus was taken for granted as an autonomous and discretely demarcated category, and anglocentrically restricted to the literature of, specifically, England (for all that Q himself remained a card-carrying Cornish regionalist.) That inward turn away from internationalism was also an inward turn methodologically, towards the text and its intrinsic qualities.

In Cambridge in particular, various literary scholars were reforming poetical and formal criticism. The aesthetic connoisseurship of the old-school critics (the Bloomsbury circle, Gosse, Quiller-Couch) was outflanked by the works of two men associated (at the time) with Magdalene College: I. A. Richards (*The Principles of Literary Criticism*, 1926; *Practical Criticism*, 1929) and William Empson (*Seven Types of Ambiguity*, 1930). Between them, Richards and Empson developed formalized and non-judgemental text-analytical approaches which would after 1940 be taken up by American academics under the name of 'New Criticism' (Fry 2000, Wood 2000). A concomitant of this approach was an averseness to contextual reading of literary texts. Biographical explanations adducing the author's personal investment were taboo: the emphasis was exclusively on an intratextual 'close reading', in what was originally an obvious backlash against older, posivistic/historicist approaches — and which became, in due course, itself a rictus.

A different type of modernized criticism was at the same time being worked out by F. R. Leavis (Bell 2000). *The Great Tradition* was as yet some years in the future (1948), but Leavis had already begun, through his articles and editorship of *Scrutiny* (founded in 1932) to develop a new critical approach, which placed literature in the context of, or in response to, a more generalized notion of the 'literary culture' of a society at a given historical stage. The tone was set by his 1924 doctoral thesis on *The Relationship of Journalism to Literature*, and perhaps even better by *Fiction and the Reading Public* (1932) by his wife Q. D. Leavis (1906–1981; née Roth; the pair had married in 1929, and her book was based on her 1923 thesis under I. A. Richards). As a critic, Leavis also felt (in the Arnoldian sense) that he had a mission to intervene in the literary debates, tastes and developments of his day. Even before the foundation of *Scrutiny,* his *New Directions in English Poetry* laid down a poetical agenda for the modern age by a judicious distribution of praise and blame, attention and disregard. Over time, this would lead to fiercely agonistic judgementalism. In the process, the old link between criticism (academic or periodical) and literary art was, as a result, strengthened. Among the intellectuals involved in *Scrutiny* were Empson, Richards, Herbert Read and Michael Oakeshott (cf. Day 1996, Hilliard 2012).

The main literary review with which *Scrutiny* had to contend, and which pursued literary criticism as a meta-literary form of reflection, was *The Criterion*, founded by T. S. Eliot in 1922 and edited by him until 1939. It attracted leading literati (also internationally) of the 1920s and 1930s and pursued a cosmopolitan and somewhat elitist vision of literary culture as a transnational bastion of values in a troubled age. Eliot also used the journal to propound his poetics of a sere traditionalism expressing itself in anti-nostalgic, experimental form (Menand 2000).

The periodical criticism attracted by such eminent journals also manifested itself in book form. As a critic, Eliot published his *The Sacred Wood* in 1920 and *The Use of Poetry and the Use of Criticism* in 1933. Other literati also offered intelligent and insightful comments on their craft: C. S. Lewis with *The Allegory of Love* (1936), E. M. Forster with *Aspects of the Novel* (1927).

Eng.Lit. as it developed in the interwar years focused on literary techniques and achievements, or social or regional forcefields and tensions, and did this usually on the basis of two unquestioned assumptions: one, the authority of the critic to sit in judgement and to dispense, as he saw fit, and often by mere assertion, praise or blame; the other, the framework of 'Englishness' or of an (implicitly or explicitly English) 'Tradition'. English Literature was prone to the very definition of methodological nationalism: the a priori assumption of a mono-national frame both as a valid circumscription of the working corpus and as a valid analytical horizon. This was exacerbated by an anglocentric gravitation: English Literature focused around 'the literature of England'. Although England and its literary production might be deeply divided by regional and class distinctions, the discipline was nonetheless held together by an overriding quiddity, something that could make Smollett, Austen, Dickens, Trollope, George Eliot, and D. H. Lawrence siblings under the skin. That assumption was at the bottom of the Leavises' problematization of modernity as a cultural challenge, suffused F. R. Leavis's *The Great Tradition* and lay at the core of Q. D. Leavis's theories on 'The Englishness of the English Novel'.

The Victorian and Edwardian literary construction of a notional 'Englishness' (continuing unabated in film and TV productions from *Chariots of Fire* to *Downton Abbey*) has in the past decades drawn considerable critical attention (see p. 157, below). We should not neglect the fact that it was to no small extent also constructed by the critics in English Literature departments and in the literary reviews. This was due in part, perhaps, to the fact that from the New Criticism onwards, reflections on the nature of poetry, literature and a critical method tended to develop in a transatlantic intellectual 'anglosphere'. American 'New Critics' were intensely involved, but did so from altogether differently-organized educational institutions. That curious half-symmetry (cf. Martin 2000) may have stimulated Eng.Lit. critics on the European side of the Atlantic to deal with, specifically, the cisatlantic wing of the English literary traditions. Be that as it may, the anglocentrism of English Studies, its neglect (comparatively speaking) of non-England-based literary corpuses, necessitated a corrective: the rise, in the 1960s and 1970s, of dedicated specialisms focusing on its neglected margins. Such specializations — 'Anglo-Irish' or 'Commonwealth Literature' — foreshadowed, and were later folded into, postcolonial studies (cf. below, 156). But those correctives developed alongside, rather than in tandem with, Comparative Literature.

Comparatists *avant la lettre*, and among them a slightly larger representation of women, can be found in the study either of Classics and ancient philologies, or of Modern Languages other than English.

Literary anthropology at Cambridge

An exemplary and colourful presence on the Cambridge scene was the unusual woman of letters Eliza Marian (Elsie) Butler, alumna of Newnham College, who was assistant lecturer at Cambridge prior to 1917, a nurse in the Eastern theatre in the Great War, and lecturer under Karl Breul from 1920 until 1936. She was to take a chair at Manchester in 1936, and returned to Cambridge when she obtained the Schröder Professorship in 1944.

Butler had already in 1926 published a study on *The Saint-Simonian Religion in Germany*. The book that has made her famous was *The Tyranny of Greece over Germany* (1935), on German philhellenism and the internalization of a 'Greek' self-image by the German Romantics. It was both a study in literary imagology (although it was marked by a pronounced and quite essentialist mistrust of 'the' German character on Butler's own part, cf. Peacock 2006) and a political critique of a German self-beguilement. That topic had obvious relevance in 1935, but also foreshadowed some of the arguments in Martin Bernal's *Black Athena* (1987). The book's standing in Britain profited from its being banned in the Third Reich. In later years, Butler's work came increasingly to reflect the influence of her lifelong companion Isaline Horner, expert in Pali studies and, like Butler, a Newnham graduate. Her late work, a trilogy on the Faust figure (*The Myth of the Magus*, 1948; *Ritual Magic*, 1950; *The Fortunes of Faust*, 1952) returns almost to the literary ethnography of the tradition of Max Müller, E. B. Tylor and Sir James Frazer.

Fig 5.3. Eliza Marian Butler, photograph by Elliott & Fry, c. 1958
(© National Portrait Gallery, London)

Leonard Willoughby wrily commented that in Butler's later work, 'Comparative Literature shades into Comparative Demonology' (1950, 22–23). It was, in fact more directly indebted to the work of the Newnham mythological scholar Jane Ellen Harrison, who had also influenced Jessie L. Weston's *From Ritual to Romance* (1920). Weston herself (1850–1928) was a private scholar; her early work consists mainly of reworkings of medieval chivalric romances in a Pre-Raphaelite vein. In the preface to *From Ritual to Romance* (famous mainly for its inclusion in the notes to T. S. Eliot's *The Waste Land*) she acknowledges the work of Frazer, Ellison and the classical scholar Gilbert Murray (the Australian-born Regius Professor of Greek at Oxford), who shared Jane Harrison's interest in the mythological and cultic aspects of classical literature.

Through such connections (Horner, Harrison, Weston, Murray) Butler's work can be aligned with the circle of the 'Cambridge ritualists', classical scholars whose interest in ancient literature was mainly concerned with its mythological and ritualistic undercurrents and who as a result had a strong affinity for Comparative Religion — a discipline whose early history, from the days of Max Müller onwards, has intriguing parallels and overlaps with that of Comparative Literature. Willoughby's quip about 'Comparative Demonology', though flippant, made a serious point. Under the presiding genius of Sir James Frazer, based at Trinity College Cambridge, the ritual-mythological approach breathed the pervasive influence of the Swiss antiquarian Johann Jacob Bachofen and his *Das Mutterrecht* of 1861, on matrilinearity and matriarchy in the ancient world. From Harrison and Butler, the post-1945 repercussions of that tradition include Robert Graves's interpretations of the Greek myths and, in particular, *The White Goddess* (1948), a book which Graves himself subtitled 'A Historical Grammar of Poetic Myth'. Graves's book in turn became a relay point for feminist New Age 'Goddess' theories in the 1970s and 80s, with some influence on Celtic studies and literary criticism. Whereas the myth-ritual circle (Harrison, *Prolegomena to the Study of Greek Religion*, 1903; Murray, *Four Stages of Greek Religion*, 1913) were strictly focused on classical and Biblical antiquity, Butler cast her net wider across the ancient world.

Others pursuing this revival of mythographical anthropology at Cambridge were the husband-and-wife team of Hector Munro Chadwick and Nora Kershaw Chadwick. H. M. Chadwick (1870–1974) had been appointed in 1912 to the Professorship of Anglo-Saxon and fostered a closer collaboration between the study of ancient Nordic literatures with archaeology and medieval history. His early work accordingly echoes the mythological-cum-sociological interests of scholars like Sir Henry Maine and Freeman: *The Myth of Othin* (1899), *Studies in Anglo-Saxon Institutions* (1905) and *The Making of the English Nation* (1907). His interest in a 'Heroic Age' in literature followed to some extent W. P. Ker's *Epic and Romance* and the attempts to align both classical-Homeric and non-classical ancient literatures as reflections of a tribal warrior society; that vision became dominant in the twentieth century, as evidenced by Maurice Bowra's *Heroic Poetry* of 1952 and the seminal studies by Milman Parry and Alfred Lord on epic orality. A Newnham alumna who, inspired by Chadwick, was to carry forward the philological tradition of Celtic Medieval Studies, was Rachel Bromwich (née Amos, 1915–2010; on her, Morgan 2005).

Fig 5.4. Nora Kershaw Chadwick (courtesy of the British Academy)

Chadwick, whom his Newnham students praised for his encouragement, 'inclusivity and gender blindness' (Straubhaar 2005, 368), collaborated most closely with his former student and wife Nora (née Kershaw; 1891–1972), yet another alumna of Newnham College, who was later to become a leading authority on the Celtic cultures of ancient Britain. The couple embarked on a very ambitious and wide-ranging survey of early literary traditions. Between 1932 and 1940, a massive three-volume, 2300-page study appeared called *The Growth of Literature*. Its first volume covers the ancient literatures of Europe, ordered, not by language, but by genre and thematics; volume two deals with orally transmitted Slavic (Russian and South-Slavic), Indic and Hebraic literature, and volume three with orally transmitted literatures among Tatars, Polynesians and some African nations. In 1969, Nora Kershaw Chadwick was to follow this up with a thoroughly reworked survey of Turkic oral literatures, *Oral Epics of Central Asia*, in collaboration with V. I. Žirmunskij, based on the third volume of *The Growth of Literature* (which itself was reprinted in 1968).

The preface to the third volume states succinctly that 'the science of literature should be recognized as an essential branch of anthropology' (Chadwick/Chadwick 1932–40, III, xxiv); and the entire work does precisely what it says in the preface. Questions of poetics and what makes literary texts different from other verbal utterances are of minor importance, addressed only to account for the memorability and transgenerational survival of texts in pre-literate societies; the study of influences, changing tastes, forms and themes is likewise of secondary importance, and literature is seen largely as a form of verbal archaeology, a window on primitive societal structures (much as in *A Comparative Study of the Literatures of Egypt, Palestine, and Mesopotamia* by the great Egyptologist T. E. Peet, 1931). That being said, the transnational scope is truly remarkable, already foreshadowing 'world literature' interests of later decades at a time when narrow Eurocentric and presentist attitudes to what 'literature' meant were still all-pervasive. It was as if the ambition of Posnett, which Posnett himself had only delivered in flawed form, was now brought to full fruition: as global a conspectus as it was possible to put together in those days on literature in pre-literate societies. As the Chadwicks themselves phrased their research questions:

> Is it possible to trace the operations of any general principle in the growth of literature? We shall endeavour to answer this question by a comparative study of the literary genres found in various countries and languages and in different periods of history.
>
> For such a comparative study the modern literatures of the West offer only a very limited amount of material. Owing to the constant interactions of these literatures upon one another for several centuries past, and before that to the common influence of Latin upon all of them, they have had little chance of independent development. The most valuable material for our purpose comes from ancient records unaffected, or only partially affected, by the influence of Latin or other languages of wide circulation, and from isolated or backward communities of the present day which are still unaffected by cosmopolitan literature. (Chadwick/Chadwick 1932–40, I, ix)

As Haun Saussy insightfully points out (2006, 15), the approach followed by the Chadwicks is paradigmatically typological, juxtaposing separate traditions, and as such is of a quite different 'comparative' nature from the more historical French school exemplified by Paul Van Tieghem, which is more interested in influences, connections and transfers. This ambivalence in the very notion of comparison — typological juxtaposition or connection and exchange — remained a point of incoherence at the core of the discipline's self-definition. One must wonder, especially in the light of modern interest in 'World Literature', if the point has ever been really argued out, and to which extent the ambivalence reflects a global as opposed to an intra-European scope (cf. Domínguez, Saussy & Villanueva 2015).

As an aside to this crux, it is of some interest to note that H. M. Chadwick in 1945 published a book of an altogether different slant: *The Nationalities of Europe and the Growth of National Ideologies*. Here, Chadwick moves from the global-typological to the European-historical mode, drawing on his medievalist expertise concerning tribal ethnicities in the early Middle Ages in order to deconstruct their later instrumentalization as ideological origin-myths for the modern nation-state. This work anticipates to some extent the more recent work by the American medievalist Patrick J. Geary (*The Myth of Nations*, 2002), and the 'new medievalism' of the decades after 1980 when scholars have become increasingly concerned with the 'reception history of the Middle Ages', the historical transmissions and historical after-effects of medieval texts. British representatives of this trend (meanwhile inflected by the notion of the 'invented tradition', i.e. the realization that latter-day views of the past are creatively adapted appropriations rather than passive reflections of that past) are Thomas Shippey, Andrew Wawn, Joanne Parker and Ian Wood; similar interests have also manifested themselves in the study of Welsh literature (Mary-Ann Constantine) and in Irish Studies.

Modern languages, joint honours and 'littérature comparée'

Comparative literary studies, as exemplified by George Robertson and Edna Purdie, wound their course, then, between the two poles of anthropological preoccupation with ancient traditions and the critical practice of literary appreciation and textual interpretation. Institutionally, the anchoring points seem initially to have been the dedicated professorships (the Taylorian of Fiedler, the Schröder Professorship of Breul, the Anglo-Saxon of Chadwick), later bolstered by a new development: the joint honours system, which consolidated the position of the modern languages as major subjects in the Arts Faculties.

At Cambridge, Breul was the mentor, not only of Butler and Purdie, but also of other Germanists: Waterhouse, Stokoe, and Stockley. Waterhouse (1888–1977) had after Cambridge taught English at Leipzig between 1911 and 1914, and became Professor of German at Trinity College Dublin in 1915; he was among those College Unionists who barricaded TCD against the Irish nationalist insurrection of 1916. In 1932 he moved to the Professorship of German at Queen's University Belfast, where he taught until 1953.[5] Violet Stockley (1893–1971), born in Canada, was a sister of the painter Walter Osborne; obtained a teaching post at Cheltenham Ladies' College;

her book on the knowledge of German literature in England (apparently a reworked MA thesis) has maintained an enduring authority in its field and is still relied upon in contemporary research. It was complemented in the 1950's by Eudo C. Mason's work on German and English Romanticism. Mason (1901–1969), a leading Rilke scholar, had studied both in Oxford and Cambridge, taught at Leipzig between 1932 and 1939 and at Basel between 1939 and 1946, and was appointed first lecturer, then professor of German in Edinburgh after the war.

As for the Romance-language dimension of comparatist studies, the dominant influence on this field is that of William Entwistle (1895–1952). Again, his personal life was markedly international: born to missionaries in China, he maintained a working knowledge of Chinese throughout his life. A graduate of Aberdeen with distinctions in Greek and Comparative Philology, and severely wounded in 1917, he studied in Madrid on a Carnegie grant in 1920, broadening his linguistic abilities to include Spanish, Catalan, Basque and Arabic. As lecturer in Spanish at Manchester (from 1925) he published *The Arthurian Legend in the Literatures of the Spanish Peninsula* (1925); his subsequent academic career took him by way of Glasgow to Oxford, where, as Alfonso XIII Professor of Spanish, he also set up a Portuguese Studies programme, took over the editorship of the *Modern Language Review*, and published his *European Balladry* in 1939. He was also among the contributors to the wartime journal *Comparative Literature Studies* (below, 130).

Typically, the other Romance scholar at Oxford with a comparatist outlook, being a woman, flourished much more tardily than Entwistle, although she was of the same generation. Dublin-born Enid Starkie (1897–1970) became a lecturer at Somerville College (from where she had graduated in 1920) in 1928, having won acclaim for her thesis on Emile Verhaeren. Her faculty career led, ultimately, to a Readership in 1946, her flamboyant personality and behaviour preventing her, perhaps, from attaining a professorship while making her a memorable and inspiring figure about town. She explored cross-national aspects of her specialism in publications after the war, notably her *From Gautier to Eliot: The Influence of France on English Literature, 1851–1939* (1960).

The scholars holding chairs and lectureships in Modern Languages were only grudgingly recognized by the older-established disciplines, and some rivalry also existed between individual language departments; the various philologies (English, French, German, with a smaller adjunct of Spanish, Italian, Scandinavian and Slavic) largely worked in isolation. All this was less than conducive to effecting a comparatist synthesis between them. This diffractive tendency was counterbalanced, however, by a system of 'joint honours' programmes, in which students combined two modern languages in their curriculum. The Scottish universities in particular offered a propitious environment:

> At Glasgow, during and after World War I, one was provided by a course of lectures on English and Italian studies. At St Andrews, in the 1920s and after, students taking a double-language course were examined, in a three-hour paper, on some literary theme or period common to both the literatures studied, e.g. Shakespeare in France, French Romanticism and Germany. Though no formal lectures were given there was some informal instruction with advice as to reading. In Aberdeen every candidate for Honours in English

Fig 5.5. Wiliam James Entwistle, photograph by Walter Stoneman, 1950 (© National Portrait Gallery, London)

FIG 5.6. Enid Starkie, photograph by Henry Parker
(courtesy Principal and Fellows, Somerville College, Oxford)

and a foreign language prepared a dissertation on a subject common to English
and French or German literature. At Edinburgh Honours English candidates
take a paper on the classical background of English literature. (Roe 1954, 8 ff;
cf also McCutchion 1966, 145).

The inter-war cohort of joint-honours graduates would from the later 1920s onwards increasingly tackle topics linking two literatures — something which tallied with the direction that *Vergleichende Literaturgeschichte* was taking in the German-speaking world and *littérature comparée* in France. Paul Van Tieghem (1871–1948), in his influential model for a comparatist discipline, even went so far as to reserve the appellation *littérature comparée* exclusively for the study of literary-cultural transfers and connections between one literature and another (e.g. his own *Ossian en France*, 1917); the synoptic study of movements, periods or trends affecting a plurality of literary traditions he called, rather, *littérature générale* — something which he triumphantly practised in his studies on European pre-romanticism and romanticism. Van Tieghem's distinction between *littérature comparée* and *littérature générale* alerts us to the rise, during the interwar years and among Continental scholars, of transnational literary histories often shading into *mentalité* history or intellectual history. One can think, alongside Van Tieghem, of Johan Huizinga's *The Waning of the Middle Ages* (1919) and of Paul Hazard's *La crise de la conscience européenne* (1935) and, for the post-WW2 continuation of that trend, of Erich Auerbach's *Mimesis* (1946) and of Ernst Robert Curtius's *Europäische Literatur und lateinisches Mittelalter* (1948). It is no coincidence to see that Entwistle's work shares this medievalist focus in its period, or that Entwistle himself cited the great French medievalist Gaston Paris as one of his scholarly ideals. That genre of transnational literary-cultural histories had some affinity with the intellectual histories in Britain which we have noted from Hallam and Buckle to John Theodore Merz and Frazer's *The Golden Bough*. If, in such large synoptic studies, the literary source material was often subordinated to a wider scope (that of *mentalité* or culture-at-large), the specific study of literary texts tended often, if it did look at cross-border transfers, to thematize at best binary traffic-flows between a specific source and a specific target.

This approach proved especially attractive for those British joint-honours graduates who combined English with a foreign literature — often French. A good few of them oriented themselves towards the Department of *Littérature comparée* at the Sorbonne, which flourished in the 1920s under Fernand Baldensperger (1871–1958). In 1921, Baldensperger himself was invited to University College Aberystwyth to give an eight-part lecture series on European literature. Does that amount to an 'unofficial recognition' of comparatism in Britain, as Weisstein (1968, 68) maintains? Be that as it may, 1921 was also the year that Baldensperger, together with Paul Hazard, founded the *Revue de Littérature Comparée*, which, along with its series of monographs (the *Bibliothèque de la Revue de Littérature Comparée*, BRLC) would provide an important publication platform also for British scholars.

No less than sixteen British comparatist monographs in the interwar years were published in this august forum, and no less than eight of these were by women: Killen 1915, Goulding 1924, Gunnell 1925, Purdie 1928, Jeffery 1928, Scott 1928,

Bain 1931, Duthie 1933.[6] One outstanding figure exemplifying the importance of the BRLC as a stepping-stone for the pre-1918 generation towards the post-1945 period is the aforementioned Edna Purdie, whose *The Story of Judith in German and English Literature* appeared in 1926. Her position is special since hers is almost the only British BRLC contribution to deal with a German-English topic; as such it draws attention to the overwhelmingly Anglo-French orientation of the British associates of the Baldensperger school. Robertson himself, in a review of three British contributions to the BRLC (by Roe, Lytton Sells and Goulding), deplored its Francocentric slant (*MLR* 20, 487).

But not all of the work published in the BRLC heralds the beginning of an academic career like Purdie's. Enid Lowry Duthie (1904–1993), who much later in life was to publish on the Brontë sisters and on Mrs Gaskell, as a young woman (in 1933) published a remarkable study on symbolist cross-currents from France to the *Blätter für die Kunst*. Of other authors (Janet Scott, Alfred C. Hunter, H.A Needham) we know little beyond their appearance on the BRLC list. There is an isolated glimpse of Sybil Goulding as 'the dark, pretty, gifted daughter of a Bridlington bank manager, who [at Somerville College] took a brilliant war-time First in French'; she was later Tutor in French at St Hugh's College, a position she gave up when she married (Brittain 1992, and Lemon 1958, 8). Doris Gunnell, who published in 1925 on *Sutton Sharpe et ses amis français*, had defended a doctoral thesis at the Parisian *Faculté des lettres* in 1908 on *Stendhal et l'Angleterre*.

Primarily, then, the BRLC must be seen as an outlet rather than as a seedbed; its publications bespeak a comparatist interest which as yet has few feedback channels to consolidate itself at British institutions. Those who were published in it were driven, rather, by a dearth of similar opportunities within the UK.

Of the male contributors to the BRLC, three continued a scholarly career with notable comparatist aspects: Arthur Lytton Sells, Eric Partridge and Frederick C. Roe. Arthur Lytton Sells (1895–1978), who had written his acclaimed Sorbonne thesis on *Les sources françaises de Goldsmith* under the direction of Paul Hazard, left his chair of French at Durham in 1948 to take up an appointment at Indiana. From there, he regularly published on topics of comparatist interest, returning to Durham only in 1971, well after his retirement. New-Zealand-born Eric Partridge, who later in life because a well-known lexicographer of non-standard English, in 1924 published his Oxford B.Litt. thesis on *The French Romantics' Knowledge of English Literature* in the BRLC. Partridge taught at London and Manchester universities in 1925–27 before turning to freelance writing, and in that period he published a remarkable *Critical Medley* (1926), subtitled *Essays, Studies, and Notes in English, French and Comparative Literature*. It contains a separate section under the heading of *Comparative Literature*, with articles on 'Fenimore Cooper's Influence on French Literature', 'Deux dettes anglaises de Gautier', and, most importantly, a lengthy essay on 'The Comparative Study of Literature, with especial References to Anglo-French Relations and to French and English Critics'.

That 60-page essay is, after Gregory Smith's of 1901 and H. V. Routh's of 1913, among the first important signs of the discipline's reflection upon itself as a special academic enterprise, and is far better historically grounded than Smith's. It covers sections on the present state of the discipline, a 'summary sketch' of its past developments, largely taken from Louis-Paul Betz, some extracts from comparatist theory and reflections on the discipline's outlook. Partridge reflects the situation of the 1920s when he designs future Comparative Literature departments largely on the basis of English literature with a foreign adjunct; at British universities, he suggests,

> [...] departments should have, as exponents, English scholars in the main and should deal primarily with the relations of England and other countries, secondarily with the relations between those countries which, either by loan or debt, have been the most associated with England [...] As France is that country which has had the closest association with England, the professor and one lecturer (who should perhaps be the senior lecturer) must be conversant with that province; the department should also have one lecturer for Anglo-German, one for Anglo-Italian, one for Anglo-Spanish, and another for Anglo-Scandinavian and Danish relations; both for completeness and for the allurement of foreign students there should be a lecturer for Franco-German, another for Franco-Italian, Spanish relations, while yet another for Germano-Italian, Spanish would undoubtedly prove an interesting experiment.

In the light of university funding and departmental policies almost a century later, the contemporary reader can only sigh. Partridge was nothing if not ambitious, not only in the structure and staffing of his proposed comparatist departments, but also in their spread:

> Surely Oxford, Cambridge and London should open the campaign: the other universities (especially those of Dublin, Edinburgh and Manchester) would soon follow suit, although they might at first confine themselves to the relations with other countries. (Partridge 1926, 226)

Finally, another author in the BRLC, Frederick Roe (1894–1958), was to remain active in academic comparatism for longer. His book on *Taine et l'Angleterre* (1923) had been his Parisian doctoral thesis and had been honoured with the *Prix Bordin* of the *Académie française*. He had studied under John Churton Collins at Birmingham, and also at Lyons (where he had taught between 1916 and 1920). In 1920 he returned to Birmingham, where he taught until 1925. After three years at St Andrews, he obtained a chair in French literature at the newly founded university of Hull in 1928, moving to Aberdeen in 1932. Under his professorship, a student association for Comparative Literature was founded there in 1948, the 'Aberdeen University Society for the Study of Comparative European Literature' (it was operative until 1952). He edited a volume of travel writing, *French Travellers in Britain, 1800–1926*, in 1928, and delivered the Taylorian Lecture of 1957 on 'Sir Thomas Urquhart and Rabelais'. At the fifth *Congrès International des Langues et Littératures Modernes* (Florence, 1951), he gave a paper on 'Taine et l'art anglais', and in 1954 he reported on the state of Comparative Literature in Britain in an article for the third volume of the American *Yearbook of Comparative and General Literature*; at this moment, the subject was definitively and finally finding solid ground under its feet at British universities (the lectureship in Manchester having been established in 1953). While Roe exemplifies a tenuous but unbroken tradition of comparatist interest from the days of John Churton Collins, his teacher, to the 1950s, his 1954 YCGL article itself is traditionalist and more concerned with a roll-call of meritorious critics from the past than with the future possibilities of the fledgling discipline.

Bridging the Second World War: *Comparative Literature Studies*

The German occupation of France broke the connection between British talent and Parisian *littérature comparée*. To some extent the preoccupation of Anglo-French or other transnational connections remained popular, and was now pursued within Britain. There was, after all, a basis to build on. At Cambridge, F. C. Green had published his remarkable *Minuet: Literary Ideas in 18th-Century France and England* in 1935, and Humphry Trevelyan published his Eliza-Butler-influenced *Goethe and the Greeks* in 1941; at Oxford, there had been William Entwistle's *European Balladry* (1939) as well as various volumes in Fiedler's Oxford Studies in Modern Languages and Literatures (Rodgers 1936, Vincent 1936, Barnes 1937). The early critical work of the great Maurice Bowra (*The Heritage of Symbolism*, 1943; *From Virgil to Milton*, 1945) flourished during the war years.

But the most significant effort to maintain, deliberately so, a presence for *littérature Comparée* in wartime Britain occurred in Cardiff in 1940. When the Parisian *Revue de Littérature comparée* ceased publishing under German occupation, two lecturers at the Cardiff college of the University of Wales, Marcel Chicoteau and Kenneth Urwin, sought to establish a continuity by founding a replacement-in-exile for the defunct comparatist flagship. Chicoteau was a son of the French Consul in Cardiff and had had an English education, developing an interest in the connections between French and Latin literature. Urwin had originally had a more linguistic orientation, but had got to know Baldensperger during his doctoral research in Paris. The review founded by the two men was called *Comparative Literature Studies*; its first issue came out in 1941. From its sixth issue onwards it carried the subtitle *Etudes de Littérature Comparée*, changed to *Cahiers de Littérature Comparée* as of issue 10.

All in all, 19 issues were to appear (six of which were double issues, bringing the numbering up to 24) between 1941 and late 1946. By that time, the review had played out its role: the *Revue de Littérature Comparée* recommenced its publication after the Liberation, Chicoteau's career had taken him, first as French Consul to Liverpool and then as university Reader to New Zealand.

The five-year run of *Comparative Literature Studies* was a modest but by no means unsuccessful enterprise. The publication never led to financial deficits, and subscriptions were placed far and wide (the Free French government in exile subscribed to thirty copies). When *Comparative Literature Studies* ceased publishing, it was 'fortunately at a time when we could sensibly leave the field to the RLC once again', and with a sense of accomplishment rather than failure.[7]

That accomplishment was to no small extent due to the high prestige of the contributors. Among these we find W. J. Entwistle and prominent Continental comparatists such as Fernand Baldensperger, Jean-Marie Carré, Edmond Eggli and Werner Milch. Eggli (1881–1956) had studied under Gustave Lanson and Baldensperger, and had since 1920 been Professor of French in Liverpool. Milch

FIG 5.7. Leonard Ashley Willoughby, photograph by Lotte Meitner-Graf, 1965 (© The Lotte Meitner-Graf Archive, Ltd.)

(1903–1950) had fled the Third Reich after the pogroms of 1938, and had emigrated to England by way of Switzerland. During the war years he taught at University College Exeter and King's College London. He returned to Germany in 1945 as part of the German Educational Reconstruction programme, and became Professor of German and Comparative Literature at Marburg in 1949, where he died unexpectedly the next year.

The review's track record also includes an obituary on Paul Hazard[8] reprinted from *Le Temps* and a contribution from the elderly Arthur Symons. To be sure, *Comparative Literature Studies* could not do much to develop comparatism in Britain; but it certainly consolidated the discipline's presence as it had grown in the 1920s and 1930s. The mere fact of its appearance, under its tell-tale title, helped ensure a continuance across the war years; and it provided a publication platform for established scholars like the aforementioned Green and Entwistle, as well as BRLC authors like Arthur Lytton Sells and Alice Killen. If, across the war, comparatism could move on in the footsteps of the interwar generation, this small review had contributed its share to the process.

Indeed, after 1945 and into the 1950s, we see an unabated continuation of the type of publications we have encountered in the late 1930s — a greater continuity across the Second World War, perhaps, than there had been across the First. In a 1949 Festschrift for the Cambridge Professor of French R. L. Graeme Ritchie, we find articles by Arthur Lytton Sells on 'Leconte de Lisle and Robert Burns' (Sells had also read a paper on that topic before the MLA) and Roy Pascal on 'Goethe's Autobiography and Rousseau's *Confessions*'. Ronald Peacock, Professor of German at Manchester, published his essay collection *The Poet in the Theatre* (1946, encompassing Grillparzer, Chekhov, Ibsen and T. S. Eliot), and Ralph Tymms, a lecturer in Peacock's department, followed this up with a study on the *Doppelgänger* motif entitled *Doubles in Literary Psychology* (1949). J. M. Clark's *The Dance of Death in the Middle Ages and the Renaissance* appeared in 1950. Across the War and into the 1950s we see prominent names such as Leonard Willoughby (who founded the prominent review *German Life and Letters* in 1936), Mary Wilkinson, Alexander Gillies, Eudo Mason and Roy Pascal (all with a background in German studies) and Frederick Roe, R. A. Sayce, Lytton Sells and Enid Starkie (in French studies).[9]

If anything, this internal continuity was boosted by the crosswinds that reached British comparatism from the rest of the world — and here the impact of the Second World War was definitely a formative influence.

Notes to Chapter 5

1. As the title suggests, the book was intended as a continuation of Herford's *Literary Relations of England and Germany in the Sixteenth Century*.
2. She was the remarkable Australian-born Ethel Florence Richardson, suffragette and — under the pen name Henry Handel Richardson — novelist (1870–1946). On her, see Ackland 2004.
3. Thus in the obituary for Robertson in the *Revue de Littérature Comparée*, 13 (1933): 758.
4. In the *Publications of the English Goethe Society* we can note Robertson's aforementioned *Goethe and Byron* (1925), James Orrick's *Matthew Arnold and Goethe* (1928), and Alexander Gillies's *Herder and the Preparation of Goethe's 'Weltliteratur'* (1933).

5. His papers are at the School of Advanced Study's Germanic Archives.
6. Fuller details are in the chronological bibliography.
7. Personal communication from Dr Kenneth Urwin, 4 December 1978.
8. Hazard, celebrated author of *La crise de la conscience européenne* (1935) and professor of Comparative Literature at the Collège de France, had founded, with Baldensperger, the *Revue de Littérature Comparée* in 1921. Elected to the Académie française, he was prevented from taking his seat under the German occupation. He died in the spring of 1944.
9. A full list of comparatist-oriented publications in German studies from the period 1949–1952 is given by Roe 1954, 11f., and is complemented by a list in the *Revue de Littérature Comparée* 28 (1954), 241.

CHAPTER 6

Consolidation and Crises (1950–2000)

National continuities and mid-century internationalism

To a large extent, British comparatism continued to develop, across the Second World War, in the mode of personal, institution-anchored filiation (scholars at centres of learning training new generations of scholars); but developments into the second half of the century were also boosted (and buffeted) by crosswinds from the wider world.

The budding British discipline conducted its postwar business in a continuation of patterns laid out in the 1930s and 1940s, drawing on the academic personalities that had entered the scene in those years — scholars in foreign literatures with an eye for cross-national topics such as Entwistle and Lytton Sells. Historical developments took shape in a skein of personal teacher-pupil filiations (Robertson-Purdie, Collins-Roe, Herford-Willoughby-Wilkinson, Breul-Butler); occasionally, reviews and book series, often with a French orientation, served to bring comparatist activities together. A younger generation, including Roy Pascal, Donald Davie, and Enid Starkie began to make its mark in the 1950s. Pascal came from the Cambridge school of German studies, and had addressed the reception of Shakespeare in Germany in a 1937 thesis; throughout the 1950s he would continue, from his chair at Birmingham, to explore cross-national ramifications of German literature. Davie began his critical career as a Leavisite, but emphatically broadened his corpus to include Russian literature. Starkie (above, 124) published her *From Gautier to Eliot: The Influence of France on English Literature, 1851–1939* in 1960. This tradition of modern-language experts with transnationally roving eyes was manifested most strongly in the post-war decades by the charismatic stalwart Leonard Wilson Forster (1913–1997). Like many in the tradition from which he came, he had studied and found a spouse on the Continent before obtaining a chair in Britain. A former code-breaker at Bletchley Park, he occupied the Chair of German at University College London from 1950 on and held the Schröder Professorship in Cambridge (1961–79); he kept up a steady production of work of comparatist importance throughout the 1950s-1970s.

In 1953, a lectureship in Comparative Literature was established at the University of Manchester; the first appointee was Glyn Tegai Hughes (1923–2017), son of a

Welsh Methodist minister, who after his wartime service had studied German in Cambridge and obtained a doctorate there; his subsequent research addressed German and Welsh Romantics, and the Methodist hymn-writer William Williams Pantycelyn. The discipline was thus, finally, given an official academic footing — slender in its own right, but shored up by wide interest among the various Modern Languages and drawing on a strong pre-war tradition.

The postwar situation worldwide was affected by the Second World War in two ways. First, there was the great cultural migration of refugees, many of them Jewish, from totalitarian Central and Eastern Europe, with a store of unaccustomed languages and intellectual traditions. The impact of this migration on Hollywood cinema is a matter of general knowledge (cf. Horowitz 2008); Siegbert Prawer has traced its pre-history in his *Between Two Worlds: The Jewish Presence in German and Austrian Film, 1910–1933* (2005). As to the intellectual and academic migration, of which Prawer was himself such a prominent representative, the case of the Frankfurt School is paradigmatic (Wheatland 2009). The specific aspect of literary and historical studies would justify a major study in its own right (following on from Coser 1984, Fleming & Bailyn 1969, and Heilbut 1951, who focus on the US; generally for the UK: Snowman 2002). Following precursors like Isaiah Berlin and Jacob Bronowski, the names involved include Hannah Arendt, Erich Auerbach, Ernest Gellner, Ernst Gombrich, Roman Jakobson, Hans Kohn, Karl Popper, George Steiner, Péter Szondi, and René Wellek. (A straggler on the Atlantic crossing was Paul De Man in 1946, who emigrated under a different type of pressure; Barish 2014.)

We have seen the presence of Werner Milch in *Comparative Literature Studies*, and indeed that journal, as a haven for Baldensperger-style comparatism, may be seen as a sign of the winds of war filling the sails of the British discipline. Important comparatists of the postwar years (Lilian Furst, Siegbert Prawer, George Steiner, Gabriel Josipovici) reached Britain as refugees. What is more, the mobility of these very prominent wandering scholars (Steiner and Furst pursued academic careers on both sides of the Atlantic) contributed not only to a worldwide intellectual cross-pollination but also to an increasingly integrated academic 'Anglosphere', where the exchange of ideas in English-language publications was less and less institutionally bound to a home location, and spread as far and wide as scholars' publications did. The spread of the New Criticism on both shores of the Atlantic had been an early sign of this trend. By 1960, it had become almost meaningless to distinguish between Yvor Winters and Ifor Richards as 'American' and 'British' critics, respectively.

A subsequent, more complex type of impact proved more problematic for the British discipline. It consisted of the tangled, diffracted influence of Slavic structuralisms, along various conduits, on different research communities in the West. The work of Jurij Lotman, the OPOJAZ school, Vladimir Propp, Mikhail Bakhtin, and the Prague Linguistic Circle (Mukařovský, Vodička, Wellek) found its tardy and tortuous way to the rest of the world along different conduits and into different research communities. The parallel histories of the Parisian *Tel Quel* school, the Yale French school, the Konstanz hermeneutic school, and others, with their many half-communications, half-engagements and half-misunderstandings, present a comparatist topic of the highest interest in its own right; and to a large degree this involves the transnational, entangled careers of literary thinkers moving abroad under the pressures of war, persecution and oppression. These crisscrossing intellectual con-trails tended to bypass the British Isles, to the point of presenting, to the eyes of older British scholars in the 1970s and 1980s, the problematic snarl-up of something alien, 'foreign theory'. Even trained Slavicists like Donald Davie, Pasternak aficionado though he was, engaged more with Leavis than with Šklovskij; as for that other great scholar in Slavic-and-English literature, Henry Gifford, he had, as his obituary put it, 'misgivings about literary theory which strayed too far from the text'.[1]

The international mobility and enmeshment of an academic communicative ambience was also boosted by the spirit of internationalism that was so prominently part of the post-1945 climate. The world at large, though split in two along Cold War lines, recoiled from rampant nationalism by establishing reconciliation schemes and international organizations; and academia played its part. Scholars like Willoughby and Roy Pascal were deeply concerned to make sure that wartime antagonism did not destroy cultural interest in German literature altogether (Flood & Simon 2017); this stance alone already favoured a thematization of transnational topics. *Littérature comparée* in post-occupation France grasped the thorny topic of the ingrained antagonism between Romance and Germanic cultural traditions with the express aim of deconstructing that polarity (or, in the parlance of those years, 'de-ideologizing' or 'demythologizing' it). The role of literary authors in magnifying and reifying cultural antagonism became a focus of attention for the emerging specialism of imagology, following Jean-Marie Carré's *Les Écrivains francais et le mirage allemand* (1947; cf. Dyserinck 2005). As Europe staggered out of the ruins of the Second World War and turned to the task of international reconciliation, a disinterested, supranational preoccupation with cultural differences gained both academic, intellectual and political urgency.

In this context, networks and congresses took shape. British scholars were involved, and as part of their involvement they began to reflect on comparatism as something that they, as British scholars, could play a role in.

In Germany, the comparatist Kurt Wais organized a Europe-wide literary-historical congress at Tübingen in 1948. (This was partly, one feels, so as to exorcize some dark episodes in his own recent past; acclaimed pioneer of German comparatism though he was, Wais had also, in his university postings and in his writings, proved himself a pliable instrument for the Nazi regime: cf. Haussmann 1998, 267.)

Among the scholars present were two British delegates, famous as a working team; Leonard Willoughby (who was known for his fervent commitment to the post-war repair of Anglo-German relations) and his younger colleague (by 24 years) Mary Wilkinson. Wilkinson (1909–2001), had studied under J. G. Robertson, worked closely with Willoughby on Schiller editions and in the editorial management of *German Life and Letters*, and eventually succeeded him as Professor of German at University College London. Willoughby himself (1885–1977) had cut his teeth under Fiedler in Oxford, where he had published his first work in 1914

Fig 6.1. Elizabeth Mary Wilkinson (courtesy of the British Academy)

as a young lecturer on the comparatist topic of *Samuel Naylor and 'Reynard the Fox': A Study in Anglo-German Literary Relations* (1914). From 1931 until 1950 he held the chair of German at University College London as Wilkinson's predecessor. And at Wais's conference, Willoughby contributed by addressing the 'state and tasks of Comparative Literary History in England'.

A similar reflection on the 'tasks' of the discipline was offered around the same time by Alexander Gillies, who had taken his PhD in Göttingen, had become Professor of German at Leeds in 1945, and who had joined and later succeeded William Entwistle as Editor of the *Modern Language Review*. Gillies also reflected the internationalism of the post-war years when he stressed, in 1952:

> Comparative Literature has *relevance* of a kind that few other branches of study possess. It is a contribution not only to the study of literature but above all to the study of history. (Gillies 1952, 25)

Gillies's remarks emanate from, but also look forward to, a more historical and international orientation in British literary studies, as opposed to textual analysis and criticism; they were published in the first volume of the *Yearbook of Comparative and General Literature*, then just established in what was to become one of the main hubs of American comparatism, the University of Indiana at Bloomington. (The YCGL was two years later, in 1954, to offer another reflection on the prospects of a British comparatist discipline, the previously mentioned one by F. C. Roe.) The US, where many European exiles and émigrés had obtained comparatist posts at universities, offered a sounding board for British initiatives and was a driving force towards the establishment of Comparative Literature as a self-organizing worldwide discipline. A Comparative Literature section was founded within the MLA in 1947; and it was largely through a joining of American and Continental-European forces that the International Comparative Literature Association (ICLA) was founded (1955). It is against this international background that we must situate the endorsements of a British comparatist discipline by scholars who had established their credentials in the 1930s (Gillies, Roe, Willoughby); and it is also in this context that we must view the foundation of the Manchester lectureship in 1953.

The most important long-term impact of these developments was an informal but widely-shared assumption of what the core business of Comparative Literature was all about. Reflecting the approach of American comparatists like Ulrich Weisstein, the bibliographies in the YCGL were rubricated in a specific thematic array that was in turn taken over, from 1979 on, by *Comparative Criticism*, the annual house journal of the British Comparative Literature Association. They encompassed the following:

1. 'World and General Literature', also including generalized and theoretical reflections on literature as such, and critical methodology;
2. Themes and motifs;
3. Genres, types and forms;
4. Epochs, currents and movements;
5. The Bible and Classical Antiquity;
6. Individual countries (i.e. in their mutual relations);

7. Individual authors (i.e. in their cross-national contexts, inspirations, and reception);
8. Literature and the other arts (a comparison involving, not different countries, but different fields of cultural production).

The transnational element was the core characteristic of all these rubrics, revolving around the ideas of cross-border influence and reception of specific schools, genres, and authors. Buried deep within this mapping of the comparatist field was the idea that a proper understanding or typology of literature would need the cross-calibration of samples from different contexts so as to allow a solidly-based generalized extrapolation. In addition, there was a growing idea that this project could best be pursued by, or under the aegis of, an organization that was itself transnational, and which would allow for the pooling of the necessary intellectual resources worldwide. One of the main tasks that the ICLA set itself, accordingly, was a huge (and still ongoing) encyclopaedic enterprise, a world history of world literatures. The official title of that project bespoke the unreflected eurocentrism that was also deeply embedded in this post-1945 internationalism: the *Comparative History of Literatures in European Languages*. What pretended to be a global discipline, in the tradition of Goethe's *Weltliteratur*, was in fact blinkered to anything except Europe-rooted literary traditions; these were, after all, the decades before even the notion of a 'Third World' was coined to complement Cold War bipolarity. What appears now, egregiously, as the blind spot of post-1945 Comparative Literature was first pointed out by René Etiemble in his *Essais de littérature (vraiment) générale* of 1974. It was not only as a symptom of that colonial cognitive supremacism which Edward Said exposed shortly afterwards in his *Orientalism*, but also the result of a Cold-War academic tunnel vision, in particular a lack of familiarity with Russian scholarship. Russian comparatists, from their own imperial-orientalist origins (comparable, *mutatis mutandis*, to those of Posnett) had maintained a much greater awareness of non-Western traditions (mainly narrative and epic). Ironically, it was the aging, ethnographically-minded Nora Chadwick who was closest to that intellectual tradition when she collaborated with Viktor Žirmunskij on her *Oral Epics of Central Asia* (1969).[2]

There are other aspects where the implicit comparatist programme as reflected in this YCGL template could, in hindsight, be shown to carry the seeds of its post-1980 obsolescence; we shall return to that issue further on. Throughout the 1950s, '60s and '70s, however, the ICLA-style comparatist working agenda offered an excellent field guide for British comparatists, and many of the best examples of the new discipline's potential reflect its focus. Most notably, perhaps, Lilian Furst's work on Romantic lyric, which she undertook from her post at Manchester, and which for decades counted as a showcase example of what the new discipline could achieve; but one can also think of Elinor Shaffer's work on Coleridge, Prawer's work on Heine and on the Frankenstein myth, Shackleton's on Voltaire and the Enlightenment, Brian Vickers on the Renaissance and Renaissance rhetoric.

Thus Comparative Literature gained a quiet, unobtrusive but powerful solidity in postwar Britain; but as we shall see, it was also affected by anguished, soul-searching debates internationally.

The ICLA, the challenge of Wellek, and the New Criticism

Postwar comparatism manifested itself at the Triennial Congress of the International Federation for Modern Languages and Literatures (FILLM), held at Oxford in 1954: among the British participants were Ronald Peacock, Garnet Rees, R. A. Sayce, Robert Shackleton and E. R. Vincent, as well as someone who was by now a senior figure: Frederick Roe.

The occasion was noteworthy, not only as marking the beginning of the British comparatist consolidation process, but also as a crucial date for the discipline worldwide, for the Oxford FILLM congress fed into the establishment of the International Comparative Literature Association (ICLA), which hoisted its flag at the first of its triennial congresses (Venice, 1955). That congress, and its organizing body, were the result of a transatlantic collaboration (we have noted the importance of the comparatist section of the MLA as another forerunner). However, immediately afterwards, the next ICLA congress (Chapel Hill, 1958) sparked off a notorious Atlantic split between 'French' and 'American' approaches, with British comparatism caught between the two.

The opening volley was René Wellek's provocative lecture on 'The Crisis of Comparative Literature'. What crisis?, one may well ask — the occasion being only the second in what was to become a flourishing tradition of ICLA congresses. Wellek's lecture is usually seen against the background of the programmatic vision he had unfolded, together with Austin Warren, in the classic handbook *Theory of Literature* (1948). True to the background of the two authors (an émigré of the Prague Linguistic Circle and an adept of the New Criticism), that handbook espoused a text-oriented (poetical, rhetorical, stylistic) study of literature in order to arrive at a general theory of what made literary texts different from other types of discourse. Wellek/Warren adapted the New Criticism to the legacy of the Russian Formalists and their search for *literaturnost'* ('literariness'), of Mukařovský's idea of a 'poetic function' characterizing a text as literary, and of Roman Ingarden's *Das literarische Kunstwerk*. The core of literary studies should be aesthetic and poetical in its aim, and text-analytical and structuralist in its method.

This predilection for what Wellek/Warren called the 'intrinsic study' of literature was, like the New Criticism that had preceded it, averse from contextual study (dismissively called the 'external approach'): anything dealing with the text's historical setting or social and ideological situatedness, or the author's biographical or social circumstances. The old positivistic reduction of literature to its 'race, milieu, moment' parameters was firmly rejected; comparison was useful only as a stepping stone towards a typology of literary strategies, dangerous as a contextual distraction. But it was precisely this more historical contextualization of the text which, as Wellek rightly noted, flourished in the internationalist enthusiasm of post-war Europe. Wellek's attack on the contextual/historical study of literature was thus aligned geographically with an American-European opposition, which soon was honed down to an American-French one. In the Cold War climate of the period, a methodological crux became an Atlanticist issue.

The impact on British comparatists could not have been more immediate. On the day after Wellek had delivered his 'Crisis' lecture, Robert Shackleton responded. He was the only British representative present at Chapel Hill and had been present at the Oxford FILLM meeting of 1954. His work on the Enlightenment — in which field he would rise to great prominence — meant that he worked in close collaboration with French literary historians and was open to the transnational historical study of literature and of its intellectual, rather than aesthetic or poetical, aspects. Undaunted by the authoritative Wellek, Shackleton opened his paper on 'Comparative Literature and the Enlightenment' with a firm statement expressing his dissent 'and the dissent, I am confident, of the majority of members of this Congress' with Wellek's pessimism; on the contrary, he affirmed his belief 'that Comparative Literature is a discipline which has a rich future before it' (Shackleton 1959, 56).

How should British comparatists negotiate this sudden French-American fork in the road? Institutionally, British comparatists relied heavily on their departmental and intellectual contacts with the European Continent: many of them were, after all, Germanists, Romanists, Italianists, Slavicists or Hispanists, often working under the inspiration of intellectual history. On the other hand, the still-strong tradition of literary and 'practical' criticism, and the transatlantic bonding factor of the English language, meant that the influence of New Criticism and Wellek's emphasis on the 'intrinsic study' of the literary text were also very strong.

This latter factor bolstered the strictly interpretative school of criticism. Henry Gifford, charismatic professor at one of the new universities (Bristol) may count as a case in point. Born in 1913, he was a product of the pre-war tradition of English Studies (Harrow, Oxford, teaching stint at Eton), with a lifelong commitment to the ethical usefulness of studying and teaching literature. In addition, he had learned Russian during the war, gained celebrity as a fine Slavicist with works on Tolstoy, Pasternak and Mandelstam, and managed to incorporate a programme of Russian literature in his English department, which as a result became 'Comparative' in nature. As his obituary put it,

> students of English and Russian literature had the rare privilege of witnessing Gifford's sensitive and scrupulous mind evaluate the various Russian translations of Gray's Elegy or discourse on Pasternak's renditions of Shakespeare, while throwing in asides on Lozinsky's version of The Divine Comedy.

— a telling point, for it shows, on the downside, how comparison was neglected in favour of aesthetic appreciation of the fine qualities of a given text, and, on the upside, that in such a climate a specialism could germinate which had been completely neglected in the YCGL template of comparatist studies, namely the study of translation. This would, in later years, prove a major strength in the portfolio of British comparatism.

The danger was, however, that such fine criticism by multilingually versed scholars would become, not a Comparative Literature, but rather a 'Sampled and Savoured' Literature. To quote that same obituary once more: 'Callers at his house were invariably treated to food, drink and impromptu seminars on Kipling, Mandels'tam, Dante, Solzhenitsyn, Hardy or whatever fiction or poetry he, usually together with his wife, happened to be reading at the time'.

Postwar criticism and Eng.Lit.

Accordingly, Gifford, a Professor of English and Comparative Literature at the time of his retirement in 1976, inspiring and fine scholar though he was, never grasped the nettle of what 'Comparative' stood for. With him, as with a good many other English critics who dealt with what they called 'Comparative Literature', comparison was a hermeneutic or cognitive operation rather than a scientific method. It meant that judgements were arrived at, and critically balanced, by situating a textual encounter in a wide spectrum of other, comparable ones. And the finest minds could draw these comparable examples also from other languages than English — as in Matthew Arnold's use of 'the world' when encompassing the best that is known and thought. In 1969, Henry Gifford published a book entitled *Comparative Literature* (Posnett's title of 1886, but an altogether different book), which opened with the rather self-defeating sentence

> Comparative Literature cannot pretend to be a discipline on its own. I should rather define it as an area of interest — like that one proclaimed by Goethe when he predicted a *Weltliteratur* in which all the nations would have their voice.

This type of criticism was most firmly rooted in English Studies, and indeed left the field wide open for scholars in English Studies to formulate general theories on literary genres, movements or techniques — topics which in other countries were now firmly a comparatist remit. Eminent critics such as F. W. Bateson and Bernard Bergonzi, like Matthew Arnold or T. S. Eliot before them, could effortlessly range over materials from many different periods and languages, and in the process come up with generalized statements about genres like lyrical verse or the novel — but they would not consider this part of a comparative method, merely the informed working of a well-read and discerning critical mind. And in vindicating their work (Leavis and Bateson in particular were known for their polemics and apologias) they would formulate something like a theory of criticism, or, in the tradition of Arnold and Eliot, reflect on the function of criticism, while asserting their mistrust of anything as uncongenial as theory-driven literary science. What, to an outside reader like the present author, would be characteristic in this type of critical discourse, and betray its roots in the older criticism, was its continuing reliance on personal taste or opinion, and its unabashed use of authoritatively asserted ethical and aesthetic value judgements — a subjectivism which, in continental scholarship, the comparative method was specifically meant to prevent.

Some of these critical debates were carried out around the platform of the periodical *Essays in Criticism* (founded by Bateson and his then fellow-Oxonian W. W. Robson in 1951). Another prominent periodical was the Cambridge-based, post-Leavisite *Critical Quarterly*, founded by Brian Cox and others in 1958. While providing a platform for Leavisite criticism, it also turned to contemporary literature and emerging critics (David Lodge, Raymond Williams, and, most importantly perhaps, Frank Kermode) with an interest in more contemporary literature and questions of avant-garde, non-traditionalist poetics. But important critical debates also took place in more public forums: *The Listener*, *Encounter*, and *Times Literary*

Supplement. The TLS in particular hosted, in the course of the 1960s and 1970s, a number of formative debates by prominent and aspiring critics on topics of comparatist relevance. From the 1970s, *PN Review* (thus renamed in 1976 after its start as *Poetry Nation Review* in 1973) similarly attracted important reflections on poetry and the criticism of poetry. More rarefied in its audience outreach, the *British Journal of Aesthetics* was also an important platform for discussions of fictionality and literary poetics.

One of the more gripping public debates of the 1960s concerned pornography, which had become a hot topic during the notorious trial of *Lady Chatterley's Lover*. In 1960, the Penguin edition of that book was prosecuted under the Obscenity Act of 1959; that act noted the use of four-letter words as markers of lewdness and obscenity, but allowed for leeway if a work was deemed to have 'literary merit'. Obviously, Lawrence's novel was a test-case on both counts. Critics (what would Matthew Arnold have thought of this?) suddenly found themselves in the middle of a *cause célèbre*; among the witnesses called to help weigh the four-letter words against the literary merits were E. M. Forster, Helen Gardner, Richard Hoggart, and Raymond Williams; and a number of press reflections occurred in the wake of the court case. The sexual revolution of the 1960s kept the issue alive in a wider debate on the position of literary anticonformism (including sexual transgressiveness in Wilde, Joyce, Genet, and others). At the time, it gave the poetical topic of convention vs. innovation, and the nature of avant-garde, a topical edge. Later on, inflected by the feminist critique of pornography, it would evolve into gender approaches and 'queer' readings.

Other high-profile debates ranged from the notorious 'Two Cultures' contention, launched by C. P. Snow but relentlessly pursued by F. R. Leavis for years afterwards; Bateson and others on 'The Language of Poetry' (1967); and the TLS symposia of 1967 and 1968 ('Crosscurrents', 'The Limits of Literature', 'Civil War among the Critics', 'Crisis in Criticism' and 'The Teaching of English Literature').

The postwar generation and the new universities

In the course of these years, and *pace* Gifford, Comparative Literature had definitively become a discipline on its own, taking up a position well apart from the debates of critics in English Literature. A new generation of comparatively-minded critics followed in the footsteps of Roe, Gillies, and Rees. Prominent among these were Donald Davie, John Fletcher and Anthony Thorlby. They argued out the position and perspectives of Comparative Literature in periodicals such as TLS, *Times Higher Education Supplement* and the *Universities Quarterly*. In 1965, R. A. Sayce announced in THES that a course in Comparative and General Literature had been formed in Oxford, preparing for the B.Phil. degree and with some ten participants. In addition, the universities founded after the war (distinguished from their Victorian 'redbrick' forerunners by their plate-glass architecture, and sometimes known by that appellation) offered an environment for institutional consolidation as well: Essex (1964), Sussex (1967), East Anglia (1968), to be followed

Fig 6.3. Donald Davie (courtesy of the British Academy)

in the 1970s by Warwick and Kent. Almost immediately after their establishment, which was meant to cater for a new sense of modernity, these institutions would face the enrolment of the baby-boom demographic cohort. The result was a clash of opinions and attitudes across what became known as the 'generation gap'. Not only were teacher-student relations placed under a new strain, there was also a fresh exposure of traditional literature and literary studies to a new, edgier, and more bitingly 'critical', reassessment, deeply marked by anti-traditionalism and anti-authoritarianism. They tended to attract students from upper-middle-class backgrounds who eschewed the traditionalism of Oxford and Cambridge. In another demographic shift, lower-middle-class students profiting from scholarships and the new grammar schools began to make their way into the redbrick universities and some Oxford or Cambridge colleges.

The University of Essex, founded in Colchester in 1964, placed a 'Department of Literature' (led by Donald Davie from 1964 until 1968) in its 'School of Comparative Studies'. In the 1980s, an important series of 'Conferences on the Sociology of Literature' were held there. The University of East Anglia, founded in Norwich in 1963, established Comparative Literature, led by John Fletcher, as an interface between its 'School of English and American Studies' and its 'School of Modern Languages and European History'. It was during a Norwich conference in 1975 that the British Comparative Literature Association was founded; at its inaugural session chaired by Thorlby, the new association chose Prawer for its first president, with the Norwich hosts James Macfarlane and Elinor Shaffer on the committee, as well as Susan Bassnett (Warwick) David Bellos (Edinburgh) Simon Curtis (Manchester) Eva Fox-Gal (York) and Christopher Heywood (Sheffield). The BCLA founded two journals: *Comparative Criticism* (edited by Shaffer, from 1979) and *New Comparison* (edited by Bassnett, from 1986). In 2003, the two merged into the BCLA's new (and still current) house journal *Comparative Critical Studies*. Among the prominent critics who succeeded Prawer as President were Arthur Terry, Frank Kermode, Malcolm Bowie, Gillian Beer, Marina Warner and Susan Bassnett.

Such institutional developments went in tandem with methodological interventions. In both cases, a gravitation was noticeable towards something which would come to be called 'area studies': the integrated analysis of societies and cultures in their wider context and connections. At Essex, the School of Comparative Studies was a two-wing structure with Chairs of Literature (Davie's) and Government, respectively — something that a priori fostered a tendency to situate literature in its social or societal context. Intrinsic, in Wellek's sense of the term, the study of literature wouldn't be.

That was also asserted in 1968 as a fundamental principle by the Sussex professor Anthony Thorlby, who had studied German at Cambridge and Comparative Literature at Yale. In a substantial essay in TLS he presented Comparative Literature as something far more than a mere 'area of interest' (very much unlike Gifford), and went squarely against the text-intrinsic tradition of 'close reading' criticism:

> The most valuable implication contained in the concept of comparative literature may be that literature should be compared with something beyond itself. Literature speaks to us immediately about things other than beauty: about religious and social attitudes, about moral and emotional values, and not about these things in the abstract, but about what they feel like in practice, in the experience on subjects like fear and freedom and forgiveness which may in the end form the basis of comparative studies, in conjunction with non-literary materials on the same questions, as they have been understood by philosophers, say, or sociologists, psychologists, historians (Thorlby 1968, 80).

In his own work, Thorlby would carry out this programme in widely-scoped synoptic studies such as his *Penguin Companion to European Literature* (1969, vol. 2 in the 4-volume *Penguin Companion to World Literature* series), and the six-volume *Literature and Western Civilization* (1972 ff.). Both these ventures were co-edited together with the elder statesman David Daiches (1912–2005).

In 1970 John Fletcher, professor at East Anglia, developed similar lines in his article 'The Criticism of Comparison'. He put his finger on the sore spot that in the Arnoldian tradition comparison had become an almost meaningless term, at least methodologically. Fletcher's ambition was to transmute the comparative method from 'until now the most widespread, democratic, imprecise and perhaps primitive of approaches to literary study' into the backbone of a new discipline. For him, this meant taking the study of literature from the realm of textual appreciation and judgement into the wider field of cultural studies:

> Questions about literature lead to questions about cultures, the structures and orders of language, the relationship between literature and society, and the history of human imagination an intellect.

As a result, Fletcher opts for a staunchly anti-Wellekian view for Comparative Literature, arguing against close reading by proposing something which decades later would come to be called 'reading at a distance':

> Comparatism is irremediably extrinsic [...] The discipline overlaps too much with intellectual history and is too much interested in movements and currents, the *extra* dimension of an individual work.

These foundational considerations towards a British school of Comparative Literature were consolidated when Siegbert Prawer brought out his monograph *Comparative Literature Studies: An Introduction* (1973). Cologne-born Prawer (on him, generally Reed 2015) had come to Britain as fourteen-year-old in 1939, when his Rhineland-Jewish family had fled the Third Reich.[3] After studying German at Cambridge, as so many others had done in the history of British comparatism, he ultimately became Taylor Professor of German at Oxford in 1969.

By the early 1970s Comparative Literature had firmly established itself as a counterpart to English Studies, with an institutional base in the Joint Honours programmes and Modern Languages departments of the traditional universities (Lilian Furst in Manchester, Prawer in Oxford), as well as dedicated new institutions in the newly established 'plateglass' ones: Thorlby in Sussex (enriched by the

FIG 6.3. Siegbert Salomon Prawer in 1981 (courtesy of the British Academy)

presence of Gabriel Josipovici and, after the crushing of the Prague Spring, Eduard Goldstücker) and Fletcher in East Anglia (where the department also included scholars like Holger Klein and Elinor Shaffer; cf. also Fletcher 1985). An important consolidation point was the collection *Contemporary Criticism*, edited by Malcolm Bradbury and David Palmer (1970).

Even where separate comparatist departments struggled for consolidation (it was not without faculty opposition that Susan Bassnett, as Lecturer in Comparative Literature at Warwick, managed to establish a dedicated graduate programme), each of the new universities developed their own, modernizing profile, often with a comparatist extension to English departments. At York University, there was a department of English and Related Literatures, at Warwick English and Comparative Literary Studies, offering broad courses on general topics (like the epic, or the nineteenth-century novel) to joint-honours students. The presence of Stephen Bann at Kent ensured an interest in the interdisciplinary links between literature, history-writing and the arts.

Challenges post-1968

By 1974, however, Essex had been abandoned with some bitterness by Donald Davie, who had left for California. His career as a comparatist can be placed almost like an exemplary 'parallel life' alongside that of Henry Gifford, Slavicists both. Whereas Gifford had progressed from Harrow through Oxford, Davie belonged to the new generation of grammar school pupils and had studied on a scholarship at Cambridge. His outlook was, accordingly, deeply marked by F. R. Leavis, against whom he rebelled to the extent that he strongly advocated a turn away from the judgemental assertiveness of the traditional critics and their anglocentric tunnel vision. When, in 1974, he reported on 'British criticism' (at a conference on 'The Frontiers of Literary Criticism' in Los Angeles, with René Wellek also present), he did so under the overriding aspect of 'The Necessity for Humility', denouncing the judgementalism of the Arnoldian tradition and stating the need to break out of the comfort zone of Englishness. 'I see something extraordinarily odd in the extent to which British youth studies English literature virtually without any foreign literature to compare it with' (Davie 1974, 9).

It was this attitude which had made him a suitable first incumbent of the Chair of Literature at Essex; but he left that place in some desperation in 1968 (as another eminent comparatist would, 56 years later; cf. Warner 2014). In Davie's case it was because of a less-than-perfect spread of language traditions covered in the programme (de facto only Spanish — taught by Gordon Brotherston — and Russian), an irksome need for adjustment, and the fact that students (more than averagely critically-minded, since they had been attracted to the sociologically oriented approach at Essex) broke out in a generational revolt in May 1968, inspired by Paris and Berkeley. Davie left for Stanford, where he became Yvor Winters's successor. A similar intergenerational disenchantment befell Roy Pascal, like Davie an upwardly mobile critic who had profited from that new educational platform, the grammar school, and who by 1968 was a comparatively-oriented Professor of German at Birmingham. (It had been Pascal, incidentally, who had taken the young Siegbert Prawer under his wing as a newly-appointed lecturer in Birmingham in the 1950s.) To his great chagrin, Pascal, a lifelong Labourite and adherent of the Left, was seen by the 1968 student cohort as an icon of the punditry of the older generation, and driven to resignation in 1969 (Subiotto 1982). The pull-factor of American academia, complementing as it did the push-factors in the British universities, lured many a comparatist away. Lilian Furst, who in 1938 had fled to Britain from her native city Vienna with her parents, felt by 1970 that 'if I stayed in England, I would get stale and frustrated' (Spivey 1996; cf. Mell & Hacohen 2014). In 1974, George Steiner left Cambridge for Geneva. He had been a Fellow of Churchill College since its foundation in 1961, but his august mannerisms met with reservations, and his deep preoccupation with the Holocaust met with little empathy (Jaggi 2001).

The generational succession in some literary departments became, in the troubled 1960s, an Oedipal one, in stark contrast to the filial piety of pre-war vintage. This shift towards intergenerational antagonism was reflected and amplified in the literary genre of the campus novel — a satirical description of academic scheming and vanity, ultimately going back to the clerical intrigue novels of Anthony Trollope. Styles of academic life and theoretical positions were comically identified in the process, and often qualified through ethnotypical stock characters as 'English', 'American', or 'Continental'. Thus the campus novel fixed and popularized a certain stereotype of critical traditions and 'schools' in people's minds, from C. P. Snow's *The Masters* (1951) and Kingsley Amis's *Lucky Jim* (1954) to the successful novels of practising critics like Malcolm Bradbury (*The History Man*, 1975) and David Lodge (*Changing Places*, 1974; *Small World*, 1984). These reflected an academic system in generational transition. As Davie and Pascal had found to their grief, vehement changes and challenges were indeed washing over the British Lang. and Lit. scene from 1969 on.

The changes were coming both from within and from abroad. Within Britain, the rise of the New Left and its critique of the British class system also found expression in the critical attitudes of a younger generation of scholars. They began to criticize the institution of literary criticism as an instrument in the perpetuation of elite prestige for a rarefied class of educated gentlemen. Notions like Bourdieu's 'distinction' and 'symbolic capital' had not yet become common currency, but the tenor of his argument was in the air. Models close to Bourdieu's had been formulated by Raymond Williams, one of the *maîtres à penser* for the new generation. Williams, born into a Welsh working-class family in 1921 and a committed leftist throughout his life, had risen to intellectual prominence with important studies like *Culture and Society* (1958). Together with Richard Hoggart's *The Uses of Literacy* (1957) it had laid the basis for a left-wing, British form of cultural sociology, which in Williams's case would ultimately evolve into something he called 'cultural materialism'. His criticism ranged beyond literature in the narrow sense to fields like television (where he engaged with Marshall McLuhan and formulated a theory of new media)

Fig 6.4. Lilian R. Furst as Flora Stone Mather Visiting Professor at Case Western Reserve University, 1978. Image 02294, CWRU Archives (courtesy Case Western Reserve University)

and an early form of social communications studies. Hoggart would go on to found the benchmark Centre for Contemporary Cultural Studies (the 'Birmingham School') in 1964, which would prove to be the training ground for a plethora of critical theorists in the next generation.

Raymond Williams's most high-profile PhD student was probably Terry Eagleton, who established his own position with an initial critique of Williams in the *New Left Review*, and burst upon the critical scene like an Alien out of the chest cavity of the moribund class system, with his *Criticism & Ideology* (1976). For the next decades, Eagleton would remain the leading thinker in the development of anti-establishment critics, adopting modern Marxist thought from the Continent (Althusser, Macherey) until, following his book *After Theory* (2003), he turned to themes in Irish literary history. His introductory handbook *Literary Theory* (1983, revised 1996) was a lodestar for entire generations of students, outlining and explaining what was now becoming a widely-established narrative moving from Arnold to the breakdown of liberal essentialism and on to the revolutionary apotheosis of poststructuralism.

Another voice among the new leftists was Raman Selden, who died at the early age of 53, shortly after his appointment to a professorship at the new university of Sunderland. The son of a Hindu immigrant worker, he took a First in Classics at University College London in 1960. His PhD on English verse satire was not completed and published until 1978; this opened the door to university appointments (Durham, Lancaster, Sunderland). Selden worked both on seventeenth-century literature and on the history of criticism, with surveys like *The Theory of Criticism from Plato to the Present* (1988) and the final volume in the *Cambridge History of Literary Theory* (published posthumously in 1992). His *Guide to Contemporary Literary Theory* (1985), preceded in the year before by his *Criticism and Objectivity*, was often reprinted and widely translated.

The new critical generation, thus provided with a theoretical ground-work by the work of rebellious breakaways from English Studies, could also look to the monograph series *New Accents*. From 1969, Methuen had published an ongoing, influential series on topics in literary history, entitled *The Critical Idiom*; it contained brief, highly specialized and highly-condensed studies by the likes of Lilian Furst (Romanticism) and Gillian Beer (Romance); it all fitted effortlessly in the literary studies template as mapped by the YCGL and the ICLA. With the fresh start of an additional series, *New Accents*, a modern, theoretically informed generation of younger scholars found their platform: Susan Bassnett, Catherine Belsey, John Drakakis, Anthony Easthope, Toril Moi and Christopher Norris among them. The series, which would eventually run to 40 small volumes, both scandalized the older generation of pundit-critics and made theoretical and methodological innovations in the wider world easily accessible to students and other readers. The series editor was Terence Hawkes (1935–2014), a Shakespeare scholar based at University College Cardiff, and like many of his generation a working-class upstart in the donnish field of English Studies (Drakakis 2014); he would later go on to found the heavily theory-inflected journal *Textual Practice* (1987). Hawkes's own initial contribution to the New Accents series, in 1977, was the massively influential *Semiotics and Structuralism*. It marked the arrival of 'Continental Theory' in Britain — and Comparative Literature had little to do with it, and no control over it.

International crosswinds: The new approaches

Meanwhile, back on the Continent, Hans-Robert Jauss (1969) had proclaimed yet another crisis in literary studies — or, as he termed it in Kuhnian parlance, a 'paradigm shift'. The shift consisted, as Jauss saw it, in the overthrow of national historicism in literary studies. A new set of approaches was spreading which no longer identified literary texts by their genetic markers of production year, original language, and author's nationality. That old paradigm had arisen as part of the nationalization of cultures and the academic historicism that had engulfed all of Europe in the decades around 1800, and it had now run its course. What was also losing its *raison d'être* in the process was Comparative Literature, 'a discipline that had to be contrived to secure the comfortable old paradigm of national history, which sees single literatures as essential entities developing under autochthonous laws of development'. Strident and overstated though Jauss's dismissal was,[4] it admirably summed up an entire spectrum of new approaches which had grown up alongside, and almost behind the back of, the institutionalized Comp.Lit. departments. By now the roll-call of these approaches is familiar, and what was revolutionary then has by now acquired a slightly dated feel: the patina of vinyl Abba records, digital wristwatches and 5 1/4 inch floppy disks. All of them, while not adopted fully or wholesale by card-carrying 'schools' in Britain, were eclectically incorporated into the analytical vision of British scholars — not, be it added, without strenuous altercations. The quarrels over the new approaches lasted throughout the later 1970s and 1980s, and in them, as many a campus novel from those years can testify, generational and national prejudices played an important, and often comical role. The new approaches were often grouped together under indistinct synecdoche appellations such as 'Theory', 'Postmodernism' or 'Structuralism'. 'Structuralism' was broadly gestured at to include its nemesis, poststructuralism, which aimed to break open the fixed systematics of structuralism proper. Raman Selden's volume in the Cambridge History of Literary Criticism groups everything from the Prague School to poststructuralist psychoanalytical and Marxist theories under the rubric 'Structuralism: Its Rise, Influence and Aftermath' (Selden 1995). But while Selden's book was sympathetic to the new approaches it surveyed, this lumped-together treatment was most often used to denounce all post-Saussurean foreign follies *tutti quanti*. Thus in Laurence Lerner's collection *Reconstructing Literature* (1983); thus also, less shrilly, in *The Order of Battle at Trafalgar* (1987) by John Bayley, former student of Lord David Cecil and the first Thomas Warton Professor of English at New College Oxford. The opening essay of that book rambles effortlessly from Zbigniew Herbert by way of Julian Barnes to Henry James in order to refute Roland Barthes. But in one of the generational ironies in which these decades are so rich, Bayley himself would be succeeded on the Warton Chair in 1992 by Terry Eagleton.

Various crisscrossing developments sprang from these methodological debates and generational shifts.

Linguistic and anthropological structuralism in the tradition of Saussure and Lévi-Strauss, and applied to literature by Roland Barthes and the *Tel Quel* group, was usually linked to Barthes's slogan of the 'Death of the Author'. Initially a revolutionary rejection of the old *la vie et l'œuvre* approach, and an attempt to read cultural texts as in an ethnographically-inspired semiotics, it proved influential in loosening the philological bond between 'language and literature', loosening the critical reliance on authorial intentionalism, and instead to recontextualize literary studies as part of cultural studies generally. In subsequent decades, the notion of 'writing' (both the praxis and its end-product) came to challenge the concept of 'literature'.

The 'death of the author' was, of course, announced prematurely and with some overstatement. We can see the survival of the author in literary studies in the rise of media studies, feminism, and Foucauldian thought.

To begin with, at the time that Barthes removed authorial intentionalism from his cultural semiotics, the group of *nouvelle vague* film critics around the *Cahiers du cinéma* (a formative influence on the nascent field of film studies), were discovering what they called the *Cinéma d'auteur*. Film studies, of all fields, were the most suitable laboratory for structuralist specialisms such as semiotics and narratology (cf. Bann 1995, 98–100). Semiotics, going back to Peirce, Saussure and Lotman, for a while claimed to be nothing less than a universally applicable meta-science, a toolkit that would suit all fields and specialisms in cultural analysis. Narratology, initially elaborated in a structuralist tradition (Propp, Greimas, Genette) aimed to typify which textual elements constitute narrativity; it was later also applied to other genres than fictional tales. Ann Rigney's *The Rhetoric of Historical Representation: Three Narrative Histories of the French Revolution* (1990) is a case in point; it also testifies to a growing interest, in these decades, in non-fictional genres of narrative literature (including travel writing and autobiography). All this helped, ultimately, to invigorate that field of cultural media studies, which in the YCGL structure had often been relegated to the container category 'Literature and the Other Arts'. Thus, the thematization of 'the gaze' (a Sartre-derived concept), and the notion of focalization, so central in narratology, replaced old-school authorial intentionalism, and film studies provided an early testing ground (witness Teresa De Lauretis's *Alice Doesn't: Feminism, Semiotics, Cinema*, 1983). Within Britain, the critic/author Colin MacCabe, having been exposed to the thought of Althusser, Balibar, Barthes and Derrida during a year in Paris (1972–73), applied his new insights, once returned to English Literature at Cambridge, to film studies, mainly through his involvement with the periodical *Screen*. Accordingly, in the mid-1970s, *Screen* became a byword for 'Foreign Theory' (which MacCabe did little to mitigate, witness later titles like *Tracking the Signifier: Theoretical Essays on Film, Linguistics, Literature*, 1985). So repugnant was this stance to more traditional critics that MacCabe was denied tenure in 1981, a sign of the entrenchment of the time (cf. Forbes 1988). The sands had shifted by 1987, when MacCabe took over the editorship of the post-Leavisite

Critical Quarterly and turned it into a forum for the new approaches, hosting contributors like Derrida and Žižek.

For feminist critics (who gained a significant presence in precisely these decades), although many of them were anti-historicist and anti-essentialist, authors and authorship mattered — certainly when it came to the author's gender. Indeed, feminist literary studies were long preoccupied with the question whether gender was to be studied in the real-life, personal politics of the writer, or in the praxis (or even textuality) of writing itself. Broadly speaking, there was, as so often in literary studies, a distinction between a more social-historical orientation (e.g. the path-breaking Hazel Mews, *Frail Vessels: Woman's Role in Women's Novels from Fanny Burney to George Eliot*, 1969; Kate Flint, *The Woman Reader, 1837–1914*, 1995; the early Marina Warner), and a more interpretative-theoretical one, the latter more often inspired by Simone de Beauvoir and psychoanalysis (cf. Jacqueline Rose, *Feminine Sexuality: Jacques Lacan and the école freudienne*, 1985). The latter approach was developed mainly by the influential Lacanians Luce Irigaray and Hélène Cixous, with their concept of an *écriture féminine*. Ironically, an Atlantic-riven opposition once again swung into place in these discussions. If a more poststructuralist writing-oriented approach was 'French' in orientation, a more personalist and identitarian approach, centred on the lives, personalities and experiences of women authors, was considered more in line with American feminism. Critics like Toril Moi (*Sexual/Textual Politics*, 1986) saw it as the specific task of British feminist critics to mediate between these two traditions. Norwegian-born Moi was active in Oxford from 1969 until 1989, then moved on to the US. Other feminist scholars whose careers took them across the Atlantic were Kate Flint and Maud Ellmann.

Michel Foucault's 'Qu'est-ce qu'un auteur?' (1969) identified the author, not as an external autonomous human entity, but as a fundamental function of the text itself. Foucault's 'author function' re-thematized authorship as a valid problem in literary history — not as a validating creator, whose original intention fixes the true meaning of the text, but as the 'brand', the guarantor who identifies the provenance of the text as it reaches its audiences; the text's fundamental metadata, as it were. This link between the identity of the author and the identity of the text was taken up from the other end by Bernard Cerquiglini in his influential essay *Éloge de la variante: Histoire critique de la philologie* (1989), which criticized the philological urge to reduce the variable tradition of textual manuscript transmissions into a contradiction-free, ideal-typical *Urtext*. In all their variability, the transmissions constitute a Saussurean *langue-parole* model, and the obsession with establishing a normative fixity is a historical contingency, linked with the rise of printing, the rise of the author-function, and the rise of philology itself. Such insights were fundamental in establishing what is now termed the 'New Medievalism', strongly established in universities like Leeds, and also in the development of book history alongside literary history.

In sum: The author was, not killed off, but problematized, changed from a fixed categorical parameter to an object of analysis as complex and fluid as the text itself (Cf. Seán Burke, 1995; 2010). What was killed off in the process was, however, the romantically-rooted hero-worship of the author as authority, and of the text as his premeditated artwork.

The more specifically poststructuralist, Derrida-inspired approach was vigorously represented within Britain by Catherine Belsey and Christopher Norris at Cardiff, but also often reached Britain, by now firmly part of a global academic anglosphere, via an American detour: the Cornell review *Diacritics*, the Yale French school around Paul De Man. Between America and France, Britain had perhaps its most specifically local tradition in the class-oriented approach of the New Left tradition (Williams, Eagleton, Selden, Stuart Sim, Alan Sinfield). Marx-inspired critical theorists (like their American counterpart Fredric Jameson) had initially had some reservations concerning poststructuralism, considering it an intellectual outrider of postmodernism — which in turn was criticized as a bourgeois/late-capitalist vanity, coquetting with ontological smoke-and-mirror effects without due regard for the factual conditions and power relations in the real world. But by the mid-1980s, leftist critics were convinced by the likes of Althusser and Macherey of poststructuralism's radically subversive potential; there was also a common ground in the shared dislike of liberal humanism, which in the hands of the older generation had become such a complacent celebration of the past, its great achievements and its enduring traditions. As it turned out, Raymond Williams's 'cultural materialism' proved transgenerationally resilient enough to incorporate new insights and remained viable into the 21st century, its hidden strength lying perhaps in its capacity to be fruitfully applied to topics from older periods of literary history, such as Shakespeare, and complementing in that respect the 'New Historicism' that emerged in the US in 1990s. Critics from this tradition escaped verbal hermeticism, and used the new approaches to study literature in its social and/or historical context.

That context was often, however, mono-national, much as the literary corpus was taken from the existing national canons. A more transnational approach, studying multinational patterns from a supranational point of view, was worked out in the wake of Edward Said's *Orientalism* (1978), which opened up the field of colonial relations as an interface in intercultural encounters, cultural representations and imperial hegemony.

Postcolonialism and the new interest in World Literature

The history of postcolonial studies, a truly global, polycentric and polyphonic phenomenon, cannot be covered adequately in this constrained compass with its focus on literary studies in the British Isles. I merely note in passing its important repercussions in Irish academia, where Said was an inspiration for the Field Day group of cultural critics (Seamus Deane foremost among them, with Declan Kiberd an important kindred spirit), who began to read Irish literature and culture in postcolonial terms. There was a real political urgency justifying such an approach: between 1969 and 1998 the Northern Irish conflict amounted almost to a low-level civil war, claiming some 3500 victims. But the postcolonial approach in Irish cultural and literary studies ran counter to developments in Irish history-writing, where historians were beginning to move beyond the Manichean master narrative of 'English oppression and Irish resistance'. The ensuing, very divisive 'revisionism debates' (Brady 1999) crested in the mid-1990s and have not yet died down. Within the UK, the repercussions were noticeable in the literary criticism of Edna Longley, who denounced the Irish postcolonial approach as unreformed nationalism in a new garb (*The Living Stream: Literature and Revisionism in Ireland*, 1994), and above all in the confrontations between Terry Eagleton and Roy Foster, Professor of Irish History at Oxford and noted biographer of W. B. Yeats.

An important British antecedent to postcolonial studies was the specialism known in the 1970s as 'Commonwealth Literature', addressing the various English-language literatures of the former British Empire. The English Department at Stirling had a long-standing interest in Commonwealth Literature under A. N. Jeffares (1920–2005), a noted Yeats scholar and alumnus of Trinity College Dublin with previous experience at the universities of Adelaide and Leeds. Jeffares had developed the specialism then known as 'Anglo-Irish literature' at Leeds, where he taught from 1957. At Stirling, where he moved in 1974, this slotted into the ambit of the wider British Empire. By now a critique of post-imperial Eurocentrism was beginning to gain ground, witness the appearance of William Walsh's *Commonwealth Literature* (1973), Hugh Ridley's article in the *Revue de Littérature Comparée*, 'The Colonial Imagination', and the collection edited by Andrew Gurr and Pio Zirimu, *Black Aesthetics* (1971), based on a conference held in Nairobi, where Gurr — later to become editor of the *Modern Language Review* — taught at the time. In 1985, *Europe and its Others* followed (Francis Barker), based on a Sociology of Literature conference at Essex. British-based writers and critics from various anglophone African countries took inspiration from the African modernism and pan-Africanism of Achebe, Soyinka, E'skia Mphahlele, and Ngũgĩ wa Thiong'o (notably his *Decolonising the Mind: The Politics of Language in African Literature*, 1981). The Africa Centre in London, which had opened in 1964, provided a platform for African intellectuals, who meshed with their Caribbean counterparts, most prominently among them perhaps David Dabydeen (*The Black Presence in English Literature*, 1985). In 1978 the Association for the Teaching of Caribbean, African, Asian and Associated Literatures (ATCAL) was founded, with hubs at the universities of Warwick and Kent.

The postcolonial legacy of the Indian Raj in these years spawned both a vogue of post-imperial nostalgia (dubbed, sarcastically, 'The Raj Revival' by Salman Rushdie) and a critical engagement inspired by Edward Said and applied most influentially by Homi Bhabha. Bhabha had done graduate work and a doctorate at Oxford, where he had been tutored by, among others, Lahore-born John Bayley (himself a critic of post-Raj sentimentalism as well as a Kipling aficionado) and Terry Eagleton. Bhabha lectured at the University of Sussex throughout the 1980s before relocating to the US in 1992. Meanwhile at Essex, Gordon Brotherston helped spread an interest in Latin American and Native-American cultures and cross-Atlantic attitudes.

These various critical voices merged into a concerted approach in literary studies in the wake of the seminal study *The Empire Writes Back: Theory and Practice in Post-Colonial Literature*, by Bill Ashcroft, Gareth Griffiths, and Helen Tiffin (a New

Accents volume, 1989). While postcolonialism is by now a dominant paradigm in literary studies worldwide, the filiations arrayed here suggested that in its British developments the approach was specifically post-Imperial, and that as such the British tradition, with an important South Asian and Caribbean dimension, differed, at least in its beginnings, from the American (with its roots in the USA's race relations) or the French (with its roots in the *négritude* school and Frantz Fanon, also influential for Ngũgĩ). But whatever these local antecedents and inflections, postcolonialism has since the 1990s become the dominant approach in literary and cultural studies. National and ethnic identities, heretofore a categorical notion (a collective cultural essence underlying cultural production) were problematized into historical constructs (a self-image generated in cultural production). Partly inspired by Raphael Samuel (*Patriotism: The Making and Unmaking of British National Identity*, 1989; *The Myths We Live By*, 1990) and Benedict Anderson (*Imagined Communities*, 1983), publications like Tim Middleton and Judy Giles's sourcebook *Writing Englishness* (1995) and Anthony Easthope's *Englishness and National Culture* (1998) deconstructed the anglocentric Self as much as its imperial or colonial Other. Also, a power-inverted look is now habitually applied not only to imperial, colonial or ethnic cultural and social, but also to sexual, relations, and even to the relationship between humanity and the rest of the natural world — in ecocriticism, the posthumanist approach, or in 'Object-Oriented Ontology'. The concept of 'Orientalism' has, for better or for worse, slipped its geopolitical and historical moorings and is now being applied to any discourse that denigrates or cognitively subjects the Other, wherever or whoever that Other may be.

Most recently, the most fruitful comparative application of the postcolonial viewpoint, especially in America, was the revival of the concept at the very root of comparatism, Goethe's protean idea of a 'world literature'. The point of departure was, more specifically, the old, imperial comparatism of the likes of Posnett, but postcolonially renegotiated as to its Eurocentrist and stadialist assumptions (traces of which were still noticeable in the Daiches-Thorlby *Penguin Companion to World Literature* of 1969). David Damrosch re-opened the field with his *What is World Literature?* of 2003 and has kept up a steady production in that line since then, founding an Institute for World Literature at Harvard in 2010. Other American comparatists who have turned in this direction are Emily Apter (*The Translation Zone*, 2006), and Haun Saussy (*The Ethnography of Rhythm: Orality and Its Technologies*, 2016). Italian-born Franco Moretti developed a network-analytical approach while at Stanford, concentrating on the metadata of literary corpuses ('reading at a distance') rather than engaging in interpretative analysis. World literature was also put on the agenda by Pascale Casanova (*La République mondiale des lettres*, 1999; the book originated as a thesis under Bourdieu).

The impact of this globalization has been fourfold. It entails an awareness of global power relations in modernity (inspired by Immanuel Wallerstein, cf. *Combined and Uneven Development: Towards a New Theory of World-Literature*, by WReC [Warwick Research Collective], 2015); an interest in long-distance exchanges and *longue durée* developments; an attempt to broaden the typology of genres like myth, epic and the novel beyond their (neo-)Aristotelian a-prioris; and a new openness to orality and performativity.

Vast and complex as it is, the global framework must be primarily just that: a framework, enabling fresh ways of focusing (rather than a specific focus in its own right). The approach is also hampered by the fact that, although literature is global and long-term historical, the academic study of literature (including its methodological toolkit, its theoretical assumptions and its available expertise, and indeed its very desire to go global) is situated very much in Western modernity and postmodernity. But the reinvigoration of the global scope also gave a boost to Comparative Literature as a discipline.

Literary history, literary reception and the transnational perspective

The New Approaches, firmly anchoring their axiology and their understanding of texts ancient and modern in contemporary values, were predominantly anti-historicist. Historicism[5] had privileged a sympathetic, even submissive, understanding of the past on its own terms (*wie es eigentlich gewesen*, in Ranke's words) over its meaning for the present. The refusal of that historicism characterized all of the New Approaches, regardless of their mutual differences. Even the New Historicism and cultural materialism, for all that they engaged with the text's historicity, did so from a firmly contemporary, 'critical', anti-authoritarian value system, vindicating the subaltern against the dominant or the hegemonic.

Thus, anti-historicism meshed with another common denominator: the various New Approaches shared a fundamental, even paradigmatic anti-authoritarianism, challenging both social and textual authorities and forms of dominance, querying the power monopoly of the author over the fixed meaning of the text, and the impervious autonomy of the literary text itself as complete, self-enclosed and self-validating. What started in the spirit of 1968 has continued from Gilles Deleuze to Slavoj Žižek, Giorgio Agamben, and Jacques Rancière in more recent decades, and into the Animal Liberation criticism of posthumanism. The application of that anti-authoritarian philosophy to literary studies has by now become a pattern as recognizable as the Arnoldian paternalism of earlier vintage. Readings expose the text's apparent complacency or underlying hegemonic complicity, and in the process often read the text, rebarbatively and with rebellious gusto, 'against the grain'. That is, fundamentally, what the often-invoked words 'critique' and 'critical' stood for: a hermeneutics based, as Paul Ricœur had already noted when discussing Freud, on suspicion (Felski 2012). Criticism was no longer, in the Arnoldian sense, 'learning and propagating the best that is known and thought in the world', but attacking prior assumptions. The critic's pose has shifted from 'pronouncing refined yet authoritative judgement' to 'dauntlessly and controversially challenging the established consensus'.

Where did anti-historicism leave literary history (beyond a desire to re-write it)? And, more specifically, where did it leave Comparative Literature? After all, the entire generational upheaval of critical theory emanated largely from within the bosom of English Studies, with theoretical inspiration from Continental philosophers.

The comparative-minded departments at the new universities each developed their own point of emphasis in the new cultural/critical turn. Besides the 'Commonwealth'/postcolonial orientation of Stirling, there was a focus on women and gender studies at York. Warwick established early, if not the first, Chairs in Film Studies and Theatre Studies. But all outflanked Comparative Literature as such. As a discipline, even globally, it was taken unawares by a paradigm shift towards Theory and new departures in cultural studies specialisms. The response was, once again, a flurry of crisis proclamations predicting the discipline's future irrelevance and demise, or at least the need for a drastic self-reinvention. That tradition includes Ulrich Weisstein's 'From Ecstasy to Agony: The Rise and Fall of Comparative Literature' (1997) to Gayatri Spivak's *Death of a Discipline* (2003; for a rejoinder, see Bassnett 2006). Comparatists had failed to set trends; the best they could do was keep track of them. A 'Committee for Literary Theory' was established by the ICLA; Elinor Shaffer, in the chosen themes of the successive volumes of *Comparative Criticism*, and in her own introductions to each of these, took stock.

The New Approaches, for all that they daringly explored new viewpoints and analytical angles, and imposed a self-stoking need to abandon the old and explore the unaccustomed, applied themselves to a fairly narrow range of literary texts, more often than not from the Eng.Lit. canon. At times it seemed as if any new critical angle had to be tried out on *Heart of Darkness*, *Ulysses*, *Frankenstein*, *The Tempest* or *The Turn of the Screw*. This left the expertise needed to address more remote periods or linguistic traditions relatively unaffected, and literary history there remained strong — witness the work of Robert Shackleton, Haydn Mason and Nicholas Cronk on the Enlightenment, Brian Vickers on the Renaissance and on rhetoric, A. T. Hatto, Peter Dronke and Alastair Minnis on medieval literature. Literary historians took inspiration from Michel Foucault to move beyond a strictly poetical focus and encompass the history of mentalities and of epistemic developments as well. From the 1980s on, the comparative literary-historical study of the literatures of the British Isles profited from this approach: studies on the post-bardic Gaelic tradition in English-dominated Ireland, by the likes of Seán Ó Tuama and Breandán Ó Buachalla; on Macpherson and his Ossian as figures in the confrontation between Highland and English traditions (Howard Gaskill, Fiona Stafford), and the Celticist intellectuals of late-18th and early-19th century Wales (Mary-Ann Constantine). The 'Four Nations' view of the British Isles was adapted into an 'archipelagic' view of literary history by John Kerrigan (*Archipelagic English: Literature, History, and Politics 1603–1707*, 2008).

The historical distance between past and present remained a focus for those literary historians dealing with the comparatist vein of 'influence studies'; they, unavoidably, felt the influence of historical hermeneutics (developed by Hans-Georg Gadamer and applied to literature by Jauss's *Rezeptionsästhetik* and reception history). A revival of literary history after 2000 took the form of reception histories rather than production histories: the history of how books and authors were read across time. The nineteenth-century reception of the Middle Ages (in German known as *Mittelalterrezeption*) proved an especially fertile field. Maike Oergel (*The Return of King Arthur and the Nibelungen: National Myth in Nineteenth-Century English and German Literature*, 1998), Andrew Wawn (*The Vikings and the Victorians: Inventing the Old North in Nineteenth-century Britain*, 2000 and Joanne Parker (*'England's Darling': The Victorian Cult of Alfred the Great*, 2007) worked in the interstice of literary history and the historical study of *lieux de mémoire*. Literature was being read as cultural memory. 'Literature as Cultural Memory', the theme of the 1997 ICLA conference in Leiden, had been presaged by the ongoing Routledge 'Critical Heritage' series. From 1967 on, it has been generating many dozens of volumes presenting critical sources and commentaries from various historical periods, documenting the reception history of texts and authors. In recent decades there have also been many exciting studies of the 'afterlives' of literary figures and authors: their cultural reception history. And in a belated acceptance of Jauss's programme at Konstanz, literary history became less the history of literary production and innovations and more the history of literary dissemination and reception. Indeed, in this field British comparatism took a leading part when shortly after 2000 the benchmark series 'The Reception of British and Irish Authors in Europe' was set up under the editorship of Elinor Shaffer. It now runs to dozens of volumes tracing reception trajectories in various European countries.

An important point of reference amidst these shifting sands was provided by Susan Bassnett's handbook *Comparative Literature: A Critical Introduction* (1993), the fourth British comparatist handbook following Posnett, Gifford, and Prawer. It located the core business of the crisis-prone discipline in the specialism of Translation Studies, for which Bassnett had established a strong base at Warwick, including a graduate programme flanking the Comparative Literature MA. The case that Comparative Literature should rely on, and perhaps fold into, Translation Studies was very robustly stated at the time, and toned down afterwards (cf. Bassnett 2006); but it did express an awareness that, if Comparative Literature stood for anything specific, it was about how texts moved between reading cohorts, cultures and languages. That awareness, too, informed Shaffer's Reception series.

Comparative Literature had always, in its methodology, faced a challenge in how to deal with that aspect of cross-border literary traffic airily called 'influence'. Was 'influence' the Zeitgeist-borne wafting of disembodied ideas and fashions from one society to another, the almost intangible way in which authors would inspire and strike sympathetic chords in their readers and imitators at home and abroad? And was this cultural magnetism something that a discerning critic could infer from stylistic echoes and resemblances? The post-Jaussian study of literary reception shifted the analytical point of access in that process from the emanating to the receiving party, and accessed these processes, complex and multi-dimensional as they are, through the documentary reception record. At the same time, the study of cross-border exchanges became a more focused concern in the humanities following the development of Cultural Transfer studies and the rise of the concept of entangled histories.

Cultural Transfer was worked out as a concept by two Bourdieu-influenced scholars, Michel Espagne and Michael Werner, who studied the agency of intellectuals in institutional developments and realized that this praxis was not bounded by the perimeter of a given society's institutional infrastructure.[6] Espagne and Werner applied that insight first of all in their French-German history of Modern-Language philologies in the nineteenth century, *Philologiques* (4 vols, 1990–96). Since then, the concept has been a thriving presence in literary and intellectual history. Complemented by later variations such as *histoire croisée* or 'entangled history', it has greatly revived transnational and comparative history. This coincided with a general recoil, among historians and social scientists, from 'methodological nationalism' (the tendency to fence the historical or social analysis of causes and effects into the ambit of a single country or society, marginalizing wider, cross-border connections). Such a tendency towards national internalism is a standing gravitation for social and political historians, who rely strongly on archival study — archives themselves being the product of nation-state consolidation, and usually organized on a nation-state footing. But literary and cultural scholars deal with a corpus that is part of the communicative patterns of culture: something that is, in the root sense of the word, 'published' (i.e., made over to a public, albeit not necessarily in printed form). Literature is marked by the disseminative mobility of its airborne pollen and seeds as much as by the fixed location of its root system.

Modes of transfer: Remediation and translation

For literary studies, the notion of cultural transfer comes close to being a tautology. Culture is fundamentally a form of communication and tends to bridge distances across space and time, between one communicative situation and another. Two thresholds that can form noticeable 'bumps' in the continuum of cultural diffusion are those of language and of medium (verbal, pictorial, plastic, performative, broadcast). Exchanges between cultural media had been traditionally addressed in a specialism known as 'Literature and the Other Arts'. The impact of reception studies revitalized this somewhat rarefied aesthetic preoccupation by looking at what became known as 'remediation': how, in the course of their reception history, literary works would cross the boundaries of the textual and inspire visual artworks, music, film, or other forms of cultural production. With the rise of the graphic novel, cinema, and television, remediation became a much more foregrounded element in the dynamics of cultural diffusion. Intermediality is now a powerful analytical concept in literary studies; it has done much to bring literary reception history close to the notion of multimedia *lieux de mémoire* and the newly developing specialism of memory studies (Ann Rigney, *The Afterlives of Walter Scott*, 2015). In addition, there is a fresh interest in the field of oral literature and myth, e.g. Marina Warner's *Once upon a Time: A Short History of the Fairy Tale* (2014).

Within the medium of textuality, the most salient thresholds that literary diffusion has to negotiate are linguistic in nature. The realization that *translation*, as a cross-cultural literary praxis, lies at the heart of Comparative Literature had been little more than a tacit afterthought until well into the 1960s, but in British comparatism the role and study of translation has since then gained a higher profile — witness Henry Gifford's attention to translation as an important modality of literature's transnational dynamics. The careers of Michael Hamburger and W. G. Sebald were especially inspiring. One of the cohort of Jewish refugees from the Continent, Hamburger (1924–2007) taught at the University of Reading from 1955 onwards, gaining fame above all as a literary translator (in the distinguished tradition of Constance Garnett and C. K. Scott Moncrieff), but also as a critic. The fame of Sebald (1944–2001) as a writer needs no elaboration, but what is relevant to note here is that he was also part of the early comparatist generation at the University of East Anglia, where he submitted his thesis on Döblin in 1973 and obtained a chair in European Literature in 1987. It was in this capacity that he became the founding president of the British Centre for Literary Translation, which is at present headed by Duncan Large.

After some 30 translation-oriented articles by British critics had appeared in the course of the 1960s, the study and theory of translation developed into a specialism of its own in the 1970s. Theories developed by Itamar Even-Zohar and Gideon Toury were introduced to the UK by two Belgians who after their undergraduate studies in Ghent moved to Essex: Theo Hermans, who studied Literary Translation there and took a doctorate in Comparative Literature at Warwick in 1977, and André Lefevere, who took a PhD at Essex in 1972. The Warwick connection proved fruitful given the presence there of Susan Bassnett, who had started the journal *Comparison* (forerunner of the above-mentioned *New Comparison*) in 1975. Theo Hermans's 'Translation, Comparison, Diachrony' appeared in *Comparison* in 1979. Bassnett's own *Translation* volume in the New Accents series (1980) was widely translated, and has never gone out of print since then; Hermans's edited volume *The Manipulation of Literature: Studies in Literary Translation* (1985) provided a further crystallizing point. Bassnett and Lefevere went on to co-author a number of seminal volumes redefining translation not narrowly as the transposition of a text from one language into another, but any process whereby a text reaches an audience with a different culture than its point of origin (*Constructing Cultures: Essays of Literary Translation*, 1996).

That broad definition brings the notion of 'translation' quite close to its Latin cognate 'transfer' and can address all cross-cultural dissemination processes of literature. In other words, translation studies, while benefiting from a tight body of theory (Even-Zohar's polysystem theory, Toury's descriptive approach) can address almost all processes of literary dynamics that were originally the province of Comparative Literature. Michael Cronin's *Translating Ireland: Translation, Languages, Culture* (1996) demonstrated precisely that point. Translation studies can encompass both the 'close' and 'distant' reading of texts, address issues of criticism and historical context, and take on board the field of intercultural hermeneutics (imagology), addressing the national self-images and hetero-stereotypes which divide the literary world into separate self-defining 'national' communities. Indeed, developments in the last decades suggest a convergence between Comparative Literature, translation studies, and World-Literature interest, given their common focus on the 'social life of texts', the ways in which texts move and the ways in which there have been changes to how we read texts.[7]

By way of conclusion; outlook

Wellek's prediction, in his 1950s lecture, that he would like to see the 'comparatism' taken out of the discipline and to see chairs of 'Literature' *tout court*, was echoed in a way by the anti-comparatist diatribe of Jauss proclaiming the 'New Paradigm' in 1967, and indeed in the establishment of new chairs of 'Literature' such as Donald Davie's at Essex. At the same time, chairs of 'Comparative Literature' were created whose appellation seemed less than trenchant, among them the Weidenfeld Professorship of Comparative Literature, first held in 1994–95 by George Steiner, and subsequently by a succession of eminent incumbents such as Martha Nussbaum, Gabriel Josipovici, Umberto Eco, Mario Vargas Llosa, Sandor Gilman, Wolf Lepenies, Ali Smith, and Marina Warner. What specific programmatic vision in literary studies does such a selection of scholars bespeak? In many cases, the 'Comparative' attribute is used as a loose addition in the collocation 'English and Comparative Literature', which seems to have little more specific meaning than 'English Literature and Beyond', or 'English Literature à la mode'. The same trend is noticeable in other countries (witness the German and Austrian chairs in 'Deutsche und Vergleichende Literaturwissenschaft') and is often the relict of a merger, where a previously independent comparatist chair has been discontinued and its legacy folded into a modern-language compound. And that trend is, in turn, a sign of the steady retrenchment of humanities faculties, worldwide, since the 1980s.

In the foregoing pages, the development of Comparative Literature has been traced, not only as part of intellectual history or the history of knowledge production, but also as part of the institutional history of the humanities at British universities, and that history has in its recent decades been affected by severe constrictions. After the rise of the new universities in the 1960s and 1970s, the trend since the mid-1980s — not only in Britain — has been towards an entrepreneurial model, driven by cost-benefit efficiency and enforced by a stringent audit culture (cf. Warner 2014 and the reactions elicited thereby). That type of model has proved particularly inhospitable to the humanities and, within the humanities, to those programmes that offer no direct preparation for specific job market demands — such as Comparative Literature.

Few will deny that third-level education in general, the humanities in particular, and Comparative Literature as a canary in that particular coalmine, have been hard hit in recent decades. This should not, however, tempt us into yet another proclamation of crisis, but rather invite us to identify, over time, the tidal changes in our discipline's history. In retrospect it appears that there were two noticeably flourishing periods: the one following Matthew Arnold, and — for all its unresolved eurocentrism — the 1970s. In the Victorian decades, comparatism flourished as part of a new cross-national method that had a capacity for discovering new facts, mapping new interrelations, opening new sightlines. In the 1970s and 1980s, literary studies took a leading role in a new, anti-authoritarian patterns of thought, deconstructing old certainties, enabling a fresh look at cultural and social relations, in a climate of anti-authoritarian emancipation. The heyday of the second wave has passed as did that of the first one. Both have left enduring insights and methods, even for the present, but the leverage of these in the academic marketplace is, for the nonce, feeble.

Two questions are to be posed in the light of this. What core business can Comparative Literature rely on to weather the current climate of academic retrenchment? What might be the future conditions in the world of learning which would give the discipline fresh traction and renewed appeal to society at large?

As to the first, it strikes me that what is needed is a firm self-awareness of what the terms 'comparative' and 'literature' stand for. Without wishing to foreclose that debate or impose my own preferences, I note that the various viewpoints surveyed in the foregoing pages seem to converge around a twofold idea of 'Comparative'. 'Comparative' can refer both to a heuristic operation — things are assessed, not in their own right and by themselves in isolation, but relationally, how they stand vis-à-vis other things — and to a deliberate focus on the transnational and the intermedial, a clear realization that literature is the very opposite of self-enclosed. Comparative Literature looks at literature as something that forms a *connection*, and that connection can only be traced if we contextualize the individual texts we study, situate them in their environment. Let me add that in my opinion, the idea of comparison as a method also imposes a need for a systematically thought-through application of that method. It seems slapdash to use the concept simply to indicate a broader-than-national framework, or a scale-enlargement of one's corpus, or an ad-hoc juxtaposition. No-one will plead for rigidity; but some rigour may be welcome. It seems timely to undertake a fresh and rigorous methodological reflection on what, precisely, the comparative method actually means in contemporary literary studies

While the pursuit of Comparative Literature is firmly and organically part of the general framework of cultural studies and cultural history, the notion of literature also imposes its own specificity. Literature, in whatever way one may wish to define or interpret that term, is not just culture as such, but, more specifically, the textual expression of culture. What is more, literature is anything but an automatic, mechanical, or naively spontaneous form of anthropological behaviour, like chewing food before we swallow or blinking our eyes, but by definition a self-aware, self-reflecting expression of culture: culture aware of itself, and consciously formulating reflections on that awareness. Literature will therefore always fractally include, and be included in, nesting levels of metaliterature: commentary, intertextuality, self-conscious poetical reflections on its own conventions and convention-negotiations. This awareness of the nesting complexities of literary representation turns literary studies into a true discipline: it has developed, in a long scholarly tradition, a technical expertise about its subject which is not readily available to other scholars, even though they may read literature and take a well-versed interest in it. Not even the better historians or museum curators know how a novel is to be read differently from a satire or a political speech, how irony works, what an intentional fallacy is, or defamiliarization, or the rhetorical effect of free indirect discourse in a narrative. Or what commonly-used terms like melodrama or narrative really stand for.

These are, I trust, fairly uncontentious home truths; they are in line with the home page of the BCLA website, which states its remit as promoting

> the scholarly study of literature, across languages and borders, national or other. We explore literature in relation to other disciplines and translations between languages and media. Our primary interests are in literature, the contexts of literature, and the interaction between literatures. (bcla.org)

It is, in fact, heartening and admirable to see how comparatists, even in the less propitious academic climate of the last decades, have continued to pursue their craft on the basis of that informal, but solid self-understanding. Comparative Literature, despite the great institutional retrenchments it has to work in, despite the lack of career prospects or decent working conditions for its graduates, is, remarkably enough, thriving intellectually. One of its great success stories of the past decades lies outside the scope of this book: its spread to non-Western universities.

All that takes place on the basis of a programme that has remained solid and stable, in spite of ever-renewed crisis proclamations, for many decades. That programme has proved itself capable of adaptation; it has accommodated newly emerging interests, new questions, new approaches, such as internationalism in the 1950s, questions of gender and power in the 1970s, and the recent interests in world literature, cultural memory, intermediality or ecocriticism. What is more, I feel that there is an urgent social need for the kind of expertise that such a scholarly study has to offer. Which brings me to my closing question: what future use is there for Comparative Literature?

Both in the Arnoldian heyday and in the anti-authoritarian climate of the 1970s and 1980s, literary studies had an obvious pedagogical justification. The point was never just to develop an appreciative form of literary wine-tasting, comparing different châteaux and vintages and capturing the character of subtle flavours in well-chosen descriptive terms. The point was always to teach people to think (clearly and critically) by means of teaching them how to read (clearly and critically): improving expert literacy and showing how to make the most of the great store of inspiration and mediated experience that literature provides. That pedagogical justification was captured admirably by Matthew Arnold in his lofty Victorian definition of the function of criticism; it has remained in force, despite all paradigm shifts since Arnold's time. It strikes me that it still stands, and that it makes comparatism more urgently needed now than ever since the 1950s.

Most critics seem to concur that the great value of literature is its power to make us think differently: to empathize, to imagine how life feels to others quite different from us. This is in line with literature's power to connect: to maintain texts in circulation over many decades and centuries, and across great distances and cultural differences, binding readers together from different centuries and backgrounds into 'affective communities' (Gandhi 2006, Steenbergh 2014). The internationalist climate of the post-war decades was obviously congenial to such a literary and critical stance. The decline of internationalism after 1990 has affected politics and academic life alike (most notably in the dwindling funding for cross-national teaching and research in the humanities); it has coincided with a decline in foreign language teaching, a key competence for comparatists. Conversely, neo-nationalist populism (on which, Leerssen 2018, 254–63; Mudde & Rovira Kaltwasser 2017; Müller 2016) is hostile to educational and research practices that involve empathetic or critical thought, and instead thrives on anti-intellectualism, fake news, fact-free politics and post-truth memes.

As Latour (2004) argues, cultural scholars are themselves partly complicit in this post-truth mentality, in which all opinions, no matter how ill-informed, are equal, and humanism is mistrusted as crypto-conservatism: we ourselves pioneered the radical epistemic scepticism of postmodern thought, and the relentless, self-devouring tendency to critique the world and everything in it.

But be all that as it may, the spread of populist neonationalism, such as it is, has occurred in tandem with the institutional decline of the humanities, including Comparative Literature, with their emphasis on transnationalism and on the power of the human mind — critical, empathetic, imaginative. The pedagogical need for people trained to think clearly and critically, and transnationally, has been proved, beyond all doubt, in the negative: much as the need for vitamin C was proved, in the negative, by scurvy. Dismiss it as useless or inconsequential, and then see what you end up with.

The pedagogical need to train personalities in transcending ethnocentric or narrowly national tunnel-vision, in imaginative and critical flexibility of mind, in transcultural literacy and competence, is, then, made obvious by the very failures we are witnessing in the national and international political field over the last decades. Society is facing a new philistinism, much as Matthew Arnold faced that of the Gradgrind Victorians of his day and age: 'the people who believe most that our greatness and welfare are proved by our being very rich, and who most give their lives and thoughts to becoming rich' (above, 68 n. 4). The disinterested endeavour to learn and propagate the best that is known and thought in the world: that is still, again, an urgent social necessity.

Notes to Chapter 6

1. 'Henry Gifford' 2003. Cf. also, more generally, Gorman 1992: his *Bibliography of Russian Formalism in English* shows few British as compared to American titles pre-1975.
2. Žirmunskij/Zhirmunsky (1891–1971), a noted Russian comparatist, was among those literary scholars who were accused of a bourgeois mentality for highlighting the transnational cross-pollinations of elite cultures in literary texts rather than their demotic/vernacular rootedness. This was denounced as 'comparativism' during the Ždanov purges of 1946–48. Hence Žirmunskij's turn to the politically safer ground of oral epic and a more ethnographical approach.
3. Most Third Reich refugees eventually, unlike Prawer, left Britain: Milch, Steiner and Furst. Mention should also be made of John (Hans) Hennig (Leipzig 1911 — Basel 1986). A Lutheran theologian by training, former student of Rothacker and Ernst Robert Curtius, friend of Karl Jaspers, Catholic convert and married to a Jewish wife, he escaped with his family to Ireland in 1939, where he changed his first name from Hans to 'John'. He made his living outside academia

but kept up a steady stream of articles on German-English and German-Irish literary relations throughout the 1950s. Although he was made a member of the Royal Irish Academy in 1948, he returned to the Continent in 1956, maintaining, however, his interest in *Irlandkunde* (Irish Studies). The academic climate in Ireland at the time was not such that Hennig's interests could mesh with anything like a comparatist trend: the Comparative Literature Association of Ireland was not founded until 2007. On Hennig as a comparatist-in-isolation, see Hölfter & Rasche 2002.

4. In the original: 'ein Fach, das erfunden werden musste, um das alte bequeme Paradigma der Nationalhistorie zu sichern, und das die Einzelliteraturen als Wesenheiten sieht, die unter autochthonen Entwicklungsgesetzen stehen' (Jauss 1969, 9). Like most revolutionary proclamations, Jauss's case has its justifications but overshoots the mark. Hugo Dyserinck robustly rebutted Jauss's wholesale dismissal of Comparative Literature in the same issue of *Linguistische Berichte*, but his voice was drowned out in the fervour of the moment.

5. In Jacob Grimm's double sense: [1] 'explaining "how things are" from "how they became that way"' (*Das Sein aus dem Werden begreifen*) and [2] 'imaginatively entering into the pastness of the text' (*wir haben [...] uns in ganz geschwundene Umstände zu versetzen*). Cf. the entry 'Grimm, Jacob and Wilhelm', in ERNiE 2018.

6. The very notion of a *transfert culturel* was itself an instance of what it stood for: the concept was calqued on, and 'transferred from', the German *Kulturaustausch*; ironically, it was subsequently reimported into German, in its Espagne/Werner inflection, as *Kulturtransfer*.

7. I here follow Susan Bassnett's suggestion to that effect. The notion of the 'social life of texts' was elaborated into a methodology for Comparative Literature by the volume *Het leven van teksten* (Brillenburg Wurth & Rigney 2011, English version 2019)

SOURCE REFERENCES

1. Obituaries and articles from the *Oxford Dictionary of National Biography*

These notices provide background knowledge on which this book relies in instances so numerous and minute that they have, for the sake of readability, not been separately referenced within the text. Undated entries without further specification are DNB articles, consulted online at <http://www.oxforddnb.com>.

ADY, C. M. (revised by Diego Zancani). 'Toynbee, Paget Jackson (1855–1932)'
AUGSTEIN, H. F. 'Prichard, James Cowles (1786–1848)'
BARBER, GILES. 1987. 'Robert Shackleton, 1919–1986', *Proceedings of the British Academy*, 73: 657-84
BELL, ALAN. 'Saintsbury, George Edward Bateman (1845–1933)'
—— and KATHERINE DUNCAN-JONES. 'Lee, Sir Sidney (1859–1926)'
BORRIE, MICHAEL. 'Madden, Sir Frederic (1801–1873)'
CHAMBERS, R. W. (revised by A. S. G. Edwards). 'Ker, William Paton (1855–1923)'
DRAKAKIS, JOHN. 2014. 'Terence Hawkes Obituary', *The Guardian*, 21 February 2014
EDWARDS, PHILIP. 1996. 'Donald Alfred Davie, 1922–1995', *Proceedings of the British Academy*, 94: 391-412
FARGHER, RICHARD. 1978. 'Obituary: Dr R. A. Sayce, 11.1.1917 — 11.8.1977', *Modern Language Review* 73.4: xxxv-xxxvi
FLOOD, JOHN L. 'Robertson, John George (1867–1933)'
FRANCE, PETER. 'Starkie, Enid Mary (1897–1970)'
FREEDEN, MICHAEL. 'Robertson, John Mackinnon (1856–1933)'
FYNES, R. C. C. 'Müller, Friedrich Max (1823–1900)'
GREEN, JONATHON. 'Partridge, Eric Honeywood (1894–1979)'
GWYNN, E. J. (revised by Arthur Sherbo). 'Dowden, Edward (1843–1913)'
HAFFENDEN, JOHN. 'Empson, Sir William (1906–1984)'
HAMER, DAVID. 'Morley, John, Viscount Morley of Blackburn (1838–1923)'
HEYCK, THOMAS WILLIAM. 'Buckle, Henry Thomas (1821–1862)'
HOSKING, GEOFFREY. 2003. 'Henry Gifford: Devoted Scholar of European and Russian Literature', *The Guardian*, Saturday 6 December
HUNTER, FRED. 'Collins, John Churton (1848–1908)'
JACKSON, KENNETH. 1974. 'Nora Kershaw Chadwick, 1891–1972', *Proceedings of the British Academy*, 58: 537-49.
KENNEDY, EDWARD D. 2010. 'Lilian Renée Furst 1931–2009', *The Comparatist*, 34: 214–16
KNOBEL, PAUL. 'Chadwick [née Kershaw], Nora (1891–1972)'
L., J. 1979. 'Arthur Lytton Sells (1895–1978)', *French Studies* 33.2: 247
LANE-POOL, STANLEY (revised by J. B. Katz). 'Rosen, Friedrich August (1805–1837)'
LANG, TIMOTHY. 'Hallam, Henry (1777–1859)'
LLOYD, J. E. (revised by Brynley F. Roberts). 'Price, Thomas [*pseud.* Carnhuanawc] (1787-1848)'

LLOYD-JONES, HUGH. 1974. 'Sir Maurice Bowra, 1898–1971', *Proceedings of the British Academy*, 58: 393-408
MACKILLOP, IAN. 'Leavis, Frank Raymond (1895–1978)'
—— 'Leavis [née Roth], Queenie Dorothy 1906–1981)'
MURDOCH, BRIAN. 'Butler, Eliza Marian [Elsie] (1885–1959)'
PAULIN, ROGER. 'Breul, Karl Hermann (1860–1932)'
'Professor Henry Gifford', *Telegraph*, 18 December 2003
REED, T. J. 2015. 'Siegbert Salomon Prawer, 1925–2012', *Biographical Memoirs of Fellows of the British Academy*, 14: 519-27
RICKS, CHRISTOPHER. 1986. 'William Empson, 1906–1984', *Proceedings of the British Academy*, 71: 539-54
RUSSELL, P. E. L. R. (rev. M. C. Curthoys), 'Entwistle, William James (1895–1952)'
SANTINI, DARIA. 'Fiedler, Hermann Georg (1862–1945)'
SHELSTON, ALAN. 'Herford, Charles Harold (1853–1931)'
SKRINE, PETER. 1999. 'Leonard Wilson Forster, 1913–1997', *Proceedings of the British Academy*, 101: 365-75
SMITH, MICHAEL DOUGLAS. 'Couch, Sir Arthur Thomas Quiller- [*pseud.* Q] (1863–1944)'
SMITH, STAN. 1992. 'Professor Raman Selden, 13 December 1937 — 26 May 1991: An obituary', *Critical Survey* 4.3: 215–17
SPENCE, JOSEPH. 'Lecky, (William) Edward Hartpole (1838–1903)'
SPIVEY, ANGELA. 1996. 'Vita: Lilian Furst', *Endeavors: Reserach and Creative Activity at UBC-Chapel Hill*, Fall issue (September 1996), online at http://endeavors.unc.edu/aut96/vita.htm, last consulted 17 July 2018
STARK, SUSANNE. 'Bunsen, Christian Karl Josias von (1791–1860)'
STEPHENSON, R. H. 2003. 'Elizabeth Mary Wilkinson, 1909–2001', *Proceedings of the British Academy*, 120: 471-89
STORER, RICHARD. 'Richards, Ivor Armstrong (1893–1979)'
SUBIOTTO, A. V. 1982. 'Roy Pascal, 1904–1980', *Proceedings of the British Academy*, 67: 442-57
SWALES, MARTIN. 'Wilkinson, (Elizabeth) Mary (1909–2001)'
—— 'Willoughby, Leonard Ashley (1885–1977)'
TELFER, W. (revised by John D. Haigh). 'Chadwick, Hector Munro (1870–1947)'
THWAITE, ANN. 'Gosse, Sir Edmund William (1849–1928)'
WAGG, SHEILA M. 'Mason, Eudo Colecestra (1901–1969)'
WILLIAMS, MERRYN. 2014. 'Simon Curtis obituary', *The Guardian*, 12 January 2014
WOOD, MICHAEL. 2016. 'John Frank Kermode, 1919–2010', *Biographical Memoirs of Fellows of the British Academy*, 15: 326-42
WRIGHT, C. J. 'Holland House set (*act.* 1797–1845)'

2. Works cited in the text

AARSLEFF, HANS. 1967. *The Study of Language in England, 1780–1860* (Princeton, NJ: Princeton University Press)
ACKLAND, MICHAEL. 2004. *Henry Handel Richardson: A Life* (Cambridge: Cambridge University Press)
ANDERSON, WARREN. 1971. 'Matthew Arnold and the Grounds of Comparatism', *Comparative Literature Studies*, 8: 287–302
ANDREU, XAVIER. 2016. *El descubrimiento de la España: Mito romántico e identidad nacional* (Barcelona: Random House Spain)
APTER, EMILY. 1995. 'Comparative Exiles: Competing Margins in the History of Comparative Literature', in *Comparative Literature in the Age of Multiculturalism*, ed. C. Bernheimer (Baltimore, MD: Johns Hopkins University Press), 86–96

ARNOLD, MATTHEW. 1962. 'On the Study of Celtic Literature', in *Complete Prose Works 3: Lectures and Essays in Criticism*, ed. R. Super (orig. 1867; Ann Arbor, MI: University of Michigan Press), 291–395; 490–514
——. 1962. 'The Function of Criticism at the Present Time', in *Complete Prose Works 3: Lectures and Essays in Criticism*, ed. R. Super (orig. 1862; Ann Arbor, MI: University of Michigan Press), 158–285
AUGSTEIN, HANNAH FRANZISKA (ed.). 1996. *Race: The Origins of an Idea, 1760–1850* (Bristol: Thoemmes)
AUGSTEIN, HANNAH FRANZISKA. 1997. 'Linguistics and Politics in the Early 19th Century: James Cowles Prichard's Moral Philology', *History of European Ideas*, 23.1: 1–18
BALDICK, CHRIS. 1987. *The Social Mission of English Criticism, 1848–1932* (Oxford: Clarendon Press)
BANN, STEPHEN. 1995. 'Semiotics', in Selden 1995, 85–109
BARISH, EVELYN. 2014. *The Double Life of Paul de Man* (New York: Norton)
BASSNETT, SUSAN. 1993. *Comparative Literature: A Critical Introduction* (Oxford: Blackwell)
——. 2006. 'Reflections on Comparative Literature in the Twenty-First Century', *Comparative Critical Studies*, 3.1: 3–11.
BEATTIE, WILLIAM (ed.). 1850. *The Life and Letters of Thomas Campbell* (3 vols; London)
BELLOT, HUGH H. L. 1929. *University College London 1826–1926* (London)
BELL, MICHAEL. 2000. 'F. R. Leavis', in Litz, Menand & Rainey 2000, 389–422.
BERGER, STEFAN & CHRIS LORENZ (eds.). 2008. *Nationalizing the Past: Historians as Nation Builders in Modern Europe* (Basingstoke: Palgrave Macmillan)
BLACK, JOEL. 2000. 'Scientific Models', in Brown 2000, 115–37
BORGES, JOSÉ LUIS. 1985. *Prosa completa* (5 vols; Barcelona: Bruguera)
BRADY, CIARÁN. 1999. *Interpreting Irish History: The Debate on Historical Revisionism, 1938–1994* (Dublin: Irish Academic Press)
BREMNER, G. A., & JONATHAN CONLIN (eds.). 2015. *Making History: Edward Augustus Freeman and Victorian Cultural Politics* (Proceedings of the British Academy, 2012; London: British Academy)
BRIGGS, ASA. 1985. 'Saxons, Normans and Victorians', in Id., *Collected Essays: Images, Problems, Standpoints and Forecasts* (Urbana, IL: University of Illinois Press), 215–35
BRITTAIN, FREDERICK. 1947. *Arthur Quiller-Couch: A Biographical Study of Q* (Cambridge: Cambridge University Press)
BRITTAIN, VERA. 1992. *Testament of Friendship: The Story of Winifred Holtby* (orig. 1940; London: Virago)
BROWN, MARSHALL (ed.). 2008. *Romanticism* (The Cambridge History of Literary Criticism, vol. 5; Cambridge: Cambridge University Press)
BUCKLE, HENRY THOMAS. 1904. *Introduction to the History of Civilization of England* (orig. 1858; ed. J. M. Robertson; London)
BURKE, PETER. 2012. *A Social History of Knowledge II: From the Encyclopaedia to Wikipedia* (Cambridge: Polity)
BURKE, SEÁN. 2010. *The Death and Return of the Author: Criticism and Subjectivity in Barthes, Foucault, and Derrida* (Edinburgh: Edinburgh University Press).
CANNON, GARLAND. 1990. *The Life and Mind of 'Oriental' Jones: Sir William Jones, the Father of Modern Linguistics* (Cambridge: Cambridge university Press)
CHADWICK, HECTOR MUNRO & NORA KERSHAW CHADWICK. 1932–40. *The Growth of Literature* (3 vols; Cambridge: Cambridge University Press)
CHANCE, JANE (ed.). 2005. *Women Medievalists and the Academy* (Madison: University of Wisconsin Press)
CHANDLER, ALICE. 1998. 'Carlyle and the Medievalism of the North', in *Medievalism in the*

Modern World: Essays in Honour of Leslie Workman, ed. R. Utz & T. Shippey (Turnhout: Brepols), no pagination

CHATTERJEE, PRANAB. 2010. *A Story of Ambivalent Modernization in Bangladesh and West Bengal: The Rise and Fall of Bengali Elitism in South Asia* (Frankfurt etc.: Lang)

CHAUDHURI, NIRAD CHANDRA. 1974. *Scholar Extraordinary: The Life of Professor the Rt. Hon. Friedrich Max Müller, PC* (London: Chatto & Windus)

CLIVE, JOHN. 1957. *Scotch Reviewers: The Edinburgh Review, 1802–1815* (London: Faber)

COLLEY, LINDA. 1992. *Britons: Forging the Nation, 1701–1837* (New Haven, CT: Yale University Press).

COLLINS, JOHN CHURTON. 1908. *Voltaire, Rousseau and Montesquieu in England* (London)

CONSTANTINE, MARY-ANN. 2007. *The Truth against the World: Iolo Morganwg and Romantic Forgery* (Cardiff: University of Wales Press)

COSER, LEWIS A. 1984. *Refugee Scholars in America: Their impact and their experiences* (New Haven, CT: Yale University Press)

COULLING, SIDNEY. 1974. *Matthew Arnold and his Critics: A Study of Arnold's Controversies* (Athens, OH: Ohio University Press)

CRABB ROBINSON, HENRY. 1869. *Diary, Letters and Reminiscences* (3 vols; London)

——. 2010. *Essays on Kant, Schelling, and German Aesthetics* (ed. James Vigus; MHRA)

CUNNINGHAM, VALENTINE. 1998. 'Darke Conceits: Churton Collins, Edmund Gosse, and the Professions of Criticism', in Treglown & Bennett 1998, 72–90

CURTIS, L. P. 1968. *Anglo-Saxons and Celts: A study of Anglo-Irish prejudice in Victorian England* (University of Bridgeport, Conference on British Studies)

——. 1997. *Apes and Angels: The Irishman in Victorian Caricature* (revised ed.; Washington, DC: Smithsonian Institution)

DAMROSCH, DAVID. 2006. 'Rebirth of a Discipline: The Global Origins of Comparative Studies', *Comparative Critical Studies*, 3.1: 99–112

DASGUPTA, SUBRATA. 2011. *Awakening: The Story of the Bengal Renaissance* (Gurgaon: Random House India)

DAVIES, ANNA MORPURGO. 1998. *Nineteenth-Century Linguistics* (London: Longman)

DAVIS, JOHN R. & ANGUS NICHOLLS. 2016. 'Friedrich Max Müller: The Career and Intellectual Trajectory of a German Philologist in Victorian Britain', *Publications of the English Goethe Society* 85.2: 67–97.

—— —— (eds.). 2017. *Friedrich Max Müller and the Role of Philology in Victorian Thought* (London: Routledge).

DAYRAT, BENOÎT. 2003. 'The Roots of Phylogeny: How Did Haeckel Build his Tree?', *Systematic Biology*, 52.4: 515–27

DEKKERS, ODIN. 1998. *J. M. Robertson: Rationalist and Literary Critic* (Aldershot: Ashgate)

DELAURA, DAVID J. 1969. *Hebrew and Hellene in Victorian England: Newman, Arnold, and Pater* (Austin, TX: University of Texas Press)

DEMATA, M. & D. WU (eds.). 2002. *British Romanticism and the Edinburgh Review* (Basingstoke: Palgrave)

DOMÍNGUEZ, CÉSAR; HAUN SAUSSY & DARIO VILLANUEVA. 2015. *Introducing Comparative Literature: New Trends and Applications* (London: Routledge)

DOWDEN, EDWARD. 1864. *Considerations on the Criticism of Literature: An Address Delivered at the Opening of the Session 1863–64 of the Undergraduate Philosophical Society of the University of Dublin* (Dublin: McGee)

——. 1889. 'Goethe and the French Revolution', *Fortnightly Review*, 77–96

——. 1895. *New Studies in Literature* (London: Kegan Paul)

——. 1897. *The French Revolution and English Literature* (London: Kegan Paul)

DOWDEN, ELIZABETH D. & HILDA M. DOWDEN (eds.). 1914. *Letters of Edward Dowden and his Correspondents* (London: Dent)

DRYDEN, JOHN. 1971. 'Of Dramatick Poesie: An Essay', in *The Works of John Dryden*, ed. H. Swedenberg (Berkeley, CA), 17: 3–81
DURING, SIMON. 2004. 'Comparative Literature', *ELH*, 71: 313–22
DYSERINCK, HUGO. 1991. *Komparatistik: Eine Einführung* (orig. 1979; 3rd edn; Bonn: Bouvier)
EAGLETON, TERRY. 1976. *Criticism and Ideology* (London: New Left Books; new edn subtitled)
EIRANEN, REETTA. 2014. 'Kruununhaan piiri: Ryhmäbiografia ja fennomaaninen verkosto', *Ennen ja nyt: Historian tietosanomat* 6. ['The Kruununhaka circle: Group biography and a Fennoman network'; online at http://www.ennenjanyt.net/2014/06/kruununhaan-piiri-ryhmabiografia-ja-fennomaaninen-verkosto/]
ERNiE. 2018. *Encyclopedia of Romantic Nationalism in Europe* (ed. J. Leerssen; 2 vols; Amsterdam: Amsterdam University Press)
ESPAGNE, MICHEL & MICHAEL WERNER (eds.). 1990. *Philologiques I: Contribution à l'histoire des disciplines littéraires en France et en Allemagne au XIXe siècle* (Paris: Maison des Sciences de l'Homme)
FASSEL, HORST (ed.). 2005. *Hugo Meltzl und die Anfänge der Komparatistik* (Frankfurt: Steiner)
FAVERTY, FREDERIC E. 1968. *Matthew Arnold the Ethnologist* (New York: AMC Press)
FELSKI, RITA. 2011. 'Critique and the Hermeneutics of Suspicion' *M/C Journal*, 15.1; online at <http://journal.media-culture.org.au/index.php/mcjournal/article/view/431>
FIRCHOW, PETER E. 1986. *The Death of the German Cousin: Variations on a Literary Stereotype, 1890–1920* (Bucknell University Press)
FIRTH, CHARLES HARDING. 1929. *Modern Languages at Oxford* (Oxford University Press)
FISCHER-TINÉ, HARALD. 2011. 'Vom "Brothering" zum "Othering": Genese, Zirkulation und Transformation des Arya-Diskurses (ca. 1780–1890)', *Nach Feierabend: Zürcher Jahrbuch für Wissensgeschichte*, 7: 147–70
FLEMING, DONALD & BERNARD BAILYN. 1969. *The Intellectual Migration: Europe and America 1930–1960* (Cambridge, MA: Harvard University Press)
FLOOD, JOHN L. & ANNE SIMON (eds.). 2017. *Glanz und Abglanz: Two Centuries of German Studies in the University of London* (London: Institute of Modern Language Research)
FORBES, JILL. 1988. 'French Film Culture and British Cinema' in *Studies in Anglo-French Cultural Relations*, ed. Ceri Crossley & Ian Small (Basingstoke: Macmillan), 154–86
FRANKLIN, MICHAEL J. 2011. *'Orientalist Jones': Sir William Jones, Poet, Lawyer, and Linguist, 1746–1794* (Oxford: Oxford University Press)
FRANTZEN, ALLEN J. & JOHN D. NILES (eds). 1997. *Anglo-Saxonism and the Construction of Social Identity* (University Press of Florida)
FRASER, MAXWELL. 1962. 'The Girlhood of Augusta Waddington (afterwards Lady Llanover), 1802–1833'. *National Library of Wales Journal* 12: 305–22.
———. 1966. 'Sir Benjamin and Lady Hall in the 1840s (1840–1845)', *National Library of Wales Journal* 14: 35–42.
———. 1968. 'Lady Llanover and her Circle', *Transactions of the Honourable Society of Cymmrodorion* 1968, 170–96.
FRY, PAUL H. 2000. 'I. A. Richards', in Litz, Menand & Rainey 2000, 181–99
GANDHI, LEELA. 2006. *Affective Communities: Anticolonial Thought, Fin-de-Siècle Radicalism, and the Politics of Friendship*. Durham, NC: Duke University Press
GILLIES, ALEXANDER. 1952. 'Some Thoughts on Comparative Literature', *Yearbook of Comparative and General Literature*, 1: 15–25
GODLEY, A. D. 1908. *Oxford in the Eighteenth Century* (London)
GOETHE, JOHANN WOLFGANG VON. 1985–99. *Sämtliche Werke, Briefe, Tagebücher und Gespräche* (ed. Friedmar Apel et al.; Frankfurt: Deutscher Klassiker Verlag)
GOLDIE, DAVID. 2013. 'Literary Studies and the Academy', in Habib 2013, 46–71
GOMME, GEORGE LAURENCE. 1908. *Folklore as an Historical Science* (London: Methuen)

GOODMAN, SUSAN & CARL DAWSON. 2005. *William Dean Howells: A Writer's Life* (University of California Press)

GORMAN, DAVID. 1992. 'A Bibliography of Russian Formalism in English', *Style* 26.4: 554–76

GOULD, STEPHEN JAY. 1981. *The Mismeasure of Man* (New York: Norton)

GROSS, JOHN. 1969. *The Rise and Fall of the English Men of Letters* (London: Weidenfeld & Nicolson)

GRUBER, EDITH. 2014. *King Arthur and the Privy Councillor: Albert Schulz as a Cultural Mediator between the Literary Fields of Nineteenth-Century Wales and Germany* (PhD thesis, Bangor University)

GUEST, REVEL & ANGELA V. JOHN. 1989. *Lady Charlotte Guest: An extraordinary life* (London: Weidenfeld & Nicolson)

GUIOMAR, JEAN-YVES. 1997. 'Le "Barzaz-Breiz" de Théodore Hersart de la Villemarqué', in: *Les lieux de mémoire*, ed. Pierre Nora (Quarto ed.; Paris: Gallimard), 3: 3479–3514

GUY, JOSEPHINE M. & IAN SMALL. 2000. 'The British "Man of Letters" and the Rise of the Professional', in Litz, Menand & Rainey 2000, 377–88

HAARDER, ANDREAS & T. A. SHIPPEY (eds.). 1998. *Beowulf* (The Critical Heritage; London: Routledge)

HABIB, M. A. R. (ed.). 2013. *The Nineteenth Century, c. 1830–1914* (The Cambridge History of Literary Criticism, vol. 4; Cambridge: Cambridge University Press)

HALLAM, HENRY. 1837–39. *Introduction to the Literature of Europe in the Fifteenth, Sixteenth, and Seventeenth Centuries* (4 vols; London)

HAMBROOK, GLYN. 2014. '"Quoiqu'elle ne pousse ni grands gestes ni grands cris...": Comparative Literature in Great Britain', *Revue de Littérature comparée* 352: 393-408

HAUSMANN, FRANK-RUTGER. 1998. 'Auch eine nationale Wissenschaft? Die deutsche Romanistik unter dem Nationalsozialismus', *Romanistische Zeitschrift für Literaturgeschichte*, 22: 1–39, 261–313

HECHTER, MICHAEL. 1975. *Internal Colonialism: The Celtic Fringe in British National Development, 1536–1966* (London: Routledge & Kegan Paul)

HEILBUT, ANTHONY. 1981. *Exiled in Paradise: German Refugee Artists and Intellectuals in America from the 1930s to the Present* (New York: Viking)

HERFORD, CHARLES HAROLD. 1886. *Studies in the Literary Relations of England and Germany in the Sixteenth Century* (Cambridge: University Press)

HESKETH, IAN. 2012. *The Science of History in Victorian Britain* (London: Pickering & Chatto)

HOLFTER, GISELA & HERMAN RASCHE (eds.). 2002. *Exil in Irland: John Hennigs Schriften zu deutsch-irischen Beziehungen* (Trier: Wissenschaftlicher Verlag WVT).

HONAN, PARK. 1981. *Matthew Arnold: A Life* (London: Weidenfeld & Nicolson) Horsman, Reginald. 1981. *Race and Manifest Destiny: The Origins of American Racial Anglo-Saxonism* (Cambridge, MA: Harvard University Press)

HOROWITZ, JOSEPH. 2008. *Artists in Exile: How Refugees from Twentieth-Century War and Revolution Transformed the American Performing Arts* (New York: Harper)

HUMMEL, PASCALE. 2003. *Philologus auctor; Le philologue et son œuvre* (Bern: Lang)

JAGGI, MAYA. 2001. 'George and his Dragons', *The Guardian*, 17 March 2001

JAY, MARTIN. 1986. *Permanent Exiles: Essays on the Intellectual Migration from Germany to America* (New York: Columbia University Press)

KLANCHER, JON. 2000. 'Criticism and the Crisis of the Republic of Letters', in Brown 2000, 296–320

KLIGER, SAMUEL. 1952. *The Goths in England: A study in Seventeenth- and Eighteenth-century Thought* (Cambridge, MA: Harvard University Press)

KLING, BLAIR B. 1977. *Partner in Empire: Dwarkanath Tagore and the Age of Enterprise in Eastern India* (University of California Press)

KOPF, DAVID. 1969. *British Orientalism and the Bengal Renaissance* (University of California Press)
LATOUR, BRUNO. 2004. 'Why has Critique Run out of Steam? From Matters of Fact to Matters of Concern', *Critical Inquiry*, 30: 225–48.
LEE, SIDNEY. 1910. *The French Renaissance in England: An Account of the Literary Relations of England and France in the Sixteenth Century* (Oxford: Clarendon Press)
LEERSSEN, JOEP. 1989. 'Outer and Inner Others: The Auto-Image of French Identity from Mme de Staël to Eugène Sue', *Yearbook of European Studies*, 2: 35–52
———. 1996. 'Celticism', in *Celticism*, ed. T. Browne (Amsterdam: Rodopi), 1–20
———. 2004. 'Ossian and the Rise of Literary Historicism', in *The Reception of Ossian in Europe*, ed. H. Gaskill (London: Continuum), 109–25
———. 2004. 'Literary Historicism: Romanticism, Philologists, and the Presence of the Past', *Modern Language Quarterly*, 65.2: 221–43
———. 2006. 'Englishness, Ethnicity and Matthew Arnold', *European Journal of English Studies*, 10.1: 63–79
———. 2010. 'Some Notes on Hutcheson Macaulay Posnett (1855–1927)', in *Back to the Future of Irish Studies*, ed. M. O'Connor (Festschrift Tadhg Foley; Frankfurt: Lang), 111–19
———. 2011. 'Viral Nationalism: Romantic Intellectuals on the Move in Nineteenth-Century Europe', *Nations and Nationalism*, 17.2: 257–71
———. 2012A. 'Oral Epic: The Nation Finds a Voice', in *Folklore and Nationalism in Europe during the Long Nineteenth Century*, ed. T. Baycroft & D. Hopkin (Leiden: Brill), 11–26
———. 2012B. 'The Rise of Philology: The Comparative Method, the Historicist Turn and the Surreptitious Influence of Giambattista Vico', in *The Making of the Humanities*, ed. R. Bod, J. Maat, and T. Weststeijn (2: *From early modern to modern disciplines*; Amsterdam: Amsterdam University Press), 23–35
———. 2015. 'Comparing What, Precisely? H. M. Posnett and the Conceptual History of "Comparative Literature"', *Comparative Critical Studies*, 12.2: 197–212
———. 2018. *National Thought in Europe: A Cultural History* (3rd ed.; Amsterdam University Press)
———. 2019. 'The North: A Stereotype between Cultural Metaphor and Racial Essentialism', in *Northern Myths, Modern Identities: The Nationalisation of Northern Mythologies since 1800* (Leiden: Brill), 13–32
LEITHMANN, PETER THEODOR. 1977. 'Moriz Carrière and the Development of Comparative Literature' (doctoral thesis; Nashville, TN: Vanderbilt University)
[LEMON, E.] 1958. 'The Gaudy', *St Hugh's College, Association of Senior Members, Newsletter* 30 (1957–58): 8–11
LENNON, JOSEPH. 2007. 'Fasting for the Public: Irish and Indian Sources of Marion Wallace Dunlop's 1909 Hunger Strike', in *Enemies of Empire: New Perspectives on Imperialism, Literature and History*, ed. E. Flannery (Dublin: Four Courts), 19–39.
LIJPHART, AREND. 1971. 'Comparative Politics and the Comparative Method', *American Political Science Review*, 65.3: 682–93
LINDEN, NANNE VAN DER. 2016. 'Dorothea Schlegel: Sociabiliteit en convivialiteit: Een proof of concept van de sociale netwerkanalyse in de cultuurgeschiedenis' (Master's thesis; University of Amsterdam)
LITZ, A. WALTON, LOUIS MENAND & LAWRENCE RAINEY (eds.). 2000. *Modernism and the New Criticism* (*The Cambridge History of Literary Criticism*, vol. 4; Cambridge: Cambridge University Press)
MACDOUGALL, HUGH. 1982. *Racial Myth in English History: Trojans, Teutons, and Anglo-Saxons* (Hanover, NH: University Press of New England)
MACHANN, CLINTON. 1998. *Matthew Arnold: A Literary Life* (Basingstoke: Macmillan)

MARTÍ MONTERDE, ANTONI. 2011. *Un somni europeu: Història intel·lectual de la Literatura Comparada: De la 'Weltliteratur' a la Literatura Comparada* (Valencia: Universitat de València)
MARTIN, WALLACE. 2000. 'Criticism and the Academy', in Litz, Menand & Rainey 2000, 269–321
MAUFROY, SANDRINE. 2011. 'Friedrich August Wolf, un modèle philologique et ses incidences européennes', *Revue germanique internationale* 14: 27–40
MCCORMACK, W. J. 1985. 'The Question of Celticism', in *Ascendancy and Tradition in Anglo-Irish Literary History from 1789 to 1939* (Oxford: Clarendon Press), 219–38
MCCUTCHION, DAVID. 1966. 'Comparative Literature in England', *Jadavpur Journal of Comparative Literature*, 6: 145–49
MCMURTRY, JO. 1985. *English Language, English Literature: The Creation of an Academic Discipline* (London: Mansell)
MCNALLY, S. J. 1976. *The Chaplains of the East India Company* (London: India Office Records)
MELL, JULIE & MALACHI HACOHEN. 2014. *Central European Jewish Émigrés and the Shaping of Postwar Culture: Studies in memory of Lilian Furst (1931–2009)* (special issue of *Religions*; Basel: MDPI)
MENAND, LOUIS. 2000. 'T. S. Eliot', in Litz, Menand & Rainey 2000, 17–56
MERZ, JOHN THEODORE. 1903–14. *A History of European Thought in the Nineteenth Century* (4 vols; Edinburgh & London)
MOORE, GREGORY. 2013. 'Literary Criticism and Models of Science', in Habib 2013, 565–87
MORGAN, GERALD. 2005. 'A Scholar of Early Britain: Rachel Bromwich (1915–)', in Chance 2005, 769–780
MORLEY, EDITH. 2016. *Before and After: Reminiscences of a Working Life*, ed. Barbara Morris (Reading: Two Rivers Press)
MOUNTFORD, JAMES. 1966. *British Universities* (London)
MUDDE, CAS & CRISTÓBAL ROVIRA KALTWASSER. 2017. *Populism: A Very Short Introduction* (Oxford: Oxford University Press)
MUKHERJEE, S. N. 1968. *Sir William Jones: A Study in Eighteenth-century British Attitudes to India* (Cambridge: Cambridge University Press)
MÜLLER, MAX. 1854. *Letters to Chevalier Bunsen on the classification of the Turanian languages* (London)
———. 1994. *Lectures on the Science of Language* (orig. 1861–64; intr. Roy Harris; 2 vols; London: Routledge/Thoemmes)
MÜLLER, JAN WERNER. 2016. *What is Populism?* (Philadelphia, PA: University of Pennsylvania Press)
NAIDITCH, P. G. 1988. *A. E. Housman at University College London: The Election of 1892* (Leiden: Brill)
NICHOLLS, ANGUS. 2015. 'Max Müller and the Comparative Method', *Comparative Critical Studies* 12.2: 213-34
———. 2018. 'The "Goethean" Discourses on *Weltliteratur* and the Origins of Comparative Literature: The Cases of Hugo Meltzl and Hutcheson Macaulay Posnett', *seminar* 54.2: 167–94.
NISBET, H. B. & C. RAWSON (eds.). 2008. *The Eighteenth Century* (The Cambridge History of Literary Criticism, vol. 3; Cambridge: Cambridge University Press)
NORMAN, FREDERICK. 1930. *Henry Crabb Robinson and Goethe* (Publications of the English Goethe Society, 6; London: English Goethe Society)
OERGEL, MAIKE. 1998. 'The Redeeming Teuton: Nineteenth-Century Notions of the "Germanic" in England and Germany', in *Imagining Nations*, ed. Geoffrey Cubitt (Manchester: Manchester University Press), 75–91.

PALMER, D. J. 1965. *The Rise of English Studies: An Account of the Study of English Language and Literature from its Origins to the Making of the Oxford English School* (London: University of Hull)

PARKER, JOANNE. 2007. *'England's Darling': The Victorian cult of Alfred the Great* (Manchester University Press)

—— (ed.). 2015. *The Harp and the Constitution: Myths of Celtic and Gothic Origin* (Leiden: Brill)

PARKER, MARK. 2000. *Literary Magazines and British Romanticism* (Cambridge: Cambridge University Press)

PARTRIDGE, ERIC H. 1926. *A Critical Medley: Essays, Studies, and Notes in English, French, and Comparative Literature* (Paris: Champion)

PEACOCK, SANDRA J. 2006. 'Struggling with the Daimon: Eliza M. Butler on Germany and Germans', *History of European Ideas*, 21: 99–115

PENNY, FRANK. 1922. *The Church in Madras: The History of the Ecclesiastical and Missionary Action of the East India Company in the Presidency of Madras from 1835 to 1861* (London: Murray)

PERKINS, DAVID. 2000. 'Literary History and Historicism', in Brown 2000, 338–61

POSNER, ROLAND. 1988. 'What is an Academic Discipline?', in *Gedankenzeichen: Festschrift für Klaus Oehler zum 60. Geburtstag*, ed. R. Claussen and R. Daube-Schakat (Tübingen: Stauffenburg), 165–85

POSNETT, HUTCHESON MACAULAY. 1886. *Comparative Literature* (London: Routledge & Kegan Paul)

——. 1901. 'The Science of Comparative Literature', *Contemporary Review*, 79: 855–72

PRATT, LYNDA, TIM FULFORD, and IAN PACKER. 2009. 'The Collected Letters of Robert Southey', online at *Romantic Circles*, <https://www.rc.umd.edu/editions/southey_letters> (last consulted 15 September 2018)

PRAWER, S. S. 1973. *Comparative Literary Studies: An Introduction* (London: Duckworth)

——. 2005. *Between Two Worlds: The Jewish Presence in German and Austrian Film, 1910–1933* (London: Berghahn)

PRICE, THOMAS. 1859. *Literary Remains* (ed. Jane Williams (Ysgafell); 2 vols; Llandovery: Rees — London: Longman)

REDDING, CYRUS. 1860. *Literary Reminiscences and Memoirs of Thomas Campbell* (2 vols; London)

RICHARDSON, W. F. 1968. *Fifty Years of of Classics: A Study of the Classics Department of the Auckland University College, 1883–1933* (Auckland, NZ)

RIDOUX, CHARLES. 2001. *Evolution des études médiévales en France de 1860 à 1914* (Paris: Champion)

RIGNEY, ANN. 2001. *Imperfect Histories. The Elusive Past and the Legacy of Romantic Historicism* (Ithaca, NY: Cornell University Press)

——. 2007. 'Being an Improper Historian', in *Manfestos for History*, ed. S. Morgan, K. Jenkins & A. Munslow (London: Routledge), 149–59

ROBERTSON, JOHN GEORGE. 1923. *Studies in the Genesis of Romantic Theory in the Eighteenth Century* (Cambridge: Cambridge University Press)

——. 1925. *Goethe and Byron* (Publications of the English Goethe Society, NS 2; London)

——. 1933. 'Charles Harold Herford', *Proceedings of the British Academy*, 17: no pagination

——. 1935. *Essays and Addresses on Literature* (ed. Edna Purdie; London: Routledge)

ROE, FREDERICK C. 1954. 'Comparative Literature in the United Kingdom', *Yearbook of Comparative and General Literature*, 3: 1–12

ROTHACKER, ERICH. 1923. 'Savigny, Grimm, Ranke: Ein Beitrag zur Frage nach dem Zusammenhang der Historischen Schule', *Historische Zeitschrift*, 128.3: 415–45

ROUTH, HAROLD VICTOR. 1913. 'The Future of Comparative Literature', *Modern Language Review*, 7: 1–14

ROYAL COMMISSION. 1852. *Report of Her Majesty's Commissioners Appointed to Inquire into the State, Discipline, and Revenues of the University and Colleges of Oxford, Presented to both Houses of Parliament by Command of Her Majesty* (London)

SAINTSBURY, GEORGE EDWARD BATEMAN. 1907. *The Later Nineteenth Century* (Edinburgh & London)

———. 1900–04. *A History of Criticism and Literary Taste in Europe from the Earliest Texts to the Present Day* (3 vols; Edinburgh & London)

SANDBACH, FRANCIS EDWARD. 1903. *The Nibelungenlied and Gudrun in England and America* (London)

SAUSSY, HAUN. 2006. 'Exquisite Cadavers Stitched from Fresh Nightmares: Of Memes, Hives, and Selfish Genes', in *Comparative Literature in an Age of Globalization*, ed. H. Saussy (Princeton, NJ: Princeton University Press), 3–42.

SCHIRMER, WALTER F. 1947. *Der Einfluß der deutschen Literatur auf die Englische im 19. Jahrhundert* (Halle /Saale)

SCHLEGEL, FRIEDRICH. 1988. 'Geschichte der alten und neuen Literatur. Vorlesungen, gehalten zu Wien im Jahre 1812', in *Kritische Schriften und Fragmente: Studienausgabe*, ed. E. Behler & H. Eichner (orig. 1815; 6 vols; Paderborn: Schöningh), 4: 1–234

———. 1995. 'Über die Sprache und Weisheit der Indier. Ein Beitrag zur Begründung der Alterthumskunde', in *Kritische Friedrich-Schlegel-Ausgabe*, ed. E. Behler (orig. 1808; Munich: Schöningh), 8: 105–443

SCRAGG, DONALD & CAROLE WEINBERG (eds.). 2000. *Literary Appropriations of the Anglo-Saxons from the Thirteenth to the Twentieth Century* (Cambridge: Cambridge University Press)

SELDEN, RAMAN (ed.). 1995. *From Formalism to Poststructuralism* (The Cambridge History of Literary Criticism, vol. 8; Cambridge: Cambridge University Press)

SHAFFER, ELINOR S. 1979. 'Comparative Literature in Britain', *Comparative Criticism: A Yearbook*, 1: ix-xix

SHATTOCK, JOANNE. 1989. *Politics and Reviewers: The Edinburgh and the Quarterly in the Early Victorian Age* (Leicester: Leicester University Press)

———. 2013. 'Contexts and Conditions of Criticism, 1830–1914', in Habib 2013, 21–45

SHIPPEY, TOM. 2008. 'The Case of Beowulf', in *Editing the Nation's Memory: Textual Scholarship and Nation-Building in 19th-Century Europe* (Amsterdam: Rodopi), 223- 239

SINCLAIR, K. 1983. *A History of the University of Auckland 1883–1983* (Auckland: Auckland University Press)

SLEZKINE, JURI. 2004. *The Jewish Century* (Princeton, NJ: Princeton University Press), esp. parts 1 and 2: 'Jews and other Nomads' and 'Jews and other Moderns'

SMALL, IAN. 1991. *Conditions for Criticism: Authority, Knowledge, and Literature in the Late Nineteenth Century* (Oxford: Clarendon Press)

SMITH, GEORGE GREGORY. 1901. 'The Foible of Comparative Literature', *Blackwood's Edinburgh Magazine*, 169: 38–48. [again in *Yearbook of Comparative and General Literature*, 19 (1970): 58–66]

SNOWMAN, DANIEL. 2002. *The Hitler Emigrés: The Cultural Impact on Britain of Refugees from Nazism* (London: Chatto & Windus)

SPENCER, TERENCE. 1954. *Fair Greece, Sad Relic: Literary Philhellenism from Shakespeare to Byron* (London: Weidenfeld & Nicolson)

SPIERING, MENNO (ed.). 1999. *Nation Building and Writing Literary History* (Yearbook of European Studies, 12; Amsterdam: Rodopi)

ST CLAIR, WILLIAM. 1972. *That Greece Might Still Be Free: The Philhellene in the War of Independence* (Oxford)

STEENBERGH, KRISTINE. 2014. 'Compassion and the Creation of an Affective Community in the Theatre: Vondel's *Mary Stuart, or Martyred Majesty* (1646)', *BMGN — Low Countries Historical Review* 129.2: 90–112.

STELZIG, EUGENE L. 2009. *Henry Crabb Robinson in Germany: A Study in Nineteenth-Century Life Writing* (Lewisburg, PA: Bucknell University Press)

STEPHEN, LESLIE. 1899. 'The Cosmopolitan Spirit in Literature', *National Review*, 34: 378-392

STOCKING, GEORGE W. 1987. *Victorian Anthropology* (New York: Free Press)

STRAUBHAAR, SANDRA BALLIF. 2008. '"An Extraordinary Sense of Powerful Restlessness": Nora Kershaw Chadwick (1891–1972)', in Chance 2005, 367–97

SUTHERLAND, JOHN. 1998. 'Journalism, Scholarship, and the University College London English Department', in Treglown & Bennett 1998, 58–71.

SWEET, PAUL ROBINSON. 1978–80. *Wilhelm von Humboldt: A Biography* (2 vols; Columbus, OH: Ohio State University Press)

TEXTE, JOSEPH. 1893. 'Les études de littérature comparée à l'étranger et en France', *Revue internationale de l'enseignement*, 85: 253–69

THIEME, HUGO P. 1901. 'Joseph Texte', *Modern Language Notes*, 16: 198–202. [columns 396–404]

THORLBY, ANTHONY. 1969. 'Comparative Literature', *Yearbook of Comparative and General Literature*, 18: 75–81

TIMPANARO, SEBASTIANO. 1963. *La genesi del metodo del Lachmann* (Firenze: Le Monnier)

Trautmann, Thomas R. 1997. *Aryans and British India* (Berkeley, CA: U of California Press)

TUCKER, T. G. 1907. *The Foreign Debt of English Literature* (London: Bell)

TREGLOWN, JEREMY & BRIDGET BENNETT (eds.). 1998. *Grub Street and the Ivory Tower: Literary Journalism and Literary Scholarship from Fielding to the Internet* (Oxford: Clarendon Press)

WAARD, MARCO DE. 2007. 'John Morley and the Liberal Imagination: The Uses of History in English Liberal Culture, 1867–1914' (unpublished doctoral thesis; Florence: European University Institute)

WARNER, MARINA. 2014. 'Diary', *London Review of Books*, 36.17 (11 September 2014): 42–43

WATSON, GEORGE. 1964. *The Literary Critics: A Study of English Descriptive Criticism* (London: Chatto & Windus)

WAWN, ANDREW. 2000. *The Vikings and the Victorians: Inventing the Old North in Nineteenth-Century Britain* (Cambridge: Brewer)

WEISSTEIN, ULRICH. 1968. *Einführung in die Vergleichende Literaturwissenschaft* (Stuttgart)

Wellek, René. 1941. *The Rise of English Literary History* (Chapel Hill, NC)

——. 1997. 'From Ecstasy to Agony: The Rise and Fall of Comparative Literature', *Neohelicon* 24.2: 95–118

WELLEK, RENÉ. 1970. 'The Name and Nature of Comparative Literature', in *Discriminations: Further Concepts of Criticism* (New Haven: University of North Carolina Press), 1–36

——. 1961–92. *A History of Modern Criticism* (London: Cape)

WHEATLAND, THOMAS. 2009. *The Frankfurt School in Exile* (Minneapolis: University of Minnesota Press)

WILLOUGHBY, LEONARD A. 1950. 'Stand und Aufgaben der Vergleichenden Literaturgeschichte in England', in *Forschungsprobleme der Vergleichenden Literaturgeschichte. Internationale Beiträge zur Tübinger Literarhistoriker-Tagung, Sept. 1950*, ed. K. Wais (2 vols; Tübingen), 1: 21–28

WISEMAN, NICHOLAS. 1866. 'On the Comparative Study of Languages', in *Twelve Lectures on the Connexion between Science and Revealed Religion, Delivered in Rome* (orig. 1835; Dublin), 34–39

WOOD, MICHAEL. 2000. 'William Empson', in Litz, Menand & Rainey 2000, 219–34
WRENN, CHARLES LESLIE. 1969. *The Idea of Comparative Literature* (MHRA)
YOUNG, ROBERT J. C. 2008. *The Idea of English Ethnicity* (Oxford: Blackwell)

APPENDIX

A Chronological List of British Publications of Comparatist Interest, 1800–1975

This list also includes Irish publications. From 1975 on, annual bibliographies were published in *Comparative Criticism: An Annual Journal* (Cambridge University Press, 1979–2003). The list here as given here has been compounded from the ones in *Comparative Criticism* 7 (1985): 303–16 (covering 1800–1950); 8 (1986): 341–59 (covering 1951–1960); 9 (1987): 339–64 (covering 1961–1965); 11 (1989): 277–98 (covering 1966–70) and 15 (1993): 293–313 (covering 1971–1974). The work of Glyn Tegai Hughes in compiling some of these is gratefully acknowledged.

This list uses the *Comparative Criticism* house style, which omits the place of publication in the case of university presses. For post-1900 publications, the place of publication (for publishers other than university presses) is London unless otherwise stated.

Abbreviations

BRLC	Bibliothèque de la Revue de Littérature Comparée
GLL	German Life and Letters
MLR	Modern Language Review
MHRA	Modern Humanities Research Association
OSMLL	Oxford Studies in Modern Languages and Literatures (ed. H. G. Fiedler)
PEGS	Publications of the English Goethe Society
PEL	Periods of European Literature (ed. G. E. B. Saintsbury; 12 vols, in all)
RLC	Revue de Littérature Comparée

1800

DIBDIN, CHARLES. *A Complete History of the English Stage: Introduced by a Comparative and Comprehensive Review of the Asian, the Grecian, the Roman, the Spanish, the Italian and Other Theatres*, 5 vols (The Author)

1802

SCOTT, WALTER. *Minstrelsy of the Scottish Border*, 3 vols (Kelso: Ballantyne). Contains 'Introductory Remarks on Popular Poetry'.

1814

DUNLOP, JOHN. *The History of Fiction: Being a Critical Account of the Most Celebrated Prose Works of Fiction, from the Earliest Greek Romances to the Novels of the Present Age*, 3 vols (Longman, Hurst, Rees, Orme & Brown)

1821

CAMPBELL, THOMAS. 'Lectures on Poetry', *New Monthly Magazine*, 1: 139 ff.

1824

SCOTT, SIR WALTER. ENTRIES 'Romance' and 'Drama', *Encyclopaedia Britannica* (supplement to the 5th edn)

1831

COLLIER, JOHN. *The History of English Dramatic Poetry to the Time of Shakespeare*, 3 vols (John Murray)

1832

HALLAM, ARTHUR H., *Oration on the Influence of Italian Works of Imagination on the same Class of Compositions in English* (Cambridge: W. Metcalfe)

1837

HALLAM, HENRY. *Introduction to the Literature of Europe in the 15th, 16th, and 17th Centuries*, 4 vols (John Murray)

1839

[HARDING, JOHN DORNEY] *An Essay on the Influence of Welsh Tradition upon European Literature; which obtained the Prize Proposed by the Abergavenny Cymreigyddion Society, October 1838* (Ibotson and Palmer)

1841

SCHULZ, ALBERT. *An Essay on the Influence of Welsh Tradition upon the Literature of Germany, France, and Scandinavia; which Obtained the Prize of the Abergavenny Cymreigyddion Society at the Eisteddvod of 1840* [trl. Charlotte Berrington] (Llandovery: William Rees)

1852

DALLAS, E. S. *Poetics: an Essay on Poetry* (Smith Elder)
PRICE, THOMAS. *The Literary Remains of the Rev. Thomas Price, Carnhuanawc*, 2 vols (Llandovery: Rees; London: Longman). Contains essays 'On the Influence which the Welsh Traditions have had on the Literature of Europe' (1838) and 'On the Comparative Merits of Ancient Literature in the Welsh, Irish, and Gaelic Languages, and their value in Elucidating the Ancient History and the Mental Cultivation of the Inhabitants of Britain, Ireland, and Gaul' (1845)

1857

BUCKLE, HENRY THOMAS. *History of Civilization in England*, 2 vols (Parker)

1861

ARNOLD, MATTHEW. *On Translating Homer* (Longman)

1864

DOWDEN, EDWARD, *Considerations on the Criticism of Literature* (Dublin: McGee)

1865

ARNOLD, MATTHEW. *Essays in Criticism,* 2nd ser (London and Cambridge: Macmillan)

1866

DALLAS, E. S. *The Gay Science,* 2 vols (Chapman & Hall)

1867

ARNOLD, MATTHEW. *On the Study of Celtic Literature* (Smith Elder)

1873

BUCHANAN, ROBERT. *Master-Spirits* (H. S. King; Contains an essay on 'Tennyson, Heine and de Musset')
PATER, WALTER. *Studies in the History of the Renaissance* (Macmillan)

1877

MEREDITH, GEORGE. 'On the Idea of Comedy, and of the Uses of the Comic Spirit', *New Quarterly Magazine*, April

1879

GOSSE, EDMUND. *Studies in the Literature of Northern Europe* (Kegan Paul)

1880

METCALFE, FREDERICK. *The Englishman and the Scandinavian; Or a Comparison of Anglo-Saxon and Old Norse Literature* (Trübner)

1886

HERFORD, C. H. *Studies in the Literary Relations of England and Germany in the Sixteenth Century* (Cambridge University Press)
POSNETT, H. M. *Comparative Literature,* International Scientific Series, 55 (Kegan Paul, Trench, Trübner)

1889

DOWDEN, EDWARD, 'Goethe and the French Revolution', *Fortnightly Review*, 77–96

1890

SYMONDS, J. A. *Essays, Speculative and Suggestive.* 2 vols (Chapman & Hall)

1892

ROBERTSON, JOHN GEORGE. *Zur Kritik Jacob Ayrers, mit besonderer Rücksicht auf sein Verhältnis zu Hans Sachs und den englischen Komedianten.* (Leipzig-Reudnitz, doctoral dissertation)

1893

ALFORD, R. G. 'Goethe's Earliest Critics in England', **PEGS**, 7

1895

DOWDEN, EDWARD. *New Studies in Literature* (Kegan Paul)

1896

SNELL, F. J. *Dante in America* (London)

1897

DOWDEN, EDWARD. *The French Revolution and English Literature* (Kegan Paul)
KER, W. P. *Epic and Romance. Essays on Medieval Literature* (Macmillan)
ROBERTSON, JOHN MACKINNON. *Montaigne and Shakespeare* (London University Press)
SAINTSBURY, GEORGE. *The Flourishing of Romance and the Rise of Allegory*, **PEL**, 2 (Edinburgh and London: Blackwood)

1898

HANNAY, DAVID. *The Later Renaissance*, **PEL**, 6 (Edinburgh and London: Blackwood)
LEWES, GEORGE H. *The Principles of Success in Literature* (1865). (Scott)

1899

CRAWFORD, VIRGINIA M. *Studies in Foreign Literature* (Duckworth)
ELTON, OLIVER. *The Augustan Ages*, **PEL**, 8 (Edinburgh and London: Blackwood)
SNELL, F. J. *The Fourteenth Century*, **PEL**, 3 (Edinburgh and London: Blackwood)
STEPHEN, LESLIE. 'The Cosmopolitan Spirit in Literature', *National Review*, 34, 378–92

1900

OMOND, T. S. *The Romantic Triumph*, **PEL**, 11 (Edinburgh and London: Blackwood)
SAINTSBURY, GEORGE. *A History of Criticism and Literary Taste in Europe from the Earliest Texts to the Present Day*, 3 vols (Edinburgh and London: Blackwood, 1900–04)
SMITH, G. GREGORY. *The Transition Period*, **PEL**, 4 (Edinburgh and London: Blackwood)

1901

[SMITH, G.GREGORY]. 'The Foible of Comparative Literature', *Blackwood's Edinburgh Magazine*, 169, 38–48. Reprinted in *Yearbook of Comparative and General Literature*, 19 (1970), 58–66
POSNETT, H. M. 'The Science of Comparative Literature', *Contemporary Review*, 79, 855–72
SAINTSBURY, GEORGE. *The Earlier Renaissance*, **PEL**, 5 (Edinburgh and London: Blackwood)
WHITTUCK, CHARLES AUGUSTUS. *The 'Good Man' of the Eighteenth Century: Monograph on Eighteenth-Century Didactic Literature* (George Allen)

1902

MILLAR, J. H. *The Mid-Eighteenth Century*, **PEL**, 9 (Edinburgh and London: Blackwood)

1903

MERZ, JOHN THEODORE. *A History of European Thought in the XlXth Century*, 4 vols (Edinburgh and London: Blackwood, 1903–14)
SANDBACH, FRANCIS EDWARD. *The Nibelungenlied and Gudrun in England and America* (David Nutt)

TOYNBEE, PAGET. 'English Translations from Dante (Fourteenth to Seventeenth Century)', *Journal of Comparative Literature*, 1, 345–65

1904

KER, W. P. *The Dark Ages*, PEL, 1 (Edinburgh and London: Blackwood)

1905

GOSSE, EDMUND. *French Profiles* (Heinemann). Contains an essay on 'The Influence of France upon English Poetry'
HUME, MARTIN. *Spanish Influences on English Literature* (Eveleigh Nash)
REA, THOMAS. 'Schiller's *Räuber* in England', *Studien zur vergleichenden Literaturgeschichte* Erg. Bd., 5, 162–70
SMITH, G. GREGORY. 'Some Notes on the Comparative Study of Literature', MLR, 1: 1–8
TOYNBEE, PAGET. 'English Translations of Dante in the Eighteenth Century', MLR, 1: 9–24

1906

GRIERSON, HERBERT J. C. *The First Half of the Seventeenth Century*, PEL, 7 (Edinburgh and London: Blackwood)
REA, THOMAS. *Schiller's Dramas and Poems in England* (Fisher Unwin)
ROBERTSON, JOHN GEORGE. 'The Knowledge of Shakespeare on the Continent at the Beginning of the XVIIIth Century', MLR, 1: 312–21
—— 'Lessing and Farquhar', MLR, 2: 56–59

1907

FITZMAURICE-KELLY, JAMES. 'Tercentenary of "Don Quixote". Cervantes in England', *Proceedings of the British Academy* 1905–06
HUTTON, W. H. 'The Influence of Dante on Spanish Literature', MLR, 3: 105–25
JONES, G. HARTWELL. 'Italian Influences on Celtic Culture', *Transactions of the Honourable Society of Cymmrodorion* 1905–06: 84–160
KASTNER, L. E. 'The Elizabethan Sonneteers and the French Poets', MLR, 3: 268–77
—— 'The Scottish Sonneteers and the French Poets', MLR, 3: 1–15
ROBERTSON, JOHN GEORGE. 'Shakespeare on the Continent', chapter 12 in The *Cambridge History of English Literature*, ed. A. W. Ward & A. R. Waller (Cambridge University Press, 1907–10), 5: 283–308
SAINTSBURY, GEORGE. *The Later Nineteenth Century*, PEL, 12 (Edinburgh and London: Blackwood)
TUCKER, T. G. *The Foreign Debt of English Literature* (George Bell)
VAUGHAN, CH.E. *The Romantic Revolt*, PEL, 10 (Edinburgh and London: Blackwood)

1908

COLLINS, JOHN CHURTON. 'The Literary Indebtedness of England to France', *Fortnightly Review*, 185–200
—— *Voltaire, Rousseau and Montesquieu in England* (Eveleigh Nash)
GUNNELL, DORIS. *Stendhal et l'Angleterre* (Paris: Champion)
KASTNER, L. E. 'Spenser's "Amoretti" and Desportes', MLR, 4: 65–69
KER, W. P. 'Dante, Guido Guinicelli and Arnaut Daniel', MLR, 4: 45–52
ROBERTSON, JOHN GEORGE. 'Milton's Fame on the Continent', *Proceedings of the British Academy* 1907–1908: 319–40

1909

HUME, MARTIN. 'Some Spanish Influences in Elizabethan Literature' (read 24 Feb. 1909), *Royal Society of the United Kingdom. Essays by Divers Hands*, 2nd ser. 24: 1–34

JONES, W. LEWIS. 'The Literary Relationships of Dafydd ap Gwilym', *Transactions of the Honourable Society of Cymmrodorion* 1907–08: 118–53

TOYNBEE, PAGET. *Dante in English Literature from Chaucer to Cary*, 2 vols (Methuen)

1910

COLLINS, JOHN CHURTON. *Greek Influence on English Poetry*, ed. Michael Macmillan (Pitman)

FITZMAURICE-KELLY, JAMES. *The Relations between Spanish and English Literature* (Liverpool University Press)

KASTNER, L. E. 'Drummond of Hawthornden and the French Poets of the Sixteenth Century', MLR, 5: 40–53

LEE, SIDNEY. *The French Renaissance in England. An Account of the Literary Relations of England and France in the Sixteenth Century* (Oxford: Carendon)

VAUGHAN, CH. E. 'Carlyle and his German Masters', *Studies by Members of the English Association*, 1: 168–96

1911

HEDGCOCK, FRANK. *Un acteur cosmopolite: David Garrick et ses amis français* (Paris: Hachette; English translation: Stanley Paul, 1912)

KASTNER, L. E. 'On the Italian and French Sources of Drummond of Hawthornden', MLR, 6: 462–70

LOCKITT, CHARLES. *Relations of French and English Society 1763–1793* (Longman)

SPURGEON, CAROLINE F. E. *Chaucer devant la critique en Angleterre et France depuis son temps jusqu'à nos jours* (Paris: Hachette)

THOMAS, ALAN BURDETT. *Moore en France. Contribution à l'histoire de la fortune des œuvres de Thomas Moore dans la littérature française, 1819–1830* (Paris: Champion)

1912

KASTNER, L. E. 'The Italian Sources of Daniel's "Delia"', MLR, 7: 153–56

WILLOUGHBY, LEONARD A. *Dante Gabriel Rossetti and German Literature* (Oxford: Henry Frowde)

1913

LINDSAY, JAMES. *A Critical Essay on European Literature* (Edinburgh: William Blackwood)

ROUTH, H. V. 'The Future of Comparative Literature', MLR, 8: 1–14

TURQUET-MILNES, GLADYS R. *The Influence of Baudelaire in France and England* (Constable)

VAUGHAN, CH. E. 'The Influence of English Poetry upon the Romantic Revival on the Continent', *Proceedings of the British Academy*, 6: 261–78

1914

ABERCROMBIE, LASCELLES. *The Epic* (Martin Seeker). In the same series ('The Art and Craft of Letters'): Gilbert Cannan, *Satire* (1914); R. H. Gretton, *History* (1914); Christopher Stone, *Parody* (1915)

CRAWFURD, RAYMOND HENRY PAYNE. *Plague and Pestilence in Literature and Art* (Oxford: Carendon)

WATERHOUSE, GILBERT. *The Literary Relations of England and Germany in the Seventeenth Century* (Cambridge University Press)

WILLOUGHBY, L. A. 'An Early Translation of Goethe's *Tasso*', **MLR**, 9: 223–34
―― *Samuel Naylor and 'Reynard the Fox'; A Study in Anglo-German Literary Relations* (Humphrey Milford)

1915

KILLEN, ALICE M. *Le 'Roman terrifiant' ou 'Roman noir' de Walpole à Anne Radcliffe, et son influence sur la littérature française jusqu'en 1840.* **BRLC**, 4 (Paris: Champion; reprinted 1924)

1916

COLLISON-MORLEY, LACY. *Shakespeare in Italy* (Stratford-upon-Avon: Shakespeare Head Press)
COOKE, M. W. 'Schiller's "Robbers" in England', **MLR**, 11: 156–75
FITZMAURICE-KELLY, JAMES. 'Cervantes and Shakespeare', *Proceedings of the British Academy*, 7.
LEE, SIDNEY. *Shakespeare and the Italian Renaissance* (British Academy; Annual Shakespeare Lecture)

1917

COLLISON-MORLEY, LACY. 'The Georgian Englishman in Contemporary Italian Eyes', **MLR**, 12: 310–18

1918

GOSSE, EDMUND. *France et Angleterre: L'avenir de leurs relations littéraires* (Hayman Christy & Lilly)

1919

HERFORD, C. H. *Norse Myth in English Poetry* (Manchester University Press)
MAGNUS, LAURIE. *A General Sketch of European Literature in the Centuries of Romance* (Kegan Paul)

1920

ELIOT, T. S. *The Sacred Wood. Essays on Poetry and Criticism* (Methuen)
WRIGHT, H. G. *Studies in Anglo-Scandinavian Literary Relations* (Bangor: Jarvis and Foster)

1921

ROUTH, H. V. 'The Origins of the Essay Compared in French and English', **MLR**, 15: 28–40, 143–51
WATKIN, MORGAN. 'French Literary Influence in Medieval Wales', *Transactions of the Honourable Society of Cymmrodorion*, Session 1919–20: 1–79
WILLIAMS, ORLO. 'The Function of Literary Criticism', *Edinburgh Review*, 233: 125–35
WILLOUGHBY, LEONARD A. 'English Translations and Adaptations of Schiller's "Robbers"', **MLR**, 16: 297–315

1922

DUNSTAN, A. C. 'The German Influence on Coleridge', **MLR**, 17: 272–81; 18: 183–201
ECCLES, FRANCIS YVON. *Racine in England.* (Clarendon; Taylorian Lecture, 1921).
ENTWISTLE, WILLIAM J. 'Geoffrey of Monmouth and Spanish Literature', **MLR**, 17: 381–91
LUCAS, FRANK LAURENCE. *Seneca and Elizabethan Tragedy* (Cambridge University Press)
THOMAS, HENRY. *Shakespeare and Spain* (Clarendon; Taylorian Lecture)

1923

CHAYTOR, H. J. *The Troubadours and England* (Cambridge University Press)
DRAPER, FREDERICK W. M. *The Rise and Fall of the French Romantic Drama, with Special Reference to the Influence of Shakespeare, Scott and Byron* (Constable)
FIEDLER, H. G. 'Goethe's Lyric Poems in English Translation', **MLR**, 18: 51–67
GOSSE, EDMUND. *More Books on the Table* (Heinemann). Contains an essay on 'Browning in France'
HOUGHTON, RALPH EDWARD CUNLIFFE. *The Influence of the Classics on the Poetry of Matthew Arnold* (Oxford: Blackwell; The Matthew Arnold Memorial Prize Essay)
KER, W. P. *The Art of Poetry* (Oxford: Carendon)
—— 'L'idée de la Comédie', RLC, 3: 5–10
ROBERTSON, JOHN GEORGE. 'Sources italiennes des paradoxes dramatiques de La Motte', RLC, 3: 369–75
—— *Studies in the Genesis of Romantic Theory in the Eighteenth Century* (Cambridge University Press)
ROE, F. C. *Taine et l'Angleterre.* **BRLC**, 6 (Paris: Champion)
SAINTSBURY, GEORGE. *Collected Essays.* 4 vols (Dent). Contains an essay from 1892 on 'The Contrasts of English and French Literature'
STAWELL, FLORENCE M., and FRANCIS S. MARVIN, *The Making of the Western Mind. A Short History of European Culture* (Methuen)

1924

BELLOC, HILAIRE. 'On Translation', *London Mercury*, June
GOULDING, SYBIL. *Swift en France*, **BRLC**, 15 (Paris: Champion)
JEFFERY, VIOLET M. 'Italian and English Pastoral Drama of the Renaissance', **MLR**, 19: 56–62, 175–87, 35–44
LARG, D. G. *Madame de Staël. La vie dans l'œuvre*, **BRLC**, 16 (Paris: Champion) English translation: Routledge, 1926
LUCAS, FRANK LAURENCE. *Euripides and his Influence* (Harrap)
MACINTOSH, W. *Scott and Goethe: German Influence on the Writings of Sir Walter Scott* (Glasgow: Fraser Asher)
O'RAHILLY, CECILE. *Ireland and Wales, Their Historical and Literary Relations* (Longmans Green)
PARTRIDGE, ERIC H. *The French Romantics' Knowledge of English Literature, 1820–1848.* **BRLC**, 14 (Paris: Champion)
ROBERTSON, JOHN GEORGE. *The Gods of Greece in German Poetry* (Oxford: Carendon)
SELLS, ARTHUR LYTTON. *Les Sources françaises de Goldsmith*, **BRLC**, 12 (Paris: Champion)
SMITH, LOGAN PEARSALL. *Four Words: Romantic, Originality, Creative, Genius* (Oxford: Carendon)
WILLOUGHBY, LEONARD A. 'Schiller's "Kabale und Liebe" in English Translation', **PEGS**, n.s. 1

1925

ENTWISTLE, WILLIAM J. *The Arthurian Legend in the Literatures of the Spanish Peninsula* (Dent)
GUNNELL, DORIS. *Sutton Sharpe et ses amis français*, **BRLC**, 26 (Paris: Champion)
HUNTER, A. C. *Un introducteur de la littérature anglaise en France: J.-B. A. Suard.* **BRLC**, 22 (Paris: Champion)
KING, R. W. 'Italian Influence on English Scholarship and Literature during the Romantic Revival', **MLR**, 20: 48–63, 295–304; 21: 24–33

NEEDHAM, H.-A. *Le Développement de l'esthétique sociologique en France et en Angleterre au XIXe siècle*, **BRLC**, 29 (Paris: Champion)
O'CONNOR, D. 'Notes on the Influence of Brant's "Narrenschiff" outside Germany', **MLR**, 20: 64–70
RICHARDS, I. A. *Principles of Literary Criticism* (Routledge & Kegan Paul)
ROBERTSON, JOHN GEORGE. 'Goethe and Byron', **PEGS**, n.s. 2
VAUGHAN, CH.E. *Studies in the History of Political Philosophy before and after Rousseau* (Manchester: the University)
VINAVER, EUGENE. *Le Roman de Tristan et Iseut dans l'œuvre de Thomas Malory* (Paris: Champion)

1926

BUTLER, ELIZA MARIAN *The Saint-Simonian Religion in Germany: A Study of the Young German Movement.* (Cambridge University Press)
LARG, D. G. 'Une exploratrice malgré elle: le premier départ de Mme de Staël pour l'Allemagne', **RLC**, 6: 207–23
MAGNUS, LAURIE. *A Dictionary of European Literature. Designed as a Companion to English Studies* (Routledge)
PARTRIDGE, ERIC H. *A Critical Medley: Essays, Studies, and Notes in English, French, and Comparative Literature* (Paris: Champion)
PEERS, E. A. 'The Influence of Young and Gray in Spain', **MLR**, 21: 404–18
PURDIE, EDNA. *The Story of Judith in German and English Literature*, **BRLC**, 39 (Paris: Champion)
ROE, FREDERICK C. 'Le voyage de Gray et Walpole en Italie', **RLC**, 6: 189–206
STOKOE, F. W. *German Influence in the English Romantic Period* (Cambridge University Press). Contains chapters on Scott, Coleridge, Shelley and Byron
VAUGHAN, C. E. 'Goethe and Hugo', *Bulletin of the John Rylands Library, Manchester*, 10: 407–34

1927

FORSTER, E. M. *Aspects of the Novel* (Arnold)
HERFORD, C. H. *The Post-War Mind of Germany and Other European Studies* (Oxford: Carendon)
MAGNUS, LAURIE. *English Literature in its Foreign Relations, 1300–1800* (Kegan Paul)
ROUTH, H. V. *God, Man and Epic Poetry. A Study in Comparative Literature.* 2 vols (Cambridge University Press)

1928

DEVONSHIRE, M. G. *The English Novel in France 1830–1870* (University of London Press)
EATON, J. W. *The German Influence in Danish Literature in the Eighteenth Century* (Cambridge University Press)
GOULDING, SYBIL. 'Le beau-père de Rivarol: Mather Flint, maître de langue anglaise à Paris', **RLC**, 8: 258–78
JEFFERY, VIOLET M. *John Lyly and the Italian Renaissance*, **BRLC**, 53 (Paris: Champion)
LARG, D. G. *Madame de Staël. La seconde vie.* **BRLC**, 57 (Paris: Champion)
—— *Henry Crabb Robinson and Madame de Staël* (Sidgwick and Jackson; reprinted from *The Review of English Studies*)
MORLEY, ENID J. ED. *Crabb Robinson in Germany 1800–1805. Extracts from his Correspondence* (Oxford University Press)
NORMAN, F. *Henry Crabb Robinson and Goethe*, Parts 1 and 2, as **PEGS** 6 and 8

ORRICK, J. B. 'Matthew Arnold and Goethe', **PEGS**, n.s. 4
SCOTT, JANET G. *Les sonnets élisabéthains: les sources et l'apport personnel*, **BRLC**, 60 (Paris: Champion)
STOCKLEY, VIOLET. *German Literature as Known in England, 1750–1830* (Routledge)
TAYLOR, A. C. *Carlyle: sa première fortune littéraire en France (1825–1865)*, **BRLC**, 61 (Paris: Champion)

1930

BOWDEN, MARJORIE. *Tennyson in France* (Manchester University Press)
GRIERSON, HERBERT J. C. 'A Note upon the "Samson Agonistes" of John Milton and "Samson of Heilige Wraeck" by Joost van den Vondel', *Mélanges d'histoire littéraire, générale et comparée* (Festschrift for Fernand Baldensperger; Paris: Champion), 1: 332–39
LEAVIS, F. R. *Mass Civilisation and Minority Culture* (Cambridge: Fraser)
ROBERTSON, JOHN GEORGE. 'Lessing's Criticism on French Drama', *Mélanges d'histoire littéraire, générale et comparée* (Festschrift for Fernand Baldensperger; Paris: Champion), 2: 200–08

1931

BAIN, MARGARET I. *Les voyageurs français en Ecosse* **BRLC**, 79 (Paris: Champion)
MATHESON, P. E. *German Visitors to England 1770–1795, and their Impressions* (Oxford: Carendon)
NICOLSON, H. *Swinburne and Baudelaire* (Oxford: Carendon)
PEET, T. E. *A Comparative Study of the Literatures of Egypt, Palestine, and Mesopotamia* (British Academy)

1932

BOYD, JAMES. *Goethe's Knowledge of English Literature*, **OSMLL** (Oxford: Carendon)
BRIDGES, ROBERT. *Collected Essays, Papers etc*, no. 8. (Oxford University Press). Contains an essay on 'Dante in English Literature'
CHADWICK, HECTOR M. and NORA K. CHADWICK. *The Growth of Literature* 3 vols (Cambridge University Press, 1932–40)
LEAVIS, Q. D. *Fiction and the Reading Public* (Chatto & Windus)
LEWIS, C. S. *What Chaucer really did to Il Filostrato* (English Association Essays, 17)
OSBORN, A. W. *Sir Philip Sydney en France*, **BRLC**, 84 (Paris: Champion)
PARKER, A., and E. A. PEERS. 'Victor Hugo in Spain', **MLR**, 27: 36–57; 28: 50–61, 205–16
THOMAS, P. G. *Aspects of Literary Theory and Practice, 1550–1870* (Heath Cranton)
THOMSON, J. A. K. 'Erasmus and England', in *England und die Antike* (Vortrage der Bibliothek Warburg, 1930–31), ed. Fritz Saxl (Leipzig: B. G. Teubner)
WRIGHT, H. G. 'Southey's Relations with Finland and Scandinavia', **MLR**, 27: 149–67

1933

BUTLER, ELIZA MARIAN. '*Mansfield Park* and Kotzebue's "Lovers' Vows"', **MLR**, 28: 326–37
ELIOT, T. S. *The Use of Poetry and the Use of Criticism* (Faber & Faber)
EWEN, F. *The Prestige of Schiller in England 1788–1850* (Oxford University Press)
GILLIES, ALEXANDER. *Herder und Ossian* (Berlin: Junker & Dünnhaupt)
——— 'Herder and the Preparation of Goethe's "Weltliteratur"', **PEGS**, n.s. 9
JONES, TREVOR D. 'English contributors to Ottilie von Goethe's "Chaos"', **PEGS**, n.s. 9,: 68–91
LUCAS, FRANK LAURENCE. *The Criticism of Poetry* (Warton Lecture; Proceedings of the British Academy, 19)

1934

HENN, THOMAS RICE. *Longinus and English Criticism* (Cambridge University Press)
KNIGHT, G. WILSON. *Shakespeare and Tolstoi* (Mitford)
LEA, KATHLEEN MARGUERITE. *Italian Popular Comedy. A Study in the Commedia dell'Arte, 1560–1620, with special reference to the English Stage*, 2 vols (Oxford: Carendon)
MAGNUS, LAURIE. *A History of European Literature* (Nicholson & Watson)
SMITH, JANET MAY. *The French Background of Middle Scots Literature* (Edinburgh and London: Oliver and Boyd)
TREVELYAN, HUMPHRY. *The Popular Background to Goethe's Hellenism* (Longmans Green)
WESTON, HAROLD. *Form in Literature. A Theory of Technique and Construction* (Rich & Cowan)
WILLOUGHBY, L. A. 'Coleridge and his German Contemporaries', **PEGS**

1935

BETTERIDGE, H. T. 'The Ossianic Poems in Herder's "Volkslieder"', **MLR**, 30: 334–38
BUTLER, ELIZA MARIAN. *The Tyranny of Greece over Germany. A Study of the Influence Exercised by Greek Art and Poetry over the Great German Writers of the Eighteenth, Nineteenth, and Twentieth Centuries* (Cambridge University Press)
GILLIES, ALEXANDER. 'A Scottish Correspondent of Wieland's and the Importation of German into Scotland', **MLR**, 30: 36–49
GREEN, F. C. *Minuet. A Critical Survey of French and English Literary Ideas in the Eighteenth Century* (Dent)
JACKSON, KENNETH H. *Studies in Early Celtic Nature Poetry* (Cambridge University Press)
JAMESON, R. D. *A Comparison of Literatures* (Kegan Paul)
MACAULAY, T. C. 'French and English Drama in the Seventeenth Century: Some Contrasts and Parallels', *Essays and Studies by Members of the English Association*
ROBERTSON, JOHN GEORGE. *Essays and Addresses on Literature*, ed. Edna Purdie (Routledge). Contains essays on 'Literary Cosmopolitanism', 'The Spirit of Travel in Modern Literature' and 'Literature in the Universities'
SEATON, ETHEL. *Literary Relations of England and Scandinavia in the 17th Century*. **OSMLL** (Oxford: Carendon)
SELLS, IRIS. *Matthew Arnold and France: The Poet* (Cambridge University Press)

1936

AIKIN-SNEATH, BETSY. *Comedy in Germany in the First Half of the Eighteenth Century*, **OSMLL** (Oxford: Carendon)
BLACK, G. A. 'James Thomson, his Translations of Heine', **MLR**, 31: 48–54
DOWNS, B. W. 'Anglo-Dutch Literary Relations, 1867–1900', **MLR**, 31: 289–346
ELIOT, T. S. *Essays Ancient & Modern* (Faber & Faber)
LEWIS, C. S. *The Allegory of Love. A Study in Medieval Tradition* (Oxford: Carendon)
LUCAS, FRANK LAURENCE *The Decline and Fall of the Romantic Ideal* (Cambridge University Press)
LUCAS, W. I. *Die epischen Dichtungen Shakespeares in Deutschland* (Diss. Heidelberg)
MATTHEW, J. 'Poe's indebtedness to French Literature', *French Review*
REES, GARNET. 'A French Influence on T. S. Eliot: Rémy de Gourmont', **RLC**, 16: 764–67
VINCENT, ERIC. *Gabriele Rossetti in England*, **OSMLL** (Oxford: Carendon)
WILLOUGHBY, LEONARD A. 'Coleridge und Deutschland', *Germanisch-romanische Monatsschrift*, 24: 112–27

1937

BARNES, BERTRAM. *Goethe's Knowledge of French Literature*, **OSMLL** (Oxford: Carendon)
GILLIES, A. 'Herder's Essay on Shakespeare: "Das Herz der Untersuchung"', **MLR**, 32: 262–80
—— 'Ludwig Tieck's English Studies at the University of Göttingen, 1792–4', *Journal of English and Germanic Philology*, 36
HENDERSON, PHILIP. *The Novel Today: Studies in Contemporary Attitudes* (Bodley Head)
LEAVIS, F. R. 'Literary Criticism and Philosophy', *Scrutiny*, June
MOORE, W. G. 'A Sidelight on Goethe's English Reading', **PEGS**, n.s. 12
MOWAT, R. B. *The Romantic Age. Europe in the Early Nineteenth Century* (Harrap)
PASCAL, ROY. *Shakespeare in Germany 1740–1815* (Cambridge University Press). Introduction in English with German texts
WEEVERS, T. 'Vondel's Influence on German Literature', **MLR**, 32: 1–23.
WEST, A. *Crisis and Criticism* (Lawrence & Wishart)

1938

BEARE, M. *The German Popular Play 'Atis' and the Venetian Opera* (Cambridge University Press)
DOWNS, B. W. 'Meredith and Fontane', **GLL**, 2
GILLIES, A. 'Ludwig Tieck's Initiation into Spanish Studies', **MLR**, 33: 396–401
GUMMER, ELLIS NORMAN. 'Dickens and Germany', **MLR**, 33: 240–47
MENNIE, D. M. 'Sir Walter Scott's Unpublished Translations of German Plays', **MLR**, 33: 234–39.
POWELL, L. F. 'Fr. v. Matthisson on Gibbon', *German Studies Presented to Professor* Fiedler (Oxford: Carendon)
PURDIE, EDNA. 'Some Adventures of *Pamela* on the Continental Stage', *German Studies Presented to Professor Fiedler* (Oxford: Carendon)
TAYLOR, A. C. *Carlyle et la pensée latine* (Paris: Boivin)
WICKELGREN, F. L. 'Matthew Arnold's Literary Relations with France', **MLR**, 33: 200–14
WILLOUGHBY, LEONARD A. 'Wordsworth and Germany'. *German Studies Presented to Professor Fiedler* (Oxford: Carendon)

1939

ELTON, O. *Essays and Addresses* (Arnold). Contains an essay on 'The Nature of Literary Criticism'
ENTWISTLE, WILLIAM J. *European Balladry* (Oxford: Carendon)
FORD, FORD MADOX. *The March of Literature, from Confucius to Modern Times* (Allen & Unwin; first published New York 1938)
HAYENS, K. C. 'Goethe and English Letters', **GLL**, 3 (April): 212–21
PETTER, GUY P. *George Meredith and his German Critics* (Witherby)
WEEVERS, T. 'Some Aspects of Heinsius' Influence on the Style of Opitz', **MLR**, 34: 230–39
—— 'The Netherlands in their Cultural Relations with Germany', **GLL**, 3 (April): 72–83

1940

BUTLER, ELIZA MARIAN 'Rilke and Tolstoy', **MLR**, 35: 494–505
GUMMER, ELLIS NORMAN. *Dickens' Works in Germany, 1837–1937*, **OSMLL** (Oxford: Carendon)
HENTSCHEL, CEDRIC. *The Byronic Teuton, 1800–1933. Aspects of German Pessimism* (Methuen)

1941

Comparative Literature Studies. Edited by Marcel Chicoteau and Kenneth Urwin. Cardiff, later Liverpool, 1941–46. Nineteen issues in all, with contributions from, among others, W. J. Entwistle, F. C. Green, Alice M. Killen and Arthur Lytton Sells

FORSTER, LEONARD. 'The *Königsberger Zwischenspiele* and the Dutch Comedy: A Study in Metrics', **MLR**, 36: 488–94

TREVELYAN, HUMPHRY. *Goethe and the Greeks* (Cambridge University Press)

WITTE, W. 'The Sociological Approach to Literature', **MLR**, 36: 86–94

1942

BATES, H. G. *The Modern Short Story. A Critical Survey* (Nelson)

GILLIES, A. 'Herder and Pascal', **MLR**, 37: 56–63

1943

BATES, E. S. *Intertraffic. Studies in Translation* (Jonathan Cape)

BOWRA, C. M. *The Heritage of Symbolism* (Macmillan)

ELIOT, T. S. *The Nature of Cultural Relations* (Anglo-Swedish Society)

LILLY, G. 'The Welsh Influence in the Poetry of Gerard Manley Hopkins', **MLR**, 38: 192–205

MACPHAIL, J. H. 'Blake and Switzerland', **MLR**, 38: 81–87

1944

DOWNS, B. W. 'Anglo-Danish Literary Relations 1867–1900', **MLR**, 39: 262–79.

1945

BOWRA, C. M. *From Virgil to Milton* (Macmillan)

CHADWICK, H. M. *The Nationalities of Europe and the Growth of National Ideologies* (Cambridge University Press)

ELIOT, T. S. *What is a Classic?* (Faber & Faber)

GAUNT, WILLIAM. *The Aesthetic Adventure* (Jonathan Cape)

HENNIG, JOHN. 'Jean Paul and Ireland', **MLR**, 40: 190–96

1946

CHAMBERS, W. W. 'Language and Nationality in German Pre-Romantic and Romantic Thought', **MLR**, 41: 382–92

PEACOCK, RONALD. *The Poet in the Theatre* (Routledge)

PRITCHETT, V. S. *The Living Novel* (Chatto & Windus)

1947

CARR, C. T. 'Carlyle's Translations from the German', **MLR**, 42: 223–32

LIDDEL, R. *A Treatise on the Novel* (Jonathan Cape)

MAURER, K. W. 'Valéry and Goethe', **PEGS**, n.s. 17: 74–100

MORSE, B. J. 'Rainer Maria Rilke and English Literature', **GLL**, n.s. 1: 215–28

SELLS, A. L. 'Boccaccio, Chaucer and Stendhal', *Revista di letterature moderne*, Sept.-Dec
—— 'Kléarista, idylle écossaise', **RLC**, 21: 39–53
—— 'Leconte de Lisle and Sir Walter Scott', *French Studies*, 1

1948

BUTLER, ELIZA MARIAN *The Myth of the Magus* (Cambridge University Press)
DOWNS, B. W. 'Anglo-Danish Literary Relations 1867–1900', **MLR**, 43: 45–74
ELIOT, T. S. *Notes towards the Definition of Culture* (Faber & Faber)
GRAVES, ROBERT. *The White Goddess. A Historical Grammar of Poetic Myth* (Faber & Faber)
WAIDSON, H. M. 'Jeremias Gotthelf's Reception in Britain and America', **MLR**, 43: 223–38

1949

BOWRA, C. M. *The Creative Experiment* (Macmillan)
BRUFORD, W. H. 'Goethe and Some Victorian Humanists', **PEGS**, n.s. 18: 34–67.
BUTLER, ELIZA MARIAN. *Ritual Magic* (Cambridge University Press)
CHICOTEAU, MARCEL. 'Phèdre et les poisons: un thème de médiation tiré d'Euripide', *Comparative Literature*, 1: 259–66
ENTWISTLE, WILLIAM J. 'The Byronism of Lermontov's *A Hero of Our Times*', *Comparative Literature*, 1: 140–46
FORSTER, LEONARD. 'T. L. Beddoes' Views on German Literature', *English Studies*, 30.5: 206–14.
GAUNT, WILLIAM. *The March of the Moderns* (Jonathan Cape)
HENNIG, JOHN. 'Irish-German Literary Relations: A Survey', **GLL**, 3: 102–10
PURDIE, EDNA. 'Some Problems of Translations in the 18th Century in Germany', *English Studies*, 30.5: 191–205 (Lüdeke Anniversary Number)
SCOTT, DOUGLAS F. S. *Some English Correspondents of Goethe* (Methuen)
SELLS, ARTHUR LYTTON. 'Leconte de Lisle and Robert Burns', in *Studies in French Language, Literature, and History* (Festschrift for R. L. Graeme Ritchie; Cambridge University Press), 196–217
THOMAS, HENRY. *Shakespeare in Spain* (Geoffrey Cumberlege). Annual Shakespeare Lecture of the British Academy
TYMMS, RALPH. *Doubles in Literary Psychology* (Cambridge: Bowes & Bowes)
VINCENT, ERIC. *Byron, Hobhouse and Foscolo; New Documents in the History of a Collaboration.* (Cambridge University Press)
WHITFIELD, JOHN HUMPHREYS. *Dante and Virgil* (Oxford: Blackwell). With an English translation of Cantos i-v of the *Inferno*
WILLOUGHBY, LEONARD A. 'Literary Relations in the Light of Goethe's Principle of *Wiederspiegelung*', *Comparative Literature*, 1: 309–23

1950

BOWRA, C. M. *The Romantic Imagination* (Oxford University Press)
BUTLER, ELIZA MARIAN. *Goethe and Byron* (Nottingham University). Byron Foundation Lecture
CLARK, J. M. *The Dance of Death in the Middle Ages and the Renaissance* (Glasgow: Jackson)
HEMMINGS, F. W. J. *The Russian Novel in France (1884–1914)* (Oxford University Press)
SELLS, ARTHUR LYTTON. 'Zanella, Coleridge and Shelley', *Comparative Literature*, 2: 16–30
TAYLOR, A. C. *Non-French Admirers and Imitators of Balzac* (Birkbeck College; inaugural lecture)
WILKINSON, E. MARY. 'Neuere Strömungen der angelsachsischen Ästhetik in ihrer Beziehung zur vergleichenden Literaturwissenschaft', in *Forschungsprobleme der Vergleichenden Literaturgeschichte. Internationale Beiträge zur Tübinger Literarhistoriker-Tagung, Sept. 1950*, ed. Kurt Wais (Tubingen: Niemeyer), 1: 141–57

WILLOUGHBY, LEONARD A. 'Stand und Aufgaben der vergleichenden Literaturgeschichte in England', in *Forschungsprobleme der Vergleichenden Literaturgeschichte. Internationale Beiträge zur Tübinger Literarhistoriker-Tagung, Sept. 1950*, ed. Kurt Wais (Tubingen: Niemeyer), 1: 21–28

1951

BATESON, F. W. 'Contributions to a Dictionary of Critical Terms: I, Comedy of Manners; II, Dissociation of Sensibility', *Essays in Criticism*, 1: 83–93, 302–12. Cf. also vol. 2 (1952): 207–14, and Watson 1953
BAYNE-POWELL, R. *Travellers in Eighteenth-Century England* (Murray).
BENN, MAURICE. 'Goethe and T. S. Eliot', GLL, 5: 151–61
BOWEN, ELIZABETH. 'A Matter of Inspiration', *Saturday Review*, 13 October, 27–28.
BOWRA, C. M. *Inspiration and Poetry* (Cambridge University Press). Rede Lecture
COX, R. G. 'Victorian Criticism of Poetry: The Minority Tradition', *Scrutiny*, 18: 2–17
DAY-LEWIS, CECIL. *The Poet's Task* (Oxford: Carendon)
—— 'On Translating Virgil', *The Listener*, 2 August, 171–72
DYER, D. G., '"Amphitryon": Plautus, Molière and Kleist', GLL, 5: 191–201
EDWARDS, KATHLEEN. 'The Use of Classical Authors by Medieval Writers', *Aberdeen University Review*, 34: 233–43
ELCOCK, W. D. 'English Indifference to Du Bellay's *Regrets*', MLR, 46: 175–84
ELIOT, T. S. *Poetry and Drama*. Faber & Faber. Cf. also *Atlantic Monthly*, 187 (February): 30–37.
ENRIGHT, D. J. 'Poetic Satire and Satire in Verse', *Scrutiny*, 18: 211–23
GREEN, F. C. 'Autour de quatre lettres inédites de Diderot à John Wilkes', RLC, 25: 449–67
HAINSWORTH, G. 'Un thème des romanciers naturalistes: La matrone d'Ephèse', *Comparative Literature*, 3: 121–51
HENNIG, JOHN. 'Goethe and Huttner', MLR, 46: 404–18
—— 'Goethe's Translation from the Annals of Philosophy, 1816', *Journal of English and Germanic Philology*, 50: 494–501
—— '*Stephen Hero* and *Wilhelm Meister*. A Study of Parallels', GLL, 5: 22–29.
HORTON-SMITH, N. 'Justus Moser and the British', GLL, 5: 47–56
HUTTON, JAMES. 'Some English Poems in Praise of Music', *English Miscellany*, 2: 1–63.
KNOX, E. V. *The Mechanism of Satire* (Cambridge University Press). The Stephen Lecture.
LUCAS, FRANK LAURENCE *Literature and Psychology* (Cassell)
MAUGHAM, W. SOMERSET. *The Writer's Point of View* (Cambridge University Press/National Book League)
MUIR, KENNETH. 'The Dramatic Function of Anachronism', *Proceedings of the Leeds Philosophical Society*, 6: 521–33
STANFORD, W. B. 'Studies in the Characterization of Ulysses', *Hermathena*, 77: 52–64, 67–83
TATE, R. B. 'Italian Humanism and Spanish Historiography of the Fifteenth Century', *Bulletin of the John Rylands Library*, 34 (1951–52): 137–67
THOMAS, DYLAN. 'How to be a Poet', *Atlantic Monthly*, 188 (July): 46–49
THOMAS, L. H. C. '*Walladmor*: A Pseudo-Translation of Sir Walter Scott', MLR, 46: 218–31
THOMSON, J. A. K. *Classical Influences on English Poetry* (Allen & Unwin)
WRIGHT, H. G. 'The Indebtedness of Painter's Translation from Boccaccio in *The Palace of Pleasure* to the French Version of Le Maçon', MLR, 46: 431–35
ZOHN, HARRY, 'Stefan Zweig and Contemporary European Literature', *German Life and Letters*, 5: 202–12

1952

BALLARD, E. G. 'Towards a Philosophy for Literature', *Hibbert Journal*, 51: 149–55

BARLOW, D. 'Fontane's English Journeys', **GLL**, 6: 169–77.

BOWRA, C. M. *Heroic Poetry* (Macmillan)

BROWN, W. NIGHTINGALE. *On Writing, Reading and Literary Appreciation. A Practical and Cultural Guide* (Altrincham: John Sherratt)

BRYANT, ARTHUR. *Literature and the Historian*. (Cambridge University Press/National Book League)

COX, R. G. 'The New Scholarship?', *Scrutiny*, 19: 82–89

CRIPPS, R. S. 'Two British Interpreters of the Old Testament: Robert Lowth (1710–1787) and Samuel Lee (1783–1852)', *Bulletin of the John Rylands Library*, 35: 385–404

DOWNS, B. W. 'Anglo-Norwegian Literary Relations, 1867–1900', **MLR**, 47: 449–94

ENRIGHT, D. J. 'Reluctant Admiration: A Note on Auden and Rilke', *Essays in Criticism*, 2: 180–95.

FLEMING, JOHN ARNOLD. *The Medieval Scots Scholar in France* (Glasgow: MacLellan)

GILLIES, ALEXANDER. 'Some Thoughts on Comparative Literature', *Yearbook of Comparative and General Literature*, 1: 15–25

GODDARD, H. G. 'Maupassant and the English', *French Studies*, 6: 35–40

HENNIG, JOHN. 'Goethe and De Candelle', *Modern Language Quarterly*, 13: 277–84

HILTON-YOUNG, WAYLAND. 'Translations of the *Pervigilium Veneris* into English Verse', *Cambridge Journal*, 5 (March): 331–54

HODGART, MATTHEW. 'The Progress of Literary Criticism: III, Psychology and Literary Criticism', *The Listener*, 11 September: 420–21

KOCH-EMMERY, E. 'Thomas Mann in English Translation', **GLL**, 6: 275–84

KNIGHT, DOROTHY. 'Thomas Blackwell and J. J. Bodmer: The Establishment of a Literary Link between Homeric Greece and Medieval Germany', **GLL**, 6: 249–58

LEAVIS, F. R. 'The Responsible Critic or the Function of Criticism at Any Time', *Scrutiny*, 19: 162–83. With reactions from F. W. Bateson and Geoffrey Walton, and a rejoinder by Leavis (317–30)

LEIGH, R. A. 'Boswell and Rousseau', **MLR**, 47: 280–318

LOUGH, JOHN. 'The *Encyclopédie* in Eighteenth-Century England', *French Studies*, 6: 289–307.

OWEN, W. J. B. '*Orlando Furioso* and Stanza-Connection in *The Faerie Queene*', *Modern Language Notes*, 67: 165–72

PARRY, I. F. 'Kafka and Gogol', **GLL**, 6: 141–45

REES, JOAN. 'Samuel Daniel's *Cleopatra* and two French Plays', **MLR**, 47: 1–10

RITCHEY, MARGARET FITZGERALD. 'The Independence of Wolfram von Eschenbach in Relation to Chrestien de Troyes as shown in *Parzival*, Books III-VI', **MLR**, 47: 350–61

SPENCER, TERENCE. 'Turks and Trojans in the Renaissance', **MLR**, 47: 330–33

STANFORD, W. B. 'Dante's Conception of Ulysses', *Cambridge Journal*, 6: 239–47

STOYE, J. W. *English Travellers Abroad (1604–1667). Their Influence in English Society and Politics* (Cape)

SUTCLIFFE, F. G. 'Hegel et Valéry', *French Studies*, 6: 53–57

THOMSON, DERICK S. *The Gaelic Sources of Macpherson's 'Ossian'* (Edinburgh: Oliver & Boyd)

THOMSON, J. A. K. *Shakespeare and the Classics* (Allen & Unwin)

TODD, F. M. 'Wordsworth in Germany', **MLR**, 47: 508–11

WATERHOUSE, GILBERT. 'Goethe's Irish Enemy', in *German Studies Presented to Professor L. A. Willoughby* (Oxford: Blackwell)

WATT, IAN. 'The Progress of Literary Criticism: II, Should Criticism be Humanist?', *The Listener*, 4 September, 378–79

—— 'Defoe and Richardson on Homer: A Study of the Relation of Novel and Epic in the Early Eighteenth Century', *Review of English Studies*, 3: 325–40
—— 'Realism and the Novel', *Essays in Criticism*, 2: 376–96
WILLIAMS, RAYMOND. *Drama from Ibsen to Eliot* (Chatto & Windus). Cf. also *Theatre Arts Monthly*, 38 (Feb. 1954), 10–12
WILLIAMS, W. D. *Nietzsche and the French. A Study of the Influence of Nietzsche's French Reading on his Thought and Writing* (Oxford: Blackwell)
WITTE, W. 'Time in *Wallenstein* and *Macbeth*', *Aberdeen University Review*, 34: 106
WOLFF, ERWIN B. 'On Goethe's Reputation as a Scientist in Nineteenth-Century England', **GLL**, 6: 92–102
YOUNG, MARGARET L. M. 'Jean des Montiers, dit Le Fresse, and his Account of Scotland', *French Studies*, 6: 1–11

1953

BLAYNEY, MARGARET STATLER. 'Sir John Fortescue and Alain Chartier's Traite de l'espérance', **MLR**, 48: 385–90
BOULTON, MARJORIE. *The Anatomy of Poetry* (Routledge). Preface by L. A. G. Strong.
BOWRA, C. M. 'Dante and Sordello', *Comparative Literature*, 5: 1–15
CHADWICK, NORA. 'Literary Tradition in the Old Norse and Celtic World', *Saga-Book of the Viking Society for Northern Research*, 14: 164–99
COCKING, J. M. 'English Influences on Proust', *The Listener*, 27 August, 345–47.
COLQUHOUN, ARCHIBALD. 'Manzoni in Inghilterra', in *Atti del V. convegno storico Toscano: Relazioni tra l'Inghilterra e Toscana nel Risorgimento* (Atti dell' Accademia Lucchese di scienze, lettere ed arti, 8), 25–26
COOMBES, H. *Literature and Criticism* (Chatto & Windus)
DAVY, G. *Thomas Hobbes and J.-J. Rousseau* (Oxford: Carendon)
FARBRIDGE, MAURICE. *Literature and the Hebrew Renaissance* (Luzac)
FLEMING, JOHN ARNOLD. *Huguenot Influence in Scotland* (Glasgow: MacLellan)
GANZ, P. F. 'The *Cancionerillo Mozarabe* and the Origin of the Middle High German *Frauenlied*', **MLR**, 48: 301–09
GIFFORD, HENRY. 'Criticism and the Public', *Essays in Criticism*, 3: 463–68.
HENNIG, JOHN. 'Goethe and *Lalla Rookh*', **MLR**, 48: 445–50
—— 'The Place of German Theology in the Works of Canon Sheehan', *Irish Ecclesiastical Record*, 5.85: 379–87
HILTON, RONALD. 'Doña Emilia Pardo Bazán and the Europeanization of Spain', *Symposium*, 6: 298–307
—— 'Spanish Preconceptions about France, as Revealed in the Works of Emilia Pardo Bazán', *Bulletin of Hispanic Studies*, 30: 193–204
KING, C. D. 'Edouard Dujardin, Inner Monologue and the Stream of Consciousness', *French Studies*, 7: 116–27
LEAKEY, F. W. 'Baudelaire and Mortimer', *French Studies*, 7: 101–15.
LIDDELL, ROBERT. *Some Principles of Fiction* (Cape)
LOCKWOOD, W. B. 'A Manuscript in the Rylands Library and Flemish-Dutch and Low German Accounts of the Life and Miracles of Saint Barbara', *Bulletin of the John Rylands Library*, 36: 23–37
LOUGH, JOHN, ED. *Locke's Travels in France, 1675–79. As related in his Journals, Correspondence and other Papers* (Cambridge University Press)
MADARIAGA, S. DE. 'On Translating Shakespeare', in *Shakespeare Survey*, ed. Allardyce Nicoll (Cambridge University Press), 106–11
MAJUT, R. 'Georg Büchner and some English Thinkers', **MLR**, 48: 310–22

PEACOCK, RONALD. 'Public and Private Problems in Modern Drama', *Bulletin of the John Rylands Library*, 36: 38–55
PRITCHETT, V. S. *Books in General* (Chatto & Windus)
REES, GAMET, 'Comparative Literature', *Modern Language Journal*, 37: 3–9
ROBSON-SCOTT, W. D. *German Travellers in England, 1400–1800* (Oxford: Blackwell)
ROE, FREDERICK C. 'La découverte de l'Écosse entre 1760 et 1830',RLC, 27: 59–75
—— 'A Double Centenary: Sir Thomas Urquhart and his Translation of Rabelais', *Aberdeen University Review*, 35: 120–29
RUSSELL, P. E. 'English Seventeenth-Century Interpretations of Spanish Literature', *Atlante*, 1: 65–77
SCOTT, D. F. 'Luke Howard and Goethe', *Durham University Journal*, 14: 94–103
SHACKLETON, ROBERT. 'Renseignements inédits sur Locke, Coste et Bouhier', RLC, 27: 319–22
STANFORD, W. B. 'Ulyssean Qualities in Joyce's Leopold Bloom', *Comparative Literature*, 5: 125–36
STERN, J. P. 'On Stylistics Analysis', *Cambridge Journal*, 7: 67–80
TURNER, MARGARET. 'The Influence of La Bruyère on the *Tatler* and the *Spectator*', MLR, 48: 10–16 Vincent, E. R. *Ugo Foscolo. An Italian in Regency England* (Cambridge University Press)
WATSON, GEORGE C. 'Contributions to a Dictionary of Critical Terms: "Imagination" and "Fancy"', *Essays in Criticism*, 3: 201–14. Cf. also Bateson 1951
WELLS, G. A. 'Herder's and Coleridge's Evaluation of the Historical Approach', MLR, 48: 167–75
WILLIAMS, RAYMOND. 'The Idea of Culture', *Essays in Criticism*, 3: 239–66
WRIGHT, HERBERT G. 'Some Sixteenth- and Seventeenth-Century Writers on the Plague', *Essays and Studies by Members of the English Association*, N. S. 6: 41–55
—— *The First English Translation of the Decameron* (Uppsala: Lundeqvist)

1954

ALLEN, WALTER. 'The Novelist's Use of People', *The Listener*, 6 October, 541–42
AUDEN, W. H. 'Balaam and the Ass: The Master-Servant Relationship in Literature', *Thought*, 29: 237–70
BARTLEY, J. O. *Teague, Shenkin and Sawney. Being an Historical Study of the Earliest Irish, Welsh and Scottish Characters in English Plays* (Cork University Press)
BRETT-JAMES, ANTONY. *The Triple Stream. Four Centuries of English, French and German Literature, 1531–1930* (Cambridge: Bowes & Bowes)
BREWSTER, DOROTHY. *East-West Passage. A Study in Literary Relationships* (Allen & Unwin)
BRILL, E. V. K. 'Raabe's Reception in England', GLL, 8: 304–12
ELIOT, T. S. 'The Three Voices of Poetry', *Atlantic Monthly*, 193 (April): 38–44
EVANS, B. IFOR. *Literature and Science* (Allen & Unwin)
FOSTER, J. R. 'Jeremias Gotthelf's Reputation outside Switzerland', GLL, 8: 208–10
GRIFFITH, G. O. 'Bunyan's Pilgrim: A Dutch Forerunner', *Hibbert Journal*, 53: 62–67
GRIMSLEY, RONALD. 'The Don Juan Theme in Molière and Kierkegaard', *Comparative Literature*, 6: 316–34
HATTO, A. T. 'The Lime-Tree and Early German, Goliard and English Lyric Poetry', MLR, 49: 193–209 Hennig, John. 'Goethe and the Edgeworths', *Modern Language Quarterly*, 15: 366–71
—— 'Ireland's Place in Nineteenth-Century German Poetry', GLL, 8: 201–07
—— 'A Note on Canon Sheehan's Interest in German Literature', MLR, 49: 352–55
HUNT, H. J. 'Balzac and the English Tongue', MLR, 49: 434–41

JARRETT-KERR, MARTIN. *Studies in Literature and Belief* (Rockliff)
KNOWLES, CHRISTINE. 'Caxton and his Two French Sources', **MLR**, 49: 417–23
MAY, T. E. and E. SARMIENTO. 'Fray Luis de Leon and Boethius', **MLR**, 49: 183–92
MORGAN, CHARLES. *Dialogue in Novels and Plays* (Ashford: Hand and Flower Press). Herman Ould Memorial Lecture
PASCAL, ROY. 'An English Iphigenie: A Version for Broadcasting', **GLL**, 8: 264–72; 9 (1955–56): 20–25
PIERCE, FRANK. 'The Place of Mythology in the Lusiads', *Comparative Literature*, 6: 97–122.
PRINCE, F. T. *The Italian Element in Milton's Verse* (Oxford: Carendon)
ROE, FREDERICK C. 'Comparative Literature in the United Kingdom', *Yearbook of Comparative and General Literature*, 3: 1–12
—— 'Venise et la littérature anglaise', in *Venezia nelle letterature moderne. Atti del Primo Congresso dell' Associazione Internazionale di Letteratura Comparata* (Venezia, 25–30 settembre 1955), ed. Carlo Pellegrini (Venezia/Roma: Istituto per la Collaborazione Culturale), 50–61
SELLS, IRIS. 'Stevenson and La Motte Fouqué', **RLC**, 28: 334–43
SPELL, J. R. 'Gorostiza and England', *Atlante*, 3: 15–31
SPENCER, T. *Fair Greece, Sad Relic: Philhellenism from Shakespeare to Byron* (Weidenfeld & Nicolson)
STANFORD, W. B. *The Ulysses Theme. A Study in the Adaptability of a Traditional Hero* (Oxford: Blackwell)
SUCKLING, NORMAN. *Paul Valéry and the Civilized Mind* (Oxford University Press / University of Durham)
THOMAS, L. H. C. 'Willibald Alexis's Knowledge of English', **MLR**, 49:216–18.
TREVELYAN, GEORGE M. *A Layman's Love of Letters* (Longmans). Clark Lectures.
VINCENT, E. R. *Ugo Foscolo esule fra gli Inglesi* (Firenze: Le Monnier)
WEIL, H. H. 'A Seventeenth-Century German Looks at Russia', **GLL**, 8, 59–64
WHITMORE, P. J. S. 'English Thought and Learning in the Works of Pierre Bayle', *French Studies*, 8: 141–48
WILLIAMS, RAYMOND. *Drama in Performance* (Muller)
—— *Preface to Film* (Film Drama)

1955

AUDEN, W. H. 'The Dyer's Hand'; 'The Poetic Process'; 'On Writing Poetry Today', *The Listener*, 16 (23 and 30 June): 1063–66; 1109–12; 1151–54
BUTLER, ELIZA MARIAN. 'Heine in England and Matthew Arnold', **GLL**, 9: 157–65
DONOGHUE, DENIS. 'Notes Towards a Critical Method. Language as Order', *Studies*, 44: 181–92.
FREIDEL, F. 'Francis Lieber: Transmitter of European Ideas to America', *Bulletin of the John Rylands Library*, 38: 342–59
GIBB, HAMILTON. 'The Influence of Islamic Culture on Medieval Europe', *Bulletin of the John Rylands Library*, 38: 82–98
GRAVES, ROBERT. 'The Integrity of the Poet', *The Listener*, 31 March, 579–80
GREEN, F. C. 'La littérature française devant l'opinion anglaise', *Cahiers de l'Association internationale des études françaises*, 7: 93–100
—— 'The Letters of *milord maréchal* to Rousseau', *French Studies*, 9: 54–59
HENNIG, JOHN. 'The Auerbachs Keller Scene and *She Stoops to Conquer*', *Comparative Literature*, 7: 193–202
—— 'Goethe's Translation from Fontenelle's *Eloge de Newton*', *Modern Language Quarterly*, 16: 330–43

—— 'A Note on Goethe and Robert Blair', MLR, 50: 187–91
HOPPE, H. R. 'English Acting Companies at the Court of Brussels in the Seventeenth Century', *Review of English Studies*, 6: 26–33
HOUGH, GRAHAM. 'The Novel and the Reader'; 'The Novel as Exploration'; 'Technical Experiment in the Novel', *The Listener*, 13, 20 and 27 January, 71–73; 114–15; 146–48
KNOWLES, DAVID. *The Historian and Character* (Cambridge University Press). Inaugural lecture
Literature and Science. Proceedings of the Sixth Triennial Congress (of the International Federation for Modern Languages and Literatures) (Oxford: Blackwell). Among British participants were Ronald Peacock, Garnet Rees, F. C. Roe, R. A. Sayce, Robert Shackleton and E. R. Vincent
MACKERNESS, E. 'The Progress of an Italophile: Thomas Gray and Music', *Italian Studies*, 12: 99–109 Majut, R. 'Some Literary Affiliations of Georg Büchner with England', MLR, 50: 30–43
MALNICK, B. 'David Garrick and the Russian Theatre', MLR, 50: 173–75
OWEN, W. J. B. 'Narrative Logic and Imitation in *The Faerie Queene*', *Comparative Literature*, 7: 324–37
PRESS, JOHN. *The Fire and the Fountain. An Essay on Poetry* (Oxford University Press)
READ, HERBERT. 'The Drift of Poetry', *Times Literary Supplement*, 11 February, 89
REES, D. G. 'Sir Thomas Wyatt's Translations from Petrarch', *Comparative Literature*, 7: 15–24
ROE, FREDERICK C. 'Deuxieme congrès de littérature comparée à Oxford, 10–15 septembre 1954', *Convivium*, N. S. 1 (Jan.-Feb.): 120
—— 'L'Image que se font les anglais de la littérature française', *Cahiers de l' Association internationale des études françaises*, 7: 101–12
—— 'A French Historian in Aberdeen (1788)', *Aberdeen University Review*, 36: 13–17'
—— 'Taine et l'art anglais', *Atti del 5. congresso internazionale di lingue e letterature moderne*, Florence: Valmartina
SELLS, ARTHUR LYTTON. 'La peinture italienne et la poésie anglaise à l'époque de la renaissance', *Atti del 5. congresso internazionale di lingue e letterature moderne* (Florence: Valmartina)
—— *Animal Poetry in French and English and the Greek Tradition* (Indiana University Press)
—— *The Italian Influence on English Poetry. From Chaucer to Southwell* (Allen & Unwin)
SHACKLETON, ROBERT. 'Montesquieu et Doria', RLC, 29: 173–83
SPENDER, STEPHEN. *The Making of a Poem* (Hamish Hamilton)
VINCENT, E. R. 'Ugo Foscolo e Margaret Compton', *Giornale storico della litteratura italiana*, 72: 257–66
WILKIE, JOHN R. 'Goethe's English Friend Lupton', GLL, 9: 29–39.
WILKINSON, ELIZABETH MARY. 'Literature and Science', GLL, 9: 246–49
WILKINSON, L. P. *Ovid Recalled* (Cambridge University Press)
—— 'Shakespeare and Horace', *Times Literary Supplement*, 6 May, 237
WILLOUGHBY, L. A. 'Goethe Looks at the English', MLR, 50: 464–84

1956

ANDREWS, JOHN S. 'The Reception of Gotthelf in British and American Nineteenth-Century Periodicals', MLR, 51: 543–54
AUDEN, W. H. *Making, Knowing and Judging* (Oxford: Carendon)
AUSTIN, R. C. *Some English Translations of Virgil* (Liverpool University Press)
BOWLEY, VICTOR. 'George Sand and Geraldine Jewsbury', RLC, 30: 396–98
BUTLER, E. M. *Byron and Goethe* (Cambridge University Press)
CARY, G. *The Medieval Alexander* (Cambridge University Press)

DAVIE, DONALD. 'Pan Tadeusz in English Verse', in Adam Mickiewicz in World Literature. A Symposium, ed. W. Lednicki (California University Press), 319–29
FURNESS, N. A. 'Georg Büchner's Translations of Victor Hugo', MLR, 51: 49–54
GARDNER, HELEN. The Limits of Literary Criticism: Reflections on the Interpretation of Poetry and Scripture (Oxford University Press / University of Durham). Riddell Memorial Lecture
GRAHAM, J. 'A Negative Note on Bergson and Virginia Woolf', Essays in Criticism, 6: 70–74
GRAVES, ROBERT. The Crowning Privilege. Collected Essays on Poetry (New York: Doubleday)
GRIMSLEY, RONALD. 'Romantic Melancholy in Chateaubriand and Kierkegaard', Comparative Literature, 8: 227–44
HALSBAND, R. 'Lady Mary Wortley Montagu as a Friend of Continental Writers', Bulletin of the John Rylands Library, 39: 57–74
HENN, T. R. The Harvest of Tragedy (Methuen)
HENNIG, JOHN. 'Goethe's Translations of Scott's Criticism of Hoffmann', MLR, 51: 369–77
LADBOROUGH, R. W. 'Pepys and Pascal', French Studies, 10: 133–39
LOUGH, JOHN. 'Madame de Staël et Earl Grey', RLC, 30: 389–90
MERCIER, VIVIAN. 'Parody: James Joyce and an Irish Tradition', Studies, 45: 194–218
O'BRIEN, KATE. 'Writers of Letters', Essays and Studies by Members of the English Association, 9: 7–20
O'FAOLÁIN, SEÁN. The Vanishing Hero. Studies in Novelists of the Twentieth Century (Eyre & Spottiswoode)
O'HIGGINS, ELIZABETH. 'Irish Words in William Blake's Mythology', Dublin Magazine, 26: 25–39
PARKER, A. A. 'Fielding and the Structure of Don Quixote', Bulletin of Hispanic Studies, 33: 1–16
PASCAL, ROY. 'Dickens and Kafka', The Listener, 26 April, 504–06
—— 'Four Fausts: From W. S. Gilbert to Ferruccio Busoni', GLL, 10: 263–74
PHELPS, GILBERT. The Russian Novel in English Fiction (Hutchinson)
PURDIE, EDNA. 'Hamann, Herder and Hamlet'. GLL, 10: 198–209
—— 'Observations on some Eighteenth-Century German Versions of the Witches' Scene in Macbeth', Shakespeare-Jahrbuch, 92: 96–109
QUINTON, ANTHONY. 'Six Virtues for Authors: I, Honesty in Fiction', The Listener, 22 November, 845–47. Reeves, James. The Critical Sense. Practical Criticism of Prose and Poetry (Heinemann)
WEDGWOOD, C. V. Literature and the Historian (Oxford University Press). English Association: presidential address
RICKARD, P. Britain in Medieval French Literature, 1100–1500 (Cambridge University Press)
ROBSON-SCOTT, D. W. 'Georg Forster and the Gothic Revival', MLR, 51: 42–48
WOODHOUSE, C. M. 'Six Virtues for Authors: V, Sympathy in Literature', The Listener, 20 December, 1039–40
—— 'The Unacknowledged Legislators. Poets and Politics', Essays by Divers Hands, 28: 48–74.
SACKER, HUGH. 'Heinrich von Veldeke's Conception of the Aeneid', GLL, 10: 210–18
SKELTON, ROBIN. The Poetic Pattern (Routledge & Kegan Paul)
STONE, L. An Elizabethan: Sir Horatio Palavicino (Oxford: Carendon)
THOMAS, LIONEL. 'Schloss Avalon: A German Historical Novel with an English Setting', GLL, 10: 97–105
THOMSON, J. A. K. Classical Influences on English Prose (Allen & Unwin)
TILLYARD, E. M. W. 'The Novel as a Literary Kind', Essays and Studies by Members of the English Association, 9: 73–86

THORNE, E. 'Vincenzo Martinelli in England, 1748–1774', *Italian Studies*, 11: 92–107
TITMUS, C. J. 'The Influence of Montchrétien's *Ecossoise* upon French Classical Tragedies with Subjects from English History', *French Studies*, 10: 224–30
WEDGWOOD, C. V. 'History as Literature', *Times Literary Supplement*, 6 January, xi.
WILLOUGHBY, LEONARD A. 'Goethe and the English Language', **GLL**, 10: 240–50

1957

AMIS, KINGSLEY. 'Laughter's to be Taken Seriously', *New York Times Book Review*, 7 July, 13.
ANDREWS, JOHN S. 'The Reception of Fontane in Nineteenth-Century Britain', **MLR**, 52: 403–06
AYRTON, M. *Golden Sections* (Methuen)
BAYLEY, J. *The Romantic Survival*. Constable
BREMNER, G. 'Millwood, Lady Milford and Maria Stuart', **GLL**, 11: 41–48.
CECIL, DAVID. *The Fine Art of Reading and Other Literary Essays* (Constable)
CHASE, RICHARD. 'Notes on Manzoni's *I Promessi Sposi* and the English and European Traditions', *English Magazine*, 8: 109–24
COVENEY, PETER. *Poor Monkey: The Child in Literature* (Rockliff)
CRANSTON, MAURICE. 'Byways of Biography', *The Listener*, 24 October, 645–46
DAY-LEWIS, CECIL. *The Poet's Way of Knowledge*. (Cambridge University Press). Henry Sidgwick Memorial Lecture
EISNER, S. *A Tale of Wonder: A Source Study of the Wife of Bath's Tale* (Wexford: John English)
ENRIGHT, D. J. *The Apothecary's Shop. Essays on Literature* (Secker & Warburg)
ESPINER-SCOTT, JANET. 'Les sonnets élisabéthains. Cupidon et l'influence d'Ovide',**RLC**: 31, 421–26
FLETCHER, I. 'Leda and Saint Anne', *The Listener*, 21 February, 305–07
FRIEL, BRIAN. 'For Export Only', *Commonweal*, 65 (15 February): 509–10
GREEN, F. C. 'Scott's French Correspondence', **MLR**, 52: 35–49
GRONDAHL, I. C. 'Henrik Wergeland and England', **GLL**, 11: 286–92
HENNIG, JOHN. 'Goethe's Extracts from Birch's History of the Royal Society', **MLR**, 52: 239–41
—— 'Goethes Irlandkunde', *Deutsche Vierteljahresschrift für Literaturwissenschaft und Geistesgeschichte,* 31: 70–83
—— 'Irish Descriptions of Goethe', **PEGS**, 25:114–24
—— 'A Note on Elizabeth Dowden's Grillparzer Translations', **MLR**, 52: 576–77; 54 (1959), 578.
HUXLEY, ALDOUS. 'On Adaptation', *Theatre Arts Monthly*, 41 (December): 28–29, 87–88
HYAMS, E., ED./TR. *Taine's Notes on England* (Thames & Hudson)
KILLEEN, J. F. 'James Joyce's Roman Prototype', *Comparative Literature*, 9: 193–203
KNOX, R. *On English Translation* (Clarendon. Romanes Lecture)
LAWRENSON, T. E. *The French Stage in the XVIIth Century. A Study in the Advent of the Italian Order* (Manchester University Press)
LERNER, LAURENCE. 'Literature as the Subject of Itself', *Twentieth Century*, 161 (June): 547–55
LUCAS, FRANK LAURENCE *Tragedy. Serious Drama in Relation to Aristotle's Poetics* (Hogarth Press)
MARSHALL, R. 'An Unpublished Story in English by Massimo D'Azeglio', *Italian Studies*, 12: 22–36
MOORE, P. A. *Science and Fiction* (Harrap)
PEACOCK, RONALD. *The Art of Drama* (Routledge & Kegan Paul)

PETTOELLO, LAURA. 'A Current Misconception concerning the Influence of Marino's Poetry on Crashaw's' **MLR**, 52: 321–28
RAY, S. *Explorations: Essays in Literary and Philosophical Criticism* (Luzac)
READ, HERBERT. *The Tenth Muse. Essays in Criticism* (Routledge & Kegan Paul)
REES, D. G. 'Wyatt and Petrarch', **MLR**, 52: 389–91
RODGER, GILLIAN. 'Hero and Leander in Scottish Balladry', *Comparative Literature*, 9: 1–16
ROE, F. C. *Sir Thomas Urquhart and Rabelais* (Oxford: Carendon). Taylorian Lecture
SAVOY, T. *The Art of Translation* (Cape)
SCOTT, J. A. 'Scott and Baudelaire', **RLC**, 31: 550–62
SPENCER, T. 'Longinus in English Criticism: Influences before Milton', *Review of English Studies*, 8: 137–43
STERN, J. P. M. 'Effi Briest: Madame Bovary: Anna Karenina', **MLR**, 52: 363–75
TAYLOR, WILLIAM A. *Historical Fiction*. Preface by A. Duggan. (Cambridge University Press/National Book League)
THODY, PHILIP. 'A Note on Camus and the American Novel', *Comparative Literature*, 9: 243–49
THOMSON, D. 'The Latin Epigram in Scotland: The Sixteenth Century', *Phoenix*, 11: 63–78
THORLBY, A. *Gustave Flaubert and the Art of Realism* (Cambridge: Bowes & Bowes)
WILKINS, E. 'Descriptions of Pagan Divinities from Petrarch to Chaucer', *Speculum*, 32: 511–22 Willoughby, Leonard A. 'Die Goethe-Forschung in England seit 1949', *Euphorion*, 51: 61–77
WRIGHT, H. G. *Boccaccio in England from Chaucer to Tennyson* (Athlone Press)

1958

ALLEN, CARLETON. 'The Literature of the Law', *Essays by Divers Hands*, 29: 37–54
ATKINSON, M. E. *August Wilhelm Schlegel as a Translator of Shakespeare. A Comparison of Three Plays with the Original* (Oxford: Blackwell)
BAGBY, PHILIP. *Culture and History* (Longmans)
BENN, M. B. 'Hölderlin and Sophocles', **GLL**, 12 (1958–59): 161–73
BISSON, L. A. 'Valéry and Virgil', **MLR**, 53: 501–11
BONGIE, LAURENCE L. 'David Hume and the Official Censorship of the *ancien régime*', *French Studies*, 12: 234–46
BROOKE-ROSE, CHRISTINE. *A Grammar of Metaphor* (Secker & Warburg)
CARSANIGA, GIOVANNI. '"The Truth" in John Ford's *The Broken Heart*', *Comparative Literature*, 10: 344–48
CARY, JOYCE. *Art and Reality* (Cambridge University Press). Clark Lectures.
GRIMSLEY, RONALD. 'Hugo, Kierkegaard and the Character of Nero', **RLC**, 32: 230–36
HUNT, H. J. 'Balzac and Lady Ellenborough', *French Studies*, 12: 247–59
KEYNES, GEOFFREY. 'Dr Donne and Scaliger', *Times Literary Supplement*, 21 February, 108
KNOX, R. A. *Literary Distractions* (Sheed & Ward)
LEWIS, NAOMI. 'In Spite of Lit. On Women in Literature', *Twentieth Century*, 164 (August): 114–25
'Literature and Language'. Series in *Essays in Criticism*, with contributions by R. A. Sayce (7: 119–33), John Stedmond (7: 475–77) and Ellis Evans (8 (1958): 111–13
MURCH, A. E. *The Development of the Detective Novel* (Peter Owen)
O'REGAN, M. J. 'Furetière and Wycherley', **MLR**, 53: 77–81
REES, R. *Brave Men. A Study of D. H. Lawrence and Simone Weil* (Gollancz)
SAYCE, R. A. 'The Use of the Term "Baroque" in French Literary History', *Comparative Literature*, 10: 246–60

VINCENT, E. R. and E. M. WILSON. 'Thomas Stanley's Translations and Borrowings', RLC, 32: 548–56
WEST, ALICK. *Mountain in the Sunlight. Studies in Conflict and Unity* (Lawrence & Wishart)
WEST, ANTHONY. *Principles and Persuasions. The Literary Essays* (Eyre & Spottiswoode)
WHITEFIELD, J. H. 'Pirandello and T. S. Eliot, An Essay in Counterpoint', *English Magazine*, 9: 329–57 Wilson, Edward M. 'Spanish and English Religious Poetry of the Seventeenth Century', *Journal of Ecclesiastical History*, 9: 38–53
WINEGARTEN, RENÉE. 'Malherbe and Góngora', MLR, 53: 17–25

1959

ALLOTT, MIRIAM. *Novelists on the Novel* (Routledge & Kegan Paul)
AUSTIN, J. L. 'Mallarmé on Music and Letters', *Bulletin of the John Rylands Library*, 42: 29–39
BENNETT, JEAN. *Poetry and Interpretation* (Oxford University Press)
BERRY, FRANCIS. 'Pronouns in Poetry', *Essays in Criticism*, 9: 196–97
COE, RICHARD H. 'Stendhal, Rossini and the "Conspiracy of Musicians"', MLR, 54: 179–93
EMDEN, CECIL S. *Poets in their Letters* (Oxford University Press)
GARDNER, HELEN. *The Business of Criticism* (Oxford University Press)
GIFFORD, HENRY. 'Anna, Lawrence, and "The Law"', *Critical Quarterly*, 1: 203–06
GOOCH, C. P. 'Voltaire in England', *Contemporary Review*, 11.22 (June): 341–52; 11.23–24 (July): 31–36, 90–93
HALVERSON, J. and I. WATT. 'The Original Nostromo: Conrad's Source', *Review of English Studies*, N. S. 10: 45–52
HENNIG, JOHN. 'A Note on Goethe's Relations with Charles Sterling', MLR, 54: 76–78
—— 'Daniel O'Connell in the Opinion of some German Poets of his Time', MLR, 54: 573–78
HEPPENSTALL, RAYNER. 'Two Voices: English and the Rest', *Times Literary Supplement*, 7 August, xxvi-xxvii
JACK, I. 'The Realm of Flora in Keats and Poussin', *Times Literary Supplement*, 10 April, 212
KERR, L. 'Swinburne and Correggio', *Times Literary Supplement*, 31 July, 447
LABOULLE, LOUISE J. 'A Note on Bertolt Brecht's Adaptation of Marlowe's *Edward II*', MLR, 54: 214–20
MARPLES, MORRIS. *Shanks' Pony: A Study of Walking* (Dent)
MASON, EUDO C. *Deutsche und englische Romantik. Eine Gegenüberstellung* (Gottingen: Vandenhoeck & Ruprecht)
MUIR, KENNETH. 'Shakespeare's Use of Pliny Reconsidered', MLR, 54: 224–25
OAKESHOTT, MICHAEL JOSEPH. *The Voice of Poetry in the Conversation of Mankind. An Essay* (Cambridge: Bowes & Bowes)
O'REAGAN, M. J. 'Two Notes on French Reminiscences in Restoration Comedy', *Hermathena*, 93: 63–70
PASCAL, ROY. 'The Autobiographical Novel and the Autobiography', *Essays in Criticism*, 9: 134–50
PRESCOTT, F. C. *The Poetic Mind* (Oxford University Press)
PRITCHETT, V. S. 'Travel and the Writer', *The Listener*, 26 June, 1061
PRYME, EILEEN E. 'Zola's Plays in England, 1870–1900', *French Studies*, 13: 28–38
RANKIN, H. D. 'Plato and Bernard Shaw, Their Ideal Communities', *Hermathena*, 93: 71–77
RICHARDS, I. A. 'Poetry as an Instrument of Research', *The Listener*, 17 September, 443–44

RICHARDSON, MAURICE. 'The Psychoanalysis of Ghost Stories', *Twentieth Century*, 166 (December): 419–31
ROE, FREDERICK C. 'Urquhart, traducteur de Rabelais', *Etudes rabelaisiennes*, 1, 112–19
SHACKLETON, ROBERT. 'Comparative Literature and the Enlightenment', in *Comparative Literature. Proceedings of the Second Congress of the ICLA at the University of North Carolina, September 8–12, 1958*, ed. W. P. Friederich (University of North Carolina Press), 1: 56–61
THOMSON, PATRICIA. 'The "Canticus Troili": Chaucer and Petrarch', *Comparative Literature*, 11: 313–28
—— 'Wyatt and the Petrarchan Commentators', *Review of English Studies*, N. S. 10: 225–33
TILLOTSON, KATHLEEN. *The Tale and the Teller: A Lecture on the Place of the Narrator in Fiction* (Hart-Davis)
TIPPETT, MICHAEL. *Moving into Aquarius* (Routledge & Kegan Paul)
TRAINER, JAMES. 'Some Unpublished Shakespeare Notes of Ludwig Tieck', **MLR**, 54: 368–77
WALSH, WILLIAM. *Autobiographical Literature and Educational Thought* (Leeds University Press)
—— *The Use of Imagination: Educational Thought and the Literary Mind* (Chatto & Windus)
WEDGWOOD, C. V. 'Art, Truth and History', *London Magazine*, 6 (May): 37–48
WITTE, W. *Schiller and Burns, and other Essays* (Oxford: Blackwell). The other essays include: 'Time in *Wallenstein* and *Macbeth*' (cf. Witte 1952), 'Scottish Influence on Schiller', 'Carlyle as a Critic of German Literature'
—— 'Zweimal Maria Stuart: Schiller auf der englischen und schottischen Bühne', *Maske und Kothurn*, 5: 221–26

1960

BAXTER, B. M. 'Verwey and Shelley. A Discussion of Verwey's Translations from Shelley's Poetical Works', **MLR**, 55: 221–33
BOULTON, MARJORIE. *The Anatomy of Drama* (Routledge & Kegan Paul)
BRAIN, RUSSELL. *Some Reflections on Genius and Other Essays* (Pitman Medical)
BRETT, R. L. *Reason and Imagination: A Study of Form and Meaning in Four Poems* (Oxford University Press, for Hull University)
BROWN, DAVID D. 'Voltaire, Archbishop Tillotson and the Invention of God', **RLC**, 34: 257–61 Chancellor, Paul. 'British Bards and Continental Composers', *Musical Quarterly*, 46: 1–11
CHAPMAN, K. P. 'Lazarillo de Tormes, a Jest-Book and Benedik', **MLR**, 55: 565–67
CHURCHILL, RICHARD. 'The Art of Autobiography', *Cornhill Magazine*, 1026 (Winter 1960–61): 449–80. Chiari, Joseph. *Realism and Imagination* (Barrie & Rockliff)
COMFORT, ALEX. 'The Play's the Thing', *The Listener*, 10 November, 841–45
CONN, HARVIE M. 'Literature and Criticism', *Westminster Theological Journal*, 23 (November): 16–32
DICK, KAY. *Pierrot* (Hutchinson)
DILLISTONE, FREDERICK WILLIAM. *The Novelist and the Passion Story* (Collins)
ELLIS-FERMOR, UNA. 'The Nature of Plot in Drama', *Essays and Studies by Members of the English Association*, 13: 65–81
ENTWISTLE, ERIC A. *A Literary History of Wallpaper* (Batsford)
ESPINER-SCOTT, JANET. 'Sénèque dans la prose anglaise (1500–1580)', **RLC**, 34: 177–95
GIBBON, F. P. 'The Truth of Fiction', *Essays in Criticism*, 10: 480–83
GILLIES, A. 'Emilie and Berlepsch and Burns', **MLR**, 55: 584–87
GOSSMAN, L. 'Berkeley, Hume and Maupertuis', *French Studies*, 14: 304–24

HAMILTON, GEORGE R. 'Poetry and Life: The Critic's Failure', *Essays by Divers Hands*, 30L 102–14 Henderson, James. 'The Gothic Novel in Wales (1790–1820)', *National Library of Wales Journal*, 11: 244–54

HENNIG, JOHN. 'A Note on the First English Translation of Schiller's *History of the Thirty Years' War*', MLR, 55: 249–54

HEWETT, R. P. *Reading and Response: An Approach to the Criticism of Literature* (Harrap)

HEYWOOD, C. 'Flaubert, Miss Braddon, and George Moore', *Comparative Literature*, 12: 151–58 Hoggart, Richard. 'The Function of Literary Criticism', *The Listener*, 29 December, 1185–89

HOLLOWAY, JOHN. *The Charted Mirror: Literary and Critical Essays* (Routledge & Kegan Paul)

HONIG, EDWIN. *Dark Conceit: The Making of Allegory* (Faber & Faber)

HORNE, COLIN J. and HUGH POWELL. 'A German Analogue for *A Tale of a Tub*', MLR, 55: 488–96

GRAVES, ROBERT. 'How to Pull a Poem Apart', *Harper's Magazine*, 218 (January), 78–80

JAMES, D. G. *Skepticism and Poetry* (Allen & Unwin)

KLIENEBERGER, H. R. 'Ireland through German Eyes, 1944–1957. The Travel-Diaries of Jakob Venedey and Heinrich Böll', *Studies*, 49: 373–88

LERNER, LAURENCE. *The Truest Poetry: An Essay on the Question: 'What is Literature?'* (Hamish Hamilton)

—— 'Sheep and Goats', *Critical Quarterly*, 2: 64–71

LUCAS, FRANK LAURENCE *The Greatest Problem and Other Essays* (Cassell)

McGEARY, GEORGE FREDERICK. *On Detective Fiction and Other Things* (Hollis & Carter)

MAY, DERWENT. 'The Novelist as Moralist and the Moralist as Critic', *Essays in Criticism*, 10: 320–28 Moore, W. G. 'Boileau and Longinus', *French Studies*, 14: 52–62

MORRIS, I. V. 'Grillparzer's Impressions of the English', GLL, 14: 1–15

MURDOCH, IRIS. 'The Sublime and Beautiful Revisited', *Yale Review*, 49: 247–71

NICOLL, ALLARDYCE. '"Tragical-Comical-Historical-Pastoral"; Elizabethan Dramatic Nomenclature', *Bulletin of the John Rylands Library*, 43.1 (September): 70–89

NICOLSON, HAROLD. *The Development of English Biography* (New issue; Hogarth Press)

PASCAL, ROY. *Design and Truth in Autobiography* (Routledge & Kegan Paul)

PRIESTLEY, J. B. *Literature and Western Man* (Heinemann)

PROUDFOOT, L. *Dryden's 'Aeneid' and its Seventeenth-Century Predecessors* (Manchester University Press)

RAMSEY, A. M. *Oratory and Literature* (Oxford University Press). English Association presidential address

RAPHAEL, DAVID DAICHES. *The Paradox of Tragedy* (Allen & Unwin). The Mahlon Powell Lecture.

SEZNEC, JEAN. 'Michelet à Oxford', *French Studies*, 14: 149–52

SMITH, BERNARD. *European Vision and the South Pacific, 1768–1850. A Study in the History of Art and Ideas* (Oxford: Carendon)

SPEAIGHT, ROBERT. *The Christian Theatre* (Bums & Oates)

STARKIE, ENID. *From Gautier to Eliot: The Influence of France on English Literature, 1851–1939* (Hutchinson)

WEDGWOOD, C. V. *Truth and Opinion* (Collins)

WILLIAMS, MARGARET A. 'Some Unpublished Documents concerning Espronceda's Exile in France', MLR, 55: 419–22

WILLIAMS, RAYMOND. 'Lawrence and Tolstoy', *Critical Quarterly*, 2: 33–39

1961

ANDERSON, M. S. 'Some British Influences on Russian Intellectual Life and Society in the Eighteenth Century', *Slavonic and East European Review*, 39: 148–63

BARBER, G. 'Galignani's and the Publication of English Books in France from 1800 to 1852: A List of English Newspapers and Magazines Published in Paris, 1814–1850', *The Library*, 16: 267–86

'Battles with Babel: The Translator as Mediator', *Times Literary Supplement*, 13 October, 732

BAYLEY, JOHN. 'The Novel and the Life Standard', *London Magazine*, 8 (February): 60–66

BOWRA, C. M. *Mediaeval Love-Song* (Athlone Press). John Coffin Memorial Lecture

BRADBROOK, B. R. 'The Literary Relationship between G. K. Chesterton and Karel Čapek', *Slavonic and East European Review*, 39: 327–38

BREWER, D. S. 'English in the University III: Language and Literature', *Essays in Criticism*, 11: 243–55

BRUMFITT, J. H. 'Voltaire and Warburton', *Studies on Voltaire and the Eighteenth Century*, 18: 35–56

BURKE, KENNETH. 'The Principle of Composition', *Poetry* 99 (October): 46–53

CAMERON, J. M. *Poetry and Dialectics* (Leeds University Press)

CANNINGS, BARBARA. 'Towards a Definition of Farce as a Literary "Genre"', MLR, 56: 558–60

COX, C. B., NORMAN St JOHN-STEVAS, DONALD DAVIE, MARTIN JARRETT-KERR and C. S. LEWIS. 'Symposium: Pornography and Obscenity', *Critical Quarterly*, 3: 99–122

CUNLIFFE, MARCUS. 'Europe and America: Transatlantic Images', *Encounter*, 17.6 (December): 19–29

CURRAN, EILEEN. 'The *Foreign Quarterly Review* on Russian and Polish Literature', *Slavonic and East European Review*, 40: 206–19

DANE, CLEMENCE. *Approaches to Drama* (Oxford University Press). Presidential Address, English Association

DONOGHUE, DENIS. 'Poetry and the Behaviour of Speech', *Hudson Review*, 14: 537–49

DRAPER, R. P. 'Style and Matter', *Revue des langues vivantes*, 27: 15–23

DYSON, A. E. 'The Critic as Connoisseur', *The Listener*, 66: 763–64

'Exchanges between Continents: Europe and the American Continent', *Times Literary Supplement*, 13 October, 738–39

FITZGIBBON, CONSTANTINE. 'Politics and the Novel', *Encounter*, 16.6 (June): 71–73

GOOCH, G. P. 'Anglo-French Contacts in the Eighteenth Century', in Id., *French Profiles: Prophets and Pioneers* (Longman), 29–43

HARDY, BARBARA. 'Formal Analysis and Common Sense', *Essays in Criticism*, 11: 112–15

HENDERSON, G. P. 'The Idea of Literature', *British Journal of Aesthetics*, 1: 217–30

HEPPENSTALL, RAYNER. 'The Anatomy of Francophobia', *Twentieth Century* 169: 238–45

—— *The Fourfold Tradition: Notes on the French and English Literatures, with some Ethnological and Historical Asides* (Barrie & Rockiff)

HONOUR, HUGH. *Chinoiserie: The Vision of Cathay* (Murray)

HOUGH, GRAHAM. 'The Allegorical Circle', *Critical Quarterly*, 3: 199–209

HOWARTH, W. D. 'The Theme of the *Droit du seigneur* in the Eighteenth-Century Theatre', *French Studies*, 15: 228–40

HOWE, IRVING. *Politics and the Novel* (New Left Books)

HOOK, SIDNEY. 'Enlightenment and Radicalism', *Encounter*, 17.2 (August): 44–50

KERMODE, FRANK. 'The "Banquet of Sense"', *Bulletin of the John Rylands Library*, 44: 68–99

—— 'The European View of Christoper Brennan', *Australian Letters*, 3: 57–63

—— 'Edmund Wilson and Mario Praz', *Encounter,* 16.5 (May): 69–73
—— 'Poet and Dancer before Diaghilev', *Partisan Review,* January, 48–75
LEVER, KATHERINE. *The Novel and the Reader* (Methuen)
LEWIS, C. S. *An Experiment in Criticism* (Cambridge University Press)
MASON, EUDO C. *Rilke, Europe, and the English-SpeakingWorld* (Cambridge University Press)
MUIR, KENNETH. *Last Periods of Shakespeare, Racine, Ibsen* (Liverpool University Press)
PICK, R. *Schiller in England, 1787–1960: A Bibliography* (University of London Institute of Germanic Studies)
PRAWER, S. S. 'Lyric Structures', **MLR**, 56: 373–77
READ, HERBERT. 'The Style of Criticism', in *English Studies Today: Second Series. Lectures and Papers Read at the Fourth Conference of the International Association of University Professors held at Lausanne and Berne, August 1959,* ed. G. Bonnard (Bern: Francke), 29–41
READ, HERBERT and EDWARD DAHLBERG. *Truth is More Sacred: A Critical Exchange on Modern Literature* (Routledge & Kegan Paul)
ROLPH, C. H., ED. *Does Pornography Matter?* (Routledge & Kegan Paul)
ROSE, WILLIAM, 'A Letter from W. B. Yeats on Rilke', GLL, 15: 62–70
ROWLEY, BRIAN A. 'Theodor Fontane: A German Novelist in the European Tradition', *GLL,* 15: 71–88
SMEED, J. W. 'Carlyle's Jean-Paul-Übersetzungen', *Deutsche Vierteljahrsschrift fur Literaturwissenschaft und Geistesgeschichte,* 35: 262–79
SNOW, C. P. 'Italo Svevo: Forerunner of Cooper and Amis', *Essays and Studies,* 14: 7–16
STEINER, GEORGE. *The Death of Tragedy* (Faber & Faber)
TILLYARD, E. M. W. *Some Mythical Elements in English Literature* (Chatto & Windus)
WHITE, BEATRICE. 'Ultima Thule: Some English Travellers to Iceland', *Essays and Studies,* 14: 81–101
WILLIAMS, RAYMOND. 'The Law and Literary Merit', *Encounter,* 17.3 (September): 66–69
—— *The Long Revolution* (Chatto & Windus)
WITTE, W. 'Das neue Schillerbild der britischen Germanistik', *Schiller-Jahrbuch,* 5: 402–13

1962

ALLEN, JOHN. *Masters of European Drama* (Dobson)
ATKINSON, MARGARET E. 'Wolf Baudissin: Translator', GLL, 16: 164–73
AUDEN, W. H. 'The Poet and the City', *Massachusetts Review,* 3: 449–74
AUTY, R. 'The Formation of the Slovene Literary Language against the Background of the Slavonic National Revival', *Slavonic and East European Review,* 41 (1962–63): 391–402
BARNETT, PAMELA R. *Theodore Haak, FRS (1605–1690): The First German Translator of 'Paradise Lost'* (The Hague: Mouton). Anglica Germanica, 3
BERRY, FRANCIS. *Poetry and the Physical Voice* (Routledge & Kegan Paul)
BLACKSTONE, BERNARD. *The LostTravellers: A Romantic Theme with Variations* (Longmans)
BOASE, A. M. 'The Definition of Mannerism', in *Actes du III congres de l'Association Internationale de Littérature Comparée/Proceedings of the IIIrd Congress of the International Comparative Literature Association (Utrecht: 21–26 VIII 1961)* (The Hague: Mouton), 43–55
BOGDANOW, FANNI. 'The Spanish baladro and the *Conte du Brait*', *Romania,* 83: 383–99
BOLTON, W. F. 'The Old Icelandic Drottkvaett: A Problem in Verse Translation', *Comparative Literature,* 14: 280–89
BOWRA, C. M. *Primitive Song* (Weidenfeld & Nicolson)
BOYD, JAMES. *Goethe und Shakespeare* (Cologne/Opladen: Westdeutscher Verlag)
BRANDT, G. W. 'Realism and Parables (From Brecht to Arden)', *Stratford-upon-Avon Studies,* 4 (Contemporary Theatre): 32–55
BROPHY, BRIGID. 'The Rococo Seducer', *London Magazine,* 2 (May): 54–71

BULLOUGH, GEOFFREY. 'Literary Relations of Shaw's "Mrs Warren"', *Philological Quarterly*, 41: 339–58
CAMPBELL, J. L. 'The Contribution of Edward Lhuyd to the Study of Scottish Gaelic', *Transactions of the Honourable Society of Cymmrodorion*, session 1962: 77–80
CECIL-WILLIAMS, JOHN. 'Spanning Two Cultures', *Transactions of the Honourable Society of Cymmrodorion*, session 1962: 161–64
CHADWICK, NORA K. 'The Vikings and the Western World', in *Proceedings of the International Congress on Celtic Studies Held in Dublin, 6–10 July, 1959*, ed. Brian Ó Cuív (Dublin: Dublin Institute for Advanced Studies), 13–42
CHANDOS, JOHN, ED. *'To Deprave and Corrupt': Original Studies in the Nature and Definition of 'Obscenity'* (Souvenir Press)
COHEN, J. M. *English Translators and Translations* (Longmans for the British Council and the National Book League)
COOPER, M. A. 'A Study of Sixteenth-Century Translations of Virgil into French'. Doctoral dissertation, Leeds
COUPE, W. A. 'Thierry, Meyer and Der Heilige', **GLL**, 16: 105–16
COURTNEY, C. P. 'David Hume et l'abbé Raynal. Une source de l'*Histoire philosophique des deux Indes*', **RLC**, 36: 565–71
——. 'Edmund Burke and Petrus Camper', *English Studies*, 43: 467–75
CRAIG, ALEC. *The Banned Books of England and Other Countries. A Study of the Conception of Literary Obscenity* (George Allen & Unwin)
CRANSTON, MAURICE. 'Culture and Anxiety', *The Listener*, 67: 978–79
——. 'Rousseau's Visit to England, 1766–7', *Essays by Divers Hands*, 31: 16–34
'Criticizing Poetry', **TLS**, 12 January, 25
CROSS, J. E. 'Aspects of Microcosm and Macrocosm in Old English Literature', *Comparative Literature*, 14: 1–22
DAVIE, DONALD. 'Conventional Language', *Dubliner*, 3 (May): 15–28
——. 'Two Analogies for Poetry', *The Listener*, 57: 598–99
——. 'Turgenev in England, 1850–1950', in *Studies in Russian and Polish Literature in Honour of Waclaw Lednicki*, ed. Z. Folejewski, F. J. Whitfield & A. Kaspin (The Hague: Mouton), 168–84
DICKINS, B. 'The Teaching of Italian in Cambridge', in *Italian Studies Presented to E. R. Vincent*, ed. C. P. Brand, K. Foster and U. Limentani (Cambridge: Heffer), 15–26
DONOGHUE, DENIS. 'The Play of Words', *The Listener*, 58: 55–57
DRAGE, C. L. 'The Anacreonta and 18th-Century Russian Poetry', *Slavonic and East European Review*, 41 (1962–63): 110–34
DYSON, A. E. 'Turning-Point for Criticism', *English*, 14 (Summer): 44–48
FLETCHER, IAN. 'Le Symbolisme français en Angleterre', **RLC**, 26: 158–59. Additions to the bibliography by G. Ross Roy: **RLC**, 34 (1960): 645–59
FLETCHER, JOHN. 'Samuel Beckett et Jonathan Swift: Vers une étude comparee', *Littératures X*, 11: 81–117
FORSTER, LEONARD, 'Der Zweite Weltkrieg brachte keinen Bruch', *Die Zeit*, 6 April, 24
FURST, LILIAN R. 'Madame Bovary and Effi Briest', *Romanistisches Jahrbuch*, 12: 124–35
GARRETT, TH. J. 'Oskars Empfang in England', *Die Zeit*, 26 October, 15
GASCOIGNE, BAMBER. *Twentieth-Century Drama* (Hutchinson)
GIFFORD, HENRY. 'English in the Universities IV: The Use of Comparative Literature', *Essays in Criticism*, 12: 67–74
GLENDINNING, NIGEL. 'The Philosophy of Henri Bergson in the Poetry of Antonio Machado', **RLC**, 36: 50–70
'Going into Europe: A Symposium', *Encounter*, 19.6 (December): 56–65; 20.1 (January 1963): 53–61; 20.2 (February 1963): 64–74; 20.3 (March 1963): 68–78

GOLDSMITH, MARGARET. 'The Christian Perspective in Beowulf', *Comparative Literature*, 14: 71–90
GRAVES, ROBERT. *Oxford Addresses on Poetry* (Cassell)
GRAY, R. D. 'J. M. W. Turner and Goethe's Colour-Theory', in *German Studies Presented to Walter Horace Bruford* (Harrap), 112–16
GREEN, MARTIN. 'A Literary Defence of "The Two Cultures"', *Critical Quarterly*, 4: 155–62
GREEN, PETER. 'Aspects of the Historical Novel', *Essays by Divers Hands*, 31: 35–50
GREGOR, IAN and BRIAN NICHOLAS. *The Moral and the Story* (Faber & Faber)
GRIMSLEY, RONALD. 'Concerning an Unpublished Note from Morellet to Hume', MLR, 57: 65–67
——. 'J.-J. Rousseau jugé par un pasteur écossais', RLC, 36: 558–60
——. 'Søren Kierkegaard as a Reader of French Literature', in *Proceedings ICLA* (see Boase 1962, 313
HARDING, D. W. 'Psychological Processes in the Reading of Fiction', *British Journal of Aesthetics*, 2: 133–47
HASSALL, CHRISTOPHER. 'D. H. Lawrence and the Etruscans', *Essays by Divers Hands*, 31: 61–78
HAWKES, TERENCE. 'The Problems of Prosody', *Review of English Literature*, 3 (April): 32–49
HEMMINGS, F. W. J. 'Julian Sorel and Julian the Apostate', *French Studies*, 16: 229–44
HOGGART, RICHARD. 'The Nostalgic, the Narkers, and the Knowing', *Encounter*, 18 (April): 59–62
HOLLOWAY, JOHN. 'The Simplicities of Poetry', *Essays by Divers Hands*, 31: 79–94
HOUGH, GRAHAM. 'The Muse and Her Chains', *The Listener*, 67: 763–65; 803–05; 843–45
HUNT, HUGH. *The Live Theatre: An Introduction to the History and Practice of the Stage* (Oxford University Press)
ILLINGWORTH, R. N. 'Celtic Tradition and the Lai of Guigemar', *Medium Aevum*, 31: 176–87
INGLEDEW, J. E. 'Chapman's Use of Lucan in Caesar and Pompey', *Review of English Studies*, 13: 283–88
'Intelligence and Servitude: the Marxist Critics', TLS, 15 February
JAMES, G. INGLI. 'The Autonomy of the Work of Art: Modern Criticism and the Christian Tradition', *Sewanee Review*, 70: 296–318
'John Disney and the Study of German in Eighteenth-Century England', GLL, 16: 186–92
JOLLES, FRANK. 'Shakespeares Sommernachtstraum in Deutschland. Einige Betrachtungen uber der Vorgang der Assimilation', GLL, 16: 229–37
JONES, DAVID. 'Use and Sign', *The Listener*, 67: 900–01
JONES, HENRY JOHN F. *On Aristotle and Greek Tragedy* (Chatto & Windus)
KELLY, JOHN C. 'C. S. Lewis's Good Reader', *Studies*, 51: 298–307
KERMODE, FRANK. 'Myth, Reality and Fiction', *The Listener*, 58: 311–13
——. *Puzzles and Epiphanies: Essays and Reviews* (Routledge & Kegan Paul)
'Kinds of Criticism', TLS, 23 February, 121
KITTO, H. D. F. 'Tragic Drama and Intellectualism', *Essays by Divers Hands*, 31: 95–113
KOESTLER, ARTHUR. 'Reflections on the Peninsula of Europe', *Essays by Divers Hands*, 31: 114–22
LEAVIS, F. R. 'Two Cultures? The Significance of C. P. Snow', *Melbourne Critical Review*, 5: 90–101. Also appeared as a brochure (Chatto & Windus), together with 'An Essay on Sir Charles Snow's Rede Lecture', by Michael Yudkin. Cf also Leavis's article 'The Significance of C. P. Snow', *The Spectator*, 9 March, 297–303

LERNER, LAURENCE. 'Novels about the Future', *The Listener*, 58: 143–44
——. 'Racine and the Elizabethans', *Essays in Criticism*, 12: 353–69
LEWIS, C. S. 'The Anthropological Approach', in *English and Medieval Studies Presented to J. R. R. Tolkien on the Occasion of His Seventieth Birthday*, ed. Norman Davis and C. L. Wrenn. George Allen & Unwin), 219–30
LINDSAY, JACK. *Our Celtic Heritage* (Weidenfeld & Nicholson)
LODGE, DAVID. 'The Contemporary Novel, and All That Jazz', *London Magazine*, 2 (August): 73–80
LUCIE-SMITH, EDWARD. 'The Tortured Yearned as Well. An Enquiry into Themes of Cruelty in Current Verse', *Critical Quarterly*, 4: 34–44
MAC CANA, PROINSIAS. 'The Influence of the Vikings on Celtic Literature', in *Proceedings of the International Congress on Celtic Studies* (see Chadwick), 78–118
MASON, EUDO C. 'Gundolf und Shakespeare', *Jahrbuch der deutschen Shakespeare-Gesellschaft*, 98: 110–77
MAXWELL, J. C. 'Keats and the Bible', *Keats-Shelley Journal*, 11: 15–16
MCCULLOUGH, NORMAN. *The Negro in English Literature: A Critical Introduction* (Ilfracombe: Stockwell)
MORRISON, MARY. 'Henri Estienne and Sappho', *Bibliothèque d'Humanisme et Renaissance*, 24: 388–91
MUIR, EDWIN. *The Estate of Poetry* (Hogarth Press). Foreword by Archibald MacLeish; Charles Eliot Norton Lectures
MUIR, KENNETH. 'Verse and Prose', *Stratford-upon-Avon Studies*, 4 (Contemporary Theatre), 95–115
NICOLL, ALLARDYCE. *The Theatre and Dramatic Theory* (Harrap)
NOWOTTNY, WINIFRED. *The Language Poets Use* (Athlone Press)
Ó MAONAIGH, CAINNEACH. 'Scribhneóiri Gaeilge an Seachtú hAois Deag', *Studia Hibernica*, 2: 182–208
O'CONNOR, FRANK. 'Adventures in Translation', *The Listener*, 67: 175–78
——. 'Censorship', *Dubliner*, 2 (March): 39–44
OWEN, D. D. R. 'The Radiance in the Grail Castle', *Romania*, 83: 108–17
PARRINDER, G. *Upanishads, Gita and Bible: A Comparative Study of Hindu and Christian Scriptures* (Leiden: Brill)
PARTRIDGE, MONICA. 'Slavonic Themes in English Poetry of the 19th Century', *Slavonic and East European Review*, 41 (1962–63): 420–41
PASCAL, ROY. 'Tense and Novel', **MLR**, 57: 1–11
PEACOCK, RONALD. 'A Type of Dramatic Structure in Lyric Poems', GLL, 15: 255–73
PIETRKIEWICZ, J. 'Polish Literature in its European Context', *Slavonic and East European Review*, 41: 101–09
PRATER, D. A. 'Stefan Zweig and England', GLL, 16: 1–13
RAWSON, CLAUDE J. 'Some Remarks on Eighteenth-Century "Delicacy" with a Note on Hugh Kelly's *False Delicacy* (1768)", *Journal of English and Germanic Philology*, 61: 1–13
RIDLEY, M. R. *Studies in Three Literatures: English, Latin, Greek. Contrasts and Comparisons* (Dent). Reviewed by George Steiner in *The Spectator*, 9 February, 180
RITCHIE, J. M. 'German Books in Glasgow and Edinburgh, 1500–1700', **MLR**, 57: 523–40
RODWAY, ALLAN. 'The Need for Formal Criticism', *The Listener*, 68: 1089–93
——. 'Terms for Comedy', *Nottingham Renaissance and Modern Studies*, 5: 102–24
ROUND, NICHOLAS G. 'Renaissance Culture and its Opponents in Fifteenth-Century Castile', **MLR**, 57: 204–15
SAYCE, R. A. 'The Definition of the Term "Style"', in *Proceedings ICLA* (see Boase), 156–66

SELDEN, SAMUEL. *The Stage in Action* (Peter Owen)
SHEED, WILFRID. 'Pornography and Literary Pleasure', *Catholic World*, 194: 222–29
SHEPHARD, LESLIE. *The Broadside Ballad* (Jenkins)
SMITH, H. A. 'Dipsychus among the Shadows', *Stratford-upon-Avon Studies*, 4 (Contemporary Theatre), 138–63
SMITH, R. D. 'Back to the Text', *Stratford-upon-Avon Studies*, 4 (Contemporary Theatre), 115–37
SNOW, C. P. *Recent Thoughts on the Two Cultures* (Birkbeck College)
SOUTHERN, RICHARD. *The Seven Ages of the Theatre* (Faber & Faber)
SPENDER, STEPHEN. 'Is a New Literature Possible?', *Saturday Review*, 22 September, 16–19
STEINER, GEORGE. 'F. R. Leavis', *Encounter*, 18.5 (May): 37–45
STYAN, J. L. 'Television Drama', *Stratford-upon-Avon Studies* 4 (Contemporary Theatre), 184–204
———. *The Dark Comedy: The Development of Modern Comic Tragedy* (Cambridge University Press)
SWARDSON, H. R. *Poetry and the Fountain of Light: Observations on the Conflict between Christian and Classical Traditions in Seventeenth-Century Poetry* (Allen & Unwin)
TANNER, MICHAEL. 'The Middle Way in Literary Criticism', *The Listener*, 68: 713–14
THOMAS, R. HINTON 'Kleist and the Thorough Bass', *PEGS*, 32: 74–94
THOMPSON, W. MEREDITH. 'Chaucer's Translation of the Bible', in *English and Medieval Studies Presented to J. R. R. Tolkien* (see Lewis), 183–99
TILLYARD, E. M. W. *Essays Literary and Educational* (Chatto & Windus)
WALSH, W. H. 'History and Theory', *Encounter*, 18: no. 6 (June), 50–54
WATKIN, MORGAN. *La Civilisation française dans les Mabinogion* (Paris: Didier). Etudes de littérature étrangère et comparée, 45
WATSON, J. R. 'Wordsworth and Constable', *Review of English Studies*, 13: 361–67; 14 (1963): 275
WEAVER, ANN. C. 'William Sotheby's Translation of Schiller's "Lied von der Glocke"', *MLR*, 57: 573–75
WEEVERS, T. 'Henriette Roland Holst and William Morris: A Case of Rhythmical Affinity in One Poetic Genre', in *Proceedings ICLA* (see Boase), 318–19. Cf also W.'s article 'On the Origins of Accentual Verse Form used by William Morris and Henriette Roland Hoist', *Neophilologus*, 46, 210–26
WESKER, ARNOLD. 'Art and Action', The Listener, 57, 805–08
WIGHTMAN, W. P. D. *Science and the Renaissance I: An Introduction to the Study of the Emergence of the Sciences in the Sixteenth Century; 2: An Annotated Bibliography of the Sixteenth-Century Books Relating to the Sciences in the University of Aberdeen* (Edinburgh: Oliver & Boyd)
WILKINSON, ELIZABETH MARY. 'The Inexpressible and the Un-Speakable. Some Romantic Attitudes to Art and Language', GLL, 16: 308–20
WILLIAMS, GWYN A. 'Morgan John Rhys and Volney's Ruins of Empires', *Bulletin of the Board of Celtic Studies*, 20: 58–73
WILLIAMS, J. E. CAERWYN 'L'Enfant sage ac Adrian et Epictitus yn Gymraeg', *Bulletin of the Board of Celtic Studies*, 19: 259–95; 20: 17–28
WILLIAMS, MARY. 'King Arthur in History and Legend', *Folklore*, 73 (Summer): 73–88
WILLIAMS, RAYMOND. 'A Dialogue on Tragedy', *New Left Review*, 13–14 (January-April): 22–35
WILSON, COLIN. *The Strength to Dream: Literature and the Imagination* (Gollancz)
WILSON, N. 'Ernest Stadler and Charles Péguy: Notes on the Fiction and Facts of a Relationship', *MLR*, 57: 551–55
WILSON-JONES, K. 'Voltaire's Letters and Notebooks in English', in *Studies in Comparative Literature*, ed. W. F. McNeir (Louisiana State University Press), 120–29

WOOLF, ROSEMARY. 'The Theme of Christ the Lover-Knight in Medieval English Literature', *Review of English Studies*, 13: 1–16
YOUNG, ANDREW. *The Poet and the Landscape* (Hart-Davis)
YUILL, W. E. '"Character is Fate": A Note on Thomas Hardy, George Eliot and Novalis', MLR, 57: 401–02

1963

ALLOTT, KENNETH. 'Matthew Arnold's "The New Sirens" and George Sand', *Victorian Poetry*, 1: 156–58
BARBER, W. H. 'L'Angleterre dans Candide', *RLC*, 37: 204–15
—— 'Voltaire and Quakerism: Enlightenment and the Inner Light', *Studies on Voltaire and the Eighteenth Century*, 24 (= Transactions of the First International Congress on the Enlightenment: 1), 81–109
BATCHELOR, R. 'Unamuno devant la littérature française', *Nottingham French Studies*, 2: 35–47; 3 (1964), 82–93
BATESON, F. W. 'The Literary Artifact', *Journal of General Education*, 15: 79–92
——. 'Work in Progress II: Renaissance Literature', *Essays in Criticism*, 13: 117–31. Reply by J. P. Cooper ('Renaissance as Inflation'), 435–37. Rejoinder by Bateson, 437
BEER, J. B. 'Coleridge and Boehme's Aurora', *Notes & Queries*, 208: 183–87
BERGONZI, BERNARD. 'The Novel No Longer Novel', *The Listener*, 70: 415–16
BRAIN (Lord). 'Diagnosis of Genius', *British Journal of Aesthetics*, 3: 114–28
BRIDGWATER, PATRICK. 'Arthur Waley and Brecht', GLL, 17: 216–32
BROMLEY, J. F. 'The Literature of Madness', *Central Literary Magazine*, December, 4–14
BROWN, IVOR. 'Critics and Creators', *Saturday Review*, 10 August: 3–39
BURGESS, ANTHONY. 'The Corruption of the Exotic', *The Listener*, 70: 465–67
BURNS, COLIN A. 'Zola in Exile. Notes on an Unpublished Diary of 1898', *French Studies*, 17: 14–26
CAMERON, J. M. 'The Poetic Imagination', *The Listener*, 59: 375–76
CARR, J. L. 'Gorgons, Gormogons, Medusists and Masons', MLR, 58: 73–78
CHADWICK, NORA, ED. *Celt and Saxon: Studies in the Early British Border* (Cambridge University Press)
COHEN, J. M. *The Baroque Lyric* (Hutchinson)
COLLIS, JOHN STEWART. *Marriage and Genius. Strindberg and Tolstoy; Studies in Tragicomedy* (Cassell)
CONQUEST, ROBERT. 'Science Fiction and Literature', *Critical Quarterly*, 5: 355–57
COULSON, PETER. 'The Attack on Leavis', *Essays in Criticism*, 13: 107–12. Reply by Frank Kermode, rejoinder by Coulson, 305
COURTNEY, C. P. *Montesquieu and Burke* (Oxford: Blackwell)
CRISPIN, EDMUND. 'Science Fiction', TLS, 25 October, 865–66
'The Critical Moment', TLS, 26 July, 535–78. Contributions by, among others, George Steiner ('Humane Literacy', 539–40), W. W. Robson ('Are Purely Literary Values Enough?', 552–54), F. R. Leavis ('Research in English', 558), John Wain ('Notes on Imagination and Judgement', 561), Graham Hough ('The Function of the Imagination', 577–78). Published as *The Critical Moment. Essays on the Nature of Literature* (Faber, 1964)
DAVIE, DONALD. *The Language of Science and the Language of Literature 1700–1740* (Sheed & Ward). Newman History and Philosophy of Science Series, 13. Review article by Graham Martin, 'Literature and Science', *Universities Quarterly*, 18 (1964): 199–211
DAY-LEWIS, CECIL. 'On Translating Poetry', *Essays by Divers Hands*, 32: 18–35
FRASER, P. M. 'Cavafy and the Elgin Marbles', MLR, 58: 66–68
FREEMAN, ROSEMARY. 'Parody as a Literary Form: George Herbert and Wilfred Owen', *Essays in Criticism*, 13: 307–22

FURNESS, RAYMOND. 'Nietzsche's Views on the English and his Concept of European Community', GLL, 17: 319–25
GARDINER, S. C. 'Translation Technique in 17th-century Russia', *Slavonic and East European Review*, 42: 110–35
GOLDSTÜCKER, E. 'Über einige Probleme der Übersetzung und Edition von Goethes Werken in der Tschechoslowakei', *Weimarer Beiträge*, 6: 1200–05
GOULD, CHARLES. '"Monsieur de Balzac": Le dandysme de Balzac, et son influence sur sa création littéraire', *Cahiers de l'Association Internationale des Etudes Françaises*, 15: 379–93
GREEN, MARTIN. 'Lionel Trilling and the Two Cultures', *Essays in Criticism*, 13: 375–85
GREENSLADE, S. L., ED. *The Cambridge History of the Bible*, 3: *The West from the Reformation to the Present Day* (Cambridge University Press)
GRIFFITHS, RICHARD. 'Some Uses of Petrarchan Imagery in Sixteenth-Century France', *French Studies*, 18: 311–21
GRIGSON, GEOFFREY, ED. *The Concise Encyclopaedia of Modern World Literature* (Hutchinson)
HARDING, D. W. *Experience into Words: Essays on Poetry* (Chatto & Windus)
HARDING, F. W. J. 'Matthew Arnold and Wales', *Transactions of the Honourable Society of Cymmrodorion*, 251–72
HARVEY, W. J. 'Work in Progress I: The Character and Context of Things', *Essays in Criticism*, 13: 50–55
HASTINGS, PAT G. 'Symbolism in the Adaptations of Greek Myth by Modern French Dramatists', *Nottingham French Studies*, 2: 25–34
HEMMINGS, F. W. J. 'A Note on the Origins of *La Chartreuse de Parme*', MLR, 58: 392–95
HEPPENSTALL, RAYNER. *The Intellectual Part* (Barrie & Rockliff)
HILL, D. M. 'Romance and Epic', *English Studies*, 44: 95–107
HOGGART, RICHARD. 'A Question of Tone: Some Problems in Autobiographical Writing' (from a lecture given at the Royal Society of Literature), *Critical Quarterly*, 5: 73–90
———. 'The Difficulties of Democratic Debate', *Critical Quarterly* 5: 197–212
HOLBROOK: DAVID. *The Quest for Love* (Methuen)
HOUGH, GRAHAM. 'The Critic and the Common Reader' (1: 'The Function of Criticism', 2: 'Morality and the Novel', 3: 'A Programme for Literary Education'), *The Listener*, 69: 707–09; 747–48; 783–84
———. *The Dream and the Task: Literature and Morals in the Culture of Today* (Duckworth)
HOWARTH, W. D. 'The Sources of *L'École des femmes*', MLR, 58: 10–14
HUXLEY, ALDOUS. *Literature and Science* (Chatto & Windus)
HUXTER, N. E. W. 'Tennyson and Juvenal', *Notes & Queries*, 208: 448–49
HYDE, H. Montgomery. *A History of Pornography* (Heinemann)
INGAMELLS, JOHN. 'An Image Shared by Blake and Henri Rousseau', *British Journal of Aesthetics*, 3: 346–52
JONES, D. GWENALLT. 'Myth a Symbol yn y Llenyddiaeth Fodern', *Efrydiau Athronyddol*, 26: 3–12
JONES, THOMAS. 'The Early Evolution of the Legend of Arthur', *Nottingham Medieval Studies*, 8: 3–21
KEENE, DENNIS. 'Engagement', *Essays in Criticism*, 14: 285–300
KELL, RICHARD. 'A Note on Versification', *British Journal of Aesthetics*, 3: 341–45
KENNEDY, MARGARET. 'The Novelist and His Public', *Essays by Divers Hands*, 32: 72–83
KITCHEN, LAURENCE. 'The Theatre of Cruelty', *The Listener*, 70: 419–21
———. 'The Wide Stage', *The Listener*, 59: 531–33
———. 'The Lion-Tamers: Violence in Art', *The Listener*, 72: 87–89
KUNA, F. M. 'T. S. Eliot's Dissociation of Sensibility and the Critics of Metaphysical Poetry', *Essays in Criticism*, 13: 241–52

LAVERS, ANNETTE. *L'usurpateur et le prétendant: Le psychologue dans la litterature contemporaine* (Paris: Minard)
LEAVIS, F. R. *'Scrutiny': A Retrospect* (Cambridge University Press)
LEWIS, ANEURIN. 'Ieuan Fardd a'r Llenorion Saesneg', *Llên Cymru*, 7: 172–92
LINDSAY, DAVID W., 'Kotzebue in Scotland, 1792–1813', **PEGS**, 33: 56–74
LOOMIS, R. S. *The Grail: From Celtic Myth to Christian Symbol* (University of Wales Press)
LUCAS, F. L. *The Drama of Chekhov, Synge, Yeats, and Pirandello* (Cassell)
——. *The Drama of Ibsen and Strindberg* (Cassell)
MAC EOIN, GEARÓID S. 'On the Legend of the Origin of the Picts', *Studia Hibernica*, 4: 138–54
MASON, EUDO C. *Exzentrische Bahnen, Studien zum Dichterbewusstsein derNeuzeit* (Göttingen: Vandenhoeck und Ruprecht)
MASON, HAYDN T. 'Voltaire and Manichean Dualism', *Studies on Voltaire and the Eighteenth Century*, 26 (= Transactions of the First International Congress on the Enlightenment, 3): 1143–60
MAY, F. 'Paulus Silentiarius and Ugo Foscolo's Lines to Callirhoe', *Italian Studies*, 18: 67–77
MORRISON, MARY. 'Catullus and the Poetry of the Renaissance in France', *Bibliothèque d'Humanisme et Renaissance*, 25: 25–56
MOWAT, C. L. 'From the Edwardian Age to the Thirties: Some Literary Memoirs', *Critical Quarterly* 5, 157–67
MYLNE: VIVIENNE. 'Changing Attitudes towards Truth in Fiction', *Nottingham Renaissance and Modern Studies*, 7: 53–77
NICHOLAS, BRIAN. 'Two Nineteenth-Century Utopias: The Influence of Renan's *L'Avenir de la science* on Wilde's *The Soul of Man under Socialism*', **MLR**, 59: 361–70
NICKLAUS, ROBERT. 'Marivaux et la comédie italienne', in *Studi in onore di Carlo Pellegrini* (Turin: Società editrice internazionale), 279–87
O'BRIEN, CONOR CRUISE. *Maria Cross: Imaginative Patterns in a Group of Catholic Writers* (Burns & Oates)
O'CONNOR, FRANK. *The Lonely Voice: A Study of the Short Story* (Macmillan)
OMAN, CAROLA. 'What They Read (Admirals Nelson and Collingwood; Generals John Moore, Arthur Wellesley, and Napoleon Buonaparte)', *Essays by Divers Hands*, 32: 84–98
RAINE, KATHLEEN. 'Blake's Debt to Antiquity', *Sewanee Review*, 71: 352–450
REED, T. J. 'Mann and Turgenev — A First Love', *GLL*, 17: 313–18
REES, D. G. 'John Florio and Anton Francesco Doni', *Comparative Literature*, 15: 33–38
RICHARDSON, JOANNA. 'The Critic and the Public', *Essays by Divers Hands*, 32: 99–111
RIGHTER, WILLIAM. *Logic and Criticism* (Routledge & Kegan Paul)
RINSLER, NORMA. 'Classical Literature in the Work of Gérard de Nerval', **RLC**, 37: 5–32
RODWAY, ALLAN. 'The Technique of Formal Criticism', *The Listener*, 69: 21–23
RUNCIMAN, STEVEN. 'Medieval History and the Romantic Imagination', *Essays by Divers Hands*, 32: 112–24
SACKER, HUGH. 'The Message of the Nibelungenlied and the Business of the Literary Critic', **MLR**, 58: 225–27
SAYERS, DOROTHY. *The Poetry of Search and the Poetry of Statement* (Gollancz)
SCREECH, M.A 'Girolamo Cardano's *De Sapientia* and the *Tiers livre de Pantagruel*', *Bibliothèque d'Humanisme et Renaissance*, 25: 97–110
SEZNEC, JEAN. *Literature and the Visual Arts in Nineteenth-Century France* (Hull University Press). Inaugural lecture
SHACKLETON, D. R. 'Bentley and Horace', *Proceedings of the Leeds Philosophical and Literary Society-Literary and Historical Section*, 10: 105–15

SHIELDS, HUGH. 'Les Quinze Signes Descendus en Angleterre: A Medieval Legend in Decline', *French Studies*, 18: 112–22

SMEED, J. W. 'Jean Pauls "Höllenbreughelianismus"', *Deutsche Vierteljahrsschrift für Literaturwissenschaft und Geistesgeschichte*, 37: 558–64

SNOW, C. P. 'The Two Cultures: A Second Look', **TLS**, 25 October, 839–44

SPENDER, STEPHEN. 'Poets and Critics: The Forgotten Difference', *Saturday Review*, 5 October, 15–18

——. *The Struggle of the Modern* (Hamish Hamilton)

SPINK, JOHN S. 'A propos des drames de Beaumarchais. Tragédie bourgeoise anglaise, drame français', **RLC**, 37: 216–26

STEINER, GEORGE. 'Die Perspektive als literaturgeschichtliche Kategorie und ihre Bedeutung für die vergleichende Literaturgeschichte', in *La Littérature comparée en Europe orientale*, ed. István Sőter (Budapest: Akademiai Kiadó), 194–201

SUCKLING, NORMAN, '"L'Ombre actuel du grand Will." A Note on Shakespeare in France', *Durham University Journal*, 56: 99–103

THOMAS, PATRICIA. 'The Three Georges' [George Sand, George, Eliot, George Henry Lewes], *Nineteenth-Century Fiction*, 18: 137–50

THOMAS, R. GEORGE. 'The Enlightenment and Wales in the 18th Century', *Studies on Voltaire and the Eighteenth Century*, 27 (= Transactions of the First International Congress on the Enlightenment, 4): 1575–91

THOMAS, R. HINTON. *Poetry and Song in the German Baroque* (Oxford: Carendon)

TOLLEY, BRUCE. 'The Source of Balzac's *Elixir de longue vie*', **RLC**, 37: 91–97

TREVOR-ROPER, HUGH. 'The Historical Philosophy of the Enlightenment', *Studies on Voltaire and the Eighteenth Century*, 27 (= Transactions of the First International Congress on the Enlightenment, 4): 1667–87

WAIN, JOHN. *Essays on Literature and Ideas* (Macmillan)

WALKER, D. P. *The Decline of Hell: Seventeenth-Century Discussions of Eternal Torment* (Routledge & Kegan Paul)

WEST, PAUL. *The Modern Novel* (Hutchinson)

WHITFIELD, J. H. 'La belle Charité: The Italian Pastoral and the French Seventeenth Century', *Italian Studies*, 18: 33–53

WILLIAMS, RAYMOND. 'Tragic Despair and Revolt', *Critical Quarterly*, 5: 103–15

——. 'Tolstoy, Lawrence, and Tragedy', *Kenyon Review*, 25: 633–50

——. 'Tragic Resignation and Sacrifice', *Critical Quarterly*, 5: 5–19

WILLSON, H. B. 'Dialectic, "Passio" and "Compassio" in the *Kudrun*', **MLR**, 58: 364–76

WITTE, W. 'The Mind's Construction: Characters at Cross-Purposes', **MLR**, 58: 325–34

WREN-LEWIS: JOHN. 'The Passing of Puritanism', *Critical Quarterly*, 5: 295–305

1964

AGES, ARNOLD, 'Voltaire's Biblical Criticism: A Study in Thematic Repetitions', *Studies on Voltaire and the Eighteenth Century*, 30: 205–21

ALDISS, BRIAN. 'C. S. Lewis Discusses Science Fiction with Kingsley Amis', *SF Horizon*, 1: 5–12

AYLEN, LEO. *Greek Tragedy and the Modern World* (Methuen)

BAINTON, R. H. *Studies on the Reformation* (Hodder & Stoughton)

BARRON, W. R. J. 'Joseph of Arimathie and the Estoire del Saint Graal', *Medium Aevum*, 33: 184–94

BATESON, F. W. 'The Alternative to Scrutiny', *Essays in Criticism*, 14: 10–20

BAYLEY: JOHN. 'Vulgarity', *British Journal of Aesthetics*, 4: 298–304

BEARD, HARRY R. 'Figaro in England: Productions of Mozart's Opera, and the Early Adaptions of it in England before 1850', *Maske und Kothurn*, 10: 498–513

BERGONZI, BERNARD. 'Before 1914: Writers and the Threat of War', *Critical Quarterly*, 6: 126–34
BOLSTER, R. 'French Romanticism and the Ireland Myth', *Hermathena*, 99: 42–48
BOWRA, C. M. *In General and in Particular* (Weidenfeld & Nicolson)
BRIGGS, K. M. 'The Influence of the Brothers Grimm in England', in *Brüder-Grimm-Gedenken 1963: Gedenkschrift zur hundertsten Wiederkehr des Todestages von Jakob Grimm*, ed. L. Denecke, I.-M. Greverus and G. Heilfurth (Marburg: Elwert), 511–24
BRISSENDEN, R. F. 'Sterne and Painting', in *Of Books and Humankind: Essays and Poems Presented to Bonamy Dobree*, ed. John Butt (Routledge), 93–108
BROOKE, NICHOLAS. 'The Characters of Drama', *Critical Quarterly*, 6: 72–82
BRUFORD, W. H. 'Interpretation and Information', *Orbis Litterarum*, 19: 3 — 11
BURGESS, ANTHONY. 'A Novelist's Sources are Myth, Language, and the Here-and-Now', *New York Times Book Review*, 19 July, 5 and 26
BURNS, COLIN A. 'Literature and Society: Aspects of the Study and Teaching of Literature with Special Reference to French Nineteenth-Century Writing', in *Literary History & Literary Criticism. Acta of the Ninth Congress, International Federation for Modern Languages and Literature, Held at New York University, August 25th, 1963*, ed. Leon Edel with Kenneth McKee and William M. Gibson (New York University Press), 221–22
CAMPBELL, CLARE. 'Music and Poetry: With some Notes on Benjamin Britten's Setting of Words', *Critical Quarterly*, 6: 253–63
CLOSS, AUGUST. 'Basic Patterns and Changing Themes and Forms in Tragedy', *Maske und Kothurn*, 10: 644–59
CRAIG, DAVID. 'A National Literature? Recent Scottish Writing', *Studies on Scottish Literature*, 1: 151–69
CROSS, A. G. 'Karamzin and England', *Slavonic and East European Review*, 43: 91–114
CROW, JOAN. 'The *Quinze joyes de mariage* in France and England', *MLR*, 59: 571–77
DAICHES, DAVID. 'Time and Sensibility', *Modern Language Quarterly*, 25: 486–92
DAWSON, S. W. 'Scrutiny and the Idea of a University', *Essays in Criticism*, 14: 1–9
EDGLEY, R. 'The Object of Literary Criticism', *Essays in Criticism*, 14: 221–36. Reply by Bateson, 416–17
FRYER, W. R. 'Romantic Literature and the European Age of Revolutions', *Renaissance and Modern Studies*, 8: 53–74
FULTON, ROBIN. 'Douglas and Virgil', *Studies in Scottish Literature*, 2: 125–28
FURBANK, P. N. 'John Bull in the German Garden', *Encounter*, 22, no. 5 (April): 85–91
GREEN, F. C. 'Robert Liston et Madame Riccoboni: Une liaison franco-écossaise du XVIIe siècle', *RLC*, 38: 550–58
——. 'Sir James Hall's Impression of France in 1791', *French Studies*, 18: 236–43
GRIFFITHS, RICHARD. 'The Influence of Formulary Rhetoric upon French Renaissance Tragedy', *MLR*, 59: 201–08
GRIMBLE, IAN. 'A Lost Literature. The Disappearance of Early Gaelic Writings', *The Listener*, 71: 385–87
GRIMSLEY, RONALD. 'Kierkegaard and Scribe', *RLC*, 38: 512–30
HARDING, F. J. W. *Matthew Arnold the Critic and France* (Geneva: Droz)
HARDY, BARBARA. *The Appropriate Form: An Essay on the Novel* (Athlone Press)
HARWARD, T. B., ED. *European Patterns: Contemporary Patterns in European Writing* (Dublin: Dolmen)
HEYWOOD, C. 'Miss Braddon's *The Doctor's Wife*: An Intermediary between *Madame Bovary* and *The Return of the Native*', *RLC*, 38: 255–61
HIRST, DESIREE. *Hidden Riches: Traditional Symbolism from the Renaissance to Blake* (Eyre and Spottiswoode; New York: Barnes and Noble)
HOBSBAUM, PHILIP. 'A Voice in the Wilderness: On *Scrutiny*', *The Listener*, 71: 60–63

HOLLOWAY, JOHN. *The Colours of Clarity: Essays on Contemporary Literature and Education* (Routledge & Kegan Paul)
HOLLOWAY, JOHN. 'English and some Christian Traditions', in *The English Mind. Studies in the English Moralists Presented to Basil Willey*, ed. Hugh Sykes Davies and George Watson (Cambridge University Press), 279–302
HOLLOWAY, JOHN. *The Lion Hunt: A Pursuit of Poetry and Reality* (Routledge & Kegan Paul). Cf also *Hudson Review,* 17 (Spring): 21–43
IVES, MARGARET C. 'Musical Elements in Schiller's Concept of Harmony', **GLL**, 18: 111–16
JENNINGS, ELIZABETH. 'The Making of a Movement', *The Spectator*, 2 October, 446–48
JOHNSTON, ARTHUR. 'Gray's Use of the Gorchest y Beirdd in "The Bard"', **MLR**, 59: 335–38
JONES, G. L. 'Dwy Ddrama Gyfoes. Cymhariaeth rhwng *Brad* gan Saunders Lewis a *Y Ficer* gan Rolf Hochhuth', *Efrydiau Athronyddol*, 27: 38–46
KEMP, JOHN. 'The Work of Art and the Artist's Intentions', *British Journal of Aesthetics*, 4: 146–54
KERMODE, FRANK. 'Tradition and the New Art: Interviews with Harold Rosenberg and Ernst Gombrich', *Partisan Review*, 31: 241–52
KNIGHT, G. WILSON. '*Scrutiny* and Criticism', *Essays in Criticism*, 14: 32–36
KOESTLER, ARTHUR. *The Act of Creation* (Hutchinson)
LAURIE, I. S. 'Deschamps and the Lyric as Natural Music', **MLR**, 59: 561–70
LERNER, LAURENCE. 'Love and Gossip: or, How Moral is Literature?', *Essays in Criticism*, 14: 126–47
LEWIS, C. S. *The Discarded Image: An Introduction to Medieval and Renaissance Literature* (Cambridge University Press)
LODGE, DAVID. 'The Critical Moment 1964', *Critical Quarterly*, 6: 266–74
———. 'Not So Odious', **TLS**, 12 March 215. Reprinted in *Yearbook of Comparative and General Literature*, 14 (1965): 72–73
LUCIE-SMITH, EDWARD. 'A Murderous Art?', *Critical Quarterly* 6: 355–63
MACBETH, GEORGE. 'The Sick Rhetoric of War', *Critical Quarterly* 6: 154–63
MASON, EUDO C. 'Das englische und das deutsche Shakespeare-Bild', *Schweizer Monatshefte*, 44: 73–90
MAY, FREDERICK. 'A Foscolo Fragment in English', **MLR**, 59: 41–42
MERCHANT, W. MOELWYN. 'Blake's Shakespeare', *Apollo*, 79: 318–25
MILLER, B. D. H. '*Anglois Coué*: Further Evidence', *French Studies*, 18: 24–27
NICOLL, ALLARDYCE. *The World of Harlequin: A Critical Study of the Commedia dell' arte* (Cambridge University Press)
NORMAN, F. 'Medieval Literature and its Cultural Context', in *Literary History & Literary Criticism* (see Burns, above), 318–19
Ó SÚILLEABHÁIN, PÁDRAIG. 'Tuilleadh faoi Stair an Bhiobla', *Éigse*, 11.1: 51–56
OGILVIE, R. M. *Latin and Greek: A History of the Influence of the Classics on English Life from 1600 to 1918* (Routledge & Kegan Paul)
O'REGAN, M. J. 'The French Sources of Thomas Stanley's Paraphrases of Psalms 139 and 148', **MLR**, 59: 179–81
PASCAL, ROY. 'Goethe und das Tragische. Die Wandlung von Goethes Shakespeare-Bild', *Goethe-Jahrbuch der Goethe-Gesellschaft*, 26: 38–53
PHILLIPS, MARGARET MANN. *The 'Adages' of Erasmus: A Study with Translations* (Cambridge University Press)
POWELL, HUGH, ED. *Johann Elias Schlegel, 'Vergleichung Shakespears und Andreas Gryphs'* (Leicester University Press)

PRINCE, F. T. 'The Study of Form and the Renewal of Poetry', *Proceedings of the British Academy*, 50: 45–61

READ, HERBERT. 'The Poet and His Muse', *British Journal of Aesthetics*, 4: 99–108. Cf. also *Arts*, 2: 145–68

RODWAY, ALLAN. 'Crosscurrents in Contemporary English Criticism', *Comparative Literature Studies*, 1: 207–15

——. *Science and Modern Writing* (Sheed & Ward)

—— and BRIAN LEE. 'Coming to Terms', *Essays in Criticism*, 14: 109–25

SASSE, H.-C. 'Michael Denis: The Bard as Hymnographer', **GLL**, 18: 50–59

SELLS, A. LYTTON. *The Paradise of Travellers: The Italian Influence on Englishmen in the Seventeenth Century* (Allen & Unwin)

SEWELL, ELIZABETH. *The Human Metaphor* (Notre Dame University Press)

SEZNEC, JEAN. *John Martin en France* (Faber)

SHACKLETON, ROBERT. 'Montesquieu and Machiavelli: A Reappraisal', *Comparative Literature Studies*, 1: 1–14

SMEED, J. W. 'Thomas Carlyle and Jean Paul Richter', *Comparative Literature*, 16: 226–53

SMITH, A J. 'Theory and Practice in Renaissance Poetry: Two Kinds of Imitation', *Bulletin of the John Rylands Library*, 47: 212–43

SPENDER, STEPHEN. 'How Much Should a Biographer Tell?', *Saturday Review*, 25 January, 16–19

STAHL, E. L. '"Bürgerlicher Realismus"', **MLR**, 59: 245–49

STEWART, WILLIAM McC. 'The Unity of the Western Literary Tradition and the Study of European Languages Ancient and Modern', in *Literary History & Literary Criticism* (see Burns), 252–54

SYMONS, JULIAN. 'Scrutinizing *Scrutiny*', *London Magazine*, 3 (March): 21–30

TAYLOR, A. C. 'Balzac et les romanciers scandinaves', **RLC**, 38: 203–37

——. 'Literary History and Literary Criticism, with Special Reference to the Novel', in *Literary History & Literary Criticism* (see Burns), 321–22

THOMAS, R. S. *Words and the Poet* (University of Wales Press). W. D. Thomas Memorial Lecture

THWAITE, ANTHONY. 'Labelling the Poet', *The Listener*, 71: 930

TRAINER, JAMES. *Ludwig Tieck: From Gothic to Romantic* (The Hague: Mouton). Includes 'Gothic as a Literary Phenomenon in England', 12–25

TRAINER, JAMES. 'The First English Translation of Kabale und Liebe, **MLR**, 59: 65–72

VAIZEY, JOHN. '*Scrutiny* and Education', *Essays in Criticism*, 14: 36–42

VINAVER, EUGENE. 'Critical Approaches to Medieval Romance', in *Literary History & Literary Criticism* (see Burns), 16–27

——. 'From Epic to Romance', *Bulletin of the John Rylands Library*, 46: 476–503

WALSH, WILLIAM. *A Human Idiom: Literature and Humanity* (Chatto & Windus)

1965

BATLEY, E. M. 'The Inception of "Singspiel" in Eighteenth Century Southern Germany', **GLL**, 19: 167–77

BERGONZI, BERNARD. *Heroes' Twilight: A Study of the Literature of the Great War* (Constable)

BERLIN, ISAIAH. 'Herder and the Enlightenment', in *Aspects of the Eighteenth Century*, ed. Earl R. Wasserman (Johns Hopkins University Press / Oxford University Press), 47–104

BRAND, C. P. *Torquato Tasso. A Study of the Poet and of his Contribution to English Literature* (Cambridge University Press)

BROMWICH, RACHEL, 'The Celtic Inheritance of Medieval Literature', *Modern Language Quarterly*, 26: 203–27

——. 'Chwedlau'r Greal', *Llên Cymru*, 8: 48–57
——. *Matthew Arnold and Celtic Literature: A Retrospect* (Oxford: Carendon). O'Donnell lecture, 1964
BROOKE-ROSE, CHRISTINE. 'Dynamic Gradients', *London Magazine*, 4 (March), 89–96
CAUDWELL, CHRISTOPHER. *The Concept of Freedom* (Lawrence & Wishart)
BROPHY, BRIGID. 'Detective Fiction: A Modern Myth of Violence?', *Hudson Review*, 19 (Spring): 11–30
CAMPOS, CHRISTOPHE. *The View of France: From Arnold to Bloomsbury* (Oxford University Press)
CAPON, ERIC. 'Theatre and Reality', *British Journal of Aesthetics*, 5: 261–69
CARR, C. T. 'Two Words in Art History: I, Baroque', *Forum for Modern Language Studies*, 1: 175–90
CHURCH, RICHARD. 'How a Novelist Works', *Essays by Divers Hands*, 33: 56–69
CONNOLLY, CYRIL. *The Modern Movement: One Hundred Key Books from England, France and America, 1880–1950*. With a Bibliography by G. D. E. Soar (Deutsch/Hamish Hamilton)
CUNNINGHAM, C. F. *The 'Divina Commedia' in English: A Critical Bibliography, 1782–1900* (London and Edinburgh: Oliver & Boyd)
DAICHES, DAVID. 'Myth, Metaphor, and Poetry', *Essays by Divers Hands*: 33: 39–55
——. *Time and the Poet* (University of Wales Press). W. D. Thomas Memorial Lecture
——. 'Society and the Artist', *New York Times Book Review*, 28 November, 2
DAVIE, DONALD. 'A Case for Comparative Studies', *Universities Quarterly*, 19: 131–37
——, ED. *Russian Literature and Modern English Fiction* (University of Chicago Press)
DAWSON, SHEILA. 'Infinite Types of Ambiguity', *British Journal of Aesthetics*, 5: 289–95
GRAVES, ROBERT. *Mammon and the Black Goddess* (Cassell)
DAVIS, NORMAN. 'The *Litera Troili* and English Letters', *Review of English Studies*, 16: 234–44
DAY-LEWIS, CECIL. *The Lyric Impulse* (Chatto & Windus). Charles Eliot Norton Lectures, 1964–65
DAY, DOUGLAS A. 'Voltaire and Cicero', *RLC*, 39: 31–43
DILLISTONE, FREDERICK W. 'The Fall: Christian Truth and Literary Symbol', *Comparative Literature Studies*, 2: 349–62
DIVERRES, A. H. 'Jean Froissart's Journey to Scotland', *Forum for Modern Language Studies*, 1: 54–63
DOBREE, BONAMY. 'Nature Poetry in the Early Eighteenth Century', *Essays and Studies*, J8: 13–33
DRONKE, PETER. *Medieval Latin and the Rise of European Love-Lyric* 1: *Problems and Interpretations* (Oxford: Clarendon Press)
——. 'The Beginnings of the Sequence', *Beiträge zur Geschichte der deutschen Sprache und Literatur*, 87: 43–73
FLETCHER, JOHN. 'Beckett's Debt to Dante', *Nottingham French Studies*, 4: 41–52
——. 'Samuel Beckett and the Philosophers', *Comparative Literature*, 17: 43–56
FURNESS, RAYMOND. 'The Androgynous Ideal: Its Significance in German Literature', *MLR*, 60: 58–64
GALLAGHER, MARY. 'Goulston's Poetics and Tragic "Admiratio"', *RLC*, 39: 614–19
GRAY, R. *The German Tradition in Literature 1871–1945* (Cambridge University Press). Includes a chapter 'English Resistance to German Literature from Coleridge to D. H. Lawrence', 327–54
GREEN, F. C. *A Comparative View of French and British Civilisation, 1850–1870* (Dent)
GREENE, MILITSA. 'Pushkin and Sir Walter Scott', *Forum for Modern Language Studies*, 1: 207–15

GRIMSLEY, RONALD. 'Kierkegaard and Leibniz', *Journal of the History of Ideas*, 26: 383–96
HALL, H. GASTON. 'Guarini in Boileau's *Lutrin*', **MLR**, 60: 17–21:
HAMBURGER, MICHAEL. *From Prophecy to Exorcism. The Premisses of Modern German Literature* (Longmans)
HARPER, ANTHONY J. 'Brecht and Villon: Further Thoughts on some *Dreigroschenoper* Songs', *Forum for Modern Language Studies*, 1: 191–94
HARPER, ANTHONY J. 'Ferdinand Bruckners Behandlung des "Pyrrhus und Andromache"-Stoffes', *Maske und Kothurn*, 11: 97–102
HARVEY, W. J. *Character and the Novel* (Chatto & Windus)
HATTO, ARTHUR T., ED. *Eos: an Enquiry into the Theme of Lovers' Meetings and Partings at Dawn in Poetry* (The Hague: Mouton)
HEMMINGS, F. W. J. 'Emile Zola et le théâtre scandinave de son temps', *Les Cahiers naturalistes*, 11.29: 25–33
———. *The Uses of Literature* (Leicester University Press). Inaugural lecture
HOGGART, RICHARD. 'A Question of Tone: Some Problems in Autobiographical Writing', *Essays by Divers Hands*, 33, 18–38
HOLLOWAY, JOHN. 'The Critical Theory of Yvor Winters', *Critical Quarterly*, 7: 54–68
MACNEICE, LOUIS. *Varieties of Parable* (Cambridge University Press). Clark Lectures, 1963
JARRETT-KERR, MARTIN. 'The Conditions of Tragedy', *Comparative Literature Studies*, 2: 363–73
JENNINGS, ELIZABETH. *Christianity and Poetry* (Burns & Oates). Cf. also **TLS**, 1 July, 559
JOHNSON, R. 'Juan Ramon Jimenez, Rabindranath Tagore, and "La poesia desnuda"', **MLR**, 60: 534–46
JONES, A. R. 'Imagism: A Unity of Gesture', *Stratford-upon-Avon Studies*, 7 (American Poetry): 114–33
JONES, DAFYDD GLYN. 'O Flaen Pa Beth? Rhai problemau ynglŷn a'r Avant-Garde', *Traethodydd*, 120: 23–40
JONES, R. O. 'Renaissance Butterfly, Mannerist Flea: Tradition and Change in Renaissance Poetry', *MLN*, 80: 166–84
KELL, RICHARD. 'Content and Form in Poetry', *British Journal of Aesthetics*, 5: 382–85
KERMODE, FRANK. 'All Mod Cons', *New Statesman*, 16 July, 85–86
———. 'Modern Poetry and Tradition', *Yearbook of Comparative and General Literature*, 14: 5–15
KITCHIN, LAURENCE. 'Greek Tragedy Today', *The Listener*, 73: 551–53
LEWIS, C. S., KINGSLEY AMIS and BRIAN ALDISS. 'Unreal Estates', *Encounter*, 24.3 (March): 61–64
LLOYD, D. MIYRDDIN. 'Cymru ac Ewrop', *Efrydiau Athronyddol*, 27: 3–13
MASON, H. A. 'Some Versions of the Iliad', *Cambridge Quarterly*, 1: 69–80
MCALINDON, T. 'Magic, Fate, and Providence in Medieval Narrative', *Review of English Studies*, 16: 121–39
MELLERS, WILFRED. *Harmonious Meeting; A Study of the Relationship between English Music, Poetry and Theatre, c. 1600–1900* (Dobson)
MERCHANT, W. Moelwyn. *Creed and Drama: An Essay in Religious Drama* (S. P. C. K.)
MILLS, MALDWYN. 'Christian Significance and Romance Tradition in *Sir Gawain and the Green Knight*', **MLR**, 60: 483–93
MINOGUE, VALERIE. 'The Tableau in *La Colère de Samson*', **MLR**, 59: 374–78
MOLONEY, BRIAN. 'The Delia Cruscan Poets, the *Florence Miscellany* and the Leopoldine Reforms', **MLR**, 60: 48–57
MORGAN, P. T. J. 'The Abbé Pezron and the Celts', *Transactions of the Honourable Society of Cymmnrodorion*, 286–95

MUIR, WILLA. *Living with Ballads* (Hogarth)
Ó TUAMA, SEAN. 'Teamaí Iasachta i bhFilíocht Pholatiúil na Gaeilge (1600–1800)', *Éigse*, 11.3: 201–13
——. 'Dónal Ó Corcora agus Filíocht na Gaeilge', *Studia Hibernica*, 5: 29–41
O'BRIEN, CONOR CRUISE. *Writers and Politics* (Chatto & Windus)
OWEN, D. D. R. and R. S. LOOMIS. 'The Development of Arthurian Romance: Discussion', *Forum for Modern Language Studies*, 1: 64–77
PATRIDES, C. A. 'The Cessation of the Oracles: The History of a Legend', **MLR**, 60: 500–07
PRIESTLEY, J. B. 'Censor and Stage', *New Statesman*, 17 December, 967
PURDIE, EDNA. 'Herder's Quotations from Shakespeare', in Id., *Studies in German Literature of the Eighteenth Century* (Athlone Press), 1–30,
RAWSON, CLAUDE J. 'Rabelais and Horace: A Contact in the *Tiers livre*, Ch. Ill', *French Studies*, 19: 373–78
REYNOLDS, BARBARA. 'English Fashions in Translating Dante', *Forum for Modern Language Studies*, 1: 7–25
RICHARDS, I. A. 'From Criticism to Creation', **TLS**, 27 May, 438
RIGHTER, ANNE. 'Heroic Tragedy', *Stratford-upon-Avon Studies*, 6 (Restoration Theatre): 134–57
RINSLER, NORMA. 'Victor Hugo and the *Poésies allemandes* of Gérard de Nerval', **RLC**, 39: 382–95
ROBSON-SCOTT, W. D. *The Literary Background of the Gothic Revival in Germany. A Chapter in the History of Taste* (Oxford: Clarendon Press)
RODWAY, ALLAN. 'Critical Linguistics', *Filoloski Pregled*, 1–2: 111–15
SALINGAR, L. G. 'The Revenger's Tragedy: Some Possible Sources', **MLR**, 60: 3–12
SALVADORI, CORINNA. *Yeats and Castiglione: Poet and Cavalier. A Study of Some Fundamental Concepts of the Philosophy and Poetic Creed of W. B. Yeats in the Light of Castiglione's 'Il Libro del Cortegiano'* (Dublin: Allen Figgis)
SASSE, H.-C. 'Michael Denis as a Translator of Ossian', **MLR**, 60: 547–52
SAYCE, R. A. 'Comparative Literature', *Times Educational Supplement*, 26 March, 915
SCOTT, J. A. 'Pétrarque et la troisième élégie de Ronsard', **RLC**, 39: 75–77
SHARROCK, ROGER. 'Modes of Satire', *Stratford-upon-Avon Studies*, 6 (Restoration Theatre): 109–32
SISSON, C. H. *Art and Action* (Methuen)
SMETHURST, COLIN, and BRUCE TOLLEY. 'The Source of the "Post-Scriptum" of Balzac's *Physiologie du mariage*', **RLC**, 39: 434–39
STRICKLAND, GEOFFEY. 'Stendhal, Byron et John Cam Hobhouse', *Stendhal Club*, 28: 309–28
SUCKLING, NORMAN. 'Molière and English Restoration Comedy', *Stratford-upon-Avon Studies*, 6 (Restoration Theatre): 92–107
SUTTON, WALTER. 'Criticism and Poetry', *Stratford-upon-Avon Studies*, 7 (American Poetry): 174–95
TAYLOR, RONALD. 'Formal Parallels in Literature and Music', **GLL**, 19: 10–18
THOMAS, A. 'Hopkins, Welsh and Wales', *Transactions of the Honourable Society of Cymmrodorion*, 272–85
THOMSON, PATRICIA. 'Sonnet 15 of Samuel Daniel's *Delia*. A Petrarchan Imitation', *Comparative Literature*, 17: 151–57
WELLS, G. A. 'Fate-Tragedy and Schiller's *Die Braut von Messina*', *Journal of English and Germanic Philology*, 64: 191–212
WHITE, BEATRICE. 'Medieval Beasts', *Essays and Studies*, 18: 34–44

———. 'The "Green Knight's" Classical Forbears', *Neuphilologische Mitteilungen*, 66: 112–19
WILLIAMS, GLANMOR. *Dadeni, Diwygiad a Diwylliant* (University of Wales Press)
WILLOUGHBY, L. A. 'Oscar Wilde and Goethe: The Life of Art and the Art of Life', **PEGS**, 35: 1–37
WILSON, COLIN. *Eagle and Earwig: Essays on Books and Writers* (Baker)

1966

ADAMS, P. L. 'History, Literary History and Criticism. A Disagreement', *Oxford Review*, 1: 64–68
'After Lukács', **TLS**, 14 July: 605–06
ALLEN, L. 'Letters of Huysmans and Zola to Raffalovitch', *Forum for Modern Language Studies*, 2: 214–21
BARRÈRE, JEAN-BERTRAND. 'Goût, originalité et qualité', in *Actes du IVe Congres de l'Association Internationale de Litterature Comparée / Proceedings of the IVth Congress of the International Comparative Literature Association, Fribourg 1964*, ed. François Jost (2 vols. The Hague and Paris: Mouton), 2: 127–82
BATTERBY, K. A. J. *Rilke and France: A Study in Poetic Development* (Oxford University Press). Reviewed in **TLS**, 8 September, 817
BERNHARDT, W. W. 'A Note on the Structure and Rhetoric in Aeschylus' *Persae*', *Essays in Criticism*, 16: 207–11
BINNS, A. L. '"Linguistic" Reading: Two Suggestions of the Quality of Literature', in *Essays on Style and Language* (see Fowler), 118–34
BOAK, DENIS. 'Malraux and T. E. Lawrence', **MLR**, 61: 218–24
BOWRA, C. M. *Landmarks in Greek Literature* (Weidenfeld & Nicolson)
——— *Poetry and Politics, 1900–1960* (Cambridge University Press)
BRUCE, F. F. 'The Dead Sea Scrolls and Early Christianity', *Bulletin of the John Rylands Library*, 49: 69–90
BULLOUGH, GEOFFREY. *Narrative and Dramatic Sources of Shakespeare, 6: Other 'Classical' Plays: Titus Andronicus, Troilus and Cressida, Timon of Athens, Pericles Prince of Tyre* (Routledge & Kegan Paul)
CLARK, JOHN. 'Les Critiques impressionistes francais', in *ICLA Proceedings Fribourg* (see Barrère), 2: 1296–1303
COLLINS, C. 'Zamyatin, Wells and the Utopian Literary Tradition', *Slavonic and East European Review*, 44: 351–60
'Crisis in Criticism', **TLS**, 23 June, 545–46; a follow-up to 'Civil War among the Critics', **TLS**, 3 February, 83
CRONIN, ANTHONY. *A Question of Modernity* (Seeker & Warburg)
CROSS, A. G. 'N. M. Karamzin and Barthelemy's *Voyage du jeune Anacharsis*', **MLR**, 61: 467–72
DAVIES, H. NEVILLE, 'Dryden and Vossius: A Reconsideration', *Journal of the Warburg and Courtauld Institutes*, 29: 282–95, followed by D. T. Mace, 'A Reply to Mr H. Neville Davies's "Dryden and Vossius"', 296–310
DONALDSON, IAN. 'L. C. Knights and Soil Erosion', *Oxford Review*, 1: 57–63
DONOGHUE, DENIS. *Connoisseurs of Chaos* (Faber & Faber). Reviewed in **TLS**, 26 May, 477
DRONKE, PETER. 'Boethius, Alanus und Dante', *Romanische Forschungen*, 78: 119–25
———. *Medieval Latin and the Rise of the European Love-Lyric, 1: Problems and Interpretations, 2: Medieval Latin Love-Poetry. Texts Newly Edited from the Manuscripts and for the Most Part Previously Unpublished* (Oxford: Carendon)
ENRIGHT, D. J. *Conspirators and Poets* (Chatto & Windus)

FLETCHER, DENNIS J. 'The Fortunes of Bolingbroke in France in the Eighteenth Century', *Studies on Voltaire and the Eighteenth Century*, 42: 207–32
FOWLER, ROGER. 'Linguistics, Stylistics: Criticism?', *Lingua*, 16: 153–65
——, ED. *Essays on Style and Language. Linguistic and Critical Approaches to Literary Style* (Routledge & Kegan Paul). With Fowler's Preface (vii-ix), his article on 'Linguistic Theory and the Study of Literature' (1–28), and his article on '"Prose Rhythm" and Metre' (82–99). Other contributions are listed separately
FUSSELL, PAUL. *The Rhetorical World of Augustan Humanism* (Oxford: Carendon). Reviewed in **TLS**, 16 February 1967, 128
GIFFORD, HENRY. 'Imitation as a Poetic Mode', in *ICLA Proceedings Fribourg* (see Barrère), 2: 912–16
GRIFFITH, T. G. 'Italy and Wales', *Transactions of the Honourable Society of Cymmrodorion*: 281–98
GRIMSLEY, RONALD. 'Some Implications of the Use of Irony in Voltaire and Kierkegaard', in *ICLA Proceedings Fribourg* (see Barrère), 2: 1018–24
GRUBE, M. A. *The Greek and Roman Critics* (Methuen)
HAMBURGER, MICHAEL. 'Die Aufnahme Hölderlins in England', *Hölderlin-Jahrbuch*, 14: 20–34
HARDIE, C. 'Dante and the Tradition of Courtly Love', in *Patterns of Love and Courtesy: Essays in Memory of C. S. Lewis*, ed. J. Lawlor (Edward Arnold), 26–44
HAWKES, TERENCE. 'New Prosodies for Old?', *Essays in Criticism*, 16: 258–72
HENN, T. R. 'The Bible in Relation to the Study of English Literature Today', *Hermathena*, 100: 29–43
HENNINGS, J. 'Goethe und die englischsprachige Welt: Drei Mitteilungen', *Goethe-Jahrbuch*, 28: 270–78
HEYWOOD, CHRISTOPHER. 'Somerset Maugham's Debt to *Madame Bovary* and *L'Éducation sentimentale*: Structural Affinities', *Etudes Anglaises*, 19: 64–69
HOLLOWAY, JOHN. *Widening Horizons in English Verse* (Routledge & Kegan Paul)
HOSLEY, RICHARD. 'The Formal Influence of Plautus and Terence', in *Elizabethan Drama* (Stratford-upon-Avon Studies, ed. J. R. Brown and B. Harris, 9), 130–45
HOUGH, GRAHAM. *An Essay on Criticism* (Duckworth). Reviewed in **TLS**, 17 November 1966, 1050, and by A. D. Moody, *Essays in Criticism*, 17 (1967): 495–504
HYDE, J. K. 'Medieval Descriptions of Cities', *Bulletin of the John Rylands Library*, 48: 308–40
INGLIS, FRED. 'Classicism and Poetic Drama', *Essays in Criticism*, 16, 154–69
KILLHAM, JOHN. 'The "Second Self" in Novel Criticism', *British Journal of Aesthetics*, 6: 272–90
JONES, G. L. 'Lessing and Amory', **GLL**, 20 (1966–67): 298–306
JONES, W. GARETH. 'George Eliot's *Adam Bede* and Tolstoy's Conception of *Anna Karenina*', **MLR**, 61: 473–81
KERMODE, FRANK. 'The New Apocalyptists', *Partisan Review*, 33: 339–61
—— 'Language', in *Essays on Style and Language* (see Fowler), 29–52
LODGE, DAVID. *The Language of Fiction: Essays in Criticism and Verbal Analysis of the English Novel* (Routledge & Kegan Paul). Reviewed by W. J. Harvey, *Essays in Criticism*, 17 (1967): 231–32
LAWRENCE, R. F. 'The Formulaic Theory and its Application to English Alliterative Poetry', in *Essays on Style and Language* (see Fowler), 166–83
LEE, BRIAN. 'The New Criticism and the Language of Poetry', in *Essays on Style and Language* (see Fowler), 68–81
LEECH, G. N. 'Linguistics and the Figures of Rhetoric', in *Essays on Style and Language* (see Fowler), 135–56

LITTLE, J. ROGER. 'Elements of the Jason-Medea Myth in *Exil* by Saint-John Perse', **MLR**, 61: 422–25
MAJUT, RUDOLF. 'Ein englischer Besucher Rückerts, mit einem Ausblick auf die Aufnahme Rückerts in England und Amerika', *Germanisch-romanische Monatsschrift*, 16: 100–06
MALINS, EDWARD. *English Landscaping and Literature, 1660–1840* (Oxford University Press)
MARCUS, STEVEN. 'Pornotopia', *Encounter*, 27.2: 9–18. Also appeared in Marcus's *The Other Victorians: A Study of Sexuality and Pornography in Mid-Nineteenth Century England* (Weidenfeld & Nicolson). Reviewed in **TLS**, 19 January 1967, 45
MITCHELL, B. 'W. H. Auden and Christopher Isherwood: The "German Influence"', *Oxford German Studies*, 1: 163–72
MOURGUES, ODETTE DE. 'Originalité', in *ICLA Proceedings Fribourg* (see Barrère), 2: 1259–64
MYLNE, VIVIENNE. 'Illusion and the Novel', *British Journal of Aesthetics*, 6: 142–51
O'MEARA, J. J. 'Yeats, Catullus and the Lake Island', *Irish University Review*, 3.8: 15–24
O'REGAN, MICHAEL. 'Imitation, Tradition and Creation: Vicissitudes of the Phrase "Eternal Night" in French Poetry', in *ICLA Proceedings Fribourg* (see Barrère), 2: 820–26
PRIESTLEY, J. B. *The English Novel* (Ernest Benn)
RAINE, KATHLEEN. 'The Use of the Beautiful', *Southern Review*, 2: 245–63
RAWSON, C. J. 'Pope and Montaigne: A Parallel', *Notes & Queries*, 211: 459–60
REMSBURY, JOHN. '"Real Thinking": Lawrence and Cézanne', *Critical Quarterly*, 2.1 (Winter 1966–67), 117–47
RICHARDSON, MAURICE. 'It's All Been Done Before', **TLS**, 8 December, 1144–45
ROBERTS, MARK. 'The Pill and the Cherries: Sydney and the Neo-Classical Tradition', *Essays in Criticism*, 16: 22–31
ROBSON, W. W. 'English as a University Subject', *Balcony*, 4: 5–19. The first F.R. Leavis Lecture
RODWAY, A. 'By Algebra to Augustanism', in *Essays on Style and Language* (see Fowler), 53–67
ROE, W. G. *Lamennais and England* (Oxford University Press)
RUTSON, E. M. 'A Note on Jean Marot's Debt to Italian Sources', **MLR**, 61: 25–28
SAYCE, R. A. 'Comparative Literature', *Yearbook of Comparative and General Literature*, 15: 63–65
SCOTT, D. F. S. 'The Development of German Studies at Durham', *Durham University Journal*, 59: 25–29
SEWELL, ELIZABETH. 'Science and Literature', *Commonweal*, 84: 218–19
SHEPPARD, R. W. 'Rilke's "Duineser Elegien": A Critical Appreciation in the Light of Eliot's "Four Quartets"', **GLL**, 20: 205–18
SHERGOLD, N. D. and PETER URE. 'Dryden and Calderón: A New Spanish Source for "The Indian Emperour"', **MLR**, 61: 369–83
SHERRY, NORMAN. *Conrad's Eastern World* (Cambridge University Press). Reviewed in **TLS**, 3 November, 992–93
SINCLAIR, J.McH. 'Taking a Poem to Pieces', in *Essays on Style and Language* (see Fowler), 68–81
SKRINE, PETER. 'A Flemish Model for the Tragedies of Lohenstein', **MLR**, 61: 64–70
SMEED, J. W. 'Jean Paul und die Tradition des theophrastischen "Charakters"', *Jahrbuch der Jean Paul-Gesellschaft*, 1: 53–77
SPENDER, STEPHEN. *Chaos and Control in Poetry. A Lecture Delivered at the Library of Congress, October 11, 1965* (Washington, D. C.: Library of Congress)
STEINER, GEORGE. 'To Traduce or Transfigure: Modern Verse Translation', *Encounter*, 27.2: 48–54

STIMSON, F. S. 'Dario's "Estival" and Leconte de Lisle's "Le rêve du jaguar"', *Hispanic Review*, 34: 53–58
SULLIVAN, J. P. *Ezra Pound and Sextus Propertius. A Study in Creative Translation* (Faber & Faber). Reviewed in **TLS**, 29 September, 900
TANNER, MICHAEL. 'Wittgenstein and Aesthetics', *Oxford Review*, 3: 5–13
THOMPSON, DAVID. 'Religion and the Arts: Playing with Mystery', **TLS**, 3 March, 166
'Two Kinds of Criticism', **TLS**, 17 November, 1050
WEBSTER, T. B. L. 'The Myth of Ariadne from Homer to Catullus', *Greece & Rome*, 13: 22–31
WELLS, STANLEY. 'Shakespeare and Romance', in *Later Shakespeare* (Stratford-upon-Avon Studies, ed. J. R. Brown and B. Harris, 8), 48–79
WEXLER, P. J. 'Distych and Sentence in Corneille and Racine', in *Essays on Style and Language* (see Fowler), 100–17
WHITE, JOHN J. 'Mathematical Imagery in Musil's *Young Törless* and Zamyatin's *We*', *Comparative Literature*, 18: 71–78
WILLIAMS, DAVID. *Voltaire: Literary Critic* (Geneva: Institut et Musée Voltaire). Studies on Voltaire and the Eighteenth Century, 48
WILLIAMS, RAYMOND. *Modern Tragedy* (Chatto & Windus)
WITTE, W. 'Is That the Law', *Forum for Modern Language Studies*, 2: 1 — 13
YATES, FRANCES A. *The Art of Memory* (Routledge & Kegan Paul)

1967

BATESON, F. W. 'Editorial Commentary', *Essays in Criticism*, 17: 1–5. Followed by J. C. Maxwell's 'Textual Criticism and its Problems', 383–85. Bateson's rejoinder, 385–91. Maxwell replies 18 (1968): 87–88. Bateson again, 96–100. Maxwell, 237–38; Bateson closes the debate (in which Paul G. Zomberg also participated), 460
——. 'The Language of Poetry', **TLS**, 27 July, 688–89. Elicited letters by Stanley Williams and Roger Fowler in subsequent issues
BEER, GAVIN DE, and ANDRÉ-MICHEL ROUSSEAU, EDS. *Voltaire's British Visitors* (Geneva: Institut et Musée Voltaire). Studies in Voltaire and the Eighteenth Century, 49
BOWRA, C. M. *Ancient Greek Literature* (Oxford University Press)
BRIGGS, KATHARINE MARY. *The Fairies in Tradition and Literature* (Routledge & Kegan Paul)
BRUMFITT, J. H. 'Scotland and the French Enlightenment', in *The Age of the Enlightenment. Studies Presented to Theodore Bestermann*, ed. W. H. Barber (University of St Andrews), 318–29
BURGESS, ANTHONY. *The Novel Now: A Student's Guide to Contemporary Fiction* (Faber and Faber). Reviewed in **TLS**, 27 June 1968, 680
BUSST, A. J. L. 'The Image of the Androgyne in the Nineteenth Century', in *Romantic Mythologies* (see Fletcher), 1–95
CASEY, JOHN. *The Language of Criticism* (Methuen). Reviewed in **TLS**, 17 August, 744, and by James Griffin, *Essays in Criticism*, 17 (1967): 374–82
CLARK, CECILY. 'Byrhtnoth and Roland: A Contrast', *Neophilologus*, 51: 288–93
COLMER, JOHN. *Approaches to the Novel* (Oliver & Boyd)
COOPER, DAVID. 'Poetic Justice', **TLS**, 27 July, 687. See also 'Crosscurrents'
COURTNEY, C. P. 'Autour de Benjamin Constant. Lettres inédites de Juste de Constant à Sir Robert Murray Keith', *Revue d'histoire littéraire de la France*, 67: 97–100
CRAIG, DAVID. 'Fiction and the Rising Industrial Classes', *Essays in Criticism*, 17: 64–74
'Crosscurrents', **TLS**, special issue, 27 July, opening with 'Limits of Literature', 651. Other contributions listed separately. A second issue on 'Crosscurrents' appeared 28 September,

with contributions by non-British luminaries: Enzensberger, Queneau, Calvino, Eco, Havel, Böll, Barthes and Goldman

DAVIE, DONALD. 'Language to Literature: The Long Way Round', *Style*, 1: 215–20

DICKSON, K. A. 'Lessing's Creative Misinterpretation of Aristotle', *Greece & Rome*, 14: 53–60

DOYLE, P. A. 'Chekhov in Erin', *Dublin Review*, 241: 263–69

DYSON, A. E. 'Literature and the Transmutation of Experience', *Essays and Studies*, 20: 1–14

ENRIGHT, D. J. 'Translating Hölderlin', *Encounter*, 29.4: 84–86

FLETCHER, DENNIS J. 'Bolingbroke and the Diffusion of Newtonianism in France', *Studies on Voltaire and the Eighteenth Century*, 53: 29–46

FLETCHER, IAN, ED. *Romantic Mythologies* (Routledge & Kegan Paul). With Fletcher's foreword, vii–xiii, and his article on 'Bedford Park: Aesthete's Elysium?', 169–207. Some other contributions are entered separately

FLETCHER, JOHN. 'Confrontations: I. Harold Pinter, Roland Dubillard, and Eugène Ionesco. II. Arnold Wesker, John Arden, and Arthur Adamov. III. David Hume, Gilbert Ryle, and Alain Robbe-Grillet', *Caliban*, 4, 149–59

FORSTER, LEONARD. 'Conventional Safety Valves: Alba, Pastourelle, and Epithalamium', in *Lebende Antike: Symposium für Rudolf Sühnel* (Berlin: Schmidt), 120–38

——. *Die Niederlande und die Anfänge der Barocklyrik in Deutschland* (Groningen: Wolters)

——. *Janus Gruters English Years: Studies in the Continuity of Dutch Literature in Exile in Elizabethan England* (Oxford University Press and Leiden University Press for the Sir Thomas Browne Institute). Reviewed by T. Weevers, **MLR**, 65 (1970): 558–61

FOWLER, ROGER. 'Literature and Linguistics', *Essays in Criticism*, 17, 322–35. A reply to Helen Vendler's earlier review of his *Essays on Style and Literature* (Fowler 1966), *ibid.*, 16 (1966), 457–63. Fowler's essay was followed up by Bateson, 335–47; Fowler rejoins, *ibid.*, 18 (1968), 164–76; Bateson again, 176–82; E. B. Greenwood puts in a word: 477–78

GILMAN, ERIC. 'Some Uses of the Word "Abstraction" in Literary Criticism', *Oxford Review*, 6: 75–86

GRANSDEN, K. W. '*Paradise Lost* and the *Aeneid*', *Essays in Criticism*, 17: 281–303

GRAVES, ROBERT. *Poetic Craft and Principle* (Cassell)

GREENWOOD, E. B. 'Poetry and Paradise: A Study in Thematics', *Essays in Criticism*, 17: 6–25

GRIMSLEY, RONALD. 'Some Aspects of "Nature" and "Language" in the French Enlightenment', *Studies on Voltaire and the Eighteenth Century*, 56: 659–77 (Vols 55–58, with consecutive pagination, contained the Transactions of the Second International Congress on the Enlightenment, held at St Andrews.)

HAINSWORTH, G. 'West African Local Colour in Tamango', *French Studies*, 21: 16–23

HAMBURGER, MICHAEL. 'Art as Second Nature. The Figures of the Actor and the Dancer in the Works of Hugo von Hofmannsthal', in *Romantic Mythologies* (see Fletcher), 225–41

HARGREAVES-MAWDSLEY, W. N. *The English Della Cruscans and their Time, 1783–1828* (The Hague: Martinus Nijhoff)

HAWORTH, C. M. 'Low-level Metric', *Greece & Rome*, 14: 170–73

HEBBELTHWAITE, PETER. 'How Catholic is the Catholic Novel?', **TLS**, 27 July, 678–79. See also 'Crosscurrents'

HEALD, DAVID. 'Realism in Medieval German Literature', **GLL**, 21 (1967–68): 335–45

HOPE, FRANCIS. 'Separate Spheres', **TLS**, 27 July, 662–63. See also 'Crosscurrents'

JONES, D. A. 'Politics in the Theatre', **TLS**, 27 July, 681–82. See also 'Crosscurrents'

KERMODE, FRANK. *The Sense of an Ending: Studies in the Theory of Fiction* (Oxford University Press). Reviewed in **TLS**, 7 July, 601, and by John Bayley, *Essays in Criticism*, 18 (1968): 208–18

———. 'World without End or Beginning', *Malahat Review*, 1: 113–29
KILLHAM, JOHN. 'Autonomy versus Mimesis', *British Journal of Aesthetics*, 7: 274–85
KLIENEBERGER, H. R. 'Otway's *Venice Preserved* and Hofmannsthal's *Das gerettete Venedig*', MLR, 62: 292–97
LANGMAN, F. H. 'The Idea of the Reader in Literary Criticism', *British Journal of Aesthetics*, 7: 84–95
LE BRUN, PHILIP. 'T. S. Eliot and Henri Bergson', *Review of English Studies*, 18: 149–61; 274–86
LEHMANN, A. G. 'Pierrot and Fin de Siècle', in *Romantic Mythologies* (see Fletcher), 209–23
LERNER, LAURENCE. 'Coriolanus: Brecht and Shakespeare', *Shakespeare Newsletter*, 17: 56
LUCAS, W. J. 'Wagner and Forster: *Parsifal* and *A Room with a View*', in *Romantic Mythologies* (see Fletcher), 271–97
MATTHEWS, HONOR. *The Primal Curse: The Myth of Cain and Abel in the Theatre* (Chatto & Windus)
MCLNTYRE, ALASDAIR. 'Sociology and the Novel', TLS, 27 July, 657–58. See also 'Crosscurrents'
MICHAEL, IAN. 'A Parallel between Chrétien's *Erec* and the *Libro de Alexandre*', MLR, 62: 620–28
MILLER, JONATHAN. 'Beyond Dispute', TLS, 27 July, 652. See also 'Crosscurrents'
MORLEY, MICHAEL, 'The Source of Brecht's "Abbau des Schiffes Oskawa durch die Mannschaft"', *Oxford German Studies*, 2: 149–62
MYLNE, VIVIENNE. 'Reading and Re-reading Novels', *British Journal of Aesthetics*, 7: 67–75
NISBET, H. B. 'Herder and Francis Bacon', MLR, 62: 267–83
NUTTALL, A. D. *Two Concepts of Allegory* (Routledge & Kegan Paul). Reviewed in TLS, 8 February 1968, 134
O'CONNOR, FRANK. *The Backward Look. A Survey of Irish Literature* (Macmillan). Reviewed in TLS, 20 July, 640
OSBORNE, JOHN. 'Zola, Ibsen and the Development of the Naturalist Movement in Germany', *Arcadia*, 2: 196–203
PARKER, ALEXANDER A. *Literature and the Delinquent: The Picaresque Novel in Spain and Europe 1599–1753* (Edinburgh University Press). The Norman Maccoll Lectures, 1965; reviewed in TLS, 8 February 1968, 134
PENNINGTON, A. E. 'A Sixteenth-Century English Slavist', MLR, 62: 680–86
QUAINTON, MALCOLM. 'Some Classical References, Sources and Identities in Ronsard's "Prière à la fortune"', *French Studies*, 21: 293–301
QUINTON, ANTHONY. 'Philosophy and Literature', TLS, 27 July, 673–74. See also 'Crosscurrents'
RAINE, KATHLEEN. *Defending Ancient Springs* (Oxford University Press)
RICKS, CHRISTOPHER. 'Tennyson and Persian', *English Language Notes*, 4: 46–47
RUSSELL, D. A. 'Rhetoric and Criticism', *Greece & Rome*, 14: 130–44
SHACKLETON, ROBERT. 'Jansenism and the Enlightenment', *Studies on Voltaire and the Eighteenth Century*, 57: 1387–98 (see Grimsley)
SPEARMAN, DIANA. *The Novel and Society* (Routledge & Kegan Paul)
SPINK, JOHN S. 'The Reputation of Julian the Apostate in the Enlightenment', *Studies on Voltaire and the Eighteenth Century*, 57: 1399–1416(See Grimsley)
STEINER, GEORGE. *Language and Silence. Essays 1958–1966* (Faber & Faber). Reviewed in TLS, 28 September, 889
STONE, P. W. K. *The Art of Poetry 1750–1820: Theories of Poetic Composition and Style in the Late Neo-Classic and Early Romantic Periods* (Routledge & Kegan Paul)
STRICKLAND, GEOFFREY. 'Flaubert, Pound and Eliot', *Critical Quarterly*, 2: 242–62

SUCKLING, NORMAN. 'The Enlightenment and the Idea of Progress', *Studies on Voltaire and the Eighteenth Century*, 58: 1461–80 (see Grimsley)
TAYLOR, R. 'Herder, India and the Ideals of European Culture', *Forum for Modern Language Studies*, 3: 15–26
THACKER, CHRISTOPHER. '"Wish'd, Wintry, Horrors": The Storm in the Eighteenth Century', *Comparative Literature*, 19: 36–57
——. 'Swift and Voltaire', *Hermathena*, 104: 51–66
'The Critic as Man', **TLS**, 30 November, 1121–22
THOMAS, L. H. C. 'Swift in German Literature', *Hermathena*, 104: 67–76
THORLBY, A. K., ED. *The Romantic Movement* (Longmans). Reviewed in **TLS**, 26 October, 1011
TREVOR-ROPER, HUGH. 'The Scottish Enlightenment', *Studies on Voltaire and the Eighteenth Century*, 58: 1635–58 (see Grimsley)
VINCENT, R. R. 'Il "Cortegiano" in Inghilterra', in *Rinascimento europeo e rinascimento veneziano*, ed. V. Branca (Florence: Sansoni), 97–107
WATSON, G. *The English Petrarchans: A Critical Bibliography of the 'Canzoniere'* (University of London, Warburg Institute)
WATSON-WILLIAMS, HELEN. *André Gide and the Greek Myth* (Clarendon Press)
YATES, W. E. 'Elizabethan Comedy and the "Alt-Wiener Volkstheater"', *Forum for Modern Language Studies*, 3: 27–35

1968

ADAMS, MICHAEL. *Censorship: The Irish Experience* (Dublin: Scepter). Reviewed in **TLS**, 18 July, 746
ANDERSON, MICHAEL. 'A Note on Lessing's Misinterpretation of Aristotle', *Greece & Rome*, 15: 59–62
AUDEN, W. H. *Secondary Worlds: The T. S. Eliot Memorial Lectures* (Faber & Faber). Reviewed in **TLS**, 23 January 1969, 81
BALL, PATRICIA. *The Central Self* (Athlone Press). Reviewed in **TLS**, 19 December, 1434
BATESON, F. W. 'Linguistics and Literary Criticism', in *The Disciplines of Criticism. Essays in Literary Theory, Interpretation, and History,* ed. Peter Demetz, Thomas Greene and Lowry Nelson, Jr. (Festschrift for René Wellek; Yale University Press), 3–16
BEACHCROFT, T. O. *The Modest Art: A Survey of the Short Story in English* (Oxford University Press). Reviewed in **TLS**, 30 January 1969, 102
BETTS, JOHN H. 'Classical Allusions in Shakespeare's *Henry V* with Special Reference to Homer', *Greece & Rome*, 15: 147–63
BLAKE, N. F. 'Caxton and Courtly Style', *Essays and Studies*, 21: 29–45
BRADBURY, MALCOLM. 'The Arrival of Am. Lit.', **TLS**, 25 July, 789–90. See 'Mincing Words',
BUCKLEY, VINCENT. *Poetry and the Sacred* (Chatto & Windus). Reviewed in **TLS**, 19 December, 1434
DAICHES, DAVID. *More Literary Essays* (Oliver and Boyd). Reviewed in **TLS**, 7 November, 1248
DAVIE, DONALD. 'Reflections on the Study of Russian Literature in Britain', *Association of Teachers of Russian Journal*, 17: 17–23
DICKIE, GEORGE. 'I. A. Richards's Phantom Double', *British Journal of Aesthetics*, 8: 54–59
DONOGHUE, DENIS. *The Ordinary Universe. Soundings in Modern Literature* (Faber & Faber). Reviewed in **TLS**, 3 October, 1134, and by Ruth Grogan, *Essays in Criticism*, 20 (1970): 344–53
DUCKWORTH, COLIN. 'Flaubert and the Legend of St Julian: A Non-exclusive View of Sources', *French Studies*, 22: 107–13

EATON, TREVOR. *The Semantics of Literature* (The Hague and Paris: Mouton)
EDELMAN, MAURICE. 'Talking Culture with the French', **TLS**, 21 March, 287–88
FALCK, COLIN. 'Liberal Studies', **TLS**, 25 July, 797–98. See 'Mincing Words'
FLETCHER, JOHN. *New Directions in Literature: Critical Approaches to a Contemporary Phenomenon* (Calder & Boyars)
FORSTER, LEONARD. 'Jan van der Noot und die deutsche Renaissance-Lyrik: Stand und Aufgaben der Forschung', in *Literatur und Geistesgeschichte: Festgabe fur Heinz Otto Burger*, ed. R.Grimm and C. Wiedemann (Berlin: Schmidt), 70–84
FOWLER, ROGER. 'What is Metrical Analysis?', *Anglia*, 86: 280–320
FURST, LILIAN R. 'Italo Svevo's *La coscienza di Zeno* and Thomas Mann's *Der Zauberberg*', *Contemporary Literature*, 9: 492–506
———. 'Romanticism in Historical Perspective: The Chronology of the Romantic Movements in England, France, and Germany', *Comparative Literature Studies*, 5: 115–43
GROVER, P. R. 'Mérimée's Influence on Henry James', **MLR**, 63: 810–17
HARDIE, C. 'The Oxford Dante Society', in *Atti del congresso internazionale di studi danteschi, Firenze-Verona-Ravenna, 20–27 aprile 1965* (2 vols; Florence: Sansoni), 2: 452–58
HARDISON, O. B., ED. *English Literary Criticism: The Renaissance* (Peter Owen). Reviewed in **TLS**, 23 May, 535
HEPBURN, JAMES. *The Author's Empty Purse and the Rise of the Literary Agent* (Oxford University Press). Reviewed in **TLS**, 11 July, 734
HINDE, THOMAS. 'The Writer at the University', **TLS**, 25 July, 785–86. See 'Mincing Words'
INGLIS, FRED. *An Essential Discipline: An Introduction to Literary Criticism* (Methuen)
JACK, R. D. S. 'Imitation in the Scottish Sonnet', *Comparative Literature*, 20: 313–28
JONES, GLYN. *The Dragon Has Two Tongues* (Dent). Reviewed in **TLS**, 14 November, 1267
KERMODE, FRANK. *Continuities* (Routledge & Kegan Paul). Reviewed in **TLS**, 13 March 1969, 258–59
———. 'Novel, History and Type', *Novel*, 1, 231–38
LAWRENCE, MARGARET. *Long Drums and Cannons: Nigerian Dramatists and Novelists, 1952–1966* (Macmillan)
LLEWELLYN, R. T. 'Parallel Attitudes to Form in Late Beethoven and Late Goethe: Throwing Aside the Appearance of Art', **MLR**, 63: 407–16
MACWATTERS, K. G. *Stendhal lecteur des romanciers anglais* (Lausanne: Editions du grand-chêne). Reviewed by F. W. J. Hemmings, *French Studies*, 24 (1970): 67–68
'Mincing Words', **TLS**, 25 July (special issue on 'The Teaching of English Literature'), 767–68. Other contributions to this issue of **TLS** are entered separately. A second issue on the same topic (12 September) contained non-British contributions
MOURET, FRANCOIS J. L. 'La première rencontre d'André Gide et d'Oscar Wilde', *French Studies*, 22: 37–39
O'BRIEN, CONOR CRUISE. 'Imagination and Polities', in *The Future of the Modern Humanities. Papers Delivered at the Jubilee Congress of the MHRA. August 1968* (MHRA), 73–85
O'NOLAN, K. 'Homer and the Irish Hero Tale', *Studia Hibernica*, 8: 7–20
PARK, ROY. 'Coleridge and Kant: Poetic Imagination and Practical Reason', *British Journal of Aesthetics*, 8: 335–46
PARRY, IDRIS. 'Goethe, Dada and Zen', **GLL**, 22: 111–20
RADCLIFF-UMSTEAD, D. 'Dante's Influence on the Great Dream of Gerhart Hauptmann', *Forum Italicum*, 2: 23–33
RAINE, KATHLEEN. 'Thomas Taylor, Plato and the English Romantic Movement', *British Journal of Aesthetics*, 8: 99–123
RAWLINSON, D. H. *The Practice of Criticism* (Cambridge University Press). Reviewed in **TLS**, 2 January 1969, 8, and by J. M. Newton, *Critical Quarterly*, 4 (1969): 212–16

REED, T. J. 'Critical Consciousness and Creation. The Concept *Kritik* from Lessing to Hegel', *Oxford German Studies*, 3: 87–113

ROBSON, W. W. 'The Future of English Studies', **TLS**, 25 July, 773–74. See 'Mincing Words'

ROSTON, MURRAY. *Biblical Drama in England: From the Middle Ages to the Present Day* (Faber & Faber)

ROTHWELL, W. 'The Teaching of French in Medieval England', **MLR**, 63: 37–46

RYAN, W. F. 'Aristotle in Old Russian Literature', **MLR**, 63: 650–58

SHAFFER, E. S. 'Iago's Malignity Motivated: Coleridge's Unpublished "Opus Magnum"', *Shakespeare Quarterly*, 2: 195–203

SHAW, D. L. 'The Anti-Romantic Reaction in Spain', **MLR**, 63: 606–11

SMIEJA, FLORIAN. '"The Lord Mayor of Poznan": An Eighteenth-Century Polish Version of *El alcalde de Zalamea*', **MLR**, 63: 869–71

SPENCER, MICHAEL. 'Architecture and Poetry in "Réseau Aérien"', **MLR**, 63: 57–65

STERN, J. P. 'War and the Comic Muse', *Comparative Literature*, 20: 193–216

STOPP, F. J. 'Reformation Satire in Germany. Nature, Conditions, and Form', *Oxford German Studies*, 3: 53–68

THORLBY, ANTHONY. 'Comparative Literature', **TLS**, 25 July, 793–94. See 'Mincing Words'; reprinted in *Yearbook of Comparative and General Literature*, 18 (1969): 75–81

TURNELL, MARTIN. 'The Mystic and the Critic', **TLS**, 29 February, 201–02

VICKERS, BRIAN. '*King Lear* and Renaissance Paradoxes', **MLR**, 63: 305–14

WEEVERS, T. 'Albert Verwey and Stefan George: Their Conflicting Affinities', **GLL**, 22: 79–89

WELLS, GEORGE A. 'Criteria of Historicity: De Wette on the Laws of Moses, Kopp on the Swiss Confederation', **GLL**, 22: 90–100

WIDDOWSON, H. G. 'A Case for Comparative Literature', *English*, 17: 15–18

WOODS, M. J. 'Gracian, Peregrini, and the Theory of Topics', **MLR**, 63: 854–63

——. 'Sixteenth-Century Topical Theory: Some Spanish and Italian Views', **MLR**, 63: 66–73

1969

BATESON, F. W. 'The Mode of Existence of the Criticism of Literature', *Essays in Criticism*, 19: 426–33. A reply to Cay Dollerup (420–26). E. B. Greenwood joins the discussion, *ibid.*, 20 (1970): 271–73

BRETT, R. L. *Fancy and Imagination* (Methuen). The Critical Idiom, 6

BURGESS, ANTHONY. 'Comparisons', **TLS**, 14 August, 904

——. *Urgent Copy: Literary Studies* (Jonathan Cape). Reviewed in **TLS**, 13 March, 258–59

CALDER, W. M. 'Translating Morgenstern', *Oxford German Studies*, 4: 142–54

CAVE, TERENCE. *Devotional Poetry in France, c. 1570–1613* (Cambridge University Press). Reviewed in **TLS**, 3 April, 371, and by D. Wilson, *French Studies*, 24 (1970): 395–96

CHADWICK, NORA K. and V. ZHIRMUNSKY. *Oral Epics of Central Asia* (Cambridge University Press). Reviewed in **TLS**, 12 June, 640

CROSS, A. G. 'George Borrow and Russia', **MLR**, 64: 363–71

DAICHES, DAVID. 'Literary Evaluation', in *Problems of Literary Evaluation*, ed. Joseph P. Strelka (Pennsylvania State University Press; *Yearbook of Comparative Literature*, 2), 163–81

DENVIR, BERNARD. 'Pope and the Painters', **TLS**, 27 November, 13–15

DUBOIS, E. T., E. RATCLIFF and P. J. YARROW, eds. *Eighteenth-Century French Studies: Literature and the Arts (Festschrift for Norman Suckling)* (Newcastle upon Tyne: Oriel Press)

EDMUNDS, JOHN. '*Timon of Athens* Blended with *Le Misanthrope*: Shadwell's Recipe for Satirical Tragedy', **MLR**, 64: 500–07

FERGUSON, JOHN. 'Literature and the Open University', TLS, 17 July, 781
FLETCHER, DENNIS J. 'Le Législateur and the Patriot King: A Case of Intellectual Kinship', *Comparative Literature Studies*, 6: 410 — 18
FORSTER, LEONARD. *The Icy Fire. Five Studies in European Petrarchism* (Cambridge University Press). Reviewed in TLS, 23 April 1970, 447
FOWLER, ROGER and PETER MERCER. 'Criticism and the Language of Literature: Some Traditions and Trends in Great Britain', *Style*, 3: 45–72
FRANCE, PETER. 'Oreste and Orestes', *French Studies*, 23: 131–37
FULLER, ROY. 'Philistines and Jacobins', TLS, 20 February, 183–84. Author's inaugural lecture as Professor of Poetry at Oxford
FURST, LILIAN R. 'Thomas Mann's Interest in James Joyce', MLR, 64: 605–13
———. 'A Comparison of Romanticism as Seen in Three Poems', in *Actes du Ve Congrès de l'Association Internationale de Littérature Comparée / Proceedings of the Vth Congress of the International Comparative Literature Association, Belgrade 1967*, ed. N. Banašević (University of Belgrade and Amsterdam: Swets & Zeitlinger), 209–14
———. 'Novalis' *Hymnen an die Nacht* and Nerval's *Aurelia*', *Comparative Literature*, 21: 31–46
———. *Romanticism in Perspective: A Comparative Study of the Romantic Movements in England, France and Germany* (Macmillan)
———. *Romanticism* (Methuen). The Critical Idiom, 2
GALLAGHER, PATRICK. 'Luis de León's Development, via Garcilaso, of Horace's "Beatus Ille"', *Neophilologus*, 53: 146–56
GIFFORD, HENRY. *Comparative Literature* (Routledge & Kegan Paul). Reviewed in TLS, 14 August, 904
GILBERT, M. E. 'Painter and Poet: Hogarth's "Marriage à la Mode" and Hofmannsthal's *Der Rosenkavalier*', MLR, 44: 818–27
GILLIES, ALEXANDER. *A Hebridean in Goethe's Weimar: The Reverend James McDonald and the Cultural Relations between Scotland and Germany* (Oxford: Blackwell)
GRIGSON, GEOFFREY. *Poems and Poets* (Macmillan). Reviewed in TLS, 13 March, 258–59
HAMBURGER, MICHAEL. *The Truth of Poetry. Tensions in Modern Poetry from Baudelaire to the 1960s* (Weidenfeld & Nicolson). Reviewed in TLS, 9 April 1970, 385–86
HARRIOTT, ROSEMARY. *Poetry and Criticism before Plato* (Methuen). Reviewed in TLS, 17 July, 780
HARRIS, R. W. *Romanticism and the Social Order* (Blandford)
HIGGINBOTHAM, JOHN, ED. *Greek and Latin Literature. A Comparative Survey* (Methuen). Reviewed in TLS, 31 July, 862
HINCHCLIFFE, ARNOLD P. *The Absurd* (Methuen). The Critical Idiom, 5
HOUGH, GRAHAM. *Style and Stylistics* (Routledge & Kegan Paul). Reviewed by F. W. Bateson, *Essays in Criticism*, 20 (1970): 264–68
'In Words Begin Responsibilities. Aspects of Literary Censorship in the Twentieth Century', TLS, 10 July, 741–43
JOHNSON, R. V. *Aestheticism* (Methuen). The Critical Idiom, 3
KERMODE, FRANK. 'The Structures of Fiction', *MLN*, 84: 891–915
KIMBER, IDA M. 'Barthold Heinrich Brockes: Two Unacknowledged Borrowings', MLR, 64: 806–08.Klieneberger, H. R. 'Charles Dickens and Wilhelm Raabe', *Oxford German Studies*, 4: 90–117
KNIGHT, G. WILSON. 'Poetry and the Arts', *Essays and Studies*, 22: 88–104
KNIGHT, R. C. 'Le Grand Siècle et l'érudition d'Outre-Manche', *Revue d'histoire littéraire de la France*, 69: 614–20
LEAVIS, F. R. '"English": Unrest and Continuity', TLS, 29 May, 569–72. Opening address at a colloquium on 'English' held by the University of Wales at Gregynog. Elicited letters

in subsequent issues from David Daiches, Donald Davie, Margaret Drabble, Norman Suckling and others
——. *English Literature in Our Time and the University* (Chatto & Windus). The Clark Lectures, 1967; reviewed in **TLS**, 4 December, 1381
—— and Q. D. LEAVIS. *Lectures in America* (Chatto & Windus). Reviewed in **TLS**, 20 March, 297–98
LEECH, GEOFFREY. *A Linguistic Guide to English Poetry* (Longmans)
LUCE, J. V. 'Homeric Qualities in the Life and Literature of the Great Blasket Island', *Greece & Rome*, 16: 151–68
MARSHALL, J. H. 'Observations on the Sources of the Treatment of Rhetoric in the "Leys d'Amors"', **MLR**, 64: 39–52
MASON, H. A. 'Creative Translation: Ezra Pound's Women of Trachis', *Critical Quarterly*, 4: 244–72
——. 'Introducing the Iliad', *Critical Quarterly*, 4: 15–37; 150–68
MCCLAIN, MEREDITH. 'Kurt Schwitters' Gedicht 25: A Musicological Addendum', **GLL**, 23: 268–70
MEADOWS, A. J. *The High Firmament: A Study of Astronomy in English Literature* (Leicester University Press)
MEWS, HAZEL. *Frail Vessels: Woman's Role in Women's Novels from Fanny Burney to George Eliot* (Athlone Press). Reviewed in **TLS**, 12 March 1970, 278
MOURET, FRANÇOIS J. L. 'Le *Vathek* de William Beckford et le *Voyage d'Urien* d'André Gide', **MLR**, 64: 774–76
OSBORNE, JOHN. 'Naturalism and the Dramaturgy of the Open Drama', **GLL**, 23 (1969–70), 119–28
PEARSALL, RONALD. *The Worm in the Bud* (Weidenfeld & Nicolson). Reviewed in **TLS**, 10 July, 741–43
POLE, DAVID. 'Cleanth Brooks and the New Criticism', *British Journal of Aesthetics*, 9: 285–97
POPE-HENNESSY, JOHN. 'Writing on Art', *Essays by Divers Hands*, 35: 101–14
RAINE, KATHLEEN. *Blake and Tradition* (Routledge & Kegan Paul, 2 vols). Reviewed in **TLS**, 25 December, 1461–62
ROLPH, C. H. *Books in the Dock* (Andre Deutsch)
ROUND, NICHOLAS G. 'Five Magicians, or the Uses of Literacy', **MLR**, 64: 793–805
SALTER, ELIZABETH. 'Medieval Poetry and the Visual Arts', *Essays and Studies*, 22: 16–32
SCHORER, MARK. *The World We Imagine: Selected Essays* (Chatto & Windus)
SHAFFER, ELINOR S. 'Coleridge's Revolution in the Standard of Taste', *Journal of Aesthetics and Art Criticism*, 2: 213–21
—— 'Coleridge's Theory of Aesthetic Interest', *Journal of Aesthetics and Art Criticism*, 4: 399–408
SHIRE, HELENA M. *Song, Dance and Poetry of the Court of Scotland under King James VI* (Cambridge University Press). Reviewed in **TLS**, 18 September 1970, 1058
'Spanish Records and Legends of Peru and the Incas: Garcilaso de la Vega's Royal Commentaries of Peru in a New Translation', **TLS**, 23 January, 73–75
SPARROW, JOHN. *Visible Worlds: A Study of Inscriptions in and as Books and Works of Art* (Cambridge University Press). Reviewed by Christopher Ricks, *Essays in Criticism*, 20 (1970): 259–64
STEIN, WALTER. *Criticism as Dialogue* (Cambridge University Press)
THOMAS, DONALD. *A Long Time Burning* (Routledge & Kegan Paul). Reviewed in **TLS**, 10 July, 741–43
THOMAS, L. H. C. '*Die Judenbuche* and English Literature', **MLR**, 64: 351–54

TORRINGA, JOHANN. 'The Icelandic Sagas and their English Translators', *Essays and Studies*, 22: 1–15

TRUMAN, R. W. 'Lázaro de Tormes and the "Homo Novus" Tradition', **MLR**, 64: 62–67

WATSON, GEORGE. *The Study of Literature* (Penguin). Reviewed in **TLS**, 2 September, 1123, and by Christopher Ricks, *Critical Quarterly*, 4: 395–403

WELLS, G. A. 'Astrology in Schiller's *Wallenstein*', *Journal of English and Germanic Philology*, 58: 100–15

WILKINSON, L. P. *The Georgics of Virgil* (Cambridge University Press). Reviewed in **TLS**, 5 February 1970, 131

———. 'Virgil, Dryden, and Tennyson', **TLS**, 9 October, 1159

WILLIAMS, GORDON. *Tradition and Originality in Roman Poetry* (Oxford: Clarendon). Reviewed in **TLS**, 31 July, 861–62

1970

ANNAN, NOEL. 'The University and the Intellect. The Miasma and the Menace', **TLS**, 30 April, 465–68. A reply to Leavis's '"Literarism" versus "Scientism"' (q.v.)

BATESON, F. W. 'Literary History: The Non-Subject par excellence', *New Literary History*, 2.1: 115–22

BEER, GILLIAN. *Romance* (Methuen). The Critical Idiom, 10

BERGONZI, BERNARD. *The Situation of the Novel* (Macmillan). Reviewed in **TLS**, 7 August, 868

BOWRA, C. M. *On Greek Margins* (Oxford: Carendon). Reviewed in **TLS**, 21 August, 915

BRADBURY, MALCOLM and DAVID PALMER, EDS. *Contemporary Criticism* (Edward Arnold). Stratford-upon-Avon Studies, 12. With Bradbury's 'Introduction: The State of Criticism Today', 10–37. The one non-British contributor was Norman Holland ("The 'Unconscious' of Literature: The Psycho-analytical Approach', 130–53); other contributions are entered separately.

BRADBURY, MALCOLM. 'Literature and Sociology', *Essays and Studies*, 23: 87–100

BUTLER, CHRISTOPHER. *Number Symbolism* (Routledge & Kegan Paul)

CARDWELL, R. A. 'The Persistence of Romantic Thought in Spain', **MLR**, 65: 803–12

CHIARI, JOSEPH. *The Aesthetics of Modernism* (Vision Press)

CRISTEA, S. N. 'Poetic Theory in Mid-Eighteenth-Century Italy', **MLR**, 65: 793–802

DAWSON, S. W. *Drama and the Dramatic* (Methuen). The Critical Idiom, 11

DIPPLE, ELIZABETH. *Plot* (Methuen). The Critical Idiom, 12

DOWNS, B. W. 'Anglo-Swedish Literary Relations, 1867–1900: The Fortunes of English Literature in Sweden', **MLR**, 65: 829–52

FLETCHER, JOHN. 'The Criticism of Comparison: The Approach through Comparative Literature and Intellectual History', in *Contemporary Criticism* (see Bradbury and Palmer), 106–29

FORSTER, LEONARD. *The Poet's Tongues: Multilingualism in Literature* (Cambridge University Press and the University of Otago Press). De Carle Lectures, 1968

FOWLER, ALASTAIR, ED. *Silent Poetry: Essays in Numerological Analysis* (Routledge & Kegan Paul)

FOWLER, ROGER. 'The Structure of Criticism and the Languages of Poetry: An Approach to their Language', in *Contemporary Criticism* (see Bradbury and Palmer), 172–93

FRASER, G. S. *Metre, Rhyme and Free Verse* (Methuen). The Critical Idiom, 9

FRASER, JOHN. 'Leavis and Winters: Professional Manners', *Critical Quarterly*, 5: 41–71

GOMBRICH, E. H. 'Criteria of Periodization in the History of European Art 3: A Comment on H. W. Janson's Article', *New Literary History*, 1: 123–25

GREENWOOD, E. B. 'Literature and Philosophy', *Essays in Criticism*, 20: 1–17

GREGOR, IAN. 'Criticism as an Individual Activity: The Approach through Reading', in *Contemporary Criticism* (see Bradbury and Palmer), 194–214
GRIBBLE, JAMES. 'Logical and Psychological Considerations in the Criticism of F. R. Leavis', *British Journal of Aesthetics*, 10: 39–57
HARVEY, JOHN. 'Tolstoy in England', *Critical Quarterly*, 5: 115–33
HEALD, DAVID. 'A Dissenting German View of Shakespeare: Christian Dietrich Grabbe', GLL, 24: 67–78
HENN, T. R. *The Bible as Literature* (Lutterworth). Reviewed in TLS, 19 March 1970, 310
HEYWOOD, CHRISTOPHER. 'A Source for *Middlemarch*: Miss Braddon's *The Doctor's Wife* and *Madame Bovary*', RLC, 44: 184–94
HOGGART, RICHARD. 'Contemporary Cultural Studies: An Approach to the Study of Literature and Society', in *Contemporary Criticism* (see Bradbury and Palmer), 154–71. Also published in 1969 as a pamphlet by the Centre for Contemporary Cultural Studies at the University of Birmingham
HOGGART, SIMON. *Speaking to Each Other* 1: *About Society*; 2: *About Literature* (Chatto & Windus). Reviewed in TLS, 5 March, 237–38
HOUGH, GRAHAM. 'Criticism as a Humanist Discipline', in *Contemporary Criticism* (see Bradbury and Palmer), 38–59
HUMBLE, M. E. 'Early British Interest in Nietzsche', GLL, 24: 327–35
JACK, R. D. S. 'William Fowler and Italian Literature', MLR, 65: 481–92
JONES, G. L. 'Gottsched's View on Providence and the Foundation of a National Literature', *Oxford German Studies*, 5: 5–13
KIRK, GEOFFREY S. *Myth* (Cambridge University Press). Reviewed in TLS, 14 August, 889–91
LANE, MICHAEL, ED. *Structuralism: A Reader* (Jonathan Cape). Reviewed in TLS, 23 April, 451
LEAVIS, F. R. '"Literarism" versus "Scientism". The Misconception and the Menace', TLS, 23 April, 441–44. See also Annan; Snow; also the flurry of readers' letters in subsequent issues
LEECH, GEOFFREY. 'The Linguistic and the Literary', TLS, 23 July, 805–06. Provoked readers' letters, e.g. from Roger Fowler, F. W. Bateson, Trevor Eaton and Anne Cluysenaar
LERNER, LAURENCE. 'An Essay on Pastoral', *Essays in Criticism*, 20: 275–97
LEVI, A. H. T., ED. *Humanism in France at the End of the Middle Ages and in the Early Renaissance* (Manchester University Press)
LONGUET-HIGGINS, H. C. 'The Language of Music', TLS, 20 November, 1351–52
LUCAS, PETER J. 'The Cloud in the Interpretation of the Old English Exodus', *English Studies*, 51: 297–311
MACQUEEN, JOHN. *Allegory* (Methuen). The Critical Idiom, 14
MASON, H. A. 'Nature in Pope and Homer 1: Similes of Inanimate Nature; 2: Similes of Animal Nature', *Critical Quarterly*, 5: 3–24; 134–59
MORRIS, BRIAN. 'Satire from Donne to Marvell', in *Metaphysical Poetry* (Stratford-upon-Avon Studies, ed. M. Bradbury and D. Palmer, 11), 210–35
MUECKE, D. C. *Irony* (Methuen). The Critical Idiom, 13
'Of Poetry and Meaning: Looking Back at the Critical Achievement of I. A. Richards', TLS, 26 February, 213–14
PALMER, D. J. 'The Verse Epistle', in *Metaphysical Poetry* (see Morris), 72–99
PARRY, IDRIS, 'The Tree of Movement', *Language and Style*, 3: 312–17
POLLARD, ARTHUR. *Satire* (Methuen). The Critical Idiom, 7
POLLARD, PATRICK. 'The Sources of André Gide's "Thésée"', MLR, 65: 290–97
RODWAY, A. 'Generic Criticism: The Approach through Type, Mode and Kind', in *Contemporary Criticism* (see Bradbury and Palmer): 82–105

SHACKLETON, ROBERT. Review of Claude Pichois and André-M. Rousseau, *La Littérature comparée* (Paris: Armand Colin, 1967), *French Studies*, 24: 416–17
SHAFFER, ELINOR S. 'The "Postulates in Philosophy" in the *Biographia Literaria*', *Comparative Literature Studies*, 3: 297–313
SMALLWOOD, E. MARY. 'Behind the New Testament', *Greece & Rome*, 17: 81–99
SNOW, C. P. THE CASE OF LEAVIS and THE SERIOUS CASE', *TLS*, 9 July, 737–40. A reply to Leavis's '"Literarism" versus "Scientism"' (see above)
STEINER, GEORGE. 'Classic Culture and Post-Classic Culture', *TLS*, 2 October, 1121–23
'The Contented Positivist. M. Foucault and the Death of Man', *TLS*, 2 July, 697–98
'The Literary Computer', *TLS*, 2 April, 368
THOMSON, PATRICIA. 'World Stage and Stage in Massinger's "Roman Actor"', *Neophilologus*, 54, 409–26
VICKERS, BRIAN. *Classical Rhetoric in English Poetry* (Macmillan). Reviewed in *TLS*, 23 July, 809
WALSH, P. G. *The Roman Novel. The Satyricon of Petronius and the Metamorphoses of Apuleius* (Cambridge University Press). Reviewed in *TLS*, 6 November, 1290
WATSON, J. R. *Picturesque Landscape and English Romantic Poetry* (Hutchinson)
WILLEY, BASIL. 'On Translating the Bible into Modern English', *Essays and Studies*, 23: 1–17
WILLIAMS, CARRINGTON B. *Style and Vocabulary: Numerical Studies* (Griffin). Reviewed in *TLS*, 2 April, 360
WILLIAMS, IOAN, ED. *Novel and Romance 1700–1800: A Documentary Record* (Routledge & Kegan Paul). Reviewed in *TLS*, 9 July, 746
WIMSATT, W. K. 'Battering the Object: The Ontological Approach', in *Contemporary Criticism* (see Bradbury and Palmer), 60–81

1971

BARR, JAMES. 'The Book of Job and its Modern Interpreters', *Bulletin of the John Rylands University Library of Manchester*, 54.1: 28–46
BATESON, F. W. *Essays in Critical Dissent* (Longman)
BAWCUTT, N. W. '*Don Quixote*, Part I, and *The Duchess of Malfi*', *MLR*, 66: 488–91
BOLGAR, R. R., ED. *Classical Influences on European Culture, AD 500–1500: Proceedings of an International Conference Held at Kings College, Cambridge, April 1971* (Cambridge University Press)
BRADBURY, MALCOLM. 'Style of Life, Style of Art and the American Novelist in the Nineteen Twenties', in *The American Novel in the Nineteen Twenties* (Edward Arnold, 269 pp.; Stratford-upon-Avon Studies, ed. M. Bradbury and J. D. Palmer, 13), 10–35
———. 'Fanny Hill and the Comic Novel', *Critical Quarterly*, 13: 263–75
———. *The Social Context of Modern English Literature* (Oxford, Blackwell)
BRAGG, MELVYN. 'Class and the Novel', *TLS*, 15 October, 1261–63
BRATHWAITE, EDWARD. 'Rehabilitations', *Critical Quarterly*, 13: 175–83
CHADWICK, CHARLES. *Symbolism* (Methuen). The Critical Idiom, 16
COLEMAN, DOROTHY. 'Rabelais and *The Water-Babies*', *MLR*, 66: 511–21
COOPER, B. 'Pushkin and the Anacreonta', *Slavonic and East European Review*, 52: 182–87
CROSS, A. G. 'An Oxford Don in Catherine the Great's Russia', *Journal of European Studies*, 1: 166–74
CULLER, JONATHAN. 'Jakobson and the Linguistic Attributes of Literary Texts', *Language and Style*, 5: 53–66
DAICHES, DAVID. 'Politics and the Literary Imagination', in *Liberations: New Essays on the Humanities in Revolution*, ed. Ihab Hassan (Wesleyan University Press), 103–19

——, ED. *Britain and the Commonwealth* (Allen Lane and Penguin). Penguin Companion to Literature, 1
DALY, PETER M. 'Emblematic Poetry of Occasional Meditation', **GLL**, 25: 126–39
DEANE, SEAMUS F. 'John Bull and Voltaire: The Emergence of a Cultural Cliché', **RLC**, 45: 581–94
DICKSON, KEITH. 'In Defence of "Comparative" Criticism', **GLL**, 25: 327–34
DIXON, PETER. *Rhetoric* (Methuen). The Critical Idiom, 19
DOWNS, B. W. 'Three Seventeenth-Century Hamlets', in *European Context* (see King and Vincent), 151–63
DRAPER, R. P. 'Concrete Poetry', *New Literary History*, 2: 329–40
DUDLEY, D. R. and D. M. LANG, EDS. *Classical and Byzantine, Oriental and African* (Allen Lane and Penguin). Penguin Companion to Literature, 4
EDWARDS, MICHAEL. 'Racinian Tragedy', *Critical Quarterly*, 13: 329–48
ELAND, ROSAMUND G. 'Problems in the Middle Style: La Fontaine in Eighteenth-Century England', **MLR**, 66: 731–37
ELLMANN, RICHARD. *Literary Biography* (Oxford: Carendon)
'Epistula ad Pisones and the Poetry of Antiquity', **TLS**, 14 May, 549–50
ETTINGHAUSEN, HENRY. 'Neo-Stoicism in Pictures: Lipsius and the Engraved Title-Page and Portrait in Quevedo's *Epicteto y Phocilides*', **MLR**, 66: 94–100
EVANS, S. 'Odyssean Echoes in Propertius IV.8', *Greece & Rome*, 18: 51–53
FORREST-THOMSON, VERONICA. 'Irrationality and Artifice: A Problem in Recent Poetics', *British Journal of Aesthetics*, 11: 123–33
FORSTER, LEONARD. 'Charles Utenhove and Germany', in *European Context* (see King and Vincent), 60–80
FOWLER, ALASTAIR. 'The Life and Death of Literary Forms', *New Literary History*, 2: 199–216
FOWLER, ROGER. 'Literature and Linguistics: 1950–1970', *Dutch Quarterly Review of Anglo-American Letters*, 2: 65–81
FURST, LILIAN R. 'Lessing and Mme de Staël vis-à-vis the Literature of the Mediterranean', *Journal of European Studies*, 1: 161–65
—— and PETER N. SKRINE. *Naturalism* (Methuen). The Critical Idiom, 18
GILLIES, A. 'John Osborn, FRS and Goethe', **MLR**, 66: 353–54
GILMAN, E. 'Literary and Moral Values', *Essays in Criticism*, 21: 180–94
GORDON, CATHERINE. 'The Illustration of Sir Walter Scott. Nineteenth-Century Enthusiasm and Adaptation', *Journal of the Warburg and Courtauld Institutes*, 34: 297–317
GRIMSLEY, RONALD. 'Two Philosophical Views of the Literary Imagination: Sartre and Bachelard', *Comparative Literature Studies*, 8: 42–57
GROVER, P. R. 'Two Modes of Possessing — Conquest and Appreciation: *The Princess Casamassima* and *L'éducation sentimentale*', **MLR**, 66: 760–71
GUEST, TANIS M. 'Hadewych and Minne', in *European Context* (see King and Vincent), 14–29
GULLEY, NORMAN. *Aristotle on the Purposes of Literature* (University of Wales Press)
HATTO, A. T. *Shamanism and Epic Poetry in Northern Asia* (School of Oriental and African Studies, University of London)
HOLCOMB, ADELE M. 'Turner and Scott', *Journal of the Warburg and Courtauld Institutes*, 34: 386–97
HUMBLE, M. E. 'Early British Interest in Nietzsche', **GLL**, 24: 327–35
HUXLEY, GEORGE. 'Crete in Aristotle's Polities', *Greek, Roman and Byzantine Studies*, 12: 505–16
JONES, MALCOLM. 'Some Echoes of Hegel in Dostoyevsky', *Slavonic and East European Review*, 49: 500–20

JOSIPOVICI, GABRIEL. *The World and the Book: A Study of Modern Fiction* (Macmillan)

KELLEY, D. J. 'Delacroix, Ingres et Poe: Valeurs picturales et valeurs littéraires dans l'œuvre critique de Baudelaire', *Revue d'histoire littéraire de la France*, 71: 606–14

KILLHAM, JOHN. 'A Novel's Relevance to Life', *British Journal of Aesthetics*, 11: 63–73

KING, CHRISTINE M. 'Seneca's *Hercules Oetaeus*: A Stoic Interpretation of the Greek Myth', *Greece & Rome*, 18: 215–22

KING, JONATHAN H. 'Philosophy and Experience: French Intellectuals and the Second World War', *Journal of European Studies*, 1: 198–212

KING, P. K. and P. F. VINCENT, EDS. *European Context. Studies in the History and Literature of the Netherlands Presented to Theodoor Weevers* (MHRA)

KOLNAI, AUREL. 'Contrasting the Ethical with the Aesthetical', *British Journal of Aesthetics*, 11: 178–88; 12 (1972), 331–43

KRAILSHEIMER, A. J., ED. *The Continental Renaissance, 1500–1600* (Penguin). Pelican Guides to European Literature

LITTLE, ROGER. 'Saint-John Perse and Music', *French Studies*, 25: 305–13

LUCAS, JOHN, ED. *Literature and Politics in the Nineteenth Century* (Methuen)

MAINLAND, WILLIAM F. 'In Pursuit of Flemish: Escape or the Homeward Journey?', in *European Context* (see King and Vincent), 386–99

MANN, NICHOLAS. 'Humanisme et patriotisme en France au XVe siècle', *Cahiers de l'Association Internationale des études françaises*, 23: 51–66

MARGOLIS, JOSEPH. 'Critics and Literature', *British Journal of Aesthetics*, 11: 368–84

MASKELL, D. W. 'The Transformation of History into Epic: the *Stuartide* (1611) of Jean de Schelandre', **MLR**, 66: 53–65

—— 'In Praise of the Contemporary Critic', *Cambridge Quarterly*, 5: 327–34

MASON, H. A. 'The Young Critic', *Cambridge Quarterly*, 5: 311–26

MCFARLANE, I. D. 'Notes on the Composition and Reception of George Buchanan's Psalm Paraphrases', *Forum for Modern Language Studies*, 7: 319–60

MCINNES, EDWARD. 'Drama as Protest and Prophecy: The Historical Drama of the Jungdeutsche', *Maske und Kothurn*, 17: 190–202

MENHENNET, A. 'Between Baroque and Rococo: The "Galant Style" of Christian Holmann', **MLR**, 66: 343–52

MERCHANT, PAUL. *The Epic* (Methuen). The Critical Idiom, 17

MEW, PETER. 'Metaphor and Truth', *British Journal of Aesthetics*, 11, 189–95. See also Kipp 1973

MOTTRAM, ERIC. 'The Hostile Environment and the Survival Artist: A Note on the Twenties', in *The American Novel and the Nineteen Twenties* (see Bradbury, 'Style of Life'), 232–62

——, MALCOLM BRADBURY and JEAN FRANCO, EDS. *USA and Latin America* (Allen Lane and Penguin). Penguin Companion to Literature, 3

MOURET, FRANCOIS. 'Le voyage d'André Gide en littérature anglaise', *Romanistisches Jahrbuch*, 22, 162–77

'New Frontiers in the Theory of Fiction', **TLS**, 3 September, 1005–06

NEWTON DE MOLINA, DAVID. 'Sceptical Library Historicism: A Fictional Analogue in Jorge Luis Borges', *Essays in Criticism*, 21: 57–73

NEWTON, J. M. 'Literary Criticism, Universities, Murder', *Cambridge Quarterly*, 5: 335–54. Originally read at the Institute of Contemporary Arts, London, as part of a course of lectures by different people on 'Literary Criticism as Discipline and Language'

PARRY, IDRIS. 'Margiad Evans and Tendencies in European Literature', *Transactions of the Honourable Society of Cymmrodorion*, 224–36

PRESS, JOHN. *The Lengthening Shadows* (Oxford University Press)

Rees, Christine. 'The Metamorphosis of Daphne in Sixteenth- and Seventeenth-Century English Poetry', **MLR**, 66: 252–63

Robson-Scott, W. D. 'Goethe and the Art of the Netherlands', in *European Context* (see King and Vincent), 194–208

Sagarra, Eda. *Tradition and Revolution: German Literature and Society 1870–1890* (Weidenfeld and Nicolson)

Sayce, Olive. 'Chaucer's "Retractions": The Conclusion of the Canterbury Tales and its Place in Literary Tradition', *Medium Aevum*, 40: 230–48

Saz, Sara M. 'Guiraldes and Kipling: A Possible Influence', *Neophilologus*, 55: 270–84

Selden, Raman. 'Roughness in Satire from Horace to Dryden', **MLR**, 66: 264–72

Sheppard, R. 'Two Liberals: A Comparison of the Humanism of Matthew Arnold and Wilhelm von Humboldt', **GLL**, 24: 219–34

Skelton, Robin. *The Practice of Poetry* (Heinemann)

Snowden, J. A. 'Sean O'Casey and Naturalism', *Essays and Studies*, 24: 56–68

Sparkes, B. A. 'The Trojan Horse in Classical Art', *Greece & Rome*, 18: 54–70

Steiner, George. *Extraterrestrial: Papers on Literature and the Language Revolution* (Faber and Faber)

——. *In Bluebeard's Castle. Some Notes towards the Re-Definition of Culture* (Faber and Faber)

Stern, J. P. *Idylls and Realities. Studies in Nineteenth-Century German Literature* (Methuen)

'The Poetics of Cultural Criticism', **TLS**, 17 December, 1565–66

'The Unity of Greek', **TLS**, 29 October, 1363–65

Thompson, C. W. 'John Martin et l'image de la ville moderne chez Vigny et Lamartine', **RLC**, 45: 5–17

Thomson, George. 'The Continuity of Hellenism', *Greece & Rome*, 18: 18–29

Thorlby, Anthony, ed. *Europe* (Allen Lane and Penguin). Penguin Companion to Literature, 2

Tompkins, J. M. S. 'Kipling and Nordic Myth and Saga', *English Studies*, 52: 147–57

Vincent, P. F. 'Menno ter Braak's Anglo-Saxon Attitudes', in *European Context* (see King and Vincent), 362–85

——. 'Sir Edmund Gosse and Frederik van Eeden: Some Reflections on an Unpublished Correspondence', **MLR**, 66: 125–38

Waddington, Patrick. 'Turgenev and George Eliot: A Literary Friendship', **MLR**, 66: 751–59

Walshe, M.O'C. '*Der Ackermann aus Böhmen* and *Elkerlijc*', in *European Context* (see King and Vincent), 52–59

Watson, George. 'Orwell and the Spectrum of European Politics ', *Journal of European Studies*, 1: 191–97

Weatherby, H. L. 'Newman and Victorian Literature: A Study in the Failure of Influence', *Critical Quarterly*, 13: 205–14

Wells, D. A. 'Source and Tradition in the *Moriaen*', in *European Context* (see King and Vincent), 30–51

West, Thomas G. 'Schopenhauer, Huysmans and French Naturalism', *Journal of European Studies*, 1: 313–24

White, J. J. 'Goethe in the Machine: Georges Perec's Computer-Based Exercises with the Repertoire of "Über allen Gipfeln"', **PEGS**, 41: 103–20

Wilson, Jean. 'The "Nineties" Movement in Poetry: Myth or Reality?', *Yearbook of English Studies*, 1: 160–74

Witte, W. 'The Literary Uses of Obscenity', **GLL**, 28: 360–73

1972

AITKEN, A. J. 'The Literary Uses of the Computer', TLS, 21 April, 456–57

AMBROSE, MARY E. '*La Donna del Lago*: The First Italian Translators of Scott', MLR, 67: 74–82

ARMSTRONG, ISOBEL. *Victorian Scrutinies: Reviews of Poetry, 1830–1870* (Athlone Press)

BANN, STEPHEN. 'L'anti-histoire de Henry Esmond', *Poétique*, 9: 61–79

BARNES, CHRISTOPHER J. 'Boris Pasternak and Rainer Maria Rilke: Some Missing Links', *Forum for Modern Language Studies*, 8: 61–68

BATESON, F. W. *The Scholar-Critic: An Introduction to Literary Research* (Routledge and Kegan Paul)

BELL, MICHAEL. *Primitivism* (Methuen). The Critical Idiom, 20

BERRY, FRANCIS. 'Commentary' (on the contributions in this issue of NLH, on 'The Language of Literature'), *New Literary History*, 4: 167–80

———. *Thoughts on Poetic Time* (Abingdon, Abbey Press)

BICKERTON, DAVID. 'A Scientific and Literary Periodical, the *Bibliothèque britannique* (1796–1815): Its Foundation and Early Development', RLC, 46: 527–47

BIGSBY, C. W. E. *Dada and Surrealism* (Methuen). The Critical Idiom, 23

BIRD, ALAN. 'Rahel Varnhagen von Ense and Some English Assessments of her Character', GLL, 26: 183–92

BLACKMAN, MAURICE. 'Gérard de Nerval et Thomas Moore: Note sur "Stances élégiaques"', *Revue d'histoire littéraire de la France*, 72: 428–31

BOWRA, C. M. *Homer* (Duckworth)

BRADBROOK, M. C. *Literature in Action. Studies in Continental and Commonwealth Society* (Chatto and Windus)

BRIDGWATER, PATRICK. *Nietzsche in Anglosaxony: A Study of Nietzsche's Impact on English and American Literature* (Leicester University Press)

BRIGGS, A. D. 'Alexander Pushkin: A Possible Influence on Henry James', *Forum for Modern Language Studies*, 8: 52–60

———. 'Someone Else's Sledge: Further Notes on Turgenev's *Virgin Soil* and Henry James's *The Princess Casamassima*', *Oxford Slavonic Papers*, 5: 52–60

BRODSLEY, LAUREL. 'Butler's Character of Hudibras and Contemporary Graphic Satire', *Journal of the Warburg and Courtauld Institutes*, 35: 401–04

BROOKS, HAROLD. 'Dryden's Aureng-Zebe: Debts to Corneille and Racine', RLC, 46: 5–34

BROTHERSTON, GORDON. 'How Aesop Fared in Nahuatl', *Arcadia*, 7: 37–42

———. 'Ubirajara, Hiawatha, Cumanda: National Virtue from American Indian Literature', *Comparative Literature Studies*, 9: 243–52

BULLEN, J. B. 'Browning's "Pictor Ignotus" and Vasari's Life of Fra Bartolommeo di San Marco', *Review of English Studies*, 23: 313–19

BUTLER, R. A. 'The Prevalence of Indirect Biography', *Essays by Divers Hands*, 37: 17–30

BUXTON, JOHN. 'A Second Supplement to Toynbee's *Dante in English Literature*', *Italian Studies*, 27: 41–43

CLOSE, A. J. 'Don Quixote and the "Intentionalist Fallacy"', *British Journal of Aesthetics*, 12: 19–39

COHEN, GILLIAN. 'The Psychology of Reading', *New Literary History*, 4: 75–90

DAICHES, DAVID and ANTHONY THORLBY, EDS. *The Classical World* (Aldus). Literature and Western Civilization, 1

DASHWOOD, JULIE R. 'Futurism and Fascism', *Italian Studies*, 27: 91–103

DAVIES, LAURENCE. 'Cunninghame Graham's South American Sketches', *Comparative Literature Studies*, 9: 253–65

DAVIES, NORMAN. 'Izaak Babel's Konarmiya Stories and the Polish-Soviet War', **MLR**, 67: 845–57
DAY, W. G. 'Sterne and Ozell', *English Studies*, 53, 434–36
DOVE, MARY. 'Gawain and the *Blasme des Femmes* Tradition', *Medium Aevum*, 41: 20–26
DYSON, ANTHONY EDWARD. *Between Two Worlds: Aspects of Literary Form* (Macmillan)
EATON, MARCIA. 'The Truth Value of Literary Statements', *British Journal of Aesthetics*, 12: 163–74
EDWARDS, MICHAEL. *La Tragédie racinienne* (Paris: La pensée universelle)
FALASCHI, ENID T. 'Giotto: The Literary Legend', *Italian Studies*, 27: 1–27
FINLEY, GERALD E. 'J. M. W. Turner and Sir Walter Scott: Iconography of a Tour', *Journal of the Warburg and Courtauld Institutes*, 35: 359–85
FORREST-THOMSON, VERONICA. 'Levels in Poetic Convention', *Journal of European Studies*, 2: 35–51
FOWLER, ALASTAIR. 'Periodization and Interart Analogies', *New Literary History*, 3: 487–510
FOWLER, ROWENA. 'Η Ερημη Χωρα: Seferis' Translation of The Waste Land', *Comparative Literature Studies*, 9: 443–54
FREEBORN, RICHARD. *The Rise of the Russian Novel* (Cambridge University Press)
FULLER, JOHN. *The Sonnet* (Methuen). The Critical Idiom, 26
GARSON, RONALD. 'The English Aristophanes', **RLC**, 46: 177–93
GENT, C. L. '*Measure for Measure* and the Fourth Book of Castiglione's *Il Cortegiano*', **MLR**, 67: 252–56
GENT, VICTORIA. '"To Flinch from Modern Varnish": The Appeal of the Past to the Victorian Imagination', in *Victorian Poetry* (Edward Arnold; Stratford-upon-Avon Studies, ed. M. Bradbury and D. Palmer, 15), 10–35
GRIGSON, GEOFFREY. 'The Writer and his Territory', **TLS**, 28 July, 859–60
HALL, KATHLEEN M. 'A Defence of Jean de la Taille as a Translator of Ariosto', **MLR**, 67: 537–42
HARBERT, BRUCE. 'The Myth of Tereus in Ovid and Gower', *Medium Aevum*, 41: 208–14
HAWKES, TERENCE. *Metaphor* (Methuen). The Critical Idiom, 25
HEALD, DAVID. 'Grillparzer and the Germans', *Oxford German Studies*, 6: 61–73
HEATH, STEPHEN. *The Nouveau Roman: A Study in the Practice of Writing* (Elek)
HEMMINGS, F. W. J. 'Emile Zola devant l'Exposition universelle de 1878', *Cahiers de l'Association internationale des études françaises*, 24: 131–53
HENRY, P. L. 'The Land of Cockaygne: Cultures in Contact in Medieval Ireland', *Studia Hibernica*, 12: 120–41
HEPBURN, RONALD. 'Poetry and "Concrete Imagination": Problems of Truth and Illusion', *British Journal of Aesthetics*, 12, 3–18
HEWITT, DOUGLAS. *The Approach to Fiction: Good and Bad Readings of Novels* (Longman)
HOGGART, RICHARD. *Only Connect. On Culture and Communication* (Chatto and Windus)
HOLBROOK, DAVID. 'Pornography and Death', *Critical Quarterly*, 14: 29–41
HUTCHINSON, PETER. '"Conditioned against us...": The East German View of the Federal Republic', *Forum for Modern Language Studies*, 8: 40–51
———. 'Franz Fühmann's *Böhmen am Meer*: A Socialist Version of The Winter's Tale', **MLR**, 67: 579–89
JACK, R. D. S. *The Italian Influence on Scottish Literature* (Edinburgh University Press)
JENKINS, RAY. 'The Development of Modern Political Biography, 1945–70', *Essays by Divers Hands*, 37: 63–74
JONES, G. L. 'The Mulde's "Half-Prodigal Son": Paul Fleming, Germany and the Thirty Years' War', **GLL**, 26: 125–36

JONES, GWYN. 'Writing for Wales and the Welsh', TLS, 28 July, 869–70
JUMP, JOHN D. *Burlesque* (Methuen). The Critical Idiom, 22
KERMODE, FRANK. *Novel and Narrative* (University of Glasgow)
KUNA, F. M. 'Art as Direct Vision: Kafka and Sacher-Masoch', *Journal of European Studies*, 2: 237–46
LAURENSON, DIANA and ALAN SWINGEWOOD. *The Sociology of Literature* (MacGibbon and Kee)
LEAVIS, F. R. *Nor Shall My Sword. Discourses on Pluralism, Compassion and Social Hope* (Chatto and Windus)
LEBANS, W. M. 'The Influence of the Classics in Donne's Epicedes and Obsequies', *Review of English Studies*, 23: 127–37
LERNER, LAURENCE. *The Uses of Nostalgia: Studies in Pastoral Poetry* (Chatto & Windus)
LERNER, MICHAEL. 'The *Revue Contemporaine* and Fin de Siècle Cosmopolitanism', *Arcadia*, 7: 281–84
LIMENTANI, U. 'Foscolo and the Wells Family', *Italian Studies*, 27: 64–84; 28 (1973), 50–51
LODGE, DAVID. 'Onions and Apricots; or, Was the Rise of the Novel a Fall from Grace? Serious Reflections on Gabriel Josipovici's *The World and the Book*', *Critical Quarterly*, 14: 171–85
——, ED. *Twentieth Century Literary Criticism* (Longman)
LOFMARK, CARL. 'Wolfram's Source References in *Parzival*', MLR, 67: 820–44
LYLE, E. B. 'Two Parallels in Macbeth to Seneca's *Hercules Oetaeus*', *English Studies*, 53: 109–12
MAINZER, CONRAD. 'John Gower's Use of the "Medieval Ovid" in the *Confessio Amantis*', *Medium Aevum*, 41: 215–29
MASON, H. A. *To Homer through Pope. An Introduction to Homer's Iliad and Pope's Translation* (Chatto and Windus)
MCINNES, EDWARD. 'Strategies of Inwardness: Gutzkow's Domestic Plays and the Liberal Drama of the 1840s', *Maske und Kothurn*, 18: 219–33
MENHENNET, A. 'Order and Freedom in Haller's "Lehrgedichte": On the Limitations and Achievements of Strict Rationalism within the "Aufklärung"', *Neophilologus*, 56: 180–87
MERCHANT, W. MOELWYN. *Comedy* (Methuen). The Critical Idiom, 21
MISTRY, F. 'Hofmannsthal's Response to China in his Unpublished "Über chinesische Gedichte"', GLL, 26: 306–14
MOORE, W. G. 'Raison et structure dans la comédie de Molière', *Revue d'histoire littéraire de la France*, 72: 800–05
MORGAN, EDWIN. 'The Resources of Scotland', TLS, 28 July, 885–86
MORRIS, C. B. *Surrealism and Spain* (Cambridge University Press)
MORRIS, J. A. 'T. S. Eliot and Antisemitism', *Journal of European Studies*, 2: 173–82
MURDOCH, J. D. W. 'Scott, Pictures, and Pointers', MLR, 67: 31–43
OWEN, D. D. R. *The Vision of Hell. Infernal Journeys in Medieval French Literature* (Scottish Academic Press)
PALMER, EUSTACE. *An Introduction to the African Novel* (Heinemann)
PEACOCK, RONALD. *Criticism and Personal Taste* (Oxford: Carendon)
PRICKETT, STEPHEN. 'Dante, Beatrice and M. C. Escher: Disconfirmation as a Metaphor', *Journal of European Studies*, 2: 333–54
RADFORD, COLIN. 'Theatre within the Theatre', *Nottingham French Studies*, 11: 76–90
REES, B. R. 'Pathos in the Poetics of Aristotle', *Greece & Rome*, 19: 1–11
REISS, HANS. 'Problems of Demarcation in the Study of Literature: Some Reflections', *Deutsche Vierteljahrsschrift für Literaturwissenschaft und Geistesgeschichte*, 46: 189–212

RIGHTER, WILLIAM. 'Myth and Interpretation', *New Literary History*, 3: 319–44
RIVERS, ISABEL. *The Poetry of Conservatism, 1600–1745. A Study of Poets and Public Affairs, from Jonson to Pope* (Cambridge: Rivers Press)
ROGERS, PAT. 'Freedom and Fidelity in Augustan Translation: An Adapted Version of Bouhours', **RLC**, 46: 360–75
ROGERS, PAT. 'Shaftesbury and the Aesthetics of Rhapsody', *British Journal of Aesthetics*, 12: 244–57
ROLFE, C.D. *Saint-Amant and the Theory of 'Ut pictura poesis'* (MHRA)
ROTHENBERG, J. 'Music in the Theatre of Jean Anouilh', *Forum for Modern Language Studies*, 8: 345–53
RYCROFT, CHARLES. 'The Artist as Patient', **TLS**, 22 September, 1089–90
SALAMAN, ESTHER. *The Great Confession. From Aksakov and De Quincey to Tolstoy and Proust* (Allen Lane)
SAYCE, RICHARD. 'Littérature et architecture au XVIIe siècle', *Cahiers de l'Association internationale des études françaises*, 24: 233–50
SCOTT, CLIVE. 'Poetics and Critics', *Journal of European Studies*, 2: 52–64
SHACKLETON, ROBERT. 'The Greatest Happiness of the Greatest Number: The History of Bentham's Phrase', *Studies on Voltaire and the Eighteenth Century*, 90 (Transactions of the Third Congress on the Enlightenment, 4): 1461–82
SHERGOLD, NORMAN D., ED. *Studies in the Spanish and Portuguese Ballad* (Tamesis)
SHIELDS, HUGH. 'Bishop Turpin and the Source of *Nicodemus Gospell*', *English Studies*, 53: 497–502
SHORT, IAN. 'A Study in Carolingian Legend and its Persistence in Latin Historiography (XII-XVI Centuries)', *Mittellateinisches Jahrbuch*, 7: 127–32
SKINNER, QUENTIN. 'Motives, Intentions, and the Interpretation of Texts', *New Literary History*, 3: 393–408
SMALL, I. C. 'Plato and Pater: Fin-de-siecle Aesthetics', *British Journal of Aesthetics*, 12: 369–83
SMITH, JAMES. 'Notes on the Criticism of T. S. Eliot', *Essays in Criticism*, 22: 333–61
STEINER, GEORGE. 'Whorf, Chomsky and the Student of Literature', *New Literary History*, 4: 15–34
STERN, J. P. 'Reflections on Realism', *Journal of European Studies*, 1: 1–31
——. *On Realism* (Routledge and Kegan Paul)
SYMONS, JULIAN. *Bloody Murder: From the Detective Story to the Crime Novel* (Faber and Faber)
'The State of English', **TLS**, various issues, 147–48, 183–84, 215–16, 251–52, 269–70, 331–32, 389–90, 411–12
THOMPSON, C. W. 'Mérimée and Pictorial Inspiration: The Sources of "Les Ames du Purgatoire"', **MLR**, 67, 62–73
THOMSON, PATRICIA. 'George Sand and English Reviewers: The First Twenty Years', **MLR**, 67, 501–16
THOMSON, PHILIP. *The Grotesque* (Methuen). The Critical Idiom, 24
TIERNEY, WILLIAM. 'Irish Writers and the Spanish Civil War', *Éire — Ireland*, 7: 36–55
TRENDALL, A. D. and T. B. L. WEBSTER. *Illustrations of Greek Drama* (Phaidon)
TUCKER, SUSIE. 'Biblical Translation in the Eighteenth Century', *Essays and Studies*, 25: 106–20
WAGNER, GEOFFREY. *Five for Freedom: A Study of Feminism in Fiction* (George Allen and Unwin)
WAIN, JOHN. 'The New Puritanism, the New Academicism, the New, the New...', *Critical Quarterly*, 14: 7–18

WALEY, PAMELA. 'The Nurse in Boccaccio's *Fiammetta*: Source and Invention', *Neophilologus*, 56: 164–74
WALSH, DOROTHY. 'Literary Art and Linguistic Meaning', *British Journal of Aesthetics*, 12: 321–30
YOUNG, KENNETH. 'The Literature of Polities', *Essays by Divers Hands*, 37: 134–52

1973

ALDISS, BRIAN. *Billion Year Spree: The History of Science Fiction* (Weidenfeld and Nicolson)
ANDREW, MALCOLM. 'Jonah and Christ in *Patience*', *Modern Philology*, 70: 230–33
AUTY, ROBERT. 'Prešeren's German Poems', *Oxford Slavonic Papers*, 6: 1–11
——. 'The Role of Poetry in the Early-Nineteenth-Century Slavonic Language Revivals', in *Expression, Communication and Experience in Literature and Language. Proceedings of the XIIth Congress of the International Federation for Modern Languages and Literatures, Held at Cambridge University, 20 to 26 August 1972*, ed. R. G. Popperwell (MHRA), 229–30
BANN, STEPHEN and JOHN E. BOWLT, eds. *Russian Formalism* (Scottish Academic Press)
BARNES, ANNIE. 'Proust et Goethe', *Oxford German Studies*, 8: 128–48
BARR, JAMES. 'Reading the Bible as Literature', *Bulletin of the John Rylands University Library of Manchester*, 56.1, 10–33
BATCHELOR, R. 'The Presence of Nietzsche in André Malraux', *Journal of European Studies*, 3: 218–29
BENNETT, P. E. 'The Literary Source of Beroul's *Godoine*', *Medium Aevum*, 42: 133–40
BERGONZI, BERNARD. 'Critical Situations: From the Fifties to the Seventies', *Critical Quarterly*, 15: 59–73
BOA, ELIZABETH and J. H. REID. *Critical Strategies: German Fiction in the Twentieth Century* (Edward Arnold)
BOWLT, J. E. 'Russian Symbolism and the "Blue Rose" Movement', *Slavonic and East European Review*, 51: 161–81
BRADBROOK, M. C. 'The Nature of Theatrical Experience in Ben Jonson, with Special Reference to the Masques', in *Expression, Communication and Experience in Literature and Language* (see Auty, 'The Role'), 103–17
BRADBURY, MALCOLM. *Possibilities* (Oxford: Carendon)
BRYAN-KINNS, MERRICK. 'Philippe Habert's *Temple de la Mort*: Probable Source of a German Baroque Allegory', *Arcadia*, 8: 296–99
BULLOCK-DAVIES, CONSTANCE. 'The Form of the Breton Lay', *Medium Aevum*, 42: 18–31
BURNS, ELIZABETH and TOM BURNS. *The Sociology of Literature and Drama* (Penguin)
BUTLER, CHRISTOPHER. 'What Is a Literary Work?', *New Literary History*, 5: 17–30
CAIN, TOM. 'Tolstoy's Use of *David Copperfield*', *Critical Quarterly*, 15: 237–46
CARDINAL, ROGER. 'Image and Word in Schizophrenic Creation', *Forum for Modern Language Studies*, 9: 103–20
CAVE, TERENCE. 'Mythes de l'abondance et de la privation chez Ronsard', *Cahiers de l'Association internationale des études françaises*, 25: 247–60
CHAPMAN, RAYMOND. *Linguistics and Literature: An Introduction to Literary Stylistics* (Edward Arnold)
CRAIG, DAVID. *The Real Foundations: Literature and Social Change* (Chatto and Windus)
DAICHES, DAVID and ANTHONY THORLBY, EDS. *The Mediaeval World* (Aldus). Literature and Western Civilization, 2
DENNY, NEVILLE, ED. *Medieval Drama* (Edward Arnold). Stratford-upon-Avon Studies, 16
DICKIE, GEORGE. 'Psychical Distance: In a Fog at Sea', *British Journal of Aesthetics*, 13: 17–29
DONAGHEY, B. S. 'Another English Manuscript of an Old French Translation of Boethius', *Medium Aevum*, 42: 38–43

DRISCOLL, IRENE JOAN. 'Visual Allusion in the Work of Theophile Gautier', *French Studies*, 27: 418–28
DUNCAN, ALISTAIR B. 'Claude Simon and William Faulkner', *Forum for Modern Language Studies*, 9: 235–52
DUTTON, DENIS. 'Criticism and Method', *British Journal of Aesthetics*, 13: 232–42
ELLIS, D. G. 'Romans français dans la prude Angleterre (1830–1870)', **RLC**, 47: 306–15
ENRIGHT, D. J. *Man is an Onion: Reviews and Essays* (Chatto and Windus)
FINDLAY, CHARLES. 'The Opera and Operatic Elements in the Fragmentary Biography of Johannes Kreisler', GLL, 27: 22–34
FLAVELL, M. K. 'Goethe, Rousseau, and the "Hyp"', *Oxford German Studies*, 7: 5–23
——. '"Arkadisch frei sei unser Glück": The Myth of the Golden Age in Eighteenth-Century Germany', **PEGS**, 43: 1–27
FOOTE, I. P. '*Otechestvennye Zapiski* and English Literature, 1868–84', *Oxford Slavonic Papers*, 6: 28–47
FORREST-THOMSON, VERONICA. 'Necessary Artifice: Form and Theory in the Poetry of *Tel Quel*', *Language and Style*, 6: 3–26
FOWLER, ALASTAIR. *Readers of Literature* (University of Edinburgh)
FOWLER, ROWENA. 'Ernest Dowson and the Classics', *Yearbook of English Studies*, 3: 243–52
FRASER, J. H. 'German Exile Publishing: The Malik-Aurora Verlag of Wieland Herzfeld', **GLL**, 27, 115–24
FURNESS, R. S. *Expressionism* (Methuen). The Critical Idiom, 29
FURST, LILIAN R. 'The Structure of Romantic Agony', *Comparative Literature Studies*, 10: 125–38
GABLE, A. T. 'Tragic Lament and Tragic Action', *Journal of European Studies*, 3: 59–69
GASKILL, P. H. 'Hölderlin's Medievalism', *Neophilologus*, 57: 353–°9
GIBBONS, TOM. 'Modernism in Poetry: The Debt to Arthur Symons', *British Journal of Aesthetics*, 13: 47–60
GILL, ROMA. 'As We Read the Living?', *Essays in Criticism*, 23: 167–75. With a reply by F. W. Bateson, 175–78
GREEN, R. J. 'Oscar Wilde's Intentions: An Early Modernist Manifesto', *British Journal of Aesthetics*, 13: 397–404
GREENWOOD, E. B. 'Eikhenbaum, Formalism, and Tolstoy', *Essays in Criticism*, 23: 372–87
GRIFFIN, NIGEL. 'Miguel Venegas and the Sixteenth-Century Jesuit School Drama', **MLR**, 68: 796–806
GURR, ANDREW and PIO ZIRIMU, eds. *Black Aesthetics: Papers from a Colloquium Held at the University of Nairobi, June 1971* (Nairobi, Kampala and Dar es Salaam, East African Literary Bureau)
HAGGIS, D. R. 'Scott, Balzac, and the Historical Novel as Social and Political Analysis: *Waverley* and *Les Chouans*', **MLR**, 68: 50–68
HAMMOND, GERALD. 'English Bible Translation', *Critical Quarterly*, 15: 361–70
HARDING, F. W. J. 'Notes on Aesthetic Theory in France in the Nineteenth Century', *British Journal of Aesthetics*, 13: 251–70
HAWTHORN, JEREMY. *Identity and Relationship: A Contribution to Marxist Theory of Literary Criticism* (Lawrence & Wishart)
HIBBERD, JOHN. 'Gessner in England', **RLC**, 47: 296–306
HIGGINS, IAN. 'Towards a Poetic Theatre: Poetry and the Plastic Arts in Verhaeren's Aesthetics', *Forum for Modern Language Studies*, 9: 1–23. Higgins edited seven essays from this issue of *FMLS* (entered separately) under the title *Literature and the Plastic Arts, 1880–1930* (Scottish Academic Press)
HONDERICH, PAULINE. 'John Calvin and Doctor Faustus', **MLR**, 68: 1–13

HUNT, TONY. 'The Structure of Medieval Narrative', *Journal of European Studies*, 3: 295–328
JEPHCOTT, E. F. N. *Proust and Rilke* (Chatto and Windus)
JONES, MICHAEL R. 'Censorship as an Obstacle to the Production of Shakespeare on the Stage of the Burgtheater in the Nineteenth Century', GLL, 27: 187–94
KELLER, R. E. 'Diglossia in German-Speaking Switzerland', *Bulletin of the John Rylands University Library of Manchester*, 56.1, 130–49
KERMODE, FRANK. 'The Use of Codes', in *Approaches to Poetics: Selected Papers from the English Institute*, ed. S. Chatman (Columbia University Press), 51–79
KIPP, DAVID. 'Metaphor, Truth and Mew on Elliott', *British Journal of Aesthetics*, 13: 30–40. See also Mew 1971
LARRY, N. M. *Dostoevsky and Dickens: A Study of Literary Influence* (Routledge and Kegan Paul)
LEWIS, HANNA B. 'Hofmannsthal, Shelley, and Keats', GLL, 27: 220–34
LYLE, E. B. 'Sir Landevale and the Fairy-Mistress Theme in Thomas of Erceldoune', *Medium Aevum*, 42: 244–50
MAKIN, PETER. 'Ezra Pound and Scotus Erigena', *Comparative Literature Studies*, 10: 60–83
MARTIN, ANGUS. 'Baculard d'Arnaud et la vogue des séries de nouvelles en France au XVIIIe siècle', *Revue d'histoire littéraire de la France*, 73: 982–92
MASON, H. A. 'Books on Catullus', *Cambridge Quarterly*, 6: 152–77
MCCLELLAND, JOHN. 'Sonnet ou quatorzain? Marot et le choix d'une forme poétique', *Revue d'histoire littéraire de la France*, 73: 591–607
MCINNES, EDWARD. 'Lessing's *Hamburgische Dramaturgie* and the Theory of the Drama in the Nineteenth Century', *Orbis Litterarum*, 28: 294–318
MCVAY, GORDON. 'Sergey Esenin in America', *Oxford Slavonic Papers*, 6: 82–91
MEECH, PETER. 'The Frog and the Star: The Role of Music in the Dramatic and Visual Works of Ernst Barlach', *Forum for Modern Language Studies*, 9: 24–34
MITCHELL, JULIAN. *Truth and Fiction* (Covent Garden Press)
MOLONEY, BRIAN. 'Svevo as a Jewish Writer', *Italian Studies*, 28: 52–63
MURDOCH, BRIAN. 'An Early Irish Adam and Eve: *Saltair na Rann* and the Traditions of the Fall', *Medieval Studies*, 35: 146–77
NOSZLOPY, GEORGE T. 'Apollinaire, Allegorical Imagery and the Visual Arts', *Forum for Modern Language Studies*, 9: 49–74
Ó TUAMA, SEAN. 'Sean Ó Riordáin agus an nuafhilíocht', *Studia Hibernica*, 13: 100–67
OLSEN, STEIN HAUGOM. 'Authorial Intention', *British Journal of Aesthetics*, 13: 219–31
PAREKH, BHIKHU and R. N. BERKI. 'The History of Political Ideas: A Critique of Q. Skinner's Methodology', *Journal of the History of Ideas*, 34: 163–84
PARKIN, JOHN. 'Machiavellism in Etienne Pasquier's *Pourparler du prince*', MLR, 68: 530–44
PATON, MARGARET. 'Hume on Tragedy', *British Journal of Aesthetics*, 13: 121–32
RENAULT, MARY. 'History in Fiction', TLS, 23 March, 315–16. See also Taylor
REYNOLDS, LORNA. 'Collective Intellect: Yeats, Synge and Nietzsche', *Essays and Studies*, 26: 83–98
RIDLEY, HUGH. 'Hans Grimm and Rudyard Kipling', MLR, 68: 863–69
——. 'The Colonial Imagination: A Comparison of Kipling with French and German Colonial Writers', RLC, 47: 574–85
RITCHIE, J. M. 'Translations of the German Expressionists in Eugène Jolas's Journal *Transition*', *Oxford German Studies*, 8: 149–58
ROBSON, VINCENT. 'Literary Criticism and the Academic Canon', *Linguistica et litteraria*, 2.1: 30–53
ROBSON-SCOTT, W. D., ED. *Essays in German and Dutch Literature* (Institute of Germanic Studies, University of London)

RODDY, KEVIN. 'Epic Qualities in the Cycle Plays', in *Medieval Drama* (see Denny), 154–71
ROE, G. M. W. 'Paul Valéry as a Literary Critic: Theory and Practice', *Nottingham French Studies*, 13: 23–32; 73–84
SECRETAN, DOMINIQUE. *Classicism* (Methuen). The Critical Idiom, 27
SELDEN, RAMAN. 'Juvenal and Restoration Modes of Translation', **MLR**, 68: 481–93
——. 'Objectivity and Theory in Literary Criticism', *Essays in Criticism*, 23: 283–97
SHEPARD, LESLIE. *The History of Street Literature: The Story of Broadside Ballads, Chapbooks, Proclamations, Election Bills, Tracts, Pamphlets, Cocks, Catchpennies, and Other Ephemera* (Newton Abbot: David and Charles)
SHIEL, JAMES. 'The Latin Aristotle', *Medium Aevum*, 42: 147–52
SHORT, M. H. 'Linguistic Criticism and Baudelaire's "Les Chats"', *Journal of Literary Semantics*, 2, 79–93
SMITH, G. S. 'The Contribution of Gluck and Paus to the Development of Russian Versification: The Evidence of Rhyme and Stanza Forms', *Slavonic and East European Review*, 51: 22–35
SMITH, JAMES L. *Melodrama* (Methuen). The Critical Idiom, 28
SOUTHALL, RAYMOND. *Literature and the Rise of Capitalism. Critical Essays Mainly on the Sixteenth and Seventeenth Centuries* (Lawrence and Wishart)
STEINER, GEORGE. 'Beyond the Parish Pump', **TLS**, 25 May, 581–82
—— 'The Way to Silence', *Semiotica*, 8: 94–96
—— 'The Writer as Remembrancer: A Note on Poetics, 9', *Yearbook of Comparative and General Literature*, 22: 51–57
STERN, J. P. 'Occlusions, Disclosures, Conclusions', *New Literary History*, 5: 149–68
STEVENS, JOHN. *Medieval Romance* (Hutchinson)
SWIFT, BERNARD. 'The Hypothesis of the French Symbolist Novel', **MLR**, 68: 776–87
SWINGEWOOD, ALAN. 'Literature and Praxis: A Sociological Commentary', *New Literary History*, 5: 169–76
TAYLOR, A. J. P. 'Fiction in History', **TLS**, 23 March, 327–28. See also Renault
THOMSON, PATRICIA. 'Wuthering Heights and Mauprat', *Review of English Studies*, 24: 26–37
THORLBY, ANT[H]ONY. 'Liberty and Self-Development: Goethe and John Stuart Mill', *Neohelicon*, 1.3–4: 91–110
TURNER, C. J. G. 'A Slavonic Version of John Cantecuzenus's *Against Islam*', *Slavonic and East European Review*, 51: 113–17
VICKERS, BRIAN. *Towards Greek Tragedy* (Longman)
WAIN, JOHN. 'The Single Mind: A Review of Lionel Trilling, *Sincerity and Authenticity*', *Critical Quarterly*, 15: 173–79
WALSH, WILLIAM. *Commonwealth Literature* (Oxford University Press)
WARNER, MARTIN. 'Black's Metaphors', *British Journal of Aesthetics*, 13: 367–72
WEIGHTMAN, JOHN. *The Concept of the Avant-Garde: Explorations in Modernism* (Alcove)
WELLS, MARGARET BRADY. 'Du Bellay and Fracastoro', **MLR**, 68: 756–61
WEST, J. D. 'Neo-Romanticism in the Russian Symbolist Aesthetic', *Slavonic and East European Review*, 51: 413–27
WEST, M. L. 'Greek Poetry 2000–700 BC', *Classical Quarterly*, 23: 179–92
WHITFIELD, J. H. 'Machiavelli Guicciardini Montaigne', *Italian Studies*, 28: 31–47
WILLIAMS, ARNOLD. 'The Comic in the Cycles', in *Medieval Drama* (see Denny), 108–23
WILLIAMS, C. E. 'Not an Inn, but a Hospital. *The Magic Mountain* and *Cancer Ward*', *Forum for Modern Language Studies*, 9, 311–32
WILLIAMS, RAYMOND. *The Country and the City* (Chatto and Windus)

1974

AXTON, RICHARD. *European Drama of the Early Middle Ages* (Hutchinson)
BANCE, A. F. 'The Kaspar Hauser Legend and its Literary Survival', **GLL**, 28: 199–210
BAWCUTT, PRISCILLA. 'Douglas and Surrey: Translators of Virgil', *Essays and Studies*, 27: 52–67
BELL, QUENTIN. 'Art and the Elite', *Critical Inquiry*, 1.1: 33–46
BINNS, J. W. *The Latin Poetry of English Poets* (Routledge and Kegan Paul)
BOND, MARTYN. 'Das Hörspiel: Epic, Lyric or Dramatic? The Critical Debate about a Literary Form', **GLL**, 28: 45–58
BREWER, D. S. 'Some Observations on the Development of Liberalism and Verbal Criticism', *Poetics* (Tokyo), 1: 71–95
BRISSENDEN, ROBERT FRANCIS. *Virtue in Distress: Studies in the Novel of Sentiment from Richardson to Sade* (Macmillan)
BRUFORD, W. H. 'Some Early Cambridge Links with German Scholarship and Literature', in *Erfahrung und Überlieferung. Festschrift for C. P. Magill* (University of Wales Press); continued in **GLL**, 28: 233–45
CHAPMAN, RAYMOND. 'Words and Sounds: Auditory Experience in the Poetry of the 1914–18 War', *Poetics* (Tokyo), 1: 46–62
CHARLTON, WILLIAM. 'Is Philosophy a Form of Literature?', *British Journal of Aesthetics*, 14: 3–16
CLOSE, ANTHONY. 'Don Quixote as a Burlesque Hero: A Re-Constructed Eighteenth-Century View', *Forum for Modern Language Studies*, 10: 365–78
CROSS, J. E. 'The Poem in Transmitted Text — Editor and Critic', *Essays and Studies*, 27: 84–97
CULLER, JONATHAN. 'Commentary' (on the contributions in this issue of NLH, on 'Metaphor'), *New Literary History*, 6: 219–29
CURRIE, ROBERT. *Genius: An Ideology in Literature* (Chatto and Windus)
DAICHES, DAVID and ANTHONY THORLBY, EDS. *The Old World: Discovery and Rebirth* (Aldus). Literature and Western Civilization, 3
DENNY, NEVILLE. 'Aspects of the Staging of Mankind', *Medium Aevum*, 43: 252–63
DOHERTY, F. 'Boyle and Tristram Shandy: "Stage-Loads of Chymical Nostrums and Peripatetic Lumber"', *Neophilologus*, 58: 339–48
DONOGHUE, DENIS. 'Between Value and Fact', **TLS**, 6 December, 1358
——. *Imagination* (Glasgow University Press). W. P. Ker Memorial Lecture
——. 'A Reply to Frank Kermode', *Critical Inquiry*, 1: 447–52. See Kermode, 'Novels'
——. 'Some Versions of Empson', **TLS**, 7 June, 589–90
EDGE, DAVID. 'Technological Metaphor and Social Control', *New Literary History*, 6: 135–48
ELLIS, A. J. 'Intention and Interpretation in Literature', *British Journal of Aesthetics*, 14: 315–25
ELLIS, JOHN M. *Narration in the German Novelle: Theory and Interpretation* (Cambridge University Press)
FIDDIAN, R. W. 'Unamuno — Bergson: A Reconsideration', **MLR**, 69: 787–95
FLETCHER, J. 'The Difficult Dialogue: Conflicting Attitudes to the Contemporary Novel', *Journal of European Studies*, 4: 274–86
FOSTER, JOHN WILSON. *Forces and Themes in Ulster Fiction* (Dublin: Gill and Macmillan)
FOWLER, FRANK M. 'Hebbel, Jeanne d'Arc und *Die Jungfrau von Orleans*', *Hebbel-Jahrbuch*, 126–38
FURST, LILIAN R. 'Stefan George's *Die Blumen des Bosen*: A Problem of Translation', **RLC**, 48: 203–17
GASKELL, P. H. 'Hölderlin's Contact with Pietism', **MLR**, 69: 805–20

GIFFORD, D. J. 'Iconographical Notes towards a Definition of the Medieval Fool', *Journal of the Warburg and Courtauld Institutes*, 37: 336–42
GREEN, D. H. 'The *Alexanderlied* and the Emergence of the Romance', **GLL**, 28: 246–62
GRIGSON, GEOFFREY. *The Contrary View: Glimpses of Fudge and Gold* (Macmillan)
GROVER, PHILIP. 'French Literature and James's Early Criticism, 1864–1874', *Forum for Modern Language Studies*, 10: 300–12
——. *Henry James and the French Novel: A Study in Inspiration* (Elek)
HAGGIS, D. R. '*Clotilde de Lusignan, Ivanhoe*, and the Development of Scott's Influence on Balzac', *French Studies*, 28: 159–68
——. 'Fiction and Historical Change: *La Cousine Bette* and the Lesson of Walter Scott', *Forum for Modern Language Studies*, 10: 323–33
HAINING, PETER, ED. *The Penny Dreadful* (Gollancz)
HALL, J. B. '*Tablante de Ricamonte* and Other Castilian Versions of Arthurian Romances', **RLC**, 48: 177–89
HALL, KATHLEEN M. 'How to Get the Corpse Off the Stage', *French Studies*, 28: 282–93
HALPERIN, JOHN, ED. *The Theory of the Novel: New Essays* (Oxford University Press)
HARDWICK, ELIZABETH. *Seduction and Betrayal: Women and Literature* (Weidenfeld and Nicolson)
HEATH, STEPHEN. *Le Vertige du déplacement* (Paris: Fayard)
HEMMINGS, F. W. J., ED. *The Age of Realism* (Penguin). Pelican Guides to European Literature
HORSFALL, NICHOLAS. 'Classical Studies in England, 1810–1825', *Greek, Roman and Byzantine Studies*, 15: 449–77
HOUGH, GRAHAM. 'Dante and Eliot', *Critical Quarterly*, 16: 293–306
HUXLEY, GEORGE. 'Aristotle's Interest in Biography', *Greek, Roman and Byzantine Studies*, 15: 203–13
JACKSON, W. H. 'Ulrich von Zatzikhoven's *Lanzelet* and the Theme of Resistance to Royal Power', **GLL**, 28: 285–97
JACOBY, E. G. 'Thomas Hobbes in Europe', *Journal of European Studies*, 4: 57–65
JONES, ROBERT MAYNARD. *Tafody lienor: Gwersi ar theori llenyddiaeth* (University of Wales Press)
JUMP, JOHN D. *The Ode* (Methuen). The Critical Idiom, 30
KERMODE, FRANK. 'A Modern Way with the Classic', *New Literary History*, 5: 415–34
——. 'Novels: Recognition and Deception', *Critical Inquiry*, 1.1: 103–21. Replied to by Denis Donoghue (see above)
KING, BRUCE, ED. *Literatures of the World in English* (Routledge and Kegan Paul)
KNOWLES, DOROTHY. 'Eugene Ionesco's Rhinoceroses: Their Romanian Origin and their Western Fortunes', *French Studies*, 28: 294–307
LESTER, G. A. 'The Caedmon Story and its Analogues', *Neophilologus*, 58: 225–37
LOW, DONALD A. 'Byron and Europe', *Journal of European Studies*, 4: 364–67
LYONS, F. S. L. 'Two Traditions in One', **TLS**, 19 July, 763
MACLEOD, C. W. 'A Use of Myth in Ancient Poetry', *Classical Quarterly*, 24: 82–93
MAGILL, C. P. *German Literature* (Oxford University Press)
MCFARLANE, I. D. *Renaissance France, 1470–1580* (Benn)
MCGURK, P. 'Computus Helperici: Its Transmission in England in the Eleventh and Twelfth Centuries', *Medium Aevum*, 43: 1–5
MENDEL, SYDNEY. *Roads to Consciousness* (Allen and Unwin)
MEYERS, JEFFREY. 'Greuze and Lampedusa's *Il Gattopardo*' **MLR**, 69: 308–15
MITCHELLS, K. '"Nur nicht lesen! Immer singen!" Goethe's "Lieder" into Schubert Lieder', **PEGS**, 44: 63–82

MOORE, GERALD. 'Reintegration with the Lost Self: A Theme in Contemporary African Literature', *RLC*, 48: 488–503

MORRISON, MARY. 'Some Aspects of the Treatment of the Theme of Antony and Cleopatra in Tragedies of the Sixteenth Century', *Journal of European Studies*, 4: 113–25

MULRYNE, J. R. 'The French Source for the Sub-plot of Middleton's *Women Beware Women*', *Review of English Studies*, 25: 439–45

MURDOCH, BRIAN. 'Transformations of the Holocaust: Auschwitz in Modern Lyric Poetry', *Comparative Literature Studies*, 11: 123–50

MURDOCH, JOHN. 'English Realism: George Eliot and the Pre-Raphaelites', *Journal of the Warburg and Courtauld Institutes*, 37: 313–29

NORRIS, CHRISTOPHER. 'Les plaisirs des clercs: Barthes's Latest Writing', *British Journal of Aesthetics*, 14: 250–57

NUTTALL, A. D. *A Common Sky: Philosophy and the Literary Imagination* (Chatto and Windus for Sussex University Press)

———. 'Fishes in the Trees', *Essays in Criticism*, 24: 20–38

PEARSALL, DEREK and ELIZABETH SALTER. *Landscapes and Seasons of the Medieval World* (Elek)

PICKERING, F. P. 'The Western Image of Byzantium in the Late Middle Ages', *GLL*, 28: 326–40

PRAWER, S. S. *Comparative Literary Studies: An Introduction* (Duckworth)

REED, T. J. 'An Alternative Germany', *TLS*, 25 October, 1199–201

RIDLEY, H. 'Germany in the Mirror of its Colonial Literature', *GLL*, 28: 375–86

RINGROSE, C. X. 'F. R. Leavis and Yvor Winters on G. M. Hopkins', *English Studies*, 55: 32–42

ROCKWELL, JOAN. *Fact in Fiction: The Use of Literature in the Systematic Study of Society* (Routledge and Kegan Paul)

ROGERS, PAT. *The Augustan Vision* (Weidenfeld and Nicolson)

SAGE, LORNA. 'The Case of the Active Victim', *TLS*, 26 July, 803–04

SHIELDS, HUGH. 'A Text of Nicole Bozon's *Proverbes de bon enseignement* in Irish Transmission', *MLR*, 69: 274–78

SILK, M. S. *Introduction to Poetic Imagery: With Special Reference to Early Greek Poetry* (Cambridge University Press)

SMITH, MICHAEL. 'English Translations and Imitations of Italian Madrigal Verse', *Journal of European Studies*, 4: 164–77

SPENDER, STEPHEN. *Love-Hate Relations* (Hamish Hamilton)

STANLEY, ERIC GERALD. 'The Oldest English Poetry Now Extant', *Poetics* (Tokyo), 1: 1–24

STEINER, GEORGE. REVIEW OF MICHEL FOUCAULT'S *The Order of Things*, *New York Times Book Review*, 28 February. Also *Diacritics*, 1.1 (Fall): 57–60, and 1.2 (Winter): 59–60

STOPP, F. J. 'Latin Plays at the Academy of Altdorf, 1577–1626', *Journal of European Studies*, 4: 189–213

THEOBALD, D. W. 'Philosophy and Fiction: The Novel as Eloquent Philosophy', *British Journal of Aesthetics*, 14: 17–25

VICINUS, MARTHA. *The Industrial Muse. A Study of Nineteenth-Century British Working Class Literature* Croom Helm)

WEBSTER, RICHARD. 'Frank Kermode's *The Sense of an Ending*', *Critical Quarterly*, 16: 311–24

WEST, REBECCA. 'And They All Lived Unhappily Ever After', *TLS*, 26 July, 779

WETHERILL, PETER MICHAEL. *The Literary Text: An Examination of Critical Methods* (Oxford: Basil Blackwell)

WHITBOURN, CHRISTINE JANET, ED. *Knaves and Swindlers: Essays on the Picaresque Novel in Europe* (Oxford University Press for the University of Hull)

WHITE, J. J. 'Signs of Disturbance: The Semiological Import of Some Recent Fiction by Michel Tournier and Peter Handke', *Journal of European Studies*, 4: 233–54
WILLIAMS, C. E. *The Broken Eagle: The Politics of Austrian Literature from Empire to Anschluss* (Elek)
WILLIAMS, DAVID. 'Observations on an English Translation of Voltaire's Commentary on Corneille', *Studies on Voltaire and the Eighteenth Century*, 124: 143–48
WILLIAMS, RAYMOND. 'The English Language and the English Tripos', **TLS**, 15 November, 1293–94
WOODMAN, A. J. 'Sleepless Poets: Catullus and Keats', *Greece & Rome*, 21: 51–53

INDEX

Aarsleff, Hans 13, 21, 27
Aberdeen 11, 12, 99, 124, 129
Abergavenny 43, 45, 48–51
Aberystwyth 87, 106, 108, 127
Achebe, Chinua 156
Adamson, Robert 107 n. 4
Adelaide 156
Agamben, Giorgio 158
Alexandra (Princess) 65
Althusser, Louis 151, 153, 155
Amis, Kingsley 128
Ampère, Jean-Jacques 3, 50, 60, 68 n. 6
Anderson, Benedict 157
anglocentrism 63, 68 n. 8, 95, 116–18, 148 157
  see also 'Englishness' and eurocentrism
Anglo-Saxon 3, 10, 25, 27, 29, 33, 35, 40, 45, 51, 57, 61, 89, 92, 120, 123
  see also Saxons, Saxonism
anglosphere 118, 135, 155
anthropology 14, 21, 22, 31, 33, 35, 51, 67, 75, 91, 118, 120
anti-authoritarianism 145, 148, 151, 158
antiquarianism 23, 24, 38, 51, 91, 113
anti-Semitism 68, 135, 146, 162
Apter, Emily 1, 83 n. 5, 157
Archer, William 96
Arendt, Hannah 135
Aristotle 11
Albert (Prince Consort) 65
Arnold, Matthew 4, 5, 9, 48, 51, 52, 55, 57–67, 68 n. 4–5, 70, 73, 75, 81, 82, 84, 85, 87, 89, 90, 92, 105, 112, 132, 142, 143, 151, 163, 165–66
Arnold, Lucy 66
Arnold, Thomas 14, 35, 55, 66, 68 n. 11, 79
'Aryan' 31, 33, 45, 48, 49, 53 n. 14, 64
  see also Indo-European
Ashcroft, Bill 156
Athenaeum 85
Atlantic Monthly 81
Auckland 77, 80
Auerbach, Erich 23, 135
axiology, *see* value judgement

Bachofen, Johann Jakob 120
Bagehot, Walter 73, 80
Bakhtin, Mikhail 135
Baldensperger, Fernand 112, 127, 128, 130, 132 n. 8, 135

Balibar, Etiene 153
Bangalore 79
Bangor 87, 113
Bann, Stephen 148
Barker, Francis 156
Barnes, Bertram 130
Barnes, Julian 152
Barthes, Roland 152, 153
Bassnett, Susan 145, 148, 151, 159, 160, 162, 167 n. 7
Bateson, F. W. 142, 143
Bayley, John 152, 156
BCLA, *see* British Comparative Literature Association
Beauvoir, Simone de 154
Beddoe, John 64
Beer, Gillian 145, 151
Belfast 57, 67 n. 1, 77, 98, 99, 123
Bellos, David 145
Belsey, Catherine 151, 155
Bengal Renaissance 48, 54 n. 21
Beowulf 7, 29, 53 n. 11
Bergonzi, Bernard 142
Berlin 13, 14, 18, 29
Berlin, Isaiah 135
Bernal, Martin 118
Betz, Louis-Paul 3, 72, 77, 81, 82, 128
Bhabha, Homi 156
Bibliothèque de la Revue de Littérature Comparée 113, 115, 127–29, 132
Bildung 14, 55, 92
Birmingham 87, 101, 108, 110, 129, 134, 149
Birmingham School 151
Boccaccio, Giovanni 9, 95
Bökendorf Circle 53 n. 19
Bonn 5, 14, 18
Bopp, Franz 22, 53 n. 16
Borges, Jorge Luis 52 n. 1
Bourdieu, Pierre 157, 161
Bouterwek, Friedrich 3, 24
Bowie, Malcolm 145
Bowra, Maurice 120, 130
Bowring, John 37, 38
Boxhorn, Marcus Zuerius 53 n. 16
Boyd, James 110
Bradbury, Malcolm 148, 149
Brandes, Georg 3, 40, 77, 95
Breslau 14
Breul, Karl 109, 118, 123, 134

Bristol 40, 87, 141
British and Foreign Bible Society 45
British Comparative Literature Association 5, 138, 145, 165
British Journal of Aesthetics 143
BRLC, see *Bibliothèque de la Revue de Littérature Comparée*
Bromwich, Rachel 122
Bronowski, Jacob 135
Brotherston, Gordon 148, 156
Brougham, Henry 17, 18
Brown, John 80, 83 n. 8
Browning, Robert 25, 94
Brunetière, Fernand 81, 99
Buckle, Henry Thomas 70, 72, 73, 79, 80, 82, 85, 90, 91, 127
Bulwer-Lytton, Edward 52 n. 7, 68 n. 10
Bunsen, Christian Karl Josias 31, 45, 49
Bürger, Gottfried 14
Burke, Peter 1, 38, 107 n. 3
Butler, Elisa Marian 6, 115, 118, 120, 123, 130, 134
Byron, George Gordon (Lord) 25, 37, 65, 112, 132

Cahiers du cinéma 153
Calcutta 13, 48, 73
Calderón de la Barca, Pedro 9
Cambridge 1, 11, 12, 57, 65, 75, 87, 91, 94, 101, 104, 106, 108–10, 115, 116, 118, 120, 123, 124, 129, 130, 132, 134, 135, 142, 145, 146, 148, 149, 151–53
Campbell, Joseph 91
Campbell, Thomas 17–19, 24, 25, 37
Cardiff 87, 98, 130, 151, 155
Carlyle, Thomas 18, 25, 31, 53 n. 12, 55, 63, 68 n. 4–5, 85, 87, 95
Caroline (Princess) 19
Casanova, Pacale 157
Case, Thomas 87
Castro, Rosalía de 53 n. 19
Cecil, (Lord) David 152
Čelakovský, František 38
Celtic/Celticism 7, 9, 22, 33, 35, 43, 45, 48–51, 53, 57, 61–67, 68 . 12, 75, 79, 83, 85, 89–91, 104, 106, 115, 120, 122, 159
Cerquiglini, Bernard 154
Chadwick, Hector Munro 120–23
Chadwick, Nora Kershaw 10, 115, 120–23, 139
Chanson de Roland 7, 50
Chasles, Philarète 50
Chaucer, Geoffrey 9, 18, 95, 108
Chicoteau, Marcel 130
Chrétien de Troyes 49, 50
Cixous, Hélène 154
Classics 9, 18, 42, 51, 77, 89, 96, 115, 118
Coleridge, Samuel 4, 14, 17, 24, 60, 85, 99, 139
Collins, John Churton 101, 104, 105, 116, 129, 134
Collins, Wilkie 84
Cologne 146

Commonwealth Literature 156
Comparative Critical Studies 145
Comparative Criticism 5, 6, 50, 138, 145, 159
Comparative Linguistics, see Linguistics
comparative method 123, 142, 164
Comparative Literature Association of Ireland 167 n.3
Comparative Politics 73, 75, 79, 82
Comte, Auguste 70, 72, 73
Constantine, Mary-Ann 50, 123, 159
Cork 57, 89
Cornhill Magazine 61, 87
cosmopolitanism 3, 9, 58, 81, 95, 101, 107, 113, 116
 see also internationalism
Criterion 4, 85, 117
Critical Idiom 151
Critical Quarterly 142, 154
criticism 1–6, 50–52, 57–59, 85, 94–96, 98–101, 115–18, 140–43
 see also value judgement
Croker, John Wilson 84
Cronk, Nicholas 159
cultural materialism 155
cultural memory 160, 165
cultural transfer 13, 106, 160, 161, 167 n. 6
Curtis, Simon 145
Curtius, Ernst Robert 98, 127, 166 n. 3
Cuvier, Georges 13, 33
Cymmreigiddion 45

Dabydeen, David 156
Daiches, David 146, 157
Damascus 72
Damrosch, David 1, 83 n. 5, 157
Dante Alighieri 9, 23, 37, 94, 104, 108, 141
Darwin, Charles / Darwinism 22, 67, 70, 73
Davie, Donald 105, 134, 136, 143, 145, 148, 149
De Man, Paul 135, 155
De Quincey, Thomas 40
De Sanctis, Francesco 3, 42
Deane, Seamus 155
Deleuze, Gilles 158
Derrida, Jacques 153–55
Diacritics 155
Dibdin, Charles 24, 52 n. 7
Dickens, Charles 25, 59, 117
Dictionary of National Biography 6, 85, 99, 168
Donne, John 9
Dowden, Edward 87, 89, 90, 92, 94–96, 101, 105, 107, 109
Drakakis, John 151
Dronke, Peter 159
Dryden, John 4, 20, 23, 24, 95
Dublin 11, 12, 57, 67 n. 1, 77, 79–81, 89, 90, 92, 95, 123, 124, 129, 156
Dumézil, Georges 91
Durham 52 n. 4, 87, 91, 128, 151

Duthie, Enid Lowrie 127, 128
Dyserinck, Hugo 1, 3, 5, 82, 83, 136, 167 n. 4

Eagleton, Terry 59, 151, 152, 155, 156
East Anglia 143, 145, 146, 148, 162
East India Company 13, 73, 75, 79
Easthope, Anthony 151
Eco, Umberto 163
Edinburgh 11–13, 17, 18, 35, 96, 98, 99, 107, 124, 129, 145
Edinburgh Review 4, 13, 49, 84
Eggli, Edmond 130
Eichhorn, Johann Gottfried 3
eisteddfod 13, 31, 43, 45, 48–51, 61–63
Eliade, Mircea 91
Eliot, George (Mary Ann Evans) 70, 84, 94, 117
Eliot, T. S. 4, 60, 85, 124, 132, 134, 142
Ellis, George 25, 49
Ellmann, Maud 154
Elton, Oliver 98, 99
Empson, William 116, 117
Encounter 17, 45, 62, 107, 142
Encyclopaedia Britannica 27, 85, 96, 99
English Goethe Society 6, 94, 106, 112, 113, 132
Englishness 10, 55, 61, 117, 148, 157
   see also anglocentrism
entangled histories 160
   see also cultural transfer
Entwistle, W. J. 124, 127, 130, 132, 134, 138
Espagne, Michel 161, 167 n. 6
Essays in Criticism 57, 142
Essex 105, 143, 145, 148, 156, 162, 163
ethnography 64, 77, 118, 157
Etiemble, René 139
eurocentrism 1, 9, 33, 59, 83, 122, 139, 156–57, 163
   see also anglocentrism
Even-Zohar, Itamar 162

Fanon, Frantz 157
Farinelli, Arturo 3, 77
Fauriel, Claude 3, 38, 50
feminist criticism 154
Fichte, Johann Gottlieb 13
Fiedler, Hermann Georg 110, 123, 136
Field Day 155
FILLM, *see* International Federation for Modern Languages and Literatures
Finnur Mágnusson 37
Fletcher, John 143, 145, 146, 148
Flint, Kate 154
Flint, Robert 107 n. 4
Foster, E. M. 117, 143
Forster, Leonard W. 6, 134
Fortnightly Review 90, 92, 96, 101
Foster, R. F. 156
Foucault, Michel 1, 159
Fox-Gal, Eva 145

Fraser's Magazine 85
Frazer, James 91, 118, 120
Freeman, E. A. 73, 75, 79, 80, 82 n. 3, 87, 95, 116, 120
Freud, Sigmund 158
Froude, James 25
Furst, Lilian R. 135, 146, 149, 151, 166 n. 3

Gadamer, Hans-Georg 159
Galway 57
Gardner, Helen 143
Garnett, Constance 162
Gaskill, Howard 159
Geary, Patrick J. 123
Geiger, Ludwig 106
Gellner, Ernest 135
gender 53 n. 19, 113–15, 118, 120–22, 127–28, 154
Genette, Gérard 153
Geoffrey of Monmouth 49
George II (king) 14, 40
Gervinus, G. G. 9
Gifford, Henry 136, 141–43, 145, 148, 160
Gillies, Alexander 132, 138, 143
Gilman, Sandor 163
Girton College 115
Glasgow 11, 12, 17–19, 91, 107, 110, 124
Goethe, Johann Wolfgang 6–9, 13, 17, 58, 60, 81, 83, 94, 95, 106, 110, 112, 113, 130, 132, 142
Goldstücker, Eduard 148
Gombrich, Ernst 135
Gomme, Lawrence 83 n. 8, 91
Gosse, Edmund 96, 101, 104, 112, 116
Göttingen 3, 14, 17, 29, 107, 138
Goulding, Sybil 127, 128
Graf, Arturo 3, 77
Green, F. C. 130
Greimas, A. J. 153
Grierson, Herbert 99
Griffiths, Gareth 156
Grimm, Jacob and Wilhelm 22, 24, 27, 29, 49, 50, 68 n. 9, 167 n.
Guest, (Lady) Charlotte 45, 53 n. 20
Gunnell, Doris 127, 128
Gurr, Andrew 156

Haeckel, Ernst 22
Hall, Benjamin 43
Hallam, Henry 38, 40, 42, 43, 49, 72, 73, 75, 80, 87, 90, 91, 95, 98, 112, 127
Hambrook, Glyn 1
Hamburger, Michael 162
Hanka, Václav 38
Hannay, David 99, 100
Hanover 14, 19, 31, 65, 109
Hardy, Thomas 84, 141
Harrison, Jane 120
Hatto, A. T. 171

Hawkes, Terence 151
Hazard, Paul 127, 128, 132 n. 8
Hazlitt, Thomas 20, 24
Hearn, Lafcadio 81
Hegel, G. W.F. 14
Heidelberg 14
Hemans, Felicia 37
Hennig, John (Hans) 166–67
Herder, Johann Gottfried 3, 7, 63, 70, 132
Herford, Charles Harold 106–07, 108 n. 7, 132, 134
Hermans, Theo 162
Herzen, Alexander 37
Heyne, C. G. 17, 25
Heywood, Christopher 145
Hoggart, Richard 143, 149, 151
Hopkins, Gerard Manley 57
Horner, Isaline 118, 120
Housman, A. E. 77
Howells, William Dean 81, 83
Hughes, Glyn Tegai 5, 134
Hughes, Thomas 55
Huizinga, Johan 127
Hull 129
Humboldt, Wilhelm v. 8, 14, 17, 33, 57, 68 n. 9
Hunter, Alfred C. 128

ICLA, *see* International Comparative Literature Association
Indian Mutiny 75
Indo-European 7, 22, 27, 31, 35, 45, 64, 68 n. 9
 see also 'Aryan'
Ingram, James 27
International Comparative Literature Association 98, 138–40, 151, 159, 160
International Federation for Modern Languages and Literatures 140–41
internationalism 37, 81, 99, 106, 107, 116, 134, 136–39, 140, 165, 166
 see also cosmopolitanism
Iolo Morganwg 43
Irigaray, Luce 154
Ireland, Irish 9, 10, 23, 24, 35, 48, 51, 53 n. 16, 57, 61, 63, 67, 68, 77, 79, 83, 87, 89, 90, 95, 123, 151, 155, 156, 160, 166

Jacob, Therese von (Talvj) 38
Jakobson, Roman 135
Jameson, Fredric 155
Jaspers, Karl 166 n. 3
Jauss, Hans Robert 152, 163, 166 n. 4
Jean-Marie Carré 130
Jeffares, A. Norman 156
Jefferson, Thomas 18, 52 n. 3
Jeffrey, Francis 17
Jena 14, 17
Jews/Jewish 12, 59, 135, 146, 162
Johnson, Samuel 4, 20

Jones, Apollonia 45
Jones, William 13, 75
Josipovici, Gabriel 135, 146, 163
Joyce, James 143

Kant, Immanuel 13
Karadžić, Vuk 37, 38
Karamzin, Nikolaj 37
Kemble, J. M. 29, 37, 57, 61, 62, 89
Kent 145, 148, 156
Ker, W. P. 27, 84, 85, 87, 98, 104, 109, 134, 148, 166
Kermode, Frank 142, 145
Kerrigan, John 159
Kiberd, Declan 155
Killen, Alice M. 127, 132
Kingsley, Charles 65, 79, 149
Kipling, Rudyard 82, 141, 156
Klein, Holger 148
Klopstock, F. G. 17
Kohn, Hans 135
Konstanz 135, 160
Kuhn, Thomas 152

Lacan, Jacques 154
Lach-Szyrma, Kyrstyn 37
Lachmann, Karl 7, 22
Lampeter 52 n. 4
Lansdowne (Lord) 55
Lanson, Gustave 130
Laplace, Noël 13
Laracor 79
Large, Duncan 162
Latour, Bruno 166
Lawrence, D. H. 117
Le Gonidec, Jean-François 45
Leavis, F. R. 106, 109, 115–17, 136, 142, 143, 148
Leavis, Q. D. 115, 117
Lee, Sidney 85, 87, 89, 105, 109
Leeds 87, 98, 138, 154, 156
Lefevere, André 162
Leibniz, Gottfried Wilhelm 53 n. 16
Leipzig 107, 110, 123, 124, 166
Lepenies, Wolf 163
Lévi-Strauss, Claude 153
Lewes, G. H. 70, 85
Lhuyd, Edward 53 n. 16
Lijphart, Arend 73
linguistics 3, 7, 10, 14, 18, 21, 22, 27, 31, 33, 35, 45, 48, 51, 64, 67, 68, 73, 79, 82, 87, 124, 130, 135, 140, 153, 159, 161
Listener 142
literary history 3, 9, 18, 22–24, 38, 42, 50, 51, 79, 92, 96, 98, 101, 107, 110, 138, 151, 154, 155, 158–60
Liverpool 62, 87, 98, 113, 130
La Villemarqué, Théodore de 45, 48–50, 54 n. 23
Llandudno 62, 66

Llanover, Augusta Hall, née Waddington (Lady) 43–49, 51, 53 n. 20
Lodge, David 142, 149
London 4, 5, 8, 13, 17, 19, 29, 37, 43, 51, 52 n. 2, 72, 77, 85, 87, 95, 98, 101, 108, 110, 113, 115, 128–30, 134, 136, 138, 151, 156
London Review of Books 4, 85
Longley, Edna 156
Lord, Alfred 120
Lotman, Jurij 135, 153

Mabinogion 45, 63
MacCabe, Colin 153
Macfarlane, James 145
Macherey, Pierre 151, 155
Mackenzie, Alastair 81
Macpherson, James, *see* Ossian
Magnus, Laurie 109
Mágnusson, Finnur 37
Maine, Henry 73, 75, 77, 79, 82, 91, 120
Malory, Thomas 9
Manchester 3, 5, 87, 91, 106, 108, 110, 118, 124, 128, 129, 132, 134, 138, 139, 145, 146
Marburg 14, 107, 132
Martineau, Harriet 70
Marx, Karl / Marxism / Marx-inspired criticism 70, 151, 155
Mason, Eudo 123, 132
Mason, Haydn 159
Maynooth 52 n. 4
McLuhan, Marshall 149
Meltzl von Lomnitz, Hugo 77, 83 n. 5
memory (cultural) 160–161
Meres, Francis 20, 23, 24
Merz, Theodore 13, 91, 127
Methodism 9, 11
methodological nationalism 2, 91, 116, 117, 161
Mews, Hazel 154
Michel, Francisque 7
Mickiewicz, Adam 37
Middleton, Tim 157
Milch, Werner 130, 135, 166 n. 3
Mill, John Stuart 70
Millar, John Hepburn 99, 107 n. 5
Minnis, Alastair 159
MLA / Modern Language Association 132, 138, 140
MLR / *Modern Language Review* 100, 104, 106, 107, 110, 112, 113, 124, 128, 138, 156
Moi, Toril 151, 154
Monnier, Gustave 3
monogenism/polygenism 33, 35
Moore, Tom 17, 37, 48, 81, 82, 85, 100
Moretti, Franco 157
Morgan, Sidney Owenson (Lady) 37, 84
Morganwg, Iolo 43
Morley, Edith 115

Morley, John 85, 90
Mphahlele, E'skia 156
Mukařovský, Jan 135
Müller, Friedrich Max 10, 29, 31, 33, 35, 38, 45, 64, 75, 82 n. 3, 83 n. 8, 89, 91, 118, 120
Munich 14, 107, 110
Murray, Gilbert 120
mythology 7, 22, 37, 120, 123, 157

Nairobi 156
nationalism 10, 27, 35, 53 n. 10, 81, 91, 95, 123, 156, 166
Needham, H. A. 128
New Accents 151–52, 162
New Comparison 145, 162
New Criticism 116, 118, 135, 140, 141
New Historicism 101, 158
Newman, John Henry 57
Newnham College 115, 119–20
Ngũgĩ wa Thiong'o 156, 157
Nibelungenlied 7, 108
Niemcewicz, Julian Ursyn 37
Nietzsche, Friedrich 8
Nobel, Alfred, *and* Nobel Prize 81, 82
Norris, Christopher 151, 155
Norwich 14, 17, 145
Nussbaum, Martha 163

Ó Buachalla, Breandán 159
Ó Tuama, Seán 159
Oakeshott, Michael 117
O'Curry, Eugene 57, 63, 67 n. 1
O'Donovan, John 63, 67 n. 1
Oehlenschläger, Adam 37
Oergel, Maike 160
Omond, T. S. 99, 100
OPOJAZ 135
Osborne, Walter 123
Ossian 7, 9, 10, 23, 24, 159
Oxford 4, 6, 11, 12, 18, 27, 29, 31, 40, 53–55, 57, 61, 64, 73, 75, 85, 87, 92, 96, 99, 101, 106, 107, 110, 113, 115, 120, 124, 128–30, 136, 140, 141, 143, 145, 146, 148, 152, 154, 156
Oxford English Dictionary 6, 85

Palmer, David 115, 148
Pardo Bazán, Emilia 53 n. 19
Paris, Gaston 99, 127
Paris, Paulin 54 n. 22
Parker, Joanne 123, 160
Parry, Milman 120
Partridge, Eric T. 50, 108 n. 6, 128, 129
Pascal, Roy 132, 134, 136, 148, 149
Peacock, Ronald 118, 132, 140
Peet, T. E. 122
Peirce, C. S. 153

Percy, Thomas (Bishop) 24, 25, 27, 80
philhellenism 2, 37, 118
philology 20–23, 25, 27, 29, 31, 33, 38, 42, 43, 45, 49–50, 57, 61, 63, 64, 82n., 89, 90, 91, 104
phylogenetic model 21–22, 27
Pictet, Adolphe 53 n. 16
Pitt Rivers, Augustus 91
PN Review 143
polygenism, *see* monogenism/polygenism
positivism 55, 57, 58, 70, 72, 73, 77, 79–80, 82, 91, 92, 94, 99–100, 112, 140
Pope, Alexander 20, 95, 101
Popper, Karl 135
pornography 143
Posner, Roland 3, 106
Posnett, H. M. 61, 70, 75, 77–83, 95, 100, 105, 122, 139, 157, 160
Posnett, Robert 77–79
postcolonialism 1, 83, 85, 118, 155–57, 159
poststructuralist criticism 155
Powell, Anthony 85
Price, Thomas 24, 35, 38, 43, 45, 48–51, 54 n. 21, 61
Prichard, J. C. 31, 35, 49, 51, 64, 73
Priestley, J. B. 85
Pritchett, V. S. 85
professorships:
    Poetry (Oxford) 55, 57, 61
    Rawlinson (Anglo-Saxon; Oxford) 27, 29, 92
    Regius (History, Greek; Oxford) 73, 120
    Rhetoric and Belles Lettres (Edinburgh and elsewhere) 18, 67, 115
    Schröder (German; Cambridge) 109, 118, 123, 134
    Taylor (Modern Languages; Oxford) 29, 31, 57, 108, 123, 129, 132, 146
    Thomas Warton (English; Oxford) 152
    Weidenfeld (Comparative Literature; Oxford) 163
Propp, Vladimir 135, 153
Puibusque, Adolphe de 50
Purdie, Edna 107, 113, 115, 123, 127, 134

Quarterly Review 84
Quiller-Couch, Arthur 106, 109, 116

Rancière, Jacques 158
Ranke, Leopold von 14, 38, 107
Rask, Rasmus 37
Rawlinson, Richard; Rawlinson Professorship 27, 29
Rea, Thomas 113
Read, Herbert 117
Reading 115, 162
reception history 110, 159–61
Rees, Garnet 140
remediation 161
Renan, Ernest 58, 66, 68 n. 12, 82 n. 3
Revue de Littérature Comparée 113, 115, 127, 130, 132
Revue des Deux Mondes 81

Rhys, John 61
Richard Price 24
Richards, I. A. 116, 117, 135
Richardson, Ethel Florence ('Hely Handel Richardson') 132 n. 2
Ricœur, Paul 158
Rig-Veda 31, 33
Rigney, Ann 153, 161
Rio, Alexis-François 45
Ritchie, R. L. Graeme 132
Ritson, Joseph 25, 27
Robertson, John George 107, 109, 110, 112, 113, 115, 123, 128, 132, 134, 136
Robertson, John Mackinnon 72, 85
Robinson, Henry Crabb 14, 17–19, 37
Robson, W. W. 142
Rod, Édouard 81
Roe, F. C. 5, 108 n. 9, 124, 128, 129, 132, 134, 138, 140, 143
Rosen, Friedrich August 29, 31
Rossetti, Gabriele 37
Rothacker, Erich 27, 166 n. 3
Routh, H. V. 4, 104, 105, 107
Roxburghe Club 24
Rugby 14, 55
Rushdie, Salman 156

Said, Edward 10, 122, 139, 155, 156
Sainte-Beuve, Charles Augustin 58
Saintsbury, George 80, 96, 98–101, 105, 107, 109, 112
Salvandy, Narcisse-Achille de 54 n. 23
Samuel, Raphael 157
Sandbach, Francis 107, 108 n. 7
Sanskrit 7, 13, 21, 22, 29, 31, 73, 79
Sassoon, Siegfried 106
Saussure, Ferdinand de 53 n. 16, 152–54
Saussy, Haun 1, 5, 122, 123, 157
Savigny, Friedrich Carl v. 17, 27
Saxons, Saxonism 25, 27, 29, 35, 50, 53 n. 12, 61–66, 68 n. 10, 73, 89
    see also Anglo-Saxon
Sayce, R. A. 132, 140, 143
Schérer, Edmond 58, 94
Scherer, Wilhelm 106
Schiller, Friedrich 14, 110, 136
Schlegel, A. W. 17–18, 24, 52 n. 2
Schlegel, Friedrich 8, 17–18, 21, 35, 52 n. 2
Schröder Professorship 109, 118, 123, 134
Schulz, Albert ('San-Marte') 49, 50
Scott, Janet 127–28
Scott, Walter 9–11, 14, 17, 24, 25, 38, 48, 49
Scott Moncrieff, C. K. 162
Screen 153
Scrutiny 11, 29, 99, 117
Sebald, W. G. 162
Selden, Raman 5, 151, 152, 155

Sells, Arthur Lytton 128, 132, 134
Semitic languages 33, 68 n. 9
Shackleton, Robert 140, 141, 159
Shaffer, Elinor 1, 5, 60, 82, 145, 148, 159, 160
Sheffield 87, 145
Shelley, Percy Bysshe 90, 94
Shippey, T. A. 123
Sim, Stuart 155
Sinfield, Alan 155
Šklovskij, Viktor 136
Smith, Ali 163
Smith, G. Gregory 98–100
Snell, F. J. 99, 108 n. 8
Snow, C. P. 143
Somerville College 113, 115, 124, 128
Sorbonne 3, 50, 99, 108, 127, 128
Southey, Robert 17, 24, 25, 27, 48
Spencer, Herbert 70, 79, 80
St Andrews 11, 12, 124, 129
St Hilda's College 115
stadialism 23, 73, 75, 79–81, 100, 157
Staël, Germaine de 3, 17, 20, 70
Stafford, Fiona 159
Starkie, Enid 124, 132, 134
Steiner, George 135, 149, 163, 166 n. 3
Stephen, Leslie 85, 87, 90, 99
Stirling 156, 159
Stockley, Violet 123
Stokes, Whitley 73, 75
Stokoe, F. W. 123
Strasbourg 107, 108, 110
Sussex 143, 145, 146, 156
Swansea 87
Swift, Jonathan 68 n. 3, 79
Symons, Arthur 96, 132
Szondi, Péter 135

Tagore, Dwarkanath 48, 49, 54 n. 21
Tagore, Rabindranath 48, 82
Taine, Hippolyte 9, 57, 80, 81, 94, 129
Talvj (Therese von Jacob) 38
Taylor, William 14, 17
Taylor Institute / Taylorian Professorship 29, 31, 57, 108, 123, 129, 132
Tel Quel 135, 153
Tengström (Finnish family network) 53
Tennyson, Alfred (Lord) 25, 52 n. 7, 68 n. 10, 101
Terry, Arthur 145
Texte, Joseph 77, 81, 113
Thackeray, W. M. 84, 87
Thiong'o, Ngũgĩ wa 156, 157
Thorkelin, Grímur Jónsson 7, 29
Thorlby, Anthony 5, 143, 145, 146, 157
Thurneysen, Rudolf 50
Tiffin, Helen 156
Times Literary Supplement 4, 85, 143, 145

Tiraboschi, Girolamo 42
TLS, *see Times Literary Supplement*
Tokyo 81, 83 n. 9
Toldy, Ferenc 37
Toury, Gideon 162
Toynbee, J. Paget 108 n. 8
translation studies 108 n. 8, 141, 160–62
Trevelyan, Humphry 130
Trinity College Dublin 11, 12, 77, 79, 80, 89, 90, 123, 156
Trithen, Heinrich 29
Trollope, Anthony 117, 149
Tsubouchi Shōyō 81
Tübingen 14, 136
Tucker, T. G. 85, 109
Tylor, E. B. 118
Tymms, Ralph 132

universities 11–14, 57, 87, *and see under the relevant place-name*
Universities Quarterly 143
Urwin, Kenneth 130, 132 n. 7

value judgement 59, 67, 82, 142, 146, 116-117
Van Tieghem, Paul 40, 95, 112, 122, 127
Vargas Llosa, Mario 163
Vaughan, C. E. 98–100
Vickers, Brian 139, 159
Vico, Giambattista 21, 22, 82 n. 1
Victoria (Queen) 31, 35
Vienna 8, 18, 21, 106, 149
Villemain, Abel-François 3, 24, 50, 60
Vincent, E. R. 140
Vodička, Felix 135

Waddington family 31, 45
Wais, Kurt 136
Wales/Welsh 8–11, 13, 31, 35, 43, 45, 49–51, 53 n. 16, 61–63, 65, 68, 87, 95, 98, 123, 130, 135, 149
Wallerstein, Immanuel 157
Warner, Marina 145, 148, 154, 163
Warren, Austin 92, 140
Warton, Thomas 24, 52 n. 7
Warton Professorship 152
Warwick 145, 148, 156, 159, 160, 162
Waterhouse, Gilbert 6, 107, 123
Wawn, Andrew 65, 123, 160
Weber, Henry William 14, 52 n. 8
Weber, Max 2
Weidenfeld Professorship 163
Weimar 14, 17, 94, 95
Weisstein, Ulrich 3, 5, 23, 60, 82, 127, 138
Wellek, René 5, 23, 24, 60, 82, 85, 92, 101, 135, 140, 141, 148
Welsh, *see* Wales
Weltliteratur, *see* world literature

Werner, Michael 161, 167 n. 6
Weston, Jessie 10, 120
Whitman, Walt 90, 94
Wieland, C. M. 14
Wilkinson, Elizabeth Mary 107, 110, 115, 132, 134, 136
Williams, Raymond 142, 143, 149
Willoughby, Leonard Ashley 60, 68 n. 6, 107, 110, 120, 132, 134, 136, 138
Windelband, Wilhelm 82 n. 1
Winters, Yvor 135
Wiseman, Nicholas (Cardinal) 33, 35, 53 n. 15
Wolf, F. A. 13, 163
Wood, Ian 123
Woolf, Virginia 87
Wordsworth, William 12, 60
world literature 1, 3, 7–9, 58, 81–82, 83 n. 5, 139, 142, 146, 155, 157, 165

Wrenn, C. L. 92

Yale 135, 145, 155
YCGL / *Yearbook of Comparative and General Literature* 129, 138, 139, 141, 151, 153
Yeats, W. B. 61, 90, 95, 156
York 82, 145, 148, 159

Zeuss, J. C. 53 n. 16, 64
Zhirmunsky, *see* Žirmunskij
Zimmer, Heinrich 50
Zirimu, Pio 156

Žirmunskij, V. I. 122, 139, 166 n. 2
Žižek, Slavoj 154, 158

www.ingramcontent.com/pod-product-compliance
Lightning Source LLC
LaVergne TN
LVHW061250060426
835507LV00017B/1987